personal
development
for life and work 10e

L. Ann Masters
Administrator, Office of the Commissioner of Education
Nebraska Department of Education
Lincoln, Nebraska

Harold R. Wallace
Professor of Occupational & Educational Studies, Emeritus
Colorado State University
Ft. Collins, Colorado

Contributing Author
Lauri Harwood
Business Consultant and Trainer
Cincinnati, Ohio

CENGAGE

Australia • Brazil • Canada • Mexico • Singapore • United Kingdom • United States

CENGAGE

Personal Development for Life and Work, 10th Edition

L. Ann Masters

Harold R. Wallace

Editorial Director: Jack W. Calhoun

Vice President/Editor-in-Chief: Karen Schmohe

Senior Acquisitions Editor: Jane Phelan

Senior Developmental Editor: Dr. Inell Bolls

Consulting Editor: Carol Ruhl

Editorial Assistant: Conor Allen

Associate Marketing Manager: Laura Stopa

Content Project Management: Pre-Press PMG

Media Editor: Lysa Kosins

Senior Manufacturing Buyer: Kevin Kluck

Production Service: Pre-Press PMG

Copyeditor: Pre-Press PMG

Senior Art Director: Tippy McIntosh

Internal Design: Pre-Press PMG

Cover Designer: Lou Ann Thesing

Cover Image: © Getty Images/Anthony Stack, Pando Hall, Picturenet, Leigh Schindler; © iStock

Permissions Acquisition Manager/Text: Mardell Glinkski-Schultz

Permissions Acquisition Manager/Photo: Don Schlotman

For product information and technology assistance, contact us at **Cengage Customer & Sales Support, 1-800-354-9706**

For permission to use material from this text or product, submit all requests online at **www.cengage.com/permissions**
Further permissions questions can be emailed to **permissionrequest@cengage.com**

ExamView® is a registered trademark of eInstruction Corp. Windows is a registered trademark of the Microsoft Corporation used herein under license. Macintosh and Power Macintosh are registered trademarks of Apple Computer, Inc. used herein under license.

Cengage WebTutor™ is a trademark of Cengage.

Library of Congress Control Number: 2009943822

ISBN-13: 978-0-538-45023-2

ISBN-10: 0-538-45023-1

Cengage
200 Pier 4 Boulevard
Boston, MA 02210
USA

To learn more about Cengage platforms and services, register or access your online learning solution, or purchase materials for your course, visit **www.cengage.com**.

Printed at CLDPC, USA, 02-21

Introducing

personal development

for life and work

PART 1

It's All About You

Strategize to improve your personal and professional skills to build self-esteem, self-confidence, a professional image, and a positive attitude.

PART 2

It's All About Communicating

Address the skills you need for communicating clearly and collaborating effectively with coworkers, supervisors, and customers.

PART 3

It's All About Working With Others

Hone your teamwork skills by exploring the topics of diversity, group decision making, working creatively with others, and being an effective meeting participant and facilitator.

PART 4

It's All About Workplace Success

Learn to manage change, develop leadership skills, get the right job, and move ahead in your career.

New Chapters Hone ....

Personal and Workplace Skills

Applying Critical Work Skills — **10** chapter

Think About It: Sonya arrives at Topco Electric a few minutes early. She hangs up her coat, pours herself a cup of coffee, logs on to her computer, and uses the first few minutes of her morning to plan the day. She views her To Do list and organizes the items in the order of importance. She reviews her e-mail to see if additional items should be added to today's priorities. An e-mail from Helen, her supervisor, requires her to make two phone calls.

Sonya adds the calls to her To Do list. She checks her electronic calendar to see what meetings or appointments are scheduled for today, pulls documents that she will need for the meetings, and finds the telephone numbers needed for today's work. She organizes her desk and checks to make sure that the copier, printer, and fax machines are loaded with paper. Many interruptions take her in different directions during the day, but she takes each interruption in stride, deals with it, and then returns to her planned list of tasks. She checks off each task as she completes it. At the end of the day, Sonya straightens up her workspace and takes a final look at her To Do list. She moves any incomplete or delayed tasks to her list for the next day.

objectives
After completing this cha able to:
1. Develop and apply ti
2. Understand the imp and work.
3. Practice techniques anger.
4. Develop skills for e
5. Take steps to devel
6. Use technology eff
7. Develop the skills a group.

Time management, multitasking, balancing life and work, being creative, managing stress, using technology effectively

Developing Customer Focus — **11** chapter

Think About It: Logan works in an exclusive shoe store. He works on commission and prides himself on being the top sales associate each month. A frequent customer comes in and buys several pair of expensive summer shoes. She continues to look around and spots a pair of jogging shoes for her husband. She asks for a size 11. Logan doesn't have that size and tells the customer that he can call the distributor and have the shoes shipped in three to five days. The customer agrees to have the shoes shipped. After the customer leaves, Logan calls the distributor and learns that there are only a few sizes left in that style because it is late in the season. Size 11 is no longer available; however, they have the shoe in size 10½. Logan says, "That's okay, send them to the customer. She'll never notice the size difference." The distributor tells Logan that the customer should receive the shoes in seven to ten days.

objectives
After completing this chapter, you sh able to:
1. Explain why customers are vital of every organization.
2. Identify what customers expect.
3. Demonstrate how to meet custo expectations.
4. Explain how to maintain good customer relations.
5. Explain why maintaining customer loyalty is important.
6. Deal with difficult customers.
7. Demonstrate proper telephone techniques.

Working with internal and external customers to make win-win relationships every time!

Developing Leadership Skills and Managing Change — **14** chapter

Think About It: When Will was in high school, he started working at Ruiz Insurance Company as a clerk. He filed documents, made copies, and entered data in the company's customer database. After he had been there about a year, Mrs. Ruiz started to assign him more responsibility. He learned enough about homeowners' and auto insurance to answer routine phone calls from customers. He wrote routine letters for Mrs. Ruiz to review. He assembled packets of information with cover letters to be mailed to prospects. He created and updated spreadsheets detailing each salesperson's prospects, proposals, and results. Will attended a local community college after he graduated from high school and went on to complete an associate degree in business. He was thinking of transferring to a university to complete a B.S. in accounting, perhaps going on for an M.B.A degree. However, Mrs. Ruiz thought he would make an excellent insurance salesperson and offered him a job just after he completed the associate's degree. Will was flattered that Mrs. Ruiz thought he was ready for such a responsible position. After talking it over, they decided that Will could work during the day and take classes at night. Will was thrilled with this opportunity, but wondered how the secretary and receptionist he had trained under might feel about his promotion over them.

objectives
After completing the chapter, you should be able to:
1. Describe the qualities and skills common to most leaders.
2. Compare various leadership styles.
3. Explain the importance of empowering others.
4. Explain how leaders can influence others.
5. Describe how leaders bring about change and innovation.

Develop the leader in you for greater recognition and career success!

Companion Website
www.cengage.com/careerreadiness/masters

New! Videos that show personal development in action

New! Video quizzes that test your mastery of concepts on the videos

New! Web activities

New! Flash cards

New! Chapter quizzes

The Instructor Resource CD contains teaching suggestions, recommended solutions, sample documents, ExamView testbank, and PowerPoint presentations.

Critical Skills Needed for the 21st Century

Personal Development for Life and Work, 10e is designed to prepare you for the challenges of work in the constantly changing job environment of the 21st century. Today's workers will change careers at least seven times in their lifetimes. New technical skills will be needed, of course. But "people skills" will become increasingly critical as we continue to work with individuals from around the globe and serve customers with unique needs and interests. More than ever, we need to build the skills necessary to work effectively in an increasingly global and diverse workplace.

The process of assessing your skills and becoming a competent professional is an ongoing process. Personal and career development isn't a one-time experience; it requires constantly revisiting and updating goals to align with your personal and professional life. We hope you will enjoy the numerous scenarios, tips, and strategies in *Personal Development for Life and Work, 10e* designed to bring you long-term success.

How the Text is Organized

Personal Development for Life and Work, 10e is an easy-to-read text. It is designed especially for those who realize that being employable is a serious topic and who are ready to learn all they can about themselves and others. This edition has been thoroughly revised and updated.

To give greater continuity, the text has been reorganized into four parts. Each part is introduced with a **Workplace Focus**, which shows how real professionals apply the chapter concepts as they share a little slice of advice on managing a career and personal life.

Part 1—It's All About You provides success strategies for improving your personal and professional skills. Through practical tips, personal evaluations, real-life stories, and case studies, *Personal Development for Life and Work, 10e* will empower you to develop a plan for building self-esteem, self-confidence, a positive attitude, and a professional image.

Part 2—It's All About Communicating addresses the skills for communicating clearly and collaborating with coworkers, supervisors, and customers. Practical tips and activities cover assertive communication; conversation energizers; questions to keep a conversation moving; being a team player; effective use of e-mail, text-messaging, and voice mail; and conflict resolution.

Part 3—It's All About Working With Others addresses such topics as working with diverse teams, applying critical-thinking and decision-making skills; and working creatively with others. Two new chapters have been added on participating and conducting meetings effectively and developing a strong customer focus.

Part 4—It's All About Workplace Success presents strategies for managing change, developing leadership skills, securing the right job, and moving ahead in your career.

To make the text an easy and engaging read, chapters are divided into smaller, more manageable sections. Each section concludes with activities called **Checkpoint** and **Applications** to immediately check your understanding and keep you engaged, motivated, and ready to move on.

Special Features to Master the Concepts

Personal Development for Life and Work, 10e has a new, visually-appealing design, and it's rich with real-life examples that make it easy for you to relate.

THINK ABOUT IT sets the stage for the chapter with a real-life glimpse into the work experience of an employee. Meaningful questions engage you right from the start.

PRACTICAL read and put-into-use tips and strategies address a wide range of topics throughout the text. Examples include Self-Esteem Builders, Relationship Builders, Stress Signals, Beat Back Information Overload, Create an Action Plan, and Avoid These Interview Errors.

APPLY IT! relates concepts to both personal and workplace situations through self-assessments, checklists, and thought-provoking questions or activities.

ON THE JOB reinforces the concepts of each section through realistic and easy-to-understand scenarios. You can problem-solve the scenarios with classmates or on your own.

More End-of-Chapter Features

Points to Remember provide a quick review of the key concepts found in each chapter.

Key Terms are reminders of vocabulary to be mastered.

Bookmark It provides links to additional chapter-related activities found on the website.

Chapter Activities feature comprehensive individual and team activities involving the application of the essential workplace skills.

Case Studies provide opportunities to think critically about issues that often have no clear-cut answers.

What's New in the 10th Edition

Chapter 4—*Image* provides a comprehensive look at one's personal and professional image. It emphasizes the impact of first impressions, the realization that perception is reality, and that image is much more than clothing and general appearance. Business and electronic communications etiquette are included.

Chapters 5, 6, and 7 all relate to the biggest problem in the workplace—*communication*. New and updated content has been added throughout these chapters. New features in the area of communication include a four-step formula for the assertive communicator, managing information overload, the problems related to the use of colloquialisms and gender-neutral language, and conversational skills (including use of small talk, conversation openers, ice breakers, conversation energizers, and questioning techniques successfully used in conversations).

New information on a key 21st-century skill—team building—highlights the characteristics of an effective team, the qualities of a team player, the advantages and disadvantages of teams in the workplace, and the evolving role of the virtual team in the ever-changing workplace.

Chapter 9—*Meeting Essentials* addresses meeting types and styles and offers strategies and tips for participanting, planning, scheduling, and conducting meetings. Electronic meetings such as webinars, webconferencing, and teleconferencing are included.

Chapter 10—*Applying Critical Work Skills* addresses some of the toughest skills to acquire in the workplace and in life. Self-management tools, time management (to-do lists, scheduling, time wasters, procrastination, and multitasking), balancing life and work, decision making, working creatively, managing stress, and using technology effectively are covered.

Chapter 11—*Developing Customer Focus* emphasizes that customers are both internal and external and that in building solid relationships, everybody wins. Effective telephone skills when serving customers is also included.

Chapter 14—*Developing Leadership Skills and Managing Change* encourages students to recognize and work toward the leadership qualities, skills, and work habits that will result in greater recognition and career success. The importance of accepting and welcoming change as an important ingredient in career growth is reinforced.

New Website and Instructor Resource CD

www.cengage.com/careerreadiness/masters

Videos correlated to each chapter show how to build better performance and relationships. Video quizzes accompany each segment to check your comprehension. Also included are web activities, flash cards, and chapter quizzes.

The Instructor Resource CD includes teaching suggestions, extra activities, recommended solutions, ExamView testbank, and PowerPoint presentations for each chapter. Various sample documents are also provided.

Reviewers

Penny Dhindsa
Institute of Technology, Clovis, CA

Pat Theriot
Hinds Community College, Vicksburg, MS

Dianna Schuster
Ivy Tech Community College, Lafayette, IN

Dorothy Dean
Illinois Central College, East Peoria, IL

Lori Brinker
University of Akron, Wayne College, Orrville, OH

ABOUT THE AUTHORS

L. Ann Masters is administrator, Office of the Commissioner of Education, Nebraska Department of Education, Lincoln, Nebraska. Her work in education includes nearly 40 years in business and career education, curriculum development, and policy work. She has taught a wide variety of communications, human relations, and business courses at both the secondary and postsecondary levels. Her administrative experience includes positions in the Nebraska Department of Education, current member of the National High School Center Advisory Board, past president and member of the National Council of State Board of Education Executives, past president and member of the National Association of Supervisors of Business Education, past board member of the American Vocational Association (now known as Association for Career and Technical Education), and past president and member of the National Board of Directors of Future Business Leaders of America. She has published texts in business communication, business English, and human relations and has been a frequent conference participant and speaker for state and national career and technical education and business education associations.

We want to remember **Dr. Harold Wallace**, a lifelong educator who was committed to helping students develop their potential. Dr. Wallace formerly of Colorado State University, Fort Collins, passed away just as we began this edition. He will be remembered for his work and dedication to education, his zest and enthusiasm for life, and his ability to recognize the importance of balancing life and work. Thank you, Dr. Wallace, for the positive influence on the lives that you have touched throughout your distinguished career in teaching and writing.

Part 1

It's all about *You*

Digital Vision/Getty Images

Workplace Focus

Clarissa Cutrell is communications director for the e-marketing firm Paulson Management Group, Inc. Nontraditional media are a big part of Clarissa's job. She helps clients market themselves through blogs, Twitter, Facebook, and other social media profiles.

Clarissa knows how important collaboration is in the workplace. "I nurture relationships with my coworkers and collaborate to build a sense of office community. We are more productive when we work as a team. We do better work and benefit from the recognition of a job well done. By working *together*, we build our individual self-esteem and expertise."

"When you love what you do, ambition comes naturally," says Clarissa. "There are so many ways to learn and grow in a job: from online publications to seeking advice from industry veterans. You can learn something from every experience. If something doesn't go quite right, find out what to do differently the next time. Most issues come down to incomplete or unclear communication. When you get an assignment, make sure that everyone involved has the same understanding about who, what, how, when, where, and why."

Clarissa believes it is important to establish a comfortable professional image. "Every office has its own vibe and image that it wants to project. It's important to follow the formal or unspoken dress code, but within that code you can develop a style that makes you feel good about yourself. When you feel confident about how you look, it shows in your work."

© Stephen Frost

Self-Esteem

© Photodisc/Getty Images

Think About It: Olivia was pleased to be employed at Watkins Advertising. She has been on the job for three months and feels comfortable with her new responsibilities. However, today everything changed. Deanna, her supervisor, asked Olivia to create a spreadsheet to forecast the costs for the product presentations in Kansas City and Denver next month. Olivia was frantic—she had worked with spreadsheets before but had only limited experience creating them from scratch. Deanna suggested that the Help feature of the software would be Olivia's best resource, but she also said she would be available if Olivia needed help getting started. Olivia replied, "Oh, no thank you. I'm sure I can figure it out. I've worked with spreadsheets." But she couldn't figure it out, and her frustrations were beginning to show. To make matters worse, she observed a coworker creating a spreadsheet with obvious ease. Olivia thought to herself, "I'll never be able to complete this spreadsheet. Maybe I shouldn't have taken this job."

Is Olivia feeling good about herself? What signs do you see that Olivia has some self-esteem issues? What would you suggest that Olivia do to complete the spreadsheet?

objectives

After completing this chapter you should be able to:

1. Explain the term self-esteem.
2. Discuss the "do's" and "don'ts" of building self-esteem.
3. Recognize the impact of low self-esteem.
4. List the rewards of a high level of self-esteem.
5. Understand how failure paves the way to success.
6. Be sensitive to feedback and use it to your benefit.
7. Trust others to help gain self-understanding.

Know and Accept Yourself

Who are you? You know your name, your likes and dislikes, your habits, and much more about yourself. You also have an image of yourself that most likely has many dimensions, such as:

- Physical appearance (attractive, handsome, average)
- Athletic ability (agile, good at sports)
- Sense of humor (hilarious, good, dry)
- Special talents (computer whiz, singer, writer, actor)
- Morals and ethics (high standards, sense of duty, ethical behavior)
- Aptitudes (natural abilities—physical or mental)
- Values and beliefs (stated and implied)

As you examine your dimensions, you begin to develop an understanding of who you are. In essence, you develop a picture of your "self," an awareness of your essential qualities that give you a unique identity—your self-image. This chapter will challenge you to think about how you feel about your self-image.

SELF-ESTEEM AND SELF-IMAGE

Belief in your abilities and your worth or value is **self-esteem**. Self-esteem is the extent to which you like, accept, and respect yourself. Figure 1-1 shows that your **self-image** (your mental picture of who you are) is made up of variables such as physical appearance, athletic ability, sense of humor, special talents, morals and ethics, aptitudes, and values and beliefs.

© Photodisc/Getty Images

You are a unique individual. Appreciate your many talents.

High self-esteem helps you to meet everyday challenges and stay on course to become all that you can be. You must be positive about yourself if you are to be successful and have a rich, full life. Self-esteem is not conceit or self-absorption. Genuine self-esteem—liking, accepting, and respecting yourself—can make you more humble, since recognizing your own worth can make you more aware of the worth of others.

"Self-esteem isn't everything. It's just that there's nothing without it."

When you dislike yourself, you have low self-esteem. Those who have low self-esteem may react by:

- Blaming others for their own weaknesses or faults.
- Becoming easily frustrated or defensive.
- Avoiding situations that make them uncomfortable.
- Feeling weak and incompetent.

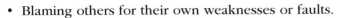

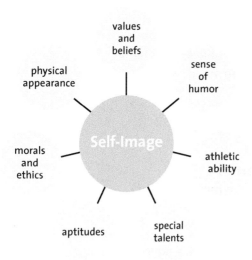

- values and beliefs
- sense of humor
- physical appearance
- **Self-Image**
- morals and ethics
- athletic ability
- aptitudes
- special talents

FIGURE 1-1 Your self-image is made up of many components.

"Friendship with one's self is all important, because without it, one cannot be friends with anyone else in the world."

- Feeling that others don't value them.
- Expressing few emotions.
- Being influenced easily by others.

Low self-esteem often leads to loneliness, anxiety, resentment, irritability, and little life satisfaction. Career, relationship, and mental health problems can often be traced to the quality of decisions and actions an individual has taken, which in turn can be traced back to low self-esteem. Review the scenario at the beginning of this chapter. What characteristics of low self-esteem does Olivia exhibit?

Having imperfections in your personality should not cause you to lose self-respect. Everyone has faults andimperfections. Just as you respect and like your friends who are not perfect, you should be able to respect and like yourself—just as you are. As Norman Vincent Peale wrote in *The Power of Positive Thinking,* "Believe in yourself. Have faith in your abilities. Without a humble yet reasonable confidence in your own powers, you cannot be successful or happy."[1]

How you feel about yourself affects your success in meeting the challenges of life and work. Having the confidence to carry out a specific task and accepting responsibility for your actions is key to developing self-esteem. If you constantly blame someone else for your actions, or feel sorry for yourself, or label yourself as a failure, you are unlikely to experience a strong sense of self-esteem. Learn from situations and attempt to do better next time. But never give up on yourself.

> *It was late, but Tayna was still hard at work at her computer trying to finish the report that was due tomorrow morning. She looked at the clock and sighed, knowing that she had no choice but to finish it before going to bed. "I should have started this sooner," she said. "I have no one to blame but myself. I will do better next time."*

Being a good person who has weaknesses is different than being an imperfect person. When you can appreciate the good in your personality (even with a clear view of your faults and inadequacies), and genuinely *like* yourself, you are ready to move ahead in planning and working to develop a personality that represents the best that you can be—with an even higher self-esteem.

We all experience problems with self-esteem at certain times in our lives—especially during the teens when we're figuring out who we are and where we fit in the world. The good news is that, because everyone's self-image changes over time, self-esteem is not fixed for life. So, if you feel that your self-esteem isn't all it could be, you can improve it.[2] Some do's and don'ts of building self-esteem follow.

Do's of Building Self-Esteem

Follow these tips to build self-esteem:

Engage in positive self-talk. Give yourself recognition, praise, and positive self-talk each day. You would do this for a friend; do it for yourself as well. Tell yourself "well done" when you do well. Remind yourself about the times you excelled, learned new skills, or treated another person well. Self-image is shaped by our own self-talk. If you tell yourself "Yes I can," chances are you will. Focus on the positive in your self-talk sessions.

Remember what you like about yourself. Know your strengths. Make a list of your good qualities and place it where you will see it each day. Some starter thoughts—you are patient, you are caring, you enjoy learning new things, you like to help others. Get the idea? Add to your list each week.

Talk with others about your good qualities. A trusted friend, relative, or counselor often sees qualities in you that you take for granted or overlook.

Focus on your achievements. Your achievements and successes, regardless of how large or small, are important to your self-image. Again, list them. Some starter thoughts—you graduated from high school, you are a good friend, you exercise each day, you do volunteer work. Get the picture? Add to your list each week.

Plan for your future. Look forward rather than dwelling on the past. Make a list of things you want to do or want to change. Visualize your dreams—what you hope to accomplish in the future. Know your weaknesses and set goals to overcome your weaknesses. You'll learn some techniques to help you work toward achieving your goals in Chapter 2.

Don'ts of Improving Self-Esteem

Avoid these pitfalls as you strive to build your self-esteem:

Don't try to imitate someone else. Attempting to imitate or be like someone else

Think about the words as you say them out loud. Repeat each sentence.

- I have the power to change myself.
- I am free to choose to live as I wish and to give priority to my needs, wants, and desires.
- I deserve happiness and success.
- I can make my own choices and decisions.
- I can choose to make changes in every aspect of my life.
- I am worthy of being loved.
- I am satisfied if I have done my best.
- I have a plan for my future, and my plan is open to change.
- I can forgive myself for mistakes.
- I will not give up on myself.

© aldomurillo/iStockphoto.com

Improve your self-esteem by participating in an activity you enjoy.

may lead to a further lack of self-worth and self-confidence. You are a unique individual, and you cannot be someone else. Strive to improve yourself rather than comparing yourself with others.

Don't think negatively about yourself. Don't criticize yourself for not being as successful, smart, popular, or attractive as someone else. Remember, you have qualities that others do not possess. If you feel others have much more of what you desire and are more worthwhile individuals than you, you may become obsessed with envy. **Envy**, a feeling of jealousy with regard to another's advantages, success, possessions, and so on, is considered by many to be the most destructive of all human emotions. However, you may pick up valuable clues to an appropriate level of self-esteem by observing family members, teachers, and friends you admire.

Don't neglect yourself. You are important. Safeguard your health and be conscientious about your grooming and appearance. Take advantage of educational opportunities. Treat yourself to a walk in the park, a trip to a museum, a couple of hours with a good book, or another activity that you enjoy. These activities are self-renewing and fulfilling. Take time to focus on your wants, needs, and desires. This is not selfishness as long as what you want doesn't injure or interfere with how others live.

Don't let setbacks get the best of you. Lack of success simply means you are not successful *yet*. Don't think of a setback as failure. Instead, think of the inevitable setbacks you will face as learning experiences or signals to change direction.

"Always be the first-rate version of yourself, instead of the second-rate version of somebody else."

on the job

Irv slumped down in his chair and stared into space. "This is the third draft of this budget report, and it still isn't right. I suppose it's because I don't write very well that I can't get the report together," he mumbled. Early drafts of the report and wadded-up papers were scattered by the computer and on the floor. Without question, his self-image was at a low point. But then Irv remembered his promise to himself—that he would not let the lack of success get the best of him. "Okay," he thought, "I need to try a different tactic. I've written short reports before—so why am I having so much difficulty with a long one?" After some thought, Irv decided to outline the report first and jot down major points under side headings—something he had learned in his communications class in school. Soon he was adding meat to the bones of his outline without a problem. When Irv was finished, he looked at the report and smiled. "I almost gave up," he said. "But in the end, I discovered that I really could do something I hadn't done before."

How might this story have ended if Irv had given up? What insight did Irv show into his own behavior?

How do you feel about yourself? Do you have a healthy, positive level of self-esteem? Think about your experiences over the past few months. Rate on a scale of 1–5 how often each statement reflects how you feel.

1—rarely   2—sometimes   3—often   4—frequently   5—usually

a. _____ I don't like going to work (or school).

b. _____ I am easily bored.

c. _____ I cannot communicate easily with others.

d. _____ I don't perform my job (or class work) up to par.

e. _____ I get into conflicts with others.

f. _____ I think my friends consider me a failure.

g. _____ I am late or fail to show up for appointments too often.

h. _____ I am not conscientious about my grooming and appearance.

i. _____ I have unattractive physical characteristics.

j. _____ I don't concentrate on anything for very long.

k. _____ I work hard but accomplish little.

l. _____ I am forgetful.

m. _____ I give up when I can't get something right the first time.

n. _____ I lack energy and enthusiasm.

Scoring:

14–20   You are doing well. Congratulations!

21–30   You are okay if you continue to build your self-esteem.

31–40   You need to do some serious self-esteem building.

41+   You appear to have very low self-esteem. Ask someone you trust and who cares about you to help you as you work to improve your self-esteem.

REWARDS OF GOOD SELF-ESTEEM

Let's look at the rewards that come with a high level of self-esteem. Positive self-esteem results from finding the positives in your life—academic success, self-control, self-acceptance, and optimism about the future. People with good self-esteem are likely to be working deliberately to strengthen and improve themselves. They understand that valuing their positive qualities is not about competing with others, but about understanding themselves and pursuing what is best for them. Think about the people you know who have high self-esteem. Chances are good that they:

- Take on responsibility (have a "can-do" attitude).
- Take pride in their accomplishments.

"You were not born a winner, and you were not born a loser. You are what you make yourself be."

- Approach challenges positively and with enthusiasm.
- Are not afraid to show a broad range of emotions.
- Feel qualified to influence others.
- Tolerate frustration, challenges, and setbacks in life.

Everyone has special gifts and unique qualities that make that person exceptional. Think about the qualities that make you unique and then strive to improve those good qualities. Remember, having healthy self-esteem enables you to project self-confidence.

checkpoint

1. What are the dimensions of your image?

_____

_____

_____

_____

2. List three tips for improving self-esteem.

_____

_____

_____

_____

3. What are two characteristics of someone with good self-esteem?

_____

_____

_____

_____

4. How can you raise your self-esteem by changing your self-talk?

_____

_____

_____

_____

5. Explain the rewards of high self-esteem.

_____

_____

_____

_____

applications

1. Write a brief description of yourself. List five characteristics or qualities that make you special.

_____

_____

_____

_____

2. List five characteristics or qualities that you would like to improve.

_____

_____

_____

_____

3. Ask someone you trust to review and comment on your responses to Applications 1 and 2. Did the reviewer know what is important to you in life? Did the reviewer add to the list of your unique qualities or to the list of characteristics/qualities you would like to improve? How did you feel after your conversation?

_____

_____

_____

_____

4. How does assessing your strengths and weaknesses help motivate you to be all that you can be?

_____

_____

_____

_____

Believe in Yourself

Ava worked as a sales associate in a discount store that went out of business. After searching for a new job, she was offered a position in a local retail store that specializes in clothing for teens. The job included selling, displaying merchandise, and keeping the shelves and racks neat. Ava accepted the job and went to work with enthusiasm. She assumed that her positive experience in the discount store was proof of her ability to work successfully in the clothing store. However, Ava had problems during her training period. She found that she could not relate to the teens shopping in the store. She objected to the way many of the teens dressed, and her opinions were expressed by her actions. Often she was dismayed by the way the teens pulled items from the shelves and made no attempt to replace them. Mr. Planck, the store owner, gave Ava low ratings on her first evaluation because she was not selling much merchandise. Also, customers had made unkind remarks about the manner in which they were treated. Many of the teen customers avoided Ava because they felt she wasn't helpful. Ava felt crushed after her first job review. She wanted to succeed, but she found herself struggling to maintain her composure when confronted with what appeared to be failure.

What should Ava do to maintain a positive, realistic self-image? How realistic was it for Ava to assume that her successful experience in a discount store was proof of her ability to work in a store that sells clothing to teens?

TURN FAILURE INTO SUCCESS

In the On the Job scenario at the beginning of this section, Ava at first made excuses for her inability to work with the primary customers of the specialty store. She told the store owner that at times she was not feeling well and this made her a bit edgy. Another excuse Ava used was that she was not trying hard enough, so she attempted to be overly friendly with the young customers. But that didn't work. The result was more criticism of her work—more failure. Finally, Ava found herself at a crossroads. If she continued to make excuses and deny the reality of her failure, she would only create more anxiety and distress for herself. It would be very stressful and, at the same time, difficult to maintain her self-esteem.

"I have not failed. I've just found 10,000 ways that won't work."

Ava made the best decision. She confronted her frustrations and gained insight about the conflict between what she valued and the evidence presented by this experience. She thought, "I tried my best to do the job well and serve the customers as my supervisor expected, but I failed. This experience tells me that I was wrong to think that my discount store experience would transfer easily to a specialty store. However, that's all right. I can accept this failure because there is much in my life that is rewarding and satisfying. I don't have to be the best at everything. My evaluations at the discount store were all good. I have good organizational skills, I'm a willing worker, and I enjoy working with people other than teens. I believe in myself and my ability to find a job where I can use my talents."

Ava was able to reflect upon her experience and keep her self-esteem intact. She assessed the situation thoughtfully and made a decision based upon her strong belief in herself and her abilities. She removed herself from a stressful situation and moved on with her life.

© Digital Vision/Getty Images

Don't let failure ruin your self-image. Instead, turn failure into success.

BE SENSITIVE TO FEEDBACK

Supervisors and coworkers give each other **feedback**, information about yourself from another's perspective that you can use to evaluate how you are doing. If you are willing to listen and observe, you will pick up all kinds of feedback. For example, "Great job in meeting that customer's needs!" "Careful, you entered the wrong amount." "I expected to get that information from you this morning; when will you have it?" If you take the initiative to ask for feedback, you will learn even more.

Always be open, alert, and sensitive to both positive and negative feedback. After evaluating the feedback, you may need to make changes within yourself.[3] Some people mistakenly go out of their way to ignore feedback that comes from negative experiences. However, these experiences provide valuable information you can use to improve. For instance, if you want to think of yourself as a good student but fear that you have done poorly, you might refuse to look at your grades. Or finding a low grade, you might feel that the teacher was being unfair. You need to interpret and use feedback wisely if you are going to grow and improve. The feedback may not always be what you want to hear—but listen, reflect on what you hear, and adjust.

Here are examples of how you might collect, interpret, and respond to evidence of praise or criticism from informal feedback.

> **Feedback:** "Our sales are off this month. If this keeps up, it may be necessary to lay off one of the sales associates."

> **Interpretation:** I'm not selling as much as I should, and I may lose my job.

Question: "Are you saying that if I don't increase my sales, I may be fired?"

Response: "No, your sales are among the highest. It's just that the economy is bad and people aren't buying as much. If this trend keeps up, I may have to lay off one of the new hires."

Feedback: "Mrs. Lucero is one of our best customers. She said to thank you for your help in getting her loan application approved."

Interpretation: One more satisfied customer. I must be doing my job well.

Feedback: "Our supervisor says we need more training in projecting a positive image for the company when we answer the telephone."

Interpretation: I may be projecting a negative image when I answer the telephone. Maybe I should improve my telephone techniques.

Feedback: Jack reviews the newspaper advertisement he wrote. The copy editor has circled several punctuation and syntax errors but has also written in the margin, "Good selling point!"

Interpretation: My technical writing skills may be weak and need work, but I have good ideas and write creatively.

There are things we can change about ourselves and things we cannot. Concentrate your energy on those things that are within your power to change. When you receive feedback:

- Don't take negative feedback personally. Concentrate your energy on the situation.
- Don't overreact if you are challenged; the feedback is about the situation, not you as a person.
- Learn from the feedback and make necessary changes.

Learn from Others

Anyone in a position to observe your behavior can give you feedback. Welcome these opportunities to learn about how others perceive you. Try not to be hurt, offended, or resentful. Even when criticism is hurtful, you can learn from it. Don't allow your anger to detract from the value of the feedback.

Close friends and associates are a good source of feedback. Counselors, teachers, and employment supervisors or coworkers can also provide you with valuable information about your behavior. But more importantly, you may feel a sense of trust and safety in talking with them. In an environment of trust, you can feel safe to reveal your real self. Only in an environment of mutual trust can honest, open, two-way communication occur. Be willing to share openly and honestly. Without that openness on your part, the person may not be willing to be open and candid about negative feedback.

checkpoint

1. What is feedback and why is it important?

   _____

   _____

   _____

2. What do employers expect of employees?

   _____

   _____

   _____

3. List five tips for improving your self-esteem.

   _____

   _____

   _____

4. Who should you ask for feedback? Why?

   _____

   _____

   _____

5. Why it important to listen to both positive and negative feedback?

   _____

   _____

   _____

applications

1. Do you have a realistic image of yourself? On the grid (page 14), place a check in the first column if the statement represents what you think you are like. In the second column, check statements that represent what others think of you. In the third column, check statements that represent what you hope will someday be true for you.

	I THINK I AM	OTHERS THINK I AM	I WANT TO BE
How I feel about myself			
Inferior to most of my peers	_____	_____	_____
Self-confident	_____	_____	_____
Lacking self-confidence	_____	_____	_____
Proud of my achievements	_____	_____	_____
Embarrassed about my achievements	_____	_____	_____
Pleased with my appearance	_____	_____	_____
Disappointed with my appearance	_____	_____	_____
How I feel toward others			
Tolerant	_____	_____	_____
Intolerant	_____	_____	_____
Friendly	_____	_____	_____
Unfriendly	_____	_____	_____
Comfortable being with strangers	_____	_____	_____
Uncomfortable being with strangers	_____	_____	_____
Enjoy being with most people	_____	_____	_____
Do not enjoy being with most people	_____	_____	_____

Which items in the first column please you the most?

Which items in the second column distress you the most?

Which items in the third column do you most want to work on?

2. Why are the items you checked in the I Want To Be column in Application 1 important for you to work toward?

_____

_____

3. Feedback is sometimes hurtful or perceived as unjust. Think of a situation in which you received feedback that you felt was unfair. How did you respond to this feedback? What could you have done to make the criticism a positive motivation for you?

_____

_____

1 points to remember

Review the following points to determine what you remember from the chapter.

- If you have good self-esteem, you appreciate your special gifts and your value as a person. You strive to do your best and to achieve your potential.
- A strong belief in your value and capabilities, coupled with proper action, can help you achieve your goals in life.
- People with healthy self-esteem work to improve themselves. They understand that believing in themselves and valuing their positive qualities is not about competing with others but about understanding themselves and pursuing what is best for them.
- Career, relationship, and mental health problems can often be traced back to low self-esteem.
- Failure can lead to success. Learn from every situation and try to do better the next time. But never give up on yourself.
- To benefit from everyday experiences, interpret and use feedback (both positive and negative) that reflects how you are doing in your life and work.
- Talking things over with a friend, counselor, or someone you can share your feelings with will give you insight and understanding.

How did you do? Did you remember the main points you studied in this chapter?

KEY terms

self-esteem

self-image

feedback

envy

Want more activities? Go to **www.cengage.com/careerreadiness/masters** to get started.

CHAPTER *activities*

1. In a conversation with a trusted friend or counselor, discuss the following questions and write your responses.

   What are your special talents and abilities?

   _____

   _____

   _____

   _____

   What events in your life seem to conflict with your ideal self-image?

   _____

   _____

   _____

   _____

   What would you like to change or improve about yourself?

   _____

   _____

   _____

   _____

   What talents and abilities do you hope to develop?

   _____

   _____

   _____

   _____

2. Think about a time when you received praise. Also, think about a time when you received constructive criticism. How did you interpret this information? Did you take criticism in the same way that you took praise?

   _____

   _____

   _____

   _____

   _____

   _____

   _____

   _____

3. Describe a situation in which you have seen someone criticized or reprimanded in a hurtful way. How did that person react? What was your reaction?

   _____

   _____

   _____

   _____

   _____

   _____

   _____

   _____

CRITICAL *thinking*

Marcy is an administrative assistant to the purchasing manager of an electronics firm. Marcy had worked happily for her supervisor Mr. DeLisi for three years. Two weeks ago, Mr. DeLisi transferred to a new position and Marcy was assigned to work with his replacement, Ms. Minzer. Marcy's new supervisor is quite capable and efficient but very short on patience. She speaks crisply and concisely to everyone. In her eagerness to please, Marcy is very self-conscious and, as a result, makes many errors. When Ms. Minzer criticizes her work rather sharply, Marcy bursts into tears. Ms. Minzer takes Marcy's tears in stride but becomes extremely irritated with Marcy's continued apologies for her previous errors. Finally, she arranges for Marcy to be transferred to another office.

1. Does Marcy have a problem with her self-esteem? What evidence do you see to support this conclusion?

   _____

   _____

   _____

   _____

2. Is Marcy expecting too much of herself? Should she see herself as a "perfectionist" and embark on a self-improvement program, or should she accept herself as a person who occasionally makes mistakes but learns from them?

   _____

   _____

   _____

   _____

3. Assume that Marcy goes to Mr. DeLisi for friendly advice. After listening to Marcy's story, what guidance and advice might he offer?

   _____

   _____

   _____

   _____

CASE 1.2 Pull Yourself Together

Madison and Hannah share an apartment and work in the same branch of a local bank. Madison is getting married in the near future, and Hannah will be responsible for the full amount of rent. Hannah does not want to leave their comfortable and convenient apartment but knows she can't afford the rent on her own. Madison tells Hannah that she had heard that the bank's marketing department plans to hire a second web developer. The position will pay a higher salary than her current position. Hannah has a webmaster certificate from the local community college, but she enjoys her current position and doesn't want to leave her friends in the loan department. However, this appears to be a perfect opportunity for Hannah to improve her salary and utilize her skills. Hannah verifies that the position is open and submits an application. She, along with several other candidates, is called in for an interview.

That evening Madison asked, "How did the interview go?" "Okay, I guess," Hannah replied. "I'm not counting on a second interview. Many others are applying for the job—applicants with better qualifications and more experience than I have. I'll bet the human resources office already has picked someone else. If I'm going to be able to stay in this apartment, I'll have to get a second job or find another roommate. Gee, I wish you weren't getting married. You are so lucky to have found Matt. I haven't had a serious date in months. Too bad I'm not the one getting married." Madison couldn't believe what she was hearing. Hannah is an intelligent young woman, a well-respected bank employee, and she has her webmaster certification. Madison was also concerned about Hannah's envious remark about her upcoming marriage. Finally, Madison said, "What's your problem? Pull yourself together and believe that position can be yours if you really want it."

1. If you were Madison, would you offer further encouragement to Hannah? Does Madison have a right to be concerned about Hannah's remarks? What might Madison say to help Hannah boost her self-esteem?

   _____

   _____

   _____

   _____

   _____

   _____

   _____

   _____

2. Why do you think Hannah is suddenly so apprehensive about her future? What do you think went through Hannah's mind when she saw many other candidates interested in the position?

_____

_____

_____

_____

_____

_____

_____

_____

3. Do you think Hannah has realistically assessed her capabilities? If not, why not? Do you predict that Hannah will be hired for the web developer position? Why or why not?

_____

_____

_____

_____

_____

_____

_____

_____

Self-Development

2 chapter

© Andresr, 2009/Used under license from Shutterstock.com

Think About It: Natalie, a shy young woman, grew up in a single-parent home with three siblings. She had to work evenings and weekends while in high school to help support her family. Her schedule left little time for socializing. After gradu-ation, Natalie landed a full-time job in a real estate office. Her receptionist duties included greeting clients and realtors and scheduling home inspections and closings. Because Natalie was shy, she struggled with the aspects of her job that required her to work with others. Another office worker, Cassandra, took the time to give Natalie some pointers on greet-ing clients, being assertive with difficult inspectors, and establishing good relationships with her cowork-ers. Natalie appreciated Cassandra's help, accepted her suggestions, and worked hard to improve her skills. Natalie had taken several computer courses in high school and was able to compile a list of websites of interest to the realtors in her office. The realtors praised Natalie for her extra effort on their behalf. Natalie's self-confidence began to soar. She taught herself to post new listings on the company's website. She enrolled in a public speaking class at the commu-nity college. She began to set goals and make plans to reach those goals.

What do you think was the turning point for Natalie? What actions did Natalie take to improve herself?

objectives

After completing this chapter, you should be able to:

1. Explain how self-confidence affects success.
2. Visualize the improvements needed to reach your potential.
3. Set long-term self-improvement goals.
4. Use behavior modification for self-improvement.
5. Develop mentoring relationships.
6. Explain tools available to predict occupational success.

2.1 Develop a Self-Improvement Plan

2.2 Improvement Requires Work

Develop a Self-Improvement Plan

If you are to take charge of yourself and become successful in your life and work, you must start with a clear, realistic image of where you are now and where you want to be in the future. Once you have a good idea of what needs to be accomplished, you are ready to begin making plans— plans for the self-improvement that is needed as you develop your success identity. A self-improvement plan is not static; rather, it is a life-long process that changes with your growth and experiences.

In this section you will learn to create a self-improvement plan that involves a realistic vision of your future self, long-term goals, and an action plan to guide you in the self-improvement process. An overview of a self-improvement plan is shown in Figure 2-1. Finally, you will learn why you must hold yourself accountable for taking the actions needed to meet your life's objectives.

Vision of your
future self

Clear, specific, and
measurable goals

Action plan for
achieving each goal

FIGURE 2-1 Overview of a self-improvement plan.

BUILD SELF-CONFIDENCE

Self-confidence influences your ability to put your self-improvement plan in motion. John Wesley defines **self-confidence** as "the difference between feeling unstoppable and feeling scared out of your wits."[1] Quite simply, self-confidence is your sense of personal strength and a belief that you are worthy and talented. What counts is what you think you can accomplish. It doesn't matter what others think you can do. Self-confidence is displayed by a pleasant demeanor, a positive outlook on life, friends, and satisfaction with life in general. Those who lack self-confidence are often timid and fear failure.

Perception is reality—the more self-confidence you have, the more likely you are to succeed. Self-confidence has a major impact on how others perceive you. Because negative events in our lives often result in a loss of self-esteem, most people can use a boost of self-confidence now and then. Apply the proven techniques that follow to build self-confidence in your career, relationships, education, health, and hobbies.

Use the talents you possess: the woods would be very silent if no birds sang there except those that sang best.

Use positive self-talk. Say positive things to yourself every day. Positive "self-talk" programs your mind to act optimistically. Use statements such as "I know I can learn this new software," or "I can raise my grade from a B to an A if I study harder," or "I'll feel better when I get this done correctly." Avoid negative expressions such as "This probably isn't right . . ." or "This may sound stupid . . ." and negative statements such as "I'm not smart enough to work this problem" or "That was dumb on my part!" Negative statements imply failure. Use positive self-talk to keep moving forward.

Increase your knowledge and skills. The foundation for a healthy self-confidence is a "bank" of knowledge and experience. At work, go beyond what is expected. Offer to take on new projects or responsibilities. Gain new skills. Learn more than you have to know about your company's and its competitors' products and services so that others can count on you for good information. Keep up with current events and read professional articles and journals. Ask questions about concepts that you don't understand. Get an education and become a lifelong learner. The more you know, the more self-confidence you will have.

Learn from mistakes. Successful people fail, but they don't stop. They rethink the situation, learn from mistakes, and try again. When you make major mistakes, analyze what went wrong, request help if necessary, correct errors where possible, and move on.

Expect to succeed. When you learn something new or take on new responsibilities, do you expect to succeed? If not, why not? Developing a "can do" attitude and raising your level of self-expectation can empower you to do well. Perhaps you're familiar with the proverb "Nothing breeds success like success." Nothing makes us happier than when we set a goal for ourself and succeed in reaching that goal. The more you succeed, the greater will be your motivation to achieve again and again.

Conquer shyness. If you consider yourself shy, know that you can conquer shyness. Force yourself into new habits. Begin by going out of your

on the job

Ramon had a lifelong dream of opening a fast-food restaurant specializing in burgers with a unique sauce of "secret" spices developed by his beloved grandmother. Although competing with the national fast-food chains would be difficult, Ramon believed his restaurant would be profitable. He developed a business plan and found financial backers. After months of preparation, he opened the Yum-Yum Burger Hut. The grand opening was a hugh success. Six months later, however, Ramon realized his business was not profitable. Ramon feared for his future. His family hears Ramon make statements like, "Why did I ever start this business? How stupid of me to think that I could make a go of my own business. Why didn't someone tell me I wouldn't make it?" Friends still feel that the business can be successful. His financial backers are concerned about Ramon's attitude. They see potential, but Ramon's focus is on failure.

How realistic are Ramon's comments? What advice would you give Ramon?

way to speak to a new person each day. Even a simple smile and saying "Good morning!" as you pass a friend or coworker is a start. As you gain confidence, move on to asking a question or making a comment. Observe people who are outgoing and learn from them. Consider whether you have characteristics of a shy person, such as looking at the floor when you speak or avoiding eye contact. With time and practice, you can break these habits and overcome your shyness.

Accept responsibility for your success. Stephen Covey defines responsibility as "the ability to choose one's response."[2] Take responsibility for creating a self-improvement plan that involves a realistic vision of your future self, long-term goals, and an action plan. By committing to your dreams, you program your brain to look for solutions to keep you going on the path to success.

VISUALIZE YOUR FUTURE

Self-improvement begins with visualizing your future self, identifying specific and measurable goals, and devising action plans to meet those goals. To visualize your potential, use a technique called **imaging**.

©wdstock/iStockphoto.com

Picture your life as you would like it to be.

Imaging refers to deliberately picturing your life as you would like it to be. Athletes have imagined (or visualized) themselves excelling in sporting events, and salespeople have imagined themselves achieving high sales. The process of growing to reach your greatest potential is called **self-actualization**.

Begin the process by finding a quiet place where you can relax and not be interrupted. Close your eyes and picture yourself being successful. Try to free your mind of anxiety, stress, depression, sadness, anger, or other distractions. Imagine the personal qualities and characteristics you will need to develop to achieve this image of success. When you complete the imaging process, write down your visualizations and review them often. Make a commitment to yourself to achieve your lofty goals and dreams. Finally, incorporate the desired qualities into your self-improvement plan.

Self-actualization is a lifelong process. Expect to reassess and redefine yourself as you move ahead in life. As you gain self-confidence and your identity evolves, you grow personally and professionally into a successful individual.

The biggest adventure you can ever take is to live the life of your dreams.

SET GOALS

All successful athletes, students, business people, and professionals have **goals**—clearly stated results they want to achieve within a specified time period. An **action plan** is an organized series of actions to achieve a specific goal. The overall process for achieving your goals is called **goal-setting**. By knowing what you want to achieve, you can direct your energy toward your goals.

Just as you might plan a trip, you must develop a plan for your life. For example, if you plan to visit the national parks in Utah, you will need to estimate the cost, determine the route to take, where you will stay, locate trails you want to hike, and so forth. Similar planning is necessary for life.

When setting goals, consider the broad aspects that are important in your life:

- Career
- Education and training
- Finances
- Relationships (family, friends, and coworkers)
- Health
- Hobbies and interests

"It is not enough to take steps which may someday lead to a goal; each step must be itself a goal and a step likewise."

VAGUE GOALS	CLEAR GOALS
Get an education.	Earn an associate's degree in graphic design within two years.
Reduce my stress level.	Lower my blood pressure eight points by attending yoga classes three nights a week this fall.
Develop my musical talents.	Take guitar lessons next semester at the community college.

FIGURE 2-2 Vague vs. clear goals.

SMART GOALS ARE:
Specific (What exactly do you want to accomplish?)
Measurable (How will you assess your progress?)
Attainable (Is your goal within your reach?)
Relevant (Is your goal important to your plan for life?)
Timely (What is your deadline for completing this goal?)

FIGURE 2-3 Criteria for SMART goals.

When you set goals for yourself, state them clearly, put them in writing, and include the date you expect to complete them. Figure 2-2 contrasts vague goals with those that are clearly stated and include a specific time. A goal that is vague or expressed like an instruction (for example, "I'd like to be more popular" or "I'd like to stop procrastinating") has limited value.

Although you may be hired as an entry-level person, employers want to hire people who care about their future and want to grow in their careers. You may be asked about your career goals in job interviews. Once hired, an employee's performance is measured by the ability to meet the goals for the position. Effective managers and supervisors help employees succeed by developing and writing specific, straightforward goals that reflect what must be accomplished in a certain timeframe. Figure 2-3 shows the criteria for preparing SMART goals as defined in many businesses.[3] SMART is a mnemonic, or memory device, in which each letter of the word stands for one of five qualities. **SMART goals** are well-focused, achievable goals.

DEVELOP ACTION PLANS

Develop an action plan as a strategy for reaching your goals. For each goal, write down the steps and timeframe that will bring you closer to achieving your long-term goals. Putting your goals and action plans in writing is essential if you are to stay focused on what you want to accomplish. Note the long-term goal and action plan that follows.

Goal: To be promoted to the position of web specialist within two years.
Action Plan:

1. Investigate the requirements for the web specialist position.
2. Shadow a web specialist to better understand the duties.
3. Enroll and complete two courses at the community college.
4. Develop a website for a charitable group.
5. Apply for the position of web specialist.

When the action plan is complete, ask yourself: "What must I do to accomplish each step in my action plan?" Here are some short-term actions that might lead to accomplishing several of the previously stated goals, and ultimately the long-term goal of being promoted to the position of web specialist:

- Contact someone in human resources to find out the specific qualifications and requirements for the position of web specialist.
- Contact the local community college and research the relevant courses.
- Contact a counselor or the registrar's office to see if I meet the prerequisites for enrolling in the courses.

Rewrite these goals in specific, measurable terms and include them in your self-improvement plan.

1. **Excellent Physical Health.** Your health is everything. Take good care of it through appropriate exercise, regular checkups, and proper nutrition.
2. **Excellence in Your Work.** A sincere commitment to your job will bring a sense of accomplishment while helping build an excellent reputation.
3. **Involvement in Your Community.** Give back to the community that has supported you in so many ways. Serving and helping others often brings a sense of personal satisfaction.
4. **Good Relationships.** Worthwhile friendships are very fulfilling. Strive to have friends and be a good friend. Make an effort to achieve harmony with coworkers.
5. **Personal Growth and Development.** Invest in yourself through enrichment activities. Lifelong learning is the norm for successful people.
6. **Self-Motivation.** Strive to be a "go-getter" by raising your level of self-expectation. Because you expect to succeed, you do succeed.

Creating a personal action plan is not difficult. It takes a little time, thought, and planning. Here's one of many ways to create an action plan:

1. Determine the goal.
2. Chart the route.
3. Define every step it will take to attain the goal and keep on track.
4. Modify the personal action plan as necessary.
5. Review the action plan.

A personal action plan is a map to attain a personal goal. It is a life-enhancement tool. As with life, detours happen. When the detours and road construction occur, be flexible, embrace them, and move on.[4]

BE ACCOUNTABLE

Your success in meeting your goals will depend on how commited you are to succeed. Too often, people fail to achieve their goals simply because they get discouraged and give up. However, if you are passionate about your goals and hold yourself accountable for taking the necessary actions to meet them, it is easier to maintain the motivation and persistence required to succeed.

Think of each goal as a contract with yourself. Keep a card file with each goal (or contract with yourself) written on a card, as shown in Figure 2-4. The contract should include the date on which the contract takes effect, what you need to do ("I promise to . . ."), a realistic date for fulfillment of the contract, and the benefit you expect to achieve. Lastly, sign the card to show your commitment to completing the task. The act of keeping your commitments may be as important, if not more important, than achieving a particular goal or dream. In this way you raise your expectations for the success of future commitments, knowing that when you make a promise to yourself, you keep it.[5]

You may wish to share your goals with those you trust and encourage them to check on your progress. Doing so provides you with important feedback and an extensive support network. Remember, you can achieve realistic goals if you carefully plan to reach them and if you hold yourself accountable for sticking with your plan.

PERSONAL CONTRACT

DATE : *May 2, 2010*

I promise to set up an appointment with Christine Glenn, Director of Human Resources for ABC Financial Services on or before May 15, 2010 to discuss the education and experience requirements for the position of web specialist.

Heidy Clayborn

FIGURE 2-4 Sample personal contract on a 5" x 7" card.

checkpoint

1. List four techniques for building your self-confidence.

   _____

   _____

   _____

   _____

2. Define imaging and explain how it relates to self-actualizing.

   _____

   _____

   _____

   _____

3. What are the criteria for preparing SMART goals?

   _____

   _____

   _____

   _____

4. How might a trusted friend help you develop appropriate self-improvement goals and action plans?

   _____

   _____

   _____

   _____

5. Explain how commitment and accountability help you reach your goals.

   _____

   _____

   _____

   _____

applications

1. Identify someone who has achieved success in a career that fits with the plans you have for yourself. Arrange an interview to discuss the planning and preparation that went into developing his or her career. If possible, observe the person at work. Some possible questions or discussion topics are:

   a. What experiences and education helped prepare you for success in your position?

b. What steps have you taken to improve yourself?

c. Who was an influential role model for you?

d. What are you doing now to expand your career options?

e. What do you see yourself doing five years from now?

2. Working with a partner, "introduce" the person interviewed in Application 1. Discuss what you learned about the person and what surprised you about this person.

3. Write a profile of yourself. Include information about your education, work experience, accomplishments, activities, and the results of any interest and aptitude tests you have taken. Include anything that suggests specific talents or abilities that may prepare you for success in life and work. How will this profile help you set your long-term goals?

_____

_____

_____

_____

_____

_____

_____

_____

4. Based on Application 3, write two realistic, clear, and measurable long-term goals.

_____

_____

_____

_____

_____

_____

_____

5. Write an action plan for accomplishing each long-term goal in Application 4.

_____

_____

_____

_____

_____

_____

_____

Improvement Requires Work

Personal development involves making a lifelong commitment to reaching your goals and being all that you can be. In Section 2.1, you learned to set goals and develop action plans to guide your self-improvement process. To be successful in your career and personal life, you must make a conscious effort to continue to grow personally and professionally. You must reassess and rewrite your goals and action plans as time passes and circumstances change.

There are many strategies, techniques, or methods to consider as you actively work to improve yourself. Some self-improvement guidelines are provided in the Self-Improvement Tips feature box in this section. Further, you may find behavior modification to be a strong motivational tool as you implement your self-improvement plan. Additional strategies described in this section are mentoring, counseling, aptitude and interest tests, and try-out experiences.

"True success is but the development of self."

CHANGE YOUR BEHAVIOR

If your self-improvement plan requires a change in behavior on your part, you may find it helpful to use behavior modification. **Behavior modification** refers to the use of techniques to improve or change behavior. It rewards people for making good decisions and discourages unwanted behavior. A reward or benefit can be a strong motivational tool to change behavior. The reward or benefit used is referred to as **reinforcement**. Rewards are generally better motivators than punishments.

If you develop your own system of rewards, begin by thinking of things you enjoy that you might use as rewards. Examples might include playing a new video game, attending a baseball game, or enjoying dinner at a favorite restaurant. Rewards for behavior modification should be realistic. Don't promise yourself an expensive digital camera if you can only afford a moderately priced one. Personal development is a step-by-step process, so plan small rewards at each step along the way.

With a potential rewards list at hand, review your self-improvement plan. Match specific activities with appropriate rewards. For example, you may decide to use more effective study skills, start tasks sooner, control your temper, or get more rest.

SELF-IMPROVEMENT TIPS

Follow these guidelines as you develop your self-improvement program.

- Start now.
- Start small. **Don't try to do everything at once. Focus on your highest priorities and add other goals as time goes by.**
- Involve others. **They can help keep you on course, listen and offer feedback, and be there to help you celebrate successes.**
- Don't give up. **Don't think of a slip as defeat—think of it as an opportunity to try again.**
- Stay focused on your goals. **Review your goals every day. Place them where you will see them each day and be reminded of their importance.**
- Acknowledge your improvements. **Recognize how far you have come, and celebrate each goal you achieve.**
- Let every success trigger a new goal. **There will always be something new to learn, something higher to attain. Keep moving forward.**
- Focus on gratitude. **Set aside time each day to mentally list what you have to be thankful for—unique skills, successes, and positive relationships.**

You may find it helpful to write a contract with yourself in which you promise that you are going to change in some way. Include the date the contract takes effect, what you need to do, a realistic date to fulfill the contract, and the reward you will receive. Lastly, sign your name to show your commitment to the change in behavior.

Stephen aspired to become manager of the Contented Cows Ice Cream Shoppe, but he knew that his people skills needed work. Too often he was abrupt with customers. Sometimes he didn't allow them to finish a sentence before he jumped in with what he wanted to say. He decided to enter into a contract with himself to change his behavior. He wrote the following on a sheet of paper: "Effective immediately, I will make an extra effort to actively listen to customers. I will not respond until the customer is finished speaking. If after three weeks I am successful in changing my behavior, I will treat myself to a day at the Wild Wild West Water Park."

LEARN FROM A MENTOR

When you begin a new job, there is a lot to learn—procedures, policies, rules (written and unwritten), as well as unspoken expectations by those who have been on the job for a while. Most coworkers are eager to welcome a new employee and help them learn their job.

Many companies recognize the benefits of establishing formal mentoring programs. Typically, someone is assigned to help new employees with on-the-job orientation and training. The person who helps an individual develop on the job is called a **mentor**. A mentor (or coach) may offer advice, answer questions, help a new employee understand the culture of the business, share expertise and experiences, and serve as a role model.

Mentoring relationships require open communication and a commitment from both parties. Typically, a mentor is someone who takes a personal interest in helping you reach your potential at work and in life. Your mentor will talk with you privately about questions or issues and do his or her best to help you achieve your self-improvement goals. A mentor's support and feedback is usually nonjudgmental and based upon honesty and trust. Take advantage of this opportunity to ask questions and learn from the more experienced person. Be open-minded and respectfully consider the mentor's advice.

©Photodisc/Getty Images

Mentoring relationships require open communication and a commitment from both parties.

Mentoring can benefit the new employee, the mentor, and the company. The employee and the mentor learn from each other, receive positive energy from the relationship, and grow professionally. The company benefits because the new employee adjusts to the job more quickly.

If you are not assigned a mentor, try to find someone in the organization or in your profession. You may need to put forth extra effort to cultivate a friendship with someone who will want to fulfill the role of mentor (or coach).

SEEK COUNSELING

A counselor or therapist can help with the process of understanding and appreciating where you are in your personal and career development. Sometimes talking with someone—a mental health professional, school or college counselor, or even a relative or a close personal friend with whom you can talk openly and honestly—allows you to explore your feelings about yourself and sort out any concerns you may have. Talking with a professional counselor can also help you appreciate the many positive aspects of your personality, your education, your employment experiences, and your natural abilities.

George has worked at Around the World Travel for three weeks. He is one of two associates responsible for handling corporate travel. Although he has booked travel in the United States, he has yet to learn the "ins and outs" of international travel. He is able to find some online help but is still not comfortable when a client comes in to book a trip to the remote corners of the world. George knows that Natasha, who has handled international travel for seven years, could be his best resource—that is, if she is willing. He approaches her and asks if she would be willing to share her expertise with him. She smiles and says, "Of course! I'd be happy to help in any way that I can. If you're willing to spend your lunch hour with me for the next week or two, I'm sure we can clear up your questions. International travel is a challenge, but it's also interesting and exciting. The corporate client you saw me talking with wants to book travel that includes London, Rome, and Athens. I suggest you buy a world map and have it on hand for our first discussion tomorrow." George felt like the weight of the world had been lifted from his shoulders. After work, he bought the map and a book on international customs. He then made a list of topics he wanted to discuss with Natasha.

Did George make the right decision when he asked Natasha for help? Do you think this mentoring relationship will work to the satisfaction of both individuals?

Large companies and government agencies may have a formal **Employee Assistance Program** (EAP) to help employees deal with personal problems that might adversely affect their job performance, health, or well-being. EAPs provide professional counseling for little or no cost to you. Information you share with an EAP counselor is strictly confidential so you should feel comfortable talking openly about your questions, concerns, and issues.

Information about EAP programs can be found in the human resources office of most companies or government agencies. If this service is provided in your new employement situation, take advantage of it. EAP services generally include assessment, short-term counseling, and referral services for employees and their household members.

TAKE APTITUDE AND INTEREST TESTS

Your local Job Service office or school career counseling center provide testing services and help with assessing your strengths and weaknesses. Career interest and aptitude tests can help you better understand your potential for success in various career fields. These tests can also identify what you need to learn to prepare for success in a career. Some tests measure characteristics that relate to the demands of various work situations. For instance:

- Do you like detail work?
- Are you by nature an orderly person?
- Do you enjoy teamwork or would you prefer to work alone?
- Do you enjoy the challenge of variety and change in your work?
- Do you work well with mechanical things?
- Do you want a 9-to-5 job or a flexible schedule?
- Do you have an aptitude for work involving math and science?

Answers to these types of questions will help you focus on your interests, aptitudes, and preferences. If you are unsure about which career field you should enter, these tests can provide you with direction. An employment or school counselor will help you interpret your tests and formulate a career strategy.

TRY OUT A WORK SITUATION

You can evaluate your potential for success in an occupation through an actual, or "try-out," work experience. A **try-out experience** provides an actual on-the-job opportunity for a limited period of time. For the musician, athlete, chef, taxi driver, and sales associate, experience provides clear and obvious signs of success and failure. For example, suppose you were considering a career in food service. An opportunity to work briefly in a restaurant would let you know if you enjoy working with people and if you can handle complaints and work intensely for several hours. Successful performance in the kitchen and compliments from the restaurant staff or customers would reinforce your career choice.

Use this checklist to help identify areas of your life that you want to improve.

_____ Do I need to improve my work skills?
_____ Do I need additional education?
_____ Is there something new I want to learn?
_____ Do I understand and use wise money management strategies?
_____ Do I take care of my physical, mental, and emotional health?
_____ Do I use my time wisely?
_____ Do I have a good relationship with my family and friends? With coworkers?
_____ Do I need to improve my communication skills?
_____ Do I treat others with respect?
_____ Do I use my unique gifts and talents?
_____ Do I have bad habits that I would like to change?

Another kind of try-out experience would be to enroll in a course related to the field you want to explore. You can find these courses in adult education programs, community colleges, career colleges and technical schools, or apprentice training programs and instruction sponsored by employers in business and industry. You may be allowed to audit a few classes without enrolling in the course.

An internship is another way to test your interests and abilities and build your self-confidence before you commit to a career program. An **internship program** coordinates classroom and laboratory training with on-the-job training in the work environment. For many college students, internships increase job opportunities after graduation because of the network of relationships developed with people outside school and home.

checkpoint

1. What is behavior modification?

_____

_____

_____

_____

2. When might you seek the services of a counselor?

_____

_____

_____

_____

3. Explain why working with a mentor requires a commitment from both parties involved.

_____

_____

_____

_____

_____

4. How might an aptitude or interest test help you decide on a career?

_____

_____

_____

_____

_____

5. Briefly explain the purpose and benefits of an internship program.

_____

_____

_____

_____

_____

applications

1. List six things you would consider as rewards or reinforcement of your self-development efforts. Will behavior modification techniques be helpful to you? Why or why not?

_____

_____

_____

_____

_____

2. What characteristics will you look for in a mentor to support you on the job? What characteristics will you look for in a personal mentor to help you with life situations?

_____

_____

_____

_____

_____

3. Visit the career counseling center of a community college or other school and gather information about the career interest and aptitude tests available. Find out if there is a charge for the tests, what information can be learned from the tests, and the procedures to take the test(s) and have the results analyzed. List the names of the tests and what they measure.

_____

_____

_____

_____

_____

_____

_____

_____

_____

_____

_____

_____

_____

_____

4. What opportunities are available to have a try-out or internship experience in the career field you are considering?

_____

_____

_____

_____

_____

_____

_____

_____

_____

_____

_____

_____

_____

_____

2 *points to* remember

Review the following points to determine what you remember from the chapter.

- Signs of a self-confident person include a pleasant demeanor, a positive outlook on life, a circle of friends, and a sense of satisfaction with life in general.

- Improve your self-confidence by reviewing your positive characteristics, talking positively to yourself, taking advantage of opportunities to build your knowledge and skills, moving on despite setbacks, increasing your expectations for yourself, and planning for self-improvement.

- Self-improvement begins with a vision of your future self, involves identifying specific goals, and devising action plans that will help you accomplish your long-term goals.

- Put your goals and action plans in writing. Stay focused on your goals and hold yourself accountable for your action plans.

- Self-actualization is a lifelong process. Expect to reassess and redefine your identity throughout your career and life.

- Behavior modification requires developing your own system. Make contracts with yourself about your goals and action plans—and keep the contracts!

- A mentoring relationship with a coworker or supervisor can help you achieve your plans for self-improvement. Mentoring relationships require open communication and a commitment from both parties.

- Employee Assistance Programs, aptitude and interest testing, try-out experiences, and internship programs are valuable self-improvement resources.

How did you do? Did you remember the main points you studied in the chapter?

KEY *terms*

self-confidence

imaging

self-actualization

goals

action plan

goal-setting

SMART goals

behavior modification

reinforcement

mentor

Employee Assistance Program

try-out experience

internship program

Want more activities? Go to **www.cengage.com/careerreadiness/masters** to get started.

CHAPTER activities

1. Your friend Elizabeth is searching for a more challenging job and is determined to improve herself. She has asked you to help her. You know the following information about Elizabeth:

   - She learns new things easily. She graduated from the local business college with a B average and is taking a Spanish class just for fun.
   - She currently works as a mail carrier for the U.S. Postal Service.
   - She uses a computer for e-mail and keeping a record of packages she delivers, but that's about all.
   - She enjoys interacting with a variety of people.
   - She has not balanced her checkbook in the past six months.
   - She earned As in her speech and English composition classes.
   - She doesn't always follow through on what she promises to do.

   a. What are Elizabeth's strong points?

   _____

   _____

   _____

   b. What areas should Elizabeth work to improve?

   _____

   _____

   _____

   c. Write two self-improvement goals that might be appropriate for Elizabeth.

   _____

   _____

   _____

   d. Write an action plan for each of the goals listed in 1-c.

   _____

   _____

   _____

2. Work with a partner to complete this activity. List as many resources as you can to assist in your self-improvement program—from first attempts at assessment through celebrating success. Consider people, websites, books, services, organizations—anything or anyone that might be helpful.

   _____

   _____

   _____

3. Think of one of your most challenging academic goals. Identify a person who could serve as a mentor to help you reach this goal and explain why the person would be a good mentor.

   _____

   _____

   _____

4. E-mail your long-term goals and action plans to a trusted friend. Ask your friend to evaluate your goals for being specific, measurable, attainable, realistic, and timely. Are the timelines for completing the goals reasonable? Print the e-mail message for your instructor. What information in your friend's response was most helpful?

   _____

   _____

   _____

CRITICAL *thinking*

CASE 2.1   Last In, First Out

Jeff has enjoyed tinkering with cars as long as he can remember. He was elated when he fulfilled his goal to earn a Certified Automotive Technician degree from the local technical institute. The placement department of the institute helped him meet another goal—a job with a local automobile manufacturer. Jeff has been on the job for ten months. He enjoys the challenges and has established a reputation for being punctual, dependable, and capable.

Unfortunately, the economy has experienced a major downturn and Jeff (a "new hire" from the standpoint of the company) is one of the first to be laid off. Jeff is shocked and devastated. He feels that he has failed. He tells his friend Dan, "I guess I'm just no good at this job. I tried my best, but I couldn't hold a job for even a year. Now what am I going to do? I need a job! But who is going to hire a loser?"

1. What is Jeff's biggest obstacle at this point in his life?

   _____

   _____

   _____

2. What does Jeff need to do to get back on track?

   _____

   _____

   _____

3. What advice might Dan give Jeff? What role could Dan play in Jeff's future?

   _____

   _____

   _____

   _____

4. Write a new long-term goal for Jeff. Develop an appropriate action plan for the new goal.

   _____

   _____

   _____

   _____

CASE 2.2 This Job is Not for Me!

Carmen enjoyed spending time with her nieces and nephew. She took them to the zoo and movies and spent an entire weekend with them when their parents were away. Based on her enjoyment and apparent success in managing her nieces and nephew, she decided to move into the field of child care. Carmen left her job as an account manager for a television station and enrolled in a child care program in a career college. She enjoyed the courses, earned excellent grades, and looked forward to completing the program and working in a daycare center. Her long-term goal was to open her own center.

As part of her coursework, Carmen eagerly accepted an internship with the Tiny Tots Daycare Center. Unfortunately, after two weeks on the job, she finds the work at Tiny Tots very stressful. The children are unruly, and working with twenty children is less satisfying than spending time with her nieces and nephew. Carmen is exhausted at the end of each day and feels that she just doesn't have the patience for this type of work. To make matters worse, she realizes the pay in a daycare center is far less than what she had been earning at the television station.

1. How could Carmen have avoided the situation she now faces?

   _____

   _____

   _____

2. Should Carmen stay in the child care field? Why or why not?

   _____

   _____

   _____

3. What suggestions do you have for Carmen at this time?

   _____

   _____

   _____

   _____

4. Have you known someone in a situation similar to Carmen's? Describe the circumstances and explain how the person resolved the situation.

   _____

   _____

   _____

   _____

Attitude

©Thinkstock Images/Jupiter Images

Think About It: Christopher and Isaac have worked at McKenzie Technology for five years. They have similar job descriptions and salaries. A new position opens up in the division where they work. This position offers job advancement, company stock options, and a significant pay raise. Christopher and Isaac both apply for the position. Christopher has been a steady worker who takes pride in his accomplishments. However, he is often abrupt with people when making a point. If his work stumps him, he moves on to something else. He participates in company gossip because, he says, "everyone else does." Christopher has refused to work extra hours on weekends because he feels weekends belong to him. Isaac comes to work each day ready to succeed. His philosophy is to say "Yes" to any reasonable task put before him, even challenging ones. He is friendly and supportive to all and ignores the company grapevine. Isaac's coworkers enjoy being around him and find him upbeat, pleasant, and helpful. He does whatever it takes to complete his work and support the mission of the company.

Christopher and Isaac are both steady workers—how do the two candidates differ? Who will likely get the new position?

objectives

After completing this chapter, you should be able to:

1. Define attitude and explain its importance in the workplace and life.
2. Explain how attitudes are developed.
3. Describe how experiences and circumstances impact attitudes.
4. Take positive steps to improve your attitude.
5. Describe how your attitudes influence others.
6. Explain how the attitudes of others impact you.

Attitude Is Important

ou are learning constantly as you grow personally and professionally. Learning is categorized into three types: knowledge, skills, and attitudes. You acquire knowledge by reading, attending classes, using the Internet, talking with others, and experiencing life. Skills such as learning to keyboard or play an instrument are gained through practice and repetition. It is easy to identify the first two types of learning, but have you given much thought to the third type of learning—how you acquire attitudes?

Attitudes are complex and develop over time. People with a high degree of optimism typically view events in their daily lives as positive, which in turn leads to a positive attitude. Others can provide you with knowledge and teach you skills, but you (and only you) can determine your attitude.

"Attitude is a little thing that makes a big difference."

WHAT IS ATTITUDE?

Attitude is your outlook on life—how you respond to people and events. More importantly, attitude is guided by your mind. If you spend your mental energies worrying about what *might* happen next, your outlook on life (your attitude) is probably negative. If you spend your mental energies taking each day as it comes and appreciating the experiences you are having and the people in your life, your attitude is probably positive and healthy.

Attitude is extremely important because it drives your behavior. **Behavior** is a manner of acting or reacting under a general set of circumstances. Your actions (behavior) and body language are a result of your mental attitude. When you exhibit an attitude, you transmit a message that everyone, consciously or unconsciously, interprets. Others around you can "tune in" to your attitude by watching your body language and listening to what you say.

Your attitude can cause others to be drawn to you—to have positive feelings or attitudes toward you. Here, for example, is what Stephen said about the new committee chair: "Alicia is so easy to work with—I'm glad she's in charge of our committee." Or, your attitudes can signal others to avoid you; for example: "Stay away from Peter; he's been grouchy all morning!"

Three important things to remember about attitude are: (1) only you control what you think, (2) attitudes can and do change over time, and (3) your attitude affects others. How attitude affects your personal and professional image will be discussed in Chapter 4.

DEVELOPING YOUR ATTITUDE

Attitudes are unique because they are developed as a result of emotion. **Emotion** is a state of feeling or a conscious mental reaction (positive or negative) toward a specific object, person, or event. Emotions such as fear, joy, anxiety, and compassion shape our feelings about the events and people in our lives.

How positive is your attitude? Check your attitude by taking this short quiz and analyzing the results.

1. I spend time thinking about what I want my future to include.
   a. I do not do this.
   b. Yes, I do this.
   c. Occasionally I do this.

2. I look for the best in people and situations.
   a. I do not do this.
   b. Yes, I do this.
   c. Occasionally I do this.

3. I believe that in every problem there is an opportunity.
   a. I do not believe this.
   b. Yes, I do believe this.
   c. Occasionally I believe this.

4. I believe I am responsible for how my day goes.
   a. I do not believe this.
   b. Yes, I do believe this.
   c. Occasionally I do believe this.

5. I enjoy learning new things and adapt well to changes.
   a. I do not do this.
   b. Yes, I do this.
   c. Occasionally I do this.

6. I speak in a positive and upbeat manner.
   a. I do not do this.
   b. Yes, I do this.
   c. Occasionally I do this.

7. I am persistent and stay with a task until it is complete.
   a. I do not do this.
   b. Yes, I do this.
   c. Occasionally I do this.

8. I spend my time seeking answers and solutions rather than whining about problems and unpleasant situations.
   a. I do not do this.
   b. Yes, I do this.
   c. Occasionally I do this.

   Analysis. Give yourself 0 points for each "a." answer, 3 points for each "b." answer and 2 points for each "c." answer. Total your points. If your score is 17–24 points, your attitude is very good. If your score is 12–16 points, your attitude is acceptable. If your score is 11 or less points, your attitude needs improvement.

When an emotion accompanies an event time after time, it creates an attitude (or predisposition to view something in a certain way) that may be very intense. For example, your attitude toward learning new things influences how favorably (or unfavorably) you react to an assignment that uses new software or requires a new procedure. Your attitude toward a coworker influences how well the two of you will work together to complete a task.

Marco was not happy. He had just learned that he and Pat must work together to develop a new advertising campaign. Although Marco hasn't worked with Pat, he has been in her company when she seemed to be a "know-it-all." Marco thinks, "I know this isn't going to work. Pat will want to make all the decisions and won't give me a chance to contribute my ideas."

Can you see how his emotions clouded Marco's judgment about his ability to work with Pat?

Figure 3-1 lists some of the many benefits in having a positive attitude. According to Remez Sasson, the owner and founder of SuccessConsciousness.com, "A positive attitude helps to cope more easily with the daily affairs of life. It brings optimism into your life, and makes it easier to avoid worry and negative thinking. With a positive attitude you see the bright side of life, become optimistic and expect the best to happen. It is certainly a state of mind that is well worth developing and strengthening."[1]

BENEFITS OF A POSITIVE ATTITUDE

A positive attitude:	
says to others, "I can achieve success!"	is liberating.
helps you achieve goals and attain success.	builds greater inner power and strength.
empowers you to succeed faster and more easily.	helps you see the glass as "half full" instead of "half empty."
gives you more energy.	enables you to overcome difficulties.
inspires and motivates others.	leads to greater happiness in life and work.

FIGURE 3-1 The benefits of a positive attitude are numerous.

In contrast, people who tend to be pessimistic often exhibit negative attitudes. Even if you've been a pessimistic, negative thinker for many years, it's not too late to change your thinking and reap the benefits of a positive attitude. Negative attitudes can be changed into positive ones, but doing so requires a genuine desire to change.

Emotional Experiences Shape Attitudes

Read the On the Job scenario on page 44 about the situation at the Rayathon Corporation. The workers at Rayathon had an attitude problem that resulted in increased work-related accidents. But, thankfully, management was quick to recognize the problem and deal with it. A supervisor came up with the idea of holding a "debriefing" after each accident. As soon as an accident happened, all work would stop. The accident victim (whenever possible) or supervisor was required to tell other workers what happened, why it happened, and how the accident might have been prevented. Once this procedure was in place, there was a dramatic reduction in accidents under that supervisor. When these impromptu meetings were held in other sections, the results were the same—a reduction in the number of accidents. Lectures on safety practices in training sessions had failed, but the emotionally charged learning that occurred in the debriefing sessions had a powerful impact on the attitude of the employees.

The Rayathon Corporation example shows how highly emotional experiences can shape attitudes, and how those attitudes can effectively influence behavior. The Rayathon workers had the knowledge they needed to follow the rules and be safe. What they lacked was the motivation to follow the safety rules. A change in atttitude provided that motivation. Attitude is very powerful in the workplace and in life. Attitude can be more important than knowledge, job skills, education, and previous success.

The management of the Rayathon Corporation, a heavy construction business, was concerned about the on-the-job safety of its workforce. Although the employee training program had stressed safety procedures and safety reminders were posted throughout the work area, the frequency of accidental injuries was high. Management presumed that the workers were thoroughly acquainted with what they should do to protect themselves from injury. However, in this case, simply knowing the safety rules did not cause the workers to behave in a safe manner. The supervisors concluded that while the workers knew what was expected, they were not compliant. Workers were found to be welding without safety glasses, and equipment was being serviced without being turned off (as safety codes required). Power tools were being operated without shields, and the workers were not wearing steel-toed shoes as required. The workers knew the safety rules, but they had not developed the proper attitude toward them. Unfortunately, the result was an increase in work-related accidents.

Considering that attitudes do change and learning new attitudes can be accomplished in a situation where emotions are high, what might the supervisors do to create positive attitudes and motivate the workers to follow the safety rules and be safety conscious?

Negative Circumstances Impact Attitudes

Everyone experiences negative moments. Negative feelings, negative comments, and negative actions depress the spirit and drag you down instead of lifting you up. "Down days" are normal, but most people need to work at looking for the bright side of life.

Negative circumstances in your life are not unending. When a tragedy or something you perceive as a tragedy strikes, you assume you will never get over it. But you *will* cope. Recovery takes time, but you will pull through and life will go on. Is there a tragedy in your past—the loss of a loved one, a fire in your home, or a broken heart? Yes, you have had bad experiences, but after an appropriate time of sorrow, you learned from the incident and moved on with your life.

Remember that a negative event is not all-encompassing. Perhaps you did not get the job that you wanted. You may have felt miserable and thought that all of your hopes and dreams were shattered. But be realistic. The lost job was simply that—a lost job. It didn't destroy your entire life. After not getting that particular job, you may have been offered a better position and all worked out for the best.

Don't think bad things happen only to you. "Why did this happen to me?" "I never get a break." "What did I do to deserve this?" These negative statements are often heard. You aren't alone in experiencing misery or joy. Good and bad things happen to everyone; recognize the fact that joy and sadness are universal. You may encounter some tough circumstances over which you have no control. But you do have control over how you respond to those circumstances. You can choose to react with a positive attitude that you will move you forward.

CHANGING YOUR ATTITUDE

If you are experiencing a negative attitude about work, a relationship, or life in general, recognize that attitudes can be changed. An attitude change can take place based on new knowledge, experiences, or a sincere desire to change. But only one person can make that change—and that person is you!

Changing negative attitudes into positive attitudes can be very satisfying, because positive attitudes are a foundation for personal satisfaction and effective human relations. When you change your attitude, you automatically change:

- Your perspective
- The way you interpret things
- The decisions you make
- The actions you take
- The results you get

Steps to Improving Your Attitude

Developing positive attitudes and eliminating negative ones is the best "first step" toward self-improvement. But where should you start? Although there is no one way for improving attitude that will work for everyone, the following

©Neustockimages/iStockphoto.com

Resolve to adopt those attitudes you want to improve.

suggestions can be helpful if you have the willingness, courage, and inner strength to try them.

Visualize the attitudes you want to improve. Picture the attitudes you want to change. Write a brief description of the image you have of yourself that you will embody after you have achieved your attitude-improvement goals. For example, you may see yourself as having more patience with classmates or coworkers. Your mental picture must be so clear and so constantly present that it can create a pattern for your behavior. Again, attitudes *do* drive behavior.

"Thought is the sculptor who can create the person you want to be."

Resolve to adopt those attitudes you want to improve. After you identify the attitudes you want to improve, make a conscious effort to change them. The changed attitudes are a reflection of your ideal personality. Your goal is to cultivate those improved qualities because they are needed as a model for your self-renewal.

Use the image of the "ideal you" as a model for your behavior. With practice and effort, the desirable behavior will come naturally, and the improved attitudes will transform you. For example, your goal may be to change your "please-don't-call-on-me" attitude when asked to participate in a class discussion. You could practice imagining yourself answering clearly and confidently when called upon. With time, you may be eager to participate in class discussions.

Choose to create a positive atmosphere around you. Every day you have choices to make, and the choice to have a positive attitude or negative attitude is one of those very choices. You can create a positive atmosphere by smiling, being pleasant, and making a genuine effort to be interested in what's going on around you. Look for positive, optimistic, good-natured, or complimentary things to say. As you look for favorable qualities in others, you will improve your attitude and create a positive environment around you.

You can even turn a negative into a positive. You and your coworker Jamie are in the elevator, when Jamie says, "I'll be glad when it's five o'clock and I can get out of this place." You might respond, "I'm looking forward to an evening with my family, too. But with the downturn in the economy, I'm happy to be working and thankful that I have a job." Your comment projects your positive attitude and may cause Jamie to rethink her attitude.

Surround yourself with positive people. It has been said that you become the average sum of the five people with whom you associate most frequently. As you think about these people, ask yourself five questions: Who am I around? What are they doing to me? What have they got me saying? Where do they have me going? What do they

BANISH NEGATIVE THOUGHTS

Your attitudes can dramatically affect your health. Next time you feel negative, try the following:

- **Sit up or stand up straight, shoulders back.** It is hard to maintain a negative attitude with really positive body language.

- **Take a deep breath and let it out slowly.** Sometimes stress affects our attitudes, and deep breathing reduces stress.

- **Laugh aloud.** Laughter brings the focus away from negative emotions in a more beneficial way than mere distractions. Also, laughter is contagious, so you can help others around you to laugh more.

- **Focus on what is good.** Think about your goals and dreams, recall a happy incident, or look at pictures of beautiful scenery.

- **Take care of yourself.** Feeling tired or stressed out often makes things seem worse than they really are.

have me thinking? What do they have me becoming? Then ask yourself the big question: Is that okay?[2]

Celebrate your successes. You need to celebrate your successes and not beat up on yourself when you have failures. Learn from setbacks, but then move forward with optimism for the future.

checkpoint

1. Define the word *attitude*.

_____

_____

_____

_____

2. List two common causes of negative attitudes.

_____

_____

_____

_____

3. List four ways to improve your attitude.

_____

_____

_____

_____

4. Explain why experts say that emotion is a critical factor in the development of attitudes.

_____

_____

_____

_____

5. Explain who can change an attitude.

_____

_____

_____

_____

_____

applications

1. Describe a situation when you demonstrated a negative attitude. How was your attitude reflected in your behavior? If the situation occurs again, how might your attitude be improved?

_____

_____

_____

2. Describe a situation when you demonstrated a positive attitude. How was your attitude reflected in your behavior?

_____

_____

_____

3. Identify someone you know who has demonstrated a negative attitude. What behavior gave you cues about this person's attitude?

_____

_____

_____

4. Think about a positive emotional experience in your life. What emotions did you feel during this experience? What attitudes did you develop from the experience? What behaviors did you exhibit as a result of the attitudes you developed?

_____

_____

_____

5. Identify someone you feel is a postive thinker and has a motivational impact on you and others. Briefly describe this persons's attitudes and behaviors that influence others.

_____

_____

_____

6. Explain what is meant by the quotation "Our attitude toward life determines life's attitude toward us."

_____

_____

_____

Attitudes Are Contagious

Have you ever wondered why people have the attitudes they have? More importantly, have you questioned where your attitudes come from? Further, is your attitude worth catching?

One person's attitude has a powerful influence on the attitudes of others. This is especially evident when people are involved in a team effort—in the workplace, on the playing field, or working as a group in the classroom. You have probably witnessed a situation where one individual causes a positive change in the attitude of a group. Likewise, one person with a negative attitude can bring everyone down.

on the job

Crystal, Simon, and Kylee are the nurses on duty at the Central City Clinic. Their charge today is giving flu shots to the employees of four large state government agencies. Employees are lined up in the hall and outside the clinic. Several employees voiced concerns about being unable to get a shot before the clinic closed. There isn't much conversation among the nurses as they work to keep the line moving and anwer questions as they administer the shots. Dr. Townsend, the clinic physician, calls out to the nurses, "How can we move this line along so everyone waiting can get a shot by closing time?" The nurses were silent. Simon rolled his eyes as he thought about how tired he was feeling. Kylee finally called out to Dr. Townsend, "I'm doing okay. If someone will get me a soft drink, I can keep working until we get everyone inoculated." Crystal said, "Me too. I'll stay until no one is left standing—I mean standing in the line!" Simon chuckled at Crystal's remark and said to Dr. Townsend, "I think you can count on us to keep these folks 'flu free' for the season." Dr. Townsend is pleased with her team of nurses. She says, "Thank you all. I'll send someone for refreshments. Keep the line moving!"

What do you see in this situation that shows the influence of one person's attitude on others?

YOUR FEELINGS SHOW

Attitudes are difficult to hide because attitudes have a profound effect on how you behave, and your behavior gives you away—those near you get a clear picture of your attitudes. Naturally, you would not want to hide a positive attitude. It shines through to create a favorable impression—an impression that is positive and "catching" to those around you. Unfortunately, a negative attitude shows through as well, creating a negative impression that can spread to others.

A positive attitude is one of the most important factors that influences a person's success. Because employers understand that much of what an individual does is based on his or her attitudes, a great deal of effort is put into determining the attitudes of job applicants. An individual's attitudes and values help to determine how focused and dedicated the worker will be, how he or she will fit into the workplace team, and how effective the worker will be in developing trusting, pleasant relationships with clients and customers. Remember: Maintaining a positive attitude will have a favorable impact on your career development.

"Ability is what you're capable of doing. Motivation determines what you do. Attitude determines how well you do it."

As your positive attitude develops, the people around you begin to respond accordingly. They think of you as being enthusiastic, willing to learn, cheerful, and friendly. Their favorable attitude toward you causes them to expect positive, productive behavior from you. As you sense these positive expectations, your motivation to live up to your image will increase. The result is a cycle of reinforcement and improvement, greater appreciation of your positive attitude, and even higher levels of self-esteem.

YOUR ATTITUDE INFLUENCES OTHERS

Attitudes are catching. When a group's attitude changes, it is because one or more individuals take the initiative to spark the change. When the leader or member of a group lets his or her positive attitudes show, the effect on the group can be electric. This can be observed when the positive energy of a team member or coach of an athletic team ignites a winning spirit in the team. Everyone seems to respond and performance improves.

This principle was in place when, after being lost in a blizzard, one mountain climber literally saved the lives of other climbers because his positive attitude inspired the others to make the effort required for survival. The principle also applies in the workplace. A positive team spirit and high morale contribute to effective job performance. **Morale** is a sense of common purpose within a group. A group of people having similar positive feelings and emotions are said to have "high morale" or "team spirit." Even in the face of adversity, a group working together for a common goal can have high morale. Success in reaching a goal helps keep morale high.

The reverse is also true. When a team experiences failure, the effect can depress everyone's emotions. However, even failure does not have to affect your attitude. Continue to focus on the intended goal and improve your efforts. This focus will help you get over negative emotions and feelings rather than letting them develop into negative attitudes. Staying positive and persevering improves your chances of being successful the next time.

NEGATIVE ATTITUDES ARE UNPRODUCTIVE

Attitudes such as impatience, conceit, boredom, and envy are negative and unproductive.

©Stockbyte/Getty Images

Attitudes are contagious — make yours positive!

Justin has just landed at O'Hare International Airport in Chicago. His flight was late because of bad weather, and he missed his connection to Dallas. He must get on the next flight to Dallas because he has an important job interview scheduled. He waits impatiently in a customer service line, eventually reaches the airline representative, and shouts at the representative, "Can't this airline ever be on time? I missed my connection because of your airline—I want a ticket on the next flight to Dallas, and I want it now!"

Justin is exhibiting a negative, unproductive attitude that is taking a considerable amount of energy on his part and causing stress for the representative and other passengers around him. Justin is wasting valuable time. If Justin needs to get the representative's maximum help, the best thing he can do is to exhibit a productive attitude that will create rapport and get the representative's cooperation.

Figure 3-2 lists productive and unproductive attitudes that you should recognize when confronted with a difficult situation. Ask yourself, "What do I want or need right now? Which attitude will serve me best?" The sooner you know what you want and the best attitude to help you get it, the sooner your body language, voice, and vocabulary will adjust to help achieve the desired outcome. In the scenario, Justin might have said to the airline representative, "I really need your help. I missed my connection to Dallas, and it's important that I get there today for a job interview. Here is my ticket. Can you possibly get me on the next available flight? Or at least on another flight later today? I know you can figure out something for me." With the correct attitude, Justin will most likely be on the next plane to Dallas.

PRODUCTIVE VS. UNPRODUCTIVE ATTITUDES

Productive Attitudes	Unproductive Attitudes
Enthusiastic	Envious
Confident	Disrespectful
Kindhearted	Conceited
Supportive	Apathetic
Helpful	Rude
Cheery	Fearful
Interested	Sarcastic
Considerate	Angry
Easy-going	Agitated
Patient	Impatient
Friendly	Pessimistic
Engaging	Anxious

FIGURE 3-2 Productive vs. unproductive attitudes.

ATTITUDES OF OTHERS AFFECT YOU

Not only do you need to deal with your own attitudes, you will frequently need to cope with the attitudes of others as well. Consumer researchers discovered that while we may not like to admit it, what other people think about something could affect what we think about it. The findings reported in the *Journal of Consumer Research* confirm that social networks greatly

Imagine that you are a person with an attitude problem about your supervisor. You feel you have been criticized too much and too often, and you let your feelings show. You failed to hide your anger. You answered abruptly, loudly, and even threatened to quit. Finally, you stormed out of the office and slammed the door behind you as your coworkers looked on.

1. How would a person with a positive attitude have responded?
2. How might the supervisor respond to your negative reaction?
3. How might the supervisor respond to a more positive reaction?
4. How might the coworkers who witnessed the exchange between you and your supervisor react?
5. Why is having a positive attitude so important in this situation?

"Our attitude toward life determines life's attitude toward us."

influence an individual's behavior. Negative opinions cause the greatest attitude shifts, not just from good to bad, but also from bad to worse.[3]

You may recall a time when the attitudes of those around you were negative and, as a result, you felt yourself becoming negative too. By being aware of the influence others have on you, you can resist and avoid negative influences on your attitudes. For example, when your coworkers get together to complain or gossip, you can opt not to participate. You *do* have a choice! You can walk away or simply ignore what you see or hear. You can choose not to chime in with additional gossip. Or, you might turn the entire dialogue around by voicing positive comments.

"Human beings, by changing their inner attitudes of their minds, can change the outer aspects of their lives."

> *Sasha was amazed by the negative talk she heard in the cafeteria about her friend Marci. Sasha thought the criticism was unkind and unfair. Rather than stay and participate, she said "I think you're wrong about Marci. She's my friend, and I think she has many good qualities." She then picked up her tray and went to another table.*

In addition to the beneficial effect of your positive attitude on your own behavior, you find yourself in a new position of power. The influence of your attitude on others allows you to persuade them—to help them improve their self-esteem and replace negative attitudes with positive attitudes.

checkpoint

1. Explain the statement "Attitudes are contagious."

_____

_____

_____

_____

2. Why is a positive attitude so important in teamwork?

_____

_____

_____

3. Classify the following attitudes as *productive* or *unproductive*.

enthusiastic	bored	supportive	conceited
helpful	patient	rude	anxious
pessimistic	cheery	interested	sarcastic
disrespectful	impatient	confident	envious

Productive attitudes

_____

_____

Unproductive attitudes

_____

_____

4. What is morale? Why is high morale important in the workplace?

_____

_____

5. Why is it important to be able to cope with the attitudes of others?

_____

_____

applications

1. Following are two examples of attitudes that an individual might want to improve. For each attitude, describe actions or behaviors that might help bring about the desired changes. Brainstorm with other students who are working on this application.

   a. <u>Present attitude</u>. *I'm so afraid to try anything new. I should consider changing jobs, but I just can't. I know I wouldn't be successful.*

      <u>Future attitude</u>. *I feel confident that I'm ready for a new job. I have the experience and knowledge to handle a new challenge.*

      To help bring about this change, I will

      _____

      _____

      _____

      _____

b. <u>Present attitude</u>. *I'm so impatient. I want things to happen fast. I'm anxious and upset when I have to wait in long lines. When I want something, I want it now.*

<u>Future attitude</u>: *I am a patient person. I can relax and feel free of stress and anxiety in situations that require patience.*

To help bring about this change, I will

_____

_____

_____

c. <u>Present attitude</u>. *I feel compulsive about sweets. I love ice cream, pastries, and chocolate. Constantly "grazing" on these foods can be an almost uncontrollable habit.*

<u>Future attitude</u>. *I feel in control of my desire for sweets. I only eat at meal times, and I rarely find myself buying or eating sweets that are not included in healthful meals.*

To help bring about this change, I will

_____

_____

_____

2. Identify two attitudes that you have resolved to improve. The examples in Application 1 illustate how you should respond. Describe each attitude as a reflection of how you feel now and how you expect to feel when you achieve your objectives for improvement. Then list the behavior you want to exhibit or actions you plan to take as you strive for improvement.

a. <u>Present attitude</u>. _____

<u>Future attitude</u>. _____

To help me change, I will

_____

_____

b. <u>Present attitude</u>. _____

<u>Future attitude</u>. _____

To help me change, I will

_____

_____

_____

3. Describe a time when someone's attitude influenced yours. Was the influence positive or negative?

_____

_____

_____

_____

_____

_____

_____

4. Observe a group of three or more people in a casual conversation. Examples might be a group at school or work or a family around the dinner table. Listen carefully to the conversation. List the attitudes and actions that you saw demonstrated.

Briefly describe the situation.

_____

_____

_____

_____

_____

_____

_____

_____

_____

Identify the attitudes and actions observed.

ATTITUDES   ACTIONS
Example: Impatience   *Example: Loud voice*

_____

_____

_____

_____

_____

_____

_____

_____

3 points to remember

Review the following points to determine what you remember from the chapter.

- Attitude is your outlook on life, which is guided by your mind and drives your behavior. You (and only you) can determine your attitude.

- Attitudes, which are developed as a result of emotion, are very complex and develop over time.

- Attitudes are affected by negative circumstances, which drag you down rather than lift you up. Negative situations will end and are not all-encompassing. You will work through difficult situations and problems and move on with your life.

- Steps for improving your attitude include visualizing and adopting the attitudes you want to improve, using the image of the "ideal you" as a model for your behavior, choosing to create a positive atmophere around you, and surrounding yourself with positive people.

- Attitudes are said to be *contagious*. One person's attitude has a powerful influence on the attitudes of others.

- Learn to recognize negative attitudes which are unproductive and not worth your energy—anger, impatience, conceit, and boredom are but a few examples.

- Others will challenge you with their negative attitudes and behaviors. But you have the power to help them improve their self-esteem and replace negative attitutudes with positive attitudes.

How did you do? Did you remember the main points you studied in the chapter?

KEY terms

attitude

behavior

emotion

morale

Want more activities? Go to **www.cengage.com/careerreadiness/masters** to get started.

CHAPTER *activities*

1. Kim Le has worked for several years in a research firm that conducts national opinion surveys. She began her career with the company conducting telephone surveys and has remained in that job. Over the years, many of her coworkers, in the same position, had been assigned to higher-level jobs positions with greater responsibility. Kim Le felt she was just as competent and productive as the coworkers who had been promoted. She applied for higher-level jobs many times. Each time she felt that she wasn't seriously considered for the promotion. Kim Le reacted by making sarcastic remarks about those who were promoted, complaining about not being recognized for her good work and attendance, and sulking and not talking to others. She knew, of course, that she was showing negative attitudes, but she wanted her supervisor Shauna and others to know how she felt. She disliked Shauna's confident, seemingly abrupt manner. Shauna was aware of Kim Le's feelings and attitude but chose to ignore them. Kim Le was convinced that Shauna did not like her because of her nationality and felt that she was stuck in her position. She was sure that Shauna would never recommend her for a promotion. You are Kim Le's friend. You have not wanted to interfere, but Shauna is your friend, too. You believe that Shauna is a fair person and that she has nothing to do with Kim Le's not being promoted to a better position.

   a. What attitudes about herself might be contributing to Kim Le's resentment?

   _____

   _____

   _____

   b. As Kim Le's friend, what would you say to her? What can she do to change her attitude toward Shauna?

   _____

   _____

   c. Would you talk to Shauna about Kim Le? If so, what would you say?

   _____

   _____

2. Review the following Monday morning carpool conversation among four coworkers. Then, in a small group, discuss the questions that follow.

   Jake says, "Well, are you prepared for another long, boring week?" Roger replies, "I ask myself every day why I continue working in this dead-end job for a company that is on the skids." Abby adds, "There must be a better place to work. I am barely earning enough to feed and clothe my kids, and our benefit package is terrible." Mark states bravely, "Oh, come on. It isn't such a bad place to work. We enjoy each other's company. We all have jobs, while many people in our community are out of work. Our benefits package may not be the greatest, but at least we have one that covers both medical and dental. It seems to me that the new production manager may be turning the company around. When sales improve, we could be in line for increased salaries and benefits."

   a. What may have caused the attitudes of Jake, Roger, and Abby? Could these attitudes be changed? How?

   _____

   _____

b. What do you think about Mark's statements? Did he go out on a limb to say what he did? How do you think the others will respond to him?

_____

_____

_____

_____

_____

c. Role play in a small group how the conversation might go if Mark's attitudes are infectious and the others begin to change their attitudes.

_____

_____

_____

_____

_____

3. Review the carpool conversation in Activity 2. Assume you are either Jake, Roger, or Abby, each of whom exhibited a negative attitude. Suppose you changed your attitude. List specific ways in which you might turn this negative atmosphere into one that is positive. For example, what positive words might you use to respond to Mark? What positive actions might you take? The outcome will be a pleasant, upbeat ride to work that will get the day started on a positive note.

_____

_____

_____

_____

_____

4. Think about someone you admire. Share your thoughts about this person with another student and have that student share thoughts about someone he or she admires. Now respond to the following question about the person you chose.

a. What are his or her outstanding qualities?

_____

_____

_____

_____

_____

_____

_____

b. Review your list of qualities. How many are attitudes that tell something about how the person feels, as compared with other qualities such as physical features, assets, accomplishments, or salary? What does this tell you about attitudes and why it is important for you to make certain that yours are positive?

_____

_____

_____

_____

_____

_____

_____

_____

CRITICAL *thinking*

CASE 3.1 Break Time at the Supermarket

Aniah was in good spirits as she began her new position in the florist shop of a large supermarket. Although the store had been open for many years, it had been newly renovated to provide more open space and include specialty areas such as the florist shop. But soon her positive attitude was threatened. At break time, she sat down with a group of coworkers from all areas of the supermarket. No one smiled or welcomed her. Everyone seemed to be unhappy. A man wearing a meat cutter's apron seemed to be leading the conversation. He talked about how "management is greedy and doesn't care about the people who do the *real* work." A checkout clerk joined the conversation and said that "the union doesn't even stand up to management." A produce worker jumped in and said that "the only way to get a fair share of overtime work is to be one of the favored few." Then the conversation turned to gossip about the personal life of the store manager.

Aniah was shocked by the negative attitudes being expressed. The clerk who had been a part of the conversation looked at her and said, "You'll understand what we are talking about when you have been here a month or two." Aniah nodded and said nothing. Aniah likes her job, needs to work, and wants to maintain her good spirit.

1. Is hearing this conversation likely to influence Aniah's attitudes about management, the union, the meat department, or the clerks? If so, how?

   _____

   _____

   _____

2. What should Aniah do in the future during break time? If she avoids her coworkers, what risk(s) is she taking? If she joins the conversation, should she express her attitude(s) even if they are different than the others? Suggest some things that Aniah could say to make the break time conversation more positive.

   _____

   _____

   _____

3. What would you do in Aniah's situation?

   _____

   _____

CASE 3.2 Will Anthony Change His Attitude?

Anthony works in a government agency responsible for services to senior citizens. Lakisha, his supervisor, has worked in government for about 30 years. She is highly competent and has been recognized publicly for her service to the agency's clients. Anthony does not like Lakisha. He is frequently rude and discourteous to her and has been heard making unkind remarks about her to the seniors. He believes Lakisha coddles them and expects too much of her employees. He has said, "Lakisha doesn't know what she is doing. I could get the work done much faster if she would let me do things my way." Antony tells other workers that it is time for Lakisha to retire. He enjoys doing imitations of her behind her back. On several occasions, Anthony has been careless and has given misinformation to seniors that confused them.

Lakisha is a caring person who prides herself on doing whatever she can to help others. She is aware of Anthony's attitudes and actions. Lakisha also recognizes Anthony's assets—he has a good education, his computer skills are excellent, and he works hard and follows the rules and regulations of the agency (for the most part). Lakisha is determined to help Anthony adjust his attitude or find him a job within the agency that suits his skills.

1. Why do you think Anthony has such an attitude? (Feel free to speculate.) How does his attitude damage the agency?

   _____

   _____

   _____

2. Does Lakisha have grounds to dismiss Anthony? Why does she want to help him with his attitude? Ultimately, who can change Anthony's attitude?

   _____

   _____

   _____

3. What suggestions do you have for Lakisha as she begins to work with Anthony? What would you say to him to start a "change" dialogue? What steps will Anthony need to take to adjust his attitude?

   _____

   _____

   _____

4. In your opinion, can Anthony be successful in another job? In another agency? Why or why not?

   _____

   _____

chapter 4

Image

©Digital Vision/Getty Images

objectives

After completing this chapter, you should be able to:

1. Explain why image is important and how perception impacts your image.
2. Identify the components that make up your image.
3. Explain why image building takes personal reflection and commitment.
4. Describe the benefits of being a professional and acting in a professional manner.
5. Identify the traits of a professional.
6. Discuss the importance of etiquette in the workplace.

Think About It: Elle walked into the Human Resources office of Zoeller Electronics and checked in at the reception desk for an interview for the position of customer service representative. Katy Griffin, the human resources director, saw Elle from an adjacent room and noted that she was an attractive, well-dressed young woman about twenty years old. As Elle sat down to wait with other applicants, Katy continued to watch her. Elle slouched comfortably into a chair and put a stick of gum in her mouth. She looked around for a wastebasket and, seeing none, wadded up the wrapper and dropped it discretely on the floor.

Do you think Katy will seriously consider Elle for the position? Why or why not? What suggestions do you have for Elle as she prepares for future interviews?

A moment later, the silence of the reception area was jarred by the loud jazz music of a ringing cell phone. Elle dug into her purse, tossing papers onto the table next to her. Finally, she found the phone and began a heated conversation with her boyfriend. Elle's loud voice and inappropriate language got the attention of others in the reception area. Elle ended the call abruptly and waited impatiently for her interview. Katy shook her head and walked back into her office. A few minutes later, the receptionist brought Elle into Katy's office and introduced her as a candidate for the customer service representative position.

4.1 Image Matters

4.2 Image in the Workplace

Image Matters

Have you ever sat in an airport or shopping mall watching people and making assumptions about them based on their appearance? Seeing how people dress and behave tells you a lot about them. It is important to note that what you see may or may not be accurate—you are making assumptions based on your perceptions. **Perception** is the process of attaining awareness or understanding based on sensory information—an immediate reaction of the senses.

The people you interact with every day constantly observe you and form opinions about your competence, character, conduct, and attitude. Other people's perceptions can dramatically shape our self-concept and self-esteem. Perceptions can also make or break a career. Whether the perceptions are accurate or not, if your actions portray laziness, rudeness, or a lack of professionalism, the perceptions of others can make or break a career path.[1]

In the opening Think About It scenario, Elle has projected an image of herself to those around her—an image she may or may not be aware was being observed by others. Katy's initial perception of Elle was positive. What Katy saw and heard later caused another reaction—a negative one based on Elle's inappropriate behavior and language. As Katy saw Elle drop a gum wrapper on the floor, carry on an inappropriate cell phone conversation, and chew gum in a business setting, Katy's perception of Elle changed significantly.

APPLY IT!

What would your perception be if you saw the individuals described below? Compare your perceptions with others in the class. The perceptions may be very different, since there are no correct answers—only perceptions. For example, assume you see a young woman with a letter in her hand crying in the park. Is she crying because she received bad news? Or, is she overcome with joy after learning that her fiancé's tour of duty is over and he's coming home?

1. An unshaven man in tattered clothing sitting on a bench.
2. A student sitting in the library wearing a headset.
3. A driver with a cell phone in one hand and pounding on the steering wheel with the other.
4. A young woman in jeans and a T-shirt carrying a backpack over her shoulder.
5. A young man in a business suit sprinting down the sidewalk.
6. A man dressed as Santa Claus in October.

WHAT IS IMAGE?

Your image is one of your most important assets. The set of qualities and characteristics that represent perceptions of you as judged by others is your **image**. Do you realize that people throughout the day are observing you and making judgments about you? They notice your dress, facial expression, hair and hands, attitude, body language, and overall conduct. Exhibiting an image of a self-confident, poised individual will give you a much better chance of achieving success in life. Because others easily detect your level of self-esteem, being unsure of yourself can be harmful to your image. Studies have shown that within the first few seconds of meeting you, a person has already formulated judgments about you. This is something to think about as you consider the image you wish to project each day.

What image do you want to project to those who are important in your life—your family, friends, coworkers, and supervisors? The more important question is "Who are you, and how do you project your true qualities?" You began to answer these questions as you worked through Chapters 1 to 3 and were introduced to the concept of imaging. Imaging is picturing your life as you would like it to be. As you complete the imaging process, you begin to establish goals for self-improvement to help you establish the image of a successful individual.

There are dozens of books, popular periodicals, and websites with tips for "dressing for success." However, your image is much more than the clothes you wear. Let's look more closely at various components that make up your image—at home, socializing with friends, and in the workplace. Several components will be discussed here as they relate primarily to your personal image. Your professional image will be discussed in the next section.

"Our self-image, strongly held, essentially determine what we become."

HOW YOU LOOK

Even before you speak, others form an opinion about you based on your appearance. Your personal appearance includes your wardrobe; your facial expression; the condition of your hair and hands; your overall fitness; your posture when walking, sitting, and standing; whether you have tattoos or body piercings; and your behavior. Quite simply, your personal appearance is the finished product of how you look when you walk out the door to attend class, go to a social function with friends, meet a first date, interview for a job, or leave for work.

Fashion trends often govern the way we dress. Designers bring out new styles on a regular basis. Some fashion trends are here to stay. Other trends will be popular fads now but in a year or two may cause you to regret some of the choices you made. If you are dressed appropriately and take pride in your appearance, others will think you take equal pride in your work. If, however, your appearance is sloppy, it will be difficult to convince others that you are an efficient, capable worker. Your clothes should be neat and clean. Instead of buying the trendiest styles, choose clothing and accessories that make you look your best.

Confidence has to come from within so positive self-talk helps. Tell your-self that you look great and feel good about yourself. Since this is easier to do when you actually do look good, careful grooming becomes a factor in self-esteem. .

HOW YOU SPEAK

Speaking is something we take for granted. You can easily tell others what is wrong with their voice (for example, too fast, too high, too soft, too loud), but do you give little thought to the sound of our own voice? Have you ever listened to a playback of your voice? Were you surprised by what you heard? Consider, for example, how slow or fast you talk, the pitch (high or low), volume, inflection, enunciation, pronunciation, and vocabu-lary. Try to speak at a moderate rate of speed so others can understand you easily. If you speak too quickly, the listener may not comprehend what you are saying.

> *Liza could hardly wait to tell Donna about her job interview. The job sounded interesting and the interviewer was enthusiastic about her qualifications. When Donna picked up the phone, Liza didn't miss a beat. She immediately started a minute-by-minute description of her busy morning. "Slow down!" Donna said. "You're not making any sense. You lost me after the first few sentences."*

The **pitch** of your voice refers to how high or low your voice sounds. When you become emotional—happy or upset—the pitch usually goes up—and a higher pitched voice tends to carry further than a lower pitched voice. Some voices are just naturally higher than others are. But each of us has an optimal pitch. You cannot change the natural pitch of your voice, but you can try to control raising it. Overall, a lower-pitched voice is more pleasant to hear.

Volume is how loud or soft your voice sounds. Have you ever noticed that it is exhausting to listen to someone who speaks too softly? Speak up so that others can hear you. Do not force others to strain to hear you or cause them to misinterpret your message because they could not hear everything you said. On the other hand, listening to a very loud voice can also be annoying. Don't assume the role of the "workplace megaphone." If you are unsure of your volume, ask others, "Can you hear me?" "Am I speaking loudly enough?" or "Am I speaking too loudly?" Then adjust your voice accordingly.

Most people instinctively do a good job with volume control by consid-ering: (1) the amount of background noise in the setting, (2) the distance between themselves and their audience, and (3) the degree to which they want to publicize a message. With the advent of the cell phone, it is all too easy to talk on the phone when and where you please. When you are on the telephone or speaking with someone in a public place, try to speak loudly enough to be heard. However, do not speak so loudly that you disrupt conversations around you or call attention to your conversation.

Inflection is the rising and falling of your voice. If you speak with no inflection, you speak in a **monotone**. A monotone is a voice that is flat. It has no expression. It always sounds the same. It can communicate the message, "I'm bored and have absolutely no interest in what we're talking about." If you have had the experience of listening to a monotonous voice, you know that it will put you to sleep in a hurry. Rather, use your voice to help express the meaning of your words. Let your voice express enthusiasm, spirit, and inner feelings. Vary your voice by stressing a word or phrase or pausing before a word or phrase. If you are unsure of your inflection, ask others if your voice is flat or always sounds the same.

Enunciation refers to pronouncing all the sounds in a word clearly. The more carefully you enunciate, the more likely you are to be understood. Speak clearly and don't run your words together. Avoid being careless. Don't drop the ends of words (especially "ing," "ed," "d," "p," and "t") and don't run words together. Take care not to leave out part of a word or syllable. (See the examples in the Practice Makes Perfect feature.) If you do not enunciate properly, the result can be slurred speech, which can be annoying and difficult to understand.

Pronunciation refers to saying a word correctly. Pronunciation requires that you know how a dictionary would tell you a word should be pronounced. Mispronouncing words makes a poor impression, and you may fail to communicate your meaning. Good pronunciation is a quality of an articulate person. If you are not sure how to pronounce a word, check a dictionary or ask others.

Vocabulary is to the sum of words used by, understood by, or at the command of a particular person or group. Your vocabulary impacts how you speak. State your ideas in simple terms and use standard English to express yourself. Choose words that convey your message in a positive and tactful manner. Eliminating problems from your speech requires practice and diligence. Often the habits you are trying to change have been a part of your speaking pattern for a long time.

HOW YOU BEHAVE

You have heard it said, "Actions speak louder than words." Always do your best to conduct yourself as a mature adult. Use common sense. Appreciate the

---

PRACTICE MAKES PERFECT

Conversation improves when your voice shows emotion. Read these sentences with enthusiasm and feeling.

1. Happy birthday!
2. Oh, I'm so sorry to hear that your visit to Disneyland was rained out.
3. That game went into extra innings. I still can't believe we won!
4. Yes, I'd be thrilled to work with you on that new project!
5. Please tell me that you can go with us to Daytona Beach for spring break.
6. Let me make sure I understand—you want me to bring what?

Avoid running together common words or phrases such as:

spostta	for	supposed to
havta	for	have to
dunno	for	don't know
uzhly	for	usually
wuncha	for	wouldn't you
can'tcha	for	can't you
gonna	for	going to

needs of others and treat others with respect. Be tolerant, and appreciate and accept individual differences. Use good manners, including proper table etiquette. Always strive to be polite and courteous. The importance of simple phrases such as "please," "thank you," and "you're welcome" cannot be overemphasized.

Respect the privacy of others. Using cell phones in public places such as restaurants and buses can be very annoying to those around you. Try to limit such calls where possible.

Control your temper. Realize that anger and being argumentative are never positive responses. Facial expressions also contribute to your overall behavior. You are more approachable if you offer a smile and pleasant look. A smile is a simple way to put yourself and others at ease.

HOW YOU WALK, SIT, AND STAND

Good posture reduces stress on muscles and joints and is an important part of your appearance. Others interpret your attitude by how you walk, sit, and stand. Confident people walk tall, sit up straight, and stand erect. Think about the posture of someone you consider successful, and you will likely picture someone with head erect, walking with purpose.

"If you see a friend without a smile, give him yours."

How you walk says something about you before you utter a single word. If you enter a room standing tall, you suggest confidence. If you enter a room slouching or stooped over, you appear insecure and unhappy. Walk or stand as though an imaginary string is lifting you by the top of your head and pulling you toward the ceiling. Looking confident doesn't mean strutting. Confidence shows up as a comfortably erect posture without too much effort.

Good posture while sitting or standing gives you an image of self-confidence. Sit up with your back straight and your shoulders back. Your buttocks should touch the back of your chair, and your body weight should be distributed evenly on both hips. Lean forward a bit to show interest and attentiveness. Bend your knees at a right angle.[2] There are several acceptable positions for the legs, which differ for men and women. EHow.com is one of several websites that provide videos that demonstrate appropriate male and female sitting positions.

When standing, place your feet side by side. Put your weight on the balls of your feet so that your heels just lightly touch the floor. Hold your head upright and look straight ahead. Lean forward ever so slightly from your hips. Keep your back straight and avoid slouching.

© AVAVA, 2009/Used under license from Shutterstock.com

Good posture is an important part of your image.

Karl, a college freshman, works part time as a clerk in the local hardware store. His supervisor, Mr. Sioudi, thinks Karl is an exceptionally mature young man. When asked why he considered Karl mature, Mr. Soiudi replied: "Seldom do we get a beginning worker, especially one who works only part time, who fits in so well and accepts responsibility as Karl does. He arrives on time for work, dresses appropriately, and always makes a good appearance. He uses good judgment when he answers customers' questions and speaks at a moderate rate of speed so others can understand him easily. He is dependable. We feel fortunate to have him here. We hope he will join us full time when he graduates."

What is Mr. Sioudi's perception of Karl? What traits did Karl exhibit that led Mr. Sioudi to hope that Karl would return as a full-time employee?

WHY ASSESS YOUR IMAGE?

You are a person worthy of the respect of others regardless of where you live, your income, the clothes you can afford, or your family background. Because your image plays an important role in getting that respect, it is important to assess your image as changes occur in your life. For example, your image as a student may be one thing, but the image you want to project as you begin your first job would be another.

During adolescence, what others say about you (or your perception of what others think), tends to act as a mirror for how you see yourself. As you mature, you will find that being true to yourself is necessary in order to actualize your potential and control how others perceive you. Only you can control your actions. However, it isn't uncommon to have a bit of adolescence resurface. If you tend to be overly concerned about what others think of you, remind yourself this is an adolescent behavior. Move on and work toward controlling what others think of you. Project the image you want others to see.

You may want to start the imaging process by determining what image people currently have of you and then set goals for improving that image. Have you ever wondered how others might describe you? You can draw inferences about your image based on your interactions with people in your life. Others often give you feedback that tells you what they think about your level of competence, character, and commitment. Other times, you may receive subtle signals about your image through questions asked, recommendations, or job assignments.

You may also want to ask hard questions of those you trust to give you accurate information. Examples: What image do I project when I walk into a room? Do I appear to be a competent person? Do I exhibit good posture? Do I speak clearly? If you ask direct questions, you will receive direct answers.

If you do not like what you hear and others do not see the image you want to project, you know who can make the changes: you, and only you.

The image-building process takes personal reflection and commitment on your part. You want to build your image so that you project the qualities and characteristics you want others to see. Believe that you have within you the power to shape your own image. Don't limit yourself by identifying with past limitations and faults. Mentally visualize yourself speaking and acting the way you want to be. When you can look in a mirror and can say: "I like what I see, I like what I am, and I am proud of what I stand for," you will know that you are happy with your image. Be sure the image in the mirror is the one that you project to others.

checkpoint

1. Define *perception*. Explain why you should be concerned about how others perceive you.

2. What is image? What parts of your image are visible to others?

3. What factors make up your personal appearance?

4. How do confident people walk?

5. What questions could you ask others to determine the image you are projecting?

applications

1. List steps you have taken to determine what others think of you. What steps do you plan in the future to check the image you project?

_____

_____

_____

2. Check your posture. Concentrate on how you walk, stand, and sit. Ask others to give you feedback on your posture and work to improve it. Where possible, have others video your walk and then critique the tape with you. State your goals for improving your posture based on the insight gained from this activity.

_____

_____

_____

3. Read a paragraph of text into a recorder. Listen to the recording and check your pronunciation and enunciation, inflection, and the volume of your voice. Ask someone to listen to the recording with you and provide additional feedback. State your goals for improving your language skills based on the insight gained from this activity.

_____

_____

_____

4. Look up these frequently mispronounced words in a dictionary or online. Write the preferred pronunciation, and practice saying the word correctly.

a. apricot _____

b. pecan _____

c. chic _____

d. pianist _____

e. route _____

f. greasy _____

g. roof _____

h. creek _____

i. aluminum _____

j. crepe _____

Image in the Workplace

The previous section discussed image from a personal standpoint. Now let's apply that knowledge to your professional image in the workplace. Professionals understand that first impressions are important because perceptions are sensory and made very quickly. Whatever job you hold, you are important to the company or organization. Never think of yourself as "just a billing clerk" or "just a dental assistant." Your role as an employee is vital to the workplace, and the image you project impacts all those with whom you come in contact.

This section discusses the most important aspects of a professional image in the workplace regardless of the occupation that interests you—computer programmer, hair stylist, educator, electrician, executive assistant, engineer, construction worker, and so on.

WHY BE A PROFESSIONAL?

There are three reasons you should strive to be a professional and act in a professional manner in the workplace:

1. The first and perhaps best reason for striving to be a professional is the heartfelt feeling that comes from within—the *pride* you feel when you know you are doing the work to the best of your ability. Seeing a task completed successfully because of the work you did is a gratifying feeling. You know the time and effort it took to complete the task, you know you made significant contributions to the final product or service, and you know you were important to the successful completion of a task that contributed to overall workplace goals. Whether your work is recognized isn't the issue. When you take pride in your work and know you are acting as a professional, your self-confidence will be enhanced and move you to greater challenges.

2. The second reason is that others will hold you in high regard for the example you set. Coworkers will want to be associated with you because of the reputation you are building and the manner in which you carry out your responsibilities. They will want to be on your team or in your work group because they know they will learn from and be motivated by you. Supervisors will appreciate your efforts and recognize the value of having a professional on staff. If you are in an occupation that directly serves customers, the customers will go the extra mile to make sure you are the person to help them. As a professional, you earned that admiration.

3. Finally, new opportunities may be made available to you. People in your workplace who can help advance your career will notice your professional image and accomplishments and may give you greater responsibilities. By pursuing these opportunities, you will expand your experiences, improve your abilities, increase your career opportunities, and do your utmost to reach your full potential.

"Being a professional is doing all the things you love to do on the days when you don't feel like doing them."

Rebecca works as a professional assistant at Appleton and Valdez, a small marketing firm. Her major responsibility is keying advertising proposals for clients. One of the firm's newest clients is TOY Talent, which manufactures educational toys for children age 5 and under. Mr. Kubiak, vice president of the company, asks Rebecca to key the marketing plan developed for TOY Talent—a plan that emphasizes the learning features of its toys. As a mom, Rebecca is always looking for learning tools for her two young children, so she takes special interest in this client. On her own time, Rebecca accesses the TOY Talent website and reviews the information about the toys produced. Rebecca is impressed by the safe product guidelines TOY Talent has established to ensure that only nontoxic paints and other nonhazardous materials are used in the production of its toys. She knows that parents are concerned about lead-based paint in toys and that toys from other manufacturers have been pulled from retailer's shelves because of unsafe production materials. Rebecca summarizes information from the website and prints a copy for Mr. Kubiak. She hands him the completed marketing plan, along with her notes about TOY Talent's use of "child safe" materials in the production of its toys. She emphasizes the importance of such guidelines to parents. Mr. Kubiak replies, "How could we have overlooked TOY Talent's use of 'child-safe' materials? These guidelines are an asset that should be included in the marketing plan. Thanks to your resourcefulness, we will have a more comprehensive plan to send to TOY Talent." Rebecca felt good about taking the initiative to call the information to Mr. Kubiak's attention.

What may be the long-term effect of Rebecca's research?
Did Rebecca receive any recognition for her initiative?
How has Rebecca enhanced her professional image?

Taking pride in your work, earning the respect of others, and being rewarded with opportunities for further success make the effort to be a professional a worthy goal.

HOW DO YOU SPOT A PROFESSIONAL?

To advance in your career, your employers must perceive you as someone who is competent and an asset to the company. Today's jobs require technical skills and knowledge, but work attitudes, character, conduct, and work ethic are also important aspects of a true professional. When you make a conscious choice to be a professional, you raise the bar on the goals you set for yourself and, more importantly, the standards you set for your performance.

You commit to conducting yourself in a mature manner, to accepting responsibility for your actions, and to striving to be all that you can be. How do you spot a professional? Professionals are spotted based on their attitude, attire, character, work ethic, conduct, competency, and the appearance of their work area.

Attitude

You learned in Chapter 2 that "attitude is everything," so it is logical to conclude that a positive attitude is a significant characteristic of a professional. A professional's attitude reflects the following:

"Whenever you are asked if you can do a job, tell 'em 'Certainly I can!' Then get busy and find out how to do it."

Professionals are team players. Team players know that no task is completed singlehandedly. Cooperation and collaboration lead to great work and the accomplishment of a common set of goals. Professionals are loyal to the team and willing to do whatever task is required for the success of the team.

Professionals recognize organizational structure and individual roles. They realize that all organizations have a structure and that each individual within that structure performs an important role. They honor and respect these structures and roles as they perform their duties. Professionals treat each person in the workplace with respect and dignity.

Professionals are persistent and determined. They stick with a task until it is completed. They persevere in the face of mistakes, deadlines, disagreements, negative forces, and delays. Professionals do not quit. They have the attitude that *"when the going gets tough, the tough get going."*

Professionals want to be helpful to others. They see requests from customers, coworkers, and supervisors as an integral component of their work responsibilities. A request from a coworker is viewed as an opportunity to help someone, not as an interruption.

Professionals are always on the lookout for unmet needs. They notice shortcomings and identify opportunities for improvement. For example, a supermarket worker spots a customer struggling with a package on a high shelf and offers to help, or an administrative assistant volunteers to update an outdated policy manual.

Professionals use good judgment. They recognize that senseless practical jokes, crude or tasteless comments, and unacceptable innuendoes are *never* appropriate in the workplace.

technotr/istockphoto.com

A professional wants to be helpful to others.

Attire

Always be aware of how you present yourself, even when you think no one is watching. It does not matter whether you work at an office, brokerage firm, retail store, or factory, always dress appropriately. Although individualism and self-expression are important, dressing appropriately is necessary for success in every line of work. However, it is difficult to set specific rules about attire for a professional image because appropriate dress differs based on the occupation, location, and company preference. For example, a business suit may be required for work in a bank or law office, while "business casual" attire would be more appropriate in a software development company.

Whether the dress code in your company is written or unwritten, you can bet there is one. If your organization's policy and procedures manual doesn't include a dress code, simply look around you. What is your supervisor wearing? What are your coworkers wearing? Extreme or faddish styles will detract from your professional image, so select your wardrobe for the workplace with care.

Troy, an executive assistant to the vice president, looked warily at the new sweater his sister gave him for his birthday. "It will be perfect for the office," she said. "I don't know," he replied. "I really like the sweater, but I think it's too casual to wear to work. However, it will be great for weekends with the guys. Thanks!"

General rules for good grooming apply to both men and women. The rules depend somewhat on the type of work you are doing. These rules could serve as a good checklist for you as you prepare for work each day.

_____ Dress appropriately for the work environment.
_____ Bath or shower daily and adopt good personal hygiene habits.
_____ Comb or brush your hair and keep it neatly cut in a style appropriate for your workplace.
_____ Brush your teeth and get regular checkups.
_____ Use mouthwash and breath mints as needed.
_____ Clean and trim your fingernails.
_____ Wear clean, pressed clothes that fit you well.
_____ Polish your shoes and keep them in good repair.
_____ Avoid excessive body piercing and tattoos.
_____ Use colognes, perfumes and other scented products sparingly. Your "scent" does not need to linger as you move from place to place.
_____ Accessorize with care. Jewelry should not interfere with your work or detract from your image.
_____ Know what not to wear. Say "No" to clothes that are too tight or too trendy.
_____ Men should wear dark-colored socks and black or brown shoes.
_____ Women should avoid short skirts and see-through or low-cut clothing.

You should feel comfortable about the way you look. Wear clothing that fits and is fit for the occasion. Follow the general rules of good grooming in the Apply It! feature. Dressing for the job you want to have, not for the one you have, may give you a competitive edge in your future career. If you are confident in your attire, you will project a secure and positive self-image.

Character and Work Ethic

If you are trustworthy, honest, responsible, and diligent, you are said to have character. **Character**, which refers to your personal qualities or personal traits, goes hand in hand with work ethic. **Work ethic** is a set of values based on the virtues of hard work, diligence, and caring about your work and your coworkers. A work ethic may include being reliable, having integrity, and showing initiative. Completing your work on time, not wasting the time of your coworkers, sending professional e-mails without keying errors, and offering help to others when they need it are qualities of people with a strong work ethic.

Companies today often get by with fewer staff doing more work, so being seen as someone with good character or a good work ethic can really help to distinguish you from others, especially during periods of downsizing or when it comes time to promote someone. The character traits of trustworthiness, honesty, responsibility, and diligence are important traits for professionals. Display these traits, and your character will never be in doubt.

Trustworthiness. Trustworthiness is a signal to others that you are dependable. You do what you say you are going to do and honor your promises. You protect the confidentiality of information shared with you. You are loyal. Others know that you can be trusted because your behavior reflects what you actually believe. You are *not* trustworthy if you disclose confidential information, fail to meet deadlines, and do not follow through on commitments made. Have the courage to do what is right, even when it is difficult.

Honesty. You have heard often that "honesty is the best policy." Honesty is more than simply telling the truth. Honesty includes being sincere, honorable, fair, and genuine. Striving to make honesty a part of your character will serve you well. Your honesty is like an invisible shield that protects you. A single act of dishonesty can destroy in a nanosecond a reputation that took an entire lifetime to build. Once people question your honesty, you may never be trusted again.

As a child, you learned not to take what belongs to others. Adhering to that principle will serve you well. The following acts are also dishonest: taking office supplies for personal use, shoplifting, taking home tools or supplies from a construction site, sliding cash into your pocket from your cashier station, stealing money from a pension fund, and copying someone else's work and identifying it as your own. But you do not have to steal or take something intentionally to be dishonest. If you lie on a job application, you are being dishonest. Cheating on an exam or your taxes or calling in sick when you are feeling fine is being dishonest. If you exaggerate the facts, mislead or withhold information, you are being dishonest.

Responsibility. Responsibility is being accountable for your conduct and obligations. You think before you act and accept the consequences of your actions. You understand your work responsibilities and are accountable for them. This includes being on time or early and doing your job in a timely manner with limited supervision. You also take responsibility for your mistakes. You are human and you will make errors. Admit your mistakes and learn from them—then work hard not to repeat them. Dwelling on a mistake is a waste of valuable work time.

"Honesty is the best image."

Diligence. Diligence means conscientiously giving total attention to each task you are given. Focus your attention on your assigned tasks and complete your duties thoughtfully and carefully. Work at a steady pace, with energy and enthusiasm. You are not being diligent if you send text messages to friends on company time, regularly return late from breaks or lunch, or send personal e-mails at work.

More responsibility and ultimately promotions often go to workers who exhibit good character and a strong work ethic. Workers who fail to exhibit a good work ethic are regarded as failing to provide fair value for the wage the employer is paying them and may not be promoted to positions of greater responsibility.

Competency

Professionals work toward excellence in their field of work. They understand the responsibilities and requirements of their jobs. They seek training, education (formal and informal), and experience. Professionals ask questions, solicit feedback, listen to those willing to mentor, and seek guidance and input from others. They continually find new, better, and faster methods of doing their work. Change does not frighten a professional—if technology or some other force changes the way their work is done, they accept and welcome the change.

Work Area

Your work area, like your personal appearance, says a lot about you. Maintain a clean, efficient, and tidy workspace because it is something you want for yourself—not to impress your supervisor or coworker or anyone else. The arrangement of your work area affects your efficiency and productivity. Keep the items for your day-to-day work

©Digital Vision/Getty Images

Your work area, like your personal appearance, says a lot about you.

A professional:

- Focuses on the work to be done.
- Addresses mistakes as they occur.
- Accepts challenging assignments.
- Completes tasks in a timely and efficient manner.
- Looks, speaks, and acts like a professional.
- Walks, sits, and stands like a professional.
- Exhibits a positive attitude.
- Stays with a job until it is completed.
- Produces more than is required.
- Takes advantage of learning opportunities.
- Keeps the work area neat and orderly.

close to you. Items that are only occasionally used should be easily accessible but out of sight. A clean and tidy area also provides a safer environment. Keep file drawers closed and power cords tucked neatly under the desk. Cables and cords should never extend into traffic areas. Avoid eating or drinking at your desk. An overturned drink can ruin hours of hard work.

Wade loved his job. He was a competent, willing worker and team player. Unfortunately, his work area sent a different message. Papers were strewn all over his desk, his monitor was littered with post-it notes, and empty and half-full cups were everywhere. Yet, he was unaware of the negative impression he was giving others.

HOW IMPORTANT IS ETIQUETTE?

Proper etiquette is an important part of being a professional and adds a "touch of class" to your professional image. Etiquette is more than knowing which fork to use. **Etiquette** refers to the customs or rules of behavior regarded as correct in social and work life. Others may feel that if you cannot be trusted not to embarrass yourself in business and social situations, you may lack the knowledge and self-control to be good at what you do.

Etiquette in the workplace focuses on rules of conduct (written or unwritten) designed to facilitate interactions between coworkers, customers, supervisors, and suppliers. Strive to incorporate these basic guidelines into your behavior:

"Good manners will open the doors the best education cannot."

"Do unto others as you would have others do unto you." Be fair, courteous, and polite. Treat others with respect. Be tolerant, and appreciate and accept individual differences. Show that you care by demonstrating generosity and compassion.

Obey company rules and regulations. If there is a policy and procedures manual, read it with care.

Be on time. Set your watch *early*. It is important that you be on time for work and appointments. If you are preparing to leave for work or for a meeting at work, break the habit of completing just one more task or accepting the last-minute phone call. Focus on the time commitment you have made. Tardiness is rude and disrespectful of the time of others.

Watch your language. Unfortunately, popular movies and television sitcoms often leave the mistaken impression that the use of four-letter words is acceptable and commonplace. Don't believe it. Vulgar language is *never* acceptable in the work environment. Unsuitable language often becomes a habit. If a coworker or supervisor uses profanity, you have two options: ignore the behavior or walk away from it. Do not lower yourself by falling into the same inappropriate habit.

Etiquette in the Electronic Age

Electronic devices offer a new set of challenges as they relate to workplace etiquette. Technology gives us the capability to reach friends, business associates, and family 24/7. However, "instant access" isn't always a good thing.

Cell phones can be lifesavers in your personal and professional life. However, be mindful that when you use a cell phone, your conversation may be overheard by coworkers and in some situations customers or even perfect strangers. Avoid making and receiving personal calls during business hours. Keep your personal cell phone off or on vibrate in the workplace so as not to disturb others. If you must answer or make a call on your cell phone, be sensitive to the fact that those around you may be distracted from their work or annoyed by your conversation.

Take care when working with confidential information to make sure that it is not accidentally available to wandering eyes.

> *Sara was entering confidential data in a spreadsheet when Ellen stopped by her workstation. Ellen had a direct view of the onscreen information. Sara smiled and said, "Give me a second," and she immediately saved and closed the file. Then she asked, "Okay, Ellen, what can I do for you?"*

E-mail is a valuable tool in the workplace. However, it is not for sending jokes, stories, pictures, or personal notes to others in or out of the office during work hours. Work-related e-mail correspondence should be professional. While it may be acceptable to include smiley faces in personal correspondence, it is not an acceptable practice in the workplace. Also, watch your language. If you could not post your message on a bulletin board for everyone to read, do not send it. Stories abound about the "private" e-mail that became a public embarrassment. Nothing is private on e-mail; it is all too easy for sensitive information to end up in the wrong inbox.[3]

checkpoint

1. Why is a professional appearance important in the workplace?

   _____

   _____

2. Give three reasons for being a professional.

   _____

   _____

3. List four characteristics of a professional.

_____

_____

_____

_____

_____

4. Why is diligence an important part of character?

_____

_____

_____

_____

_____

5. Define etiquette. Why is etiquette a characteristic of a professional?

_____

_____

_____

_____

_____

applications

1. Review the behaviors below. Place a check beside those that would not be considered appropriate professional behavior. Be prepared to discuss your checklist with your classmates.

____ being a slacker

____ talking negatively about your coworkers

____ taking initiative

____ quitting before a job is complete

____ persisting until your objective is achieved

____ dwelling on your mistakes and the mistakes of others

____ telling ethnic jokes

____ respecting a supervisor's authority

____ noticing what needs to be done

____ avoiding challenging responsibilities

____ serving and helping others

____ following company regulations

____ taking pride in your team's accomplishments

____ ignoring a coworker who wants or needs assistance

____ maintaining positive energy

____ speaking with a mouth full of food

2. Review the list in Application 1 again. Reword each behavior you checked so it reflects appropriate professional behavior.

_____

_____

_____

_____

_____

_____

3. Review the list of appropriate professional behaviors from Application 2. Categorize each behavior as exhibiting *character, attitude, competency,* or *conduct.*

_____

_____

_____

_____

_____

_____

4. Describe a situation in which you have made incorrect assumptions about someone's character based on your initial perception. How did you determine that your initial perception was incorrect? Did your perception cause anyone harm? If so, describe how.

_____

_____

_____

_____

_____

_____

5. Review the characteristics of a professional. What goals do you need to set to be considered a professional? Which goals will require the most work?

_____

_____

_____

_____

_____

4 *points to* remember

Review the following points to determine what you remember from the chapter.

✦ Perception is the immediate reaction from the senses. Others form opinions about your competency, character, conduct, and attitude based on their initial perception of you.

✦ Your image is one of your most important assets. Image includes personal appearance, behavior, posture, and voice.

✦ Build the image you want to project to others first by determining what others think of you. Ask direct questions that will provide specific information that may be of benefit to you.

✦ Reasons for having a professional image in the workplace are: *Pride* from within when a job is completed to the best of your ability, the high regard in which others hold you as a professional, and potential opportunities that could come your way as a result of demonstrating professional qualities.

✦ Professionals are identified by their attitude, attire, character, work ethic, competency, and work area. Character and work ethic include the qualities of trustworthiness, honesty, responsibility, and diligence.

✦ Professionals display proper workplace etiquette—obeying rules, being on time, using appropriate language, showing respect for others, and protecting confidential information.

How did you do? Did you remember the main points you studied in the chapter?

KEY *terms*

perception

image

pitch

volume

inflection

monotone

enunciation

pronunciation

vocabulary

character

work ethic

etiquette

Want more activities? Go to **www.cengage.com/careerreadiness/masters** to get started.

CHAPTER *activities*

1. Visualize someone you consider a professional. Describe this person and list the professional characteristics you see in this individual.

   _____

   _____

   _____

   _____

   _____

   _____

   _____

   _____

   _____

   _____

2. Think of your chosen profession. Which of the characteristics of a professional do you feel are most important? Why?

   _____

   _____

   _____

   _____

   _____

   _____

   _____

   _____

   _____

3. What do you think the message is in Julius Erving's quotation, "Being a

professional is doing all the things you love to do on the days you don't feel like doing them." Discuss your interpretation with your classmates.

   _____

   _____

   _____

   _____

   _____

   _____

   _____

   _____

4. What perception do you think others have of you? How do you know? Do you like the perception that you believe others have of you? If not, how might you change that perception?

   _____

   _____

   _____

   _____

   _____

   _____

   _____

   _____

   _____

CRITICAL thinking

CASE 4.1   Is a "Jazzed-Up" Outfit Professional?

Chelsea completed a program of study as a physical therapy assistant at a technical institute and accepted a position at a local hospital where she would support several physical therapists. The required attire for everyone working in the physical therapy unit is a blue smock and matching slacks. Chelsea received information about the required attire. While in school, she enjoyed buying clothes in vintage shops and accessorizing with wild-print handbags and lots of jewelry to achieve her own individual look. Needless to say, Chelsea found the required smock and slacks pretty dull clothing.

After purchasing the required clothes, she began to think about how she could "jazz up" the outfit. She exchanged the drawstring in the slacks for a colorful braided rope belt and tucked in her smock at the waist. She made a bracelet, dangling earrings and a necklace of large metallic blue beads to complement the smock color. Chelsea knew she would be on her feet most the day but opted to wear open sandals so that others could see the tattoos on her ankles. Chelsea's first day on the job caused quite a stir in the hospital unit. A few minutes after she arrived for work, Chelsea heard the following announcement over the intercom: "Will Chelsea Jenkins please report to the human resources office."

1. Why do you think Chelsea was called into the human resources office?

_____

_____

_____

_____

2. Does it matter that it was Chelsea's first day on the job? Why or why not?

_____

_____

_____

_____

3. List some workplaces where you have observed a strict dress code in use. Why do you think a strict dress code was necessary?

_____

_____

_____

_____

CASE 4.2 Take Him or Leave Him

Troy is a construction worker for Agee Construction, which specializes in building strip malls in large cities nationwide. Troy has worked for Agee for several years. His supervisors perceive him to be a hard-working, valuable employee with excellent job skills. Troy is well acquainted with his coworkers on the job site.

The crew is finishing a project in Miami and the next assignment is in Buffalo. Troy has told his coworkers that he is going to avoid going to Buffalo one way or another because he doesn't want to work in the cold. So Troy tells his supervisor that he has a lung condition that doesn't permit him to work in a cold climate. His coworkers know this isn't true. The supervisor reassigns Troy to a project in southern California that requires knowledge of earthquake-resistant building codes unique to California. Training classes have been established for employees before the move to California. The class is large because many companies send employees for training. After attending one session, Troy decides that sitting in a classroom is a waste of his time. From then on, he goes to class each day, signs in, and then slips out at the first opportunity.

Sean, a former coworker of Troy's, is the new site manager for the California project. He knows that Troy has not been honest in getting reassigned to the project and is not attending training classes. Sean is concerned about Troy's attitude and the impact it may have on other workers, but he also recognizes Troy's excellent job skills. Sean knows that he needs experienced workers with good skills on this project. He decides to talk with Troy before they leave for California.

1. Do you think Sean considers Troy a professional? Why or why not?

   _____

   _____

2. What professional traits are missing from the image Troy projects?

   _____

   _____

3. What topics should Sean address in his conversation with Troy?

   _____

   _____

   _____

4. If you were Sean, would you agree to have Troy on your team? Why or why not?

   _____

   _____

   _____

Part 2

It's all about Communicating

nkstock/Getty Images

Workplace Focus

Emily Greenwood is a landscape architect in Boulder, Colorado. She helps plan, design, and oversee the construction of exterior spaces such as parks, street medians, playgrounds, parking lots, and gardens.

It is crucial for Emily and her clients to understand each other perfectly. "To make sure my audience grasps my point when I speak to them, I confirm that they are listening and maintain eye contact during the conversation. I try to say only what's necessary and omit empty words and phrases such as 'like' and 'you know.' I end conversations with a verbal confirmation that my audience and I understand each other."

"It's helpful to schedule important meetings—for example, with your boss—ahead of time so you can prepare for them," recommends Emily. "In order to make your ideas sound as good verbally as they do in your mind, practice reciting them beforehand. It is also important to stay on topic. Don't let emotions or the listener's response distract you from making your point."

Emily sees meetings as opportunities to look forward to, not dread. "Be professional and friendly. Many fields have a population of older professionals who may see 'twentysomethings' as a liability. Dressing appropriately and coming overly prepared to meetings can go along way to bridge these gaps."

© Emily Greenwood

Communication Essentials

Think About It: "Good morning, Trevor, Happy Monday!" "Thanks, Blaine. How was your weekend?" "It was very interesting. I spent time with the radiology staff catching up on the latest hospital gossip. Did you know that Dr. Belemy is being sued for malpractice? Some of the radiology staff might be named in the lawsuit. I hope those of us in accounting don't get involved. One aspect of the suit involves overcharging patients." "That's news to me, Blaine. Thanks for the scoop." Later, Trevor sees Russ and asks, "Have you heard that Dr. Belemy is about to have his medical license revoked for malpractice? Blaine spent the weekend with radiology staff. They're scared stiff that they will be involved in a lawsuit against the hospital and Dr. Belemy. I've heard that the radiologists don't do a thorough job of reviewing X-rays. Everybody knows that Dr. Belemy has been overcharging patients and performing unnecessary surgeries for years. Our records are going to be scrutinized in this whole mess." "Wow, that's not good news," Russ replies. "I should give Shelley a heads-up on what is happening."

What communication problems have surfaced in this scenario? What do you think will happen when Russ gives Shelley the news?

objectives

After completing this chapter, you should be able to:

1. Describe the parts of the basic communication model.
2. Demonstrate good oral and written communication techniques.
3. Identify the types of nonverbal communication.
4. Describe the barriers to communication.
5. Identify barriers to listenening and describe good listening skills.
6. Describe the advantages of active listening.
7. Explain the importance of being able to separate fact from opinion.

Communication Basics

Think of the time you spend each day using one or more of the four basic forms of communication—reading, writing, speaking, and listening. Because you use these skills so frequently, the ability to communicate effectively is essential in your personal life and in the workplace. **Communication** is the act of transmitting information and meaning from one individual or group to another. The goal of all communication is to convey information, requests, questions, or ideas effectively.

Messages are transmitted through various communication modes or "channels." Information received in writing is called **written communication**. You may expect to receive written communication in many forms, including letters, memos, electronic messages, or even a note jotted on a scratch pad. Other communication reaches you via face-to-face conversations or by telephone, voicemail, teleconference, radio, and television. Spoken messages are called **oral communication**.

Whereas speaking and writing both involve the use of words and are considered verbal communication, you will also receive **nonverbal** (that is, no words are used) **communication**. For example, when you smile as someone passes by, you indicate your awareness of that person. Or when you repeatedly glance at the clock, you indicate your concern about time. These nonverbal indicators play an important part in everyday communication.

The fullest communication takes place between people when the entire range of information (both verbal and nonverbal) is available.

> *"Communication— the human connection—is the key to personal and career success."*

COMMUNICATION TAKES TWO

Effective communication is a two-way process. The originator of a thought, idea, or piece of information is the **sender**. The **receiver** is the individual to whom the thought, idea, or information is transmitted. The thought, idea, or information transmitted is the **message**. This message may take many forms.

- A simple request—"Please check this reference on *The New York Times* website."
- A piece of information—"The article about offline backup options is on page 20."
- A thought or opinion—"I think you should consider additional memory for your laptop."
- A question—"How long is the drive from Birmingham to Mobile?"

To know if the receiver has received your message, you watch or listen for a response. This response is called feedback. Feedback is information returned to the sender that indicates whether the message is understood. Feedback, like the message, may be verbal or nonverbal.

Assume that Melina wishes to invite Lizzie to her birthday party. Melina (the sender) calls Lizzie (the receiver) and invites Lizzie to her party next Tuesday at 1 p.m. at the Pesky Pelican restaurant (the message). Lizzie eagerly accepts the invitation and confirms the date, place, and time (feedback). In this example, the sender delivered the message and the receiver understood the message and gave feedback to the sender. Therefore, the two-way communication process was successful. When senders and receivers do not share the same understanding of a message, communication doesn't happen. Distrust, unhappiness, and confusion may result. Consider the miscommunication described in the On the Job scenario in this section.

You may find it necessary to request feedback. If, for example, you are giving directions to someone, you might ask the listener (the receiver) questions to be sure the information was received. Figure 5-1 diagrams the communication process. Communication has not taken place until the message transmitted by the sender is received by the receiver and the feedback comes back to the sender.

"Two monologues do not make a dialogue."

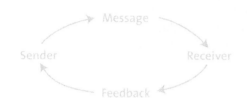

FIGURE 5-1 Diagram of the communication model.

on the job

Caleb and Ryan were talking quietly about the accounting department's new reporting form. Evelyn, an employee in accounting, overheard their conversation and assumed they were talking about the form that she had created. Caleb called out, "Evelyn, come on over. We want to talk with you." Evelyn immediately thought they were being critical of her work. She heard them mention her name several times, but she couldn't hear what they were saying. She decided to ignore their request to talk and continued her work. Caleb and Ryan wanted to compliment Evelyn on the form and explain how much it had simplified the reporting process. Evelyn missed an opportunity to communicate with coworkers and receive positive feedback about her work. Caleb and Ryan are now confused about why Evelyn didn't want to talk with them. Evelyn remains suspicious of Caleb and Ryan and avoids them for the rest of the day.

What may be the results of this ineffective communication? What could Caleb and Evelyn have done to improve the situation?

COMMUNICATION SKILLS ARE CRITICAL

"Communication works for those who work at it."

The ability to communicate effectively is one of the most important skills you can possess. Unfortunately, it is also a skill many people take for granted because it is a normal part of our everyday lives. But the truth is, personal assessment, practice, and refinement are required to develop good communication skills.

Poor communication is said to be one of the biggest problems in the workplace and in human relations. A recent survey of recruiters from companies with more than 50,000 employees cited communication skills as the single most important decisive factor in choosing managers. The survey, conducted by the University of Pittsburgh's Katz Business School, points out that communication skills, including written and oral presentations, as well as an ability to work with others, are the main factors contributing to job success.[1]

Technology in the form of instant messaging, smartphones, e-mail, teleconferencing, and cell phones with text-messaging capabilities has made it easy to commuicate with people near and far at any hour of the day or night. We spend much of our day communicating with others for business or pleasure. The better communicators we are, the more effective our interaction with others will be. The challenge in today's electronic world is to take the time to make our communications *clear, concise, courteous, complete,* and *correct.* Let's look more closely at written, oral, and nonverbal communication.

WRITTEN COMMUNICATION

The elements of good written communication include good grammar, spelling, organization, and structure. Effective written communication takes time and skill since your communication is contained in words alone; you cannot use nonverbal cues to clarify your message. Most occupations require written skills. If you were to visit several businesses, you would find many employees composing letters and e-mails, researching and preparing reports, and developing slide presentations and spreadsheets.

The ability to put your thoughts in writing is an important skill in your personal life, too. You may write a letter of application for a job or set up your own personal web page. All personal written communications need not be of the same quality. You might send a quick text message or an informal e-mail message to a friend. But a letter of application for a job would be written in a professional style using appropriate business English and revised several times before it was final. While "text speak" may be appropriate for informal text messages and e-mails to friends, it is not

EFFECTIVE WRITING TIPS

- Ask yourself: "What am I trying to achieve by this communication?"
- Use correct grammar, spelling, and punctuation. "Text speak" is not appropriate for business letters or e-mails.
- Organize your communication logically.
- Get to your point quickly. State your purpose in the first paragraph of your message.
- Make sure your message is clear, concise, courteous, complete, and correct.
- Present data to support your request, conclusions, or recommendations (where appropriate).
- Avoid use of slang words.
- Be clear about the feedback you want. Do you want a specific action or response?
- Choose an appropriate written communication method. An e-mail message may be the faster method, but a written document may better fit the circumstances.
- Proofread your text even if the spelling checker says there are no errors. Misspelled words and punctuation errors detract from your message and convey a negative impression.
- Ask others to review your work. It is difficult to spot errors in your own writing.

Words, once they are printed, have a life of their own.

appropriate for business letters or e-mails, including those that you send to your instructor.

Learning to write well takes time and practice. Begin by reviewing the Effective Writing Tips feature in this section. Then make a conscious effort to put the tips into practice.

ORAL COMMUNICATION

Newly hired employees are expected to be able to communicate orally. Employers expect workers to talk about common tasks and communicate effectively with customers, coworkers, and suppliers. Many problems in the workplace are traced to ineffective oral communication. Because tasks often require individuals to work as a team to complete the several steps necessary to get a job done, you can imagine what happens when someone misunderstands an important step in the process because of incomplete or ineffective oral communication.

Conor is part of a workgroup charged with creating a presentation to acquaint the salesforce with the new line of wireless printers. Megan says, "Conor, you are responsible for setting up the room before the presentation on Monday morning at 8:30. If you arrive by 8 a.m., you should have plenty of time to set up." Conor arrives at 8 a.m.and sets up the conference room. Megan and the others in the workgroup arrive just as the sales reps are filing into the room. Megan says, "The room looks great! Good luck on giving the presentation." "What do you mean 'giving the presentation'?" Conor asks. "You said I had to set up the room. You didn't say anything about giving the presentation. I'm not prepared to do that!"

Misunderstandings can also arise when you communicate verbally with family or friends, although they will probably be better able to infer your true meaning because they know you well. And if they don't understand, they are more likely to ask you to clarify what you said.

You learned in Chapter 4 how the rate at which you speak and your pitch, volume, inflection, enunciation, pronunciation, and vocabulary affect your image. These factors also affect your oral communication skills. It is difficult to get your message across if you speak too fast or too softly, if you mispronounce words, or if you use words the listener doesn't understand. A technique used in one situation may not be appropriate in another.

Audrey works in a factory setting and must speak loudly and emphasize key words to be heard and understood by her coworkers. When she speaks to family and friends outside the workplace, her voice is louder and stronger than necessary. The loudness of her voice doesn't match her message and often confuses her listeners.

If you are uncomfortable speaking with others in a one-to-one setting or talking with small groups, you will want to work to improve your skills so that oral communication becomes one of your strengths. Figure 5-2 lists basic do's and don'ts of good oral communication. Review these tips frequently, because they will improve your ability to communicate effectively.

NONVERBAL COMMUNICATION

"Actions speak louder than words." If your words convey one message and your nonverbal message communicates another, the nonverbal message will be stronger. For example, your words may be, "Oh, I'm so pleased to be here," but your facial expression (frown, boredom) says the opposite. Although you can stop speaking and silence your verbal output, you cannot silence your nonverbal communication.

DO'S AND DON'TS OF GOOD ORAL COMMUNICATION

DO	DON'T
Speak clearly and courteously.	Use *um* or *ah* as "fillers" between words.
Avoid the overuse of the word "I."	Be sarcastic.
Think before you speak.	Make personal attacks.
Say your main thoughts or points first and then elaborate.	Be rude or pushy.
Apologize if you err or misspeak.	Jump from topic to topic without a transition.
Consider your audience and empathize with your listener.	Use meaningless phrases or words—*you know, like*.
Use positive language.	Expect others to always agree with you.
Use standard language and enunciate words properly.	Use informal words or phrases known only to a select group.
Show interest in the listener's response.	Cut off feedback.

FIGURE 5-2 Do's and don'ts of good oral communication.

Everything about you communicates a message. Hand gestures, body language and posture, facial expression, eye contact, and touch are all forms of nonverbal communication. Research suggests that many more feelings and intentions are sent and received nonverbally than verbally. Several forms of nonverbal communication are discussed here.

Gestures

Many people use gestures as a normal part of communication when talking. If you hold up three fingers as you say, "There are three options for you to consider," this gesture adds meaning to your verbal message, and the listener may be more likely to remember the three options you mentioned.

Raymond Fullager, who writes and lectures about the British royal family, claims that Queen Elizabeth II has adopted certain motions to convey messages to her entourage. According to Fullager, Her Majesty uses her purse to send some twenty different signals to her staff. For example, when she shifts her handbag from her right arm to her left, it is a signal to her bodyguards to "Come and rescue me from this situation!"[2]

Body Language and Posture

Body language is probably the most common way of sending or receiving nonverbal messages. Leaning toward a person indicates your interest in what

"The newest computer can merely compound, at record speed, the oldest problem in the relations between human beings, and in the end the communicator will be confronted with the old problem of what to say and how to say it."

the person has to say. Someone listening with arms folded across the chest often implies a closed mind to what the other person is saying. However, such body language is personal, and it is unfair to generalize about its meaning. The individual with hands across the chest may simply find this is a comfortable way to sit.

Posture can transmit the degree of formality or informality desired. A slouched posture indicates an informal or relaxed situation. A straight, erect position indicates a more formal, serious setting. If you walk into the office of a supervisor and he or she is standing tall behind a desk, you are immediately aware that this conversation is going to be serious and your words and actions should respond accordingly. Try slouching down in a chair and sending a serious message—it doesn't work.

Facial Expressions

Facial expressions such as a raised eyebrow, frown, yawn, smile, wink, wrinkled forehead, or slight sneer all communicate a message. During a conversation, your facial expression may change many times. Some expressions are readily visible, while others are momentary. Both types can positively or negatively reinforce the spoken word and convey cues concerning emotions and attitude. A good listener constantly observes facial expressions to interpret the message of the sender. If the sender is transmitting a positive verbal message, but the facial expression appears to be a frown, beware—another message may be coming that is not so positive.

Digital Vision/Getty Images

A smile sends a positive nonverbal message.

Eye Contact

Eye contact is a powerful form of nonverbal communication. Students who frequently glance at the clock on the classroom wall rather than look at the instructor may be signaling that they are ready for a break or that they are bored with the lesson. Making direct eye contact usually conveys sincerity and a feeling of trust. Downward glances generally indicate modesty or an uneasy situation. Have you noticed that people who are busy and do not wish to be interrupted will often glance away? Or that a speaker may pause and may make direct eye contact when he or she wishes the other person to speak?

Touch

Touch is often called **tactile** (physical) **communication**. Touch not only facilitates the sending of a message, but adds an emotional impact to the message as well. When tactile communication is used appropriately, it is more direct than many words. Workers in hospitals and care facilities have long been aware of the therapeutic value of a sympathetic touch. Coworkers may "high-five" each other at the successful completion of a project and say "Congratulations!"

Used improperly, touch can build animosity, mistrust, and barriers. Use caution when touching another person in the business environment, because the meaning could be misinterpreted as sexual harrassment. If you touch a coworker's arm and the person draws back from the touch, you will know that person is uncomfortable with the tactile communication.

PERSONAL SPACE

Personal space is an important factor in nonverbal communication. The space you put between yourself and others in order to feel comfortable is called your **personal space**. You may think of this space as your "invisible boundary." You will know when someone enters your personal space because you will unconsciously step back and may feel anxious. Have you noticed how people become silent in a crowded elevator? Communication generally stops as more people enter. Occupants in a crowded elevator often look up at the floor numbers because their "invisible boundaries" are being invaded.

What nonverbal messages are sent by these actions? Compare your answers with those of your classmates. Are your interpretations the same?

Pointing a finger   _____

Winking   _____

Crossing arms over chest   _____

Shaking the index finger   _____

Nodding the head   _____

Shaking the head side to side _____

Placing hands on hips   _____

Tapping a foot   _____

Rolling the eyes   _____

Clenching a fist   _____

Yawning   _____

Stepping away from someone _____

Be aware of your space requirements and respect the requirements of others. Researchers agree that most people require 2–3 feet of personal space. However, everyone's personal space requirements are different. How close you normally stand to someone when you talk with that person depends on *whom* you are talking with and under what *circumstances*. When talking to a stranger, you may want more space; when talking with a friend, less space. When two people argue, one of them will often move in close, thereby invading the personal space of the other person (often called "getting in someone's face").

Personal space requirements are affected by environment, culture, status, and gender. People living in densely populated areas must often stand and sit close to others in crowded streets, subways, and places of business and require less personal space than someone from a rural community who is accustomed to a great deal of open space. Culture produces a wide range of differences in the way individuals use distance when communicating. What someone from North America considers acceptable conversational distance may be different from what a person from Latin America or the Middle East finds acceptable.

Studies show that when people of different status levels (positions or ranks) converse, they tend to stand farther apart than do individuals of equal status. People of higher status may close the distance between themselves and people of lower status, but seldom do people of lower status move to close the distance between themselves and a person of higher status.

Genders tend to differ in their space patterns. But the differences in part hinge on whether the communication is with someone of the same or opposite gender. In same-gender situations, men establish greater conversational distance than women do. Opposite-gender distancing depends on the relationship.

checkpoint

1. What are the three basic types of communication? Give several examples of each type.

_____

_____

_____

2. What is feedback? Why is it important?

_____

_____

_____

3. What is tactile communication? Why should it be used with caution?

_____

_____

4. Personal space requirements are based on what five factors?

_____

_____

_____

5. Why does the setting influence personal space requirements?

_____

_____

_____

applications

1. Diagram the communication model in this situation: Shari asks Erica to go to a movie on Saturday night. Erica says she cannot go because her family is having a birthday party for her brother.

2. Approach two or more friends and start a conversation about a topic of mutual interest. What nonverbal feedback (gestures, body language, facial expressions, eye contact, and touch) did you get from each person?

_____

_____

_____

3. How have advancements in technology resulted in challenges to interpersonal communication?

_____

_____

_____

4. What happens when a person who needs a large amount of personal space must interact continually with someone who likes to get "up close and personal" with others?

_____

_____

_____

Barriers to Communication

Ideal communication is straightforward. What makes it complex and sometimes frustrating are the barriers that interfere with the communication process. Barriers to effective communication can cause roadblocks in your professional and personal life and be a major hurdle in achieving your personal and career goals.

The first step to removing communication barriers is to identify them. This section will help you recognize and avoid common barriers that hinder communication. These barriers include word choice, confusing messages, information overload, interruptions, and distractions. Some barriers are easy to eliminate and others take more time, practice, and study.

WORD CHOICE

"The two words 'information' and 'communication' are often used interchangeably, but they signify quite different things. Information is giving out; communication is getting through."

Word choice is a common communication barrier. Problems begin when people don't understand the words you are using, whether it's because of differences in work or personal experiences, age, education, gender, or culture. The problem continues when a word has more than one interpretation. Word meanings vary. Take the word *spicy*, for example. For one person, this word may have a positive connotation meaning "zesty," while for another person it may have a negative connotation meaning "blisteringly hot." However, a word like *clock* probably has the same meaning for everyone. Other words, such as *cheap* and *awesome*, are vague and could be interpreted in a variety of ways.

Use precise words that are not likely to be misinterpreted. Think about the person you are communicating with as you choose your words. When you are in doubt about how someone is interpreting your words, ask. Feedback is your best tool when trying to determine if others understand your message. Use words your listeners will understand or define any words you feel may be misunderstood. Be careful when using unfamiliar words. Look at how the words are used in context and check their dictionary definitions.

Colloquialisms

Words or phrases that are often used in a geographical area and more informal settings and most common in conversation are called **colloquialisms**. These words often have multiple meanings and are also called *slang*. Americans use more figures of speech, slang, sports metaphors, and business buzzwords than perhaps any other nation on the planet. Using idioms like "flying by the seat of your pants" with someone unfamiliar with such terms can leave them wondering what planet you've beamed down from.[3]

Colloquialisms are inappropriate for formal writing and create barriers to communication for those not from the geographical area where the colloquialism originated or for people from other cultures. Figure 5-3 lists common colloquialisms. Review them carefully and think about how many of them you use without thinking.

COMMON AMERICAN COLLOQUIALISMS		
COLLOQUIALISM	**MEANING**	**COLLOQUIALISMS USED IN A SENTENCE**
Grubby	Unclean/untidy	Sally's clothes were too *grubby* to wear to school.
Hairy	Dangerous	Skydiving is *hairy* without proper instruction.
Hang loose	Relax	Just *hang loose* until everybody gets here.
Have good vibes	Feel good about	I *have good vibes* about my job interview.
Hyped up	Excited	Myra was all *hyped up* after the ballgame.
Kick out of	Enjoy	I get a *kick out of* watching her play soccer.
Megabucks	Lots of money	Alfie lost *megabucks* in that investment.
Peanuts	Practically no money	He is working for *peanuts* at that restaurant.
Touch base	Discuss a matter	I want to *touch base* with you about the driving exam.
Up in the air	Unknown/undecided	Our vacation plans are *up in the air*.

FIGURE 5-3 Examples of common American colloquialisms.

Jargon

All workplaces have a specific language that is related to the work environment. This specialized language is referred to as jargon. **Jargon** is the technical terminology or characteristic words and ideas that belong to a specific type of work or field of knowledge. Jargon tends to be most challenging in government offices, engineering facilities, law offices, and educational institutions. However, jargon can be unintelligible to someone new to any setting.

Jargon takes several forms: it may be unfamiliar terms, acronyms, abbreviations, or shortened words. For example, a coworker might say to you, "Bring me a copy of the RFP." Even if it is explained that the acronym RFP stands for *request for proposal*, you still might not understand it without further explanation.

Shortened words may also be confusing. "Bring me the Lehto contract but remove his 'soc' from it." This would mean removing Mr. Lehto's Social Security number from the contract. Jargon also includes terms that sound familiar but are defined differently in different fields. The word *mouse* means something entirely different if you work in the computer industry than it does if you are in the pest removal business.

The language of each workplace is different and can be a barrier until you learn the jargon. As you begin a new job, keep a list of unfamiliar words and terms and ask about any that are unclear. Over time, the workplace terminology will become second nature. Be sure to assist new coworkers by helping them learn the workplace jargon.

Sexist Language

Avoid sexist language in your word choice and work toward using gender-neutral terms. **Gender-neutral language** is language use that aims at minimizing assumptions about gender. For example, avoid the use of "man" in occupational terms when the person holding the job could be male or female. Replace words like *chairman, policeman,* and *mailman* with the gender-neutral terms *chairperson, police officer,* and *mail carrier* that apply to both men and women. Don't assume that a job is filled by a particular gender: many CEOs are women, and many nurses are men.

Avoid using gender-specific pronouns such as *his* and *her* or *he* and *she* by making the pronouns plural. For example, the sentence "A doctor needs to vaccinate her patients" could be changed to "Doctors need to vaccinate their patients." Or, drop the pronoun completely. The sentence, "The average student is worried about his grades" could be changed to "The average student is worried about grades."

Using gender-neutral language is ethically sound and appropriate. Speaking in a sexist manner may alienate your listeners and discourage them from communicating with you.

APPLY IT!

Sometimes the problem isn't choosing exactly the right word to express an idea—it's being "wordy." The phrases in the left column use more words where fewer will do. In the right column, suggest an appropriate (and shorter) substitute.

1. Regardless of the fact that …	
2. In all cases …	
3. I came to understand that …	
4. In the event that …	
5. They are of the opinion that …	
6. Were they able to …	
7. Due to the fact that …	
8. At that point in time …	
9. On behalf of . . .	
10. Whether or not . . .	

CONFUSING MESSAGES

You may have seen confusing messages in the classified ads. "Puppy for sale. Will eat anything. Especially likes children." Obviously, the writer is not selling a puppy who eats children, yet someone could get that message from reading the ad.

Clear messages create effective communication because they eliminate the need for requests for additional information or clarification. Confusing or muddled messages are communication barriers because the receiver is unclear about the message. Take these two messages, for example: "We'll meet tomorrow at 8 a.m." "We'll meet tomorrow at 8 a.m. in the conference room to discuss the financial report." The first sentence is confusing and requires clarification to be understood. The second message clearly indicates the time, place, and purpose of the meeting. Feedback from the receiver is the best way for a sender to be sure that the message is clear rather than muddled.

"The single biggest problem in communication is the illusion that it has taken place."

Adrien's supervisor at AERO Distributors gives him oral instructions each morning. Today, she tells him to move four pallets to Level B, Area 3. While on Level B, Adrien should pick up packets for the sales department and deliver them to Elle Ramsey. At 10:30 he should pick up Emilio Tallerico, an AERO board member, at the Atlantic Hotel and drive him to the airport. Finally, he is to stop at the post office and sign for the Certified Mail and deliver it to Marianne (and only Marianne) in the mailroom. Although Adrien was accustomed to his supervisor's oral directions, he was confused about what she wanted him to do—but he said nothing. Adrien takes the pallets to Level B, Area 3, and picks up the packets for the sales department, which he drops at Elle's desk. "So far, so good," he thought. But he couldn't remember the name of the man he is to pick up at the Atlantic Hotel nor the exact time to pick him up. He calls the hotel and asks if a man is waiting to be picked up by someone from AERO. The answer is "No, no one seems to be waiting." "When someone asks about a ride to the airport," Adrien says, "please tell him to take a cab." Adrien then drives to the post office, signs for the Certified Mail, and drops it off to no one in particular in the mailroom. He goes back to his workstation assuming that he followed his supervisor's directions.

How do you think Adrien's supervisor will react to his performance for the day? Were the supervisor's instructions clear? How could Adrien have improved their communication?

POOR CHANNEL CHOICE

Using the proper communication channel helps the receiver understand the nature and importance of the message. For example, it would be appropriate to orally wish a coworker "Good morning." A written warning to an employee who is absent excessively emphasizes to the employee that these absences are serious. A verbal expression of congratulations to a friend who has been promoted may be more personal than sending an e-mail message. You may choose to use more than one channel to get your message across. For example, an instructor may decide to give an assignment orally and also write it on the board.

Using the wrong channel of communication can result in confusion and misunderstanding. A long conversation between a contractor and a customer about the installation of a new hot tub, with neither person taking notes, will most certainly result in confusion and misunderstanding. Using a training video on handwashing techniques, along with a printed summary of key points, helps a new restaurant employee understand the importance of good sanitation practices. But detailing those same procedures only in written form might be less effective. Your goal is to choose the best channel (or channels) to get your message across.

INTERRUPTIONS, DISTRACTIONS, AND DISTANCE

The workplace is an active and lively place where interruptions are the norm rather than the exception. An interruption, a common barrier to communication, may be due to something more immediate than the work at hand, such as an unexpected visitor, a telephone call, or an emergency.

Michaela is explaining the procedure for processing purchase orders to Zaber, a new employee. Michaela's phone rings just as she is about to ask Zaber if he has any questions. A lengthy conversation with a supplier follows, and Zaber returns to his workstation. Michaela finally ends the call and leaves to attend a meeting. Later, Michaela's supervisor drops by to see how Zaber's training went. Michaela says, "Oh, I was interrupted and didn't conclude the training session. I'll call him right away!"

In this case, communication was incomplete because Michaela did not follow through to receive feedback from Zaber.

Distractions such as the slamming of a door, a siren, a conversation in an adjacent cubicle, or a noisy printer are all potential communication barriers. These distractions may be relatively easy to remedy. If office noise affects your conversation, wait for it to stop (if it is of short duration, such as a public address announcement) or move to a

The amount of information available can be overwhelming.

quieter area. If street noise becomes a problem, shut the window or move to a quieter area.

Distance can be a communication barrier when it gets in the way of sending or receiving a message. If you are in a meeting and cannot hear the speaker, for example, move closer so that you can hear what is being said and see any visuals being used. If a cell phone conversation becomes hampered by low signal strength, end the call and call back at another time.

INFORMATION OVERLOAD

You live and work in a fast-paced society where you are constantly bombarded with messages and stimuli coming from all directions. This is due in part to the ever-increasing rate of new information, an increase in the available channels of incoming information, and the ease of duplication and transmission of data across the Internet. Too much information leads to "information overload." **Information overload** refers to an excessive amount of information being provided, which makes processing and absorbing the information very difficult.

E-mail has become a major source of information overload as people struggle to keep up with the multitude of messages that keep filling up the inbox. Another source is the Internet, which provides access to billions of pages of information. In many workplaces, employees are given unrestricted access to the Web, allowing them to manage their own research. But sometimes the amount of information available is overwhelming.

Noah was doing some research on global warming, a "hot topic" he knew very little about. So he began by conducting a Google search on the topic. The number of sites totally amazed him. He clicked on the U.S. EPA link as a place to begin, only to find more links within that site. There was even a "Climate Change for Kids" link. He felt overwhelmed and wasn't sure what to do next. Noah scratched his head and began to wonder if he should have picked a topic that wasn't quite so "hot."

How should you deal with information overload? First, recognize it when it happens to you. Then try to relax and regain your focus. One way to regain focus is through organization and planning. For example, if too many e-mail messages are the problem, then work to eliminate the nonrelevant messages sitting in your inbox. Or set aside time at the beginning and end of the workday to read and respond to messages. Although you cannot control all the information that comes your way, you should try to take control of as much of it as you can. The Beat Back Information Overload feature offers helpful advice.

Feeling overwhelmed by all the information coming your way? Try these techniques for beating back information overload:

- Recognize that not all information can be examined when the volume of information available is high.
- Develop an information management strategy that works for you. Focus on the quality (not the quantity) you receive.
- Try to control the volume of information that comes your way. Keep up with the topics that are interesting and useful to you, but don't feel that you must "know it all."
- Master online search techniques to avoid getting tangled in the Web.
- Reduce paper. Handle each paper only once. Either use it and file it or toss it.

BEAT BACK INFORMATION OVERLOAD

FALSE ASSUMPTIONS OR STEREOTYPING

False assumptions and stereotyping are major barriers to communication when people assume they already know what is about to be said. As a result, they don't listen carefully to the message and miss it. A **stereotype** is a generalized perception or first impression based on oversimplified beliefs or opinions about a person, event, group, or object. For example, tall men play basketball and cars made in Sweden are better investments than cars made in the USA. Stereotyping substitutes for thinking, analyzing, and being open-minded in a new situation.

> *The class eagerly awaited the guest speaker—a former basketball forward who played on the team that won the state championship last year. But the young man was only 5'6", and many students discounted his comments. They generalized that he could not have been successful as a forward because of his stature. In reality, he was successful because of his stature—he was nimble and quick and able to move and dribble the ball better than anyone else on the team.*

Stereotyping can also work in reverse. You may give people an unfair advantage by assigning them very positive traits because of stereotyping. Stereotyping as it relates to diversity will be discussed in Chapter 12.

checkpoint

1. Give three examples of colloquialisms. Why should colloquialisms be avoided in business communications?

   _____

   _____

   _____

2. Is jargon used in your educational setting? If so, provide a few examples.

   _____

   _____

   _____

   _____

3. Give several examples of gender-neutral language. Why is it important to use this type of language?

   _____

   _____

   _____

   _____

4. List three ways of reducing information overload.

_____

_____

_____

5. Explain the term stereotype and why stereotypes are a barrier to communication. What is reverse stereotyping?

_____

_____

_____

applications

1. Are you conscious of the words you choose when speaking with others? How do the words you use with these people differ: a close friend, a parent, an instructor, and your boss?

_____

_____

2. Think of a time when a distraction or distance became a barrier to communication. Describe the situation and what you did to remedy the problem.

_____

_____

_____

3. Describe a personal experience where an interruption or muddled message became a barrier to communication. Describe the situation and what you did to remedy the problem.

_____

_____

4. Describe a situation where you experienced information overload. How did you handle it? What do you plan to do differently when you face information overload in the future?

_____

_____

5. Describe a situation where you made an assumption about someone that later proved false. What factors caused you to make the wrong assumption? What was the result?

_____

_____

Listening Skills

Have you had the experience of listening to a classroom lecture or a friend's description of a family vacation only to realize you remember nothing that has been said? You may have *heard* it, but you weren't *listening*. The process by which we make sense out of what we hear is **listening**. There is a distinction between hearing the words and really listening for the message. Hearing alone is not listening. Hearing only means that you recognize that a message is being sent—you may or may not be translating the information in the message and trying to reach a common understanding between you and the sender of the message.

By becoming a better listener, you will improve your productivity and knowledge base as well as your ability to influence, persuade, and negotiate. What's more, you'll avoid conflict and misunderstandings—all worthy goals for personal and career success.

"You can communicate best when you first listen."

BARRIERS TO LISTENING

Listening involves mentally participating in a conversation, meeting, or lecture for the purpose of comprehending what the speaker is communicating. This is especially true in the workplace, where employees are expected to exhibit effective listening skills. Unfortunately, many roadblocks or barriers can prevent you from receiving a message. Read about the following barriers to listening so that you can recognize them and take steps to eliminate them.

Distractions

You cannot allow yourself to be distracted by what is going on around you. Have you had the experience of trying to listen to a class lecture, but classmates whispering nearby broke your train of thought? Or trying to listen to someone giving you directions when a phone ringing nearby diverts your attention? You might also be distracted by the unusual attire of a speaker, a mispronounced word, or an unusual voice quality or dialect. These distractions can easily steal your thoughts away from the message.

Thinking Ahead to What You Want to Say

In a conversation, people take turns speaking and listening. Unfortunately, sometimes instead of listening, people

Listening involves more than hearing.

©Golf Money 2009/Used under license from Shutterstock.com

think about what they will say next. When this happens, you are hearing but not listening. Your reply may not make sense because you did not listen to *all* the words of the speaker. Perhaps the conversation moved to a new topic and you missed it.

> *Gemma and her supervisor Mr. Schwartz were discussing the holiday vacation schedule. Gemma was so intent on making her point that she wanted vacation during Thanksgiving week that she gave only partial attention to what Mr. Schwartz was saying. She was thinking more about what she wanted to say to him rather than listening to what he was saying to her. She didn't hear him say that the office would be closed the week of Thanksgiving!*

Mind Moving Too Fast

People can think faster than they can speak. Most speakers talk at a rate of about 120 to 150 words per minute. Most receivers listen and think at a rate exceeding 1,000 words a minute. If you are listening at the rate of 1,000 words a minute, your thoughts can wander ahead of the speaker while you are listening. You may begin to daydream, think about what you need to do later, or wonder what your friends are doing. When this happens, you miss the points the speaker is making because your mind is elsewhere and you are no longer focused on the speaker.

Lack of Attention

Too often when someone is talking we don't listen attentively. Good listening requires keeping one's thoughts on what is being said. Paying attention will prevent you from missing important information. For example, if you are being given directions on the job and you are not paying close attention, you may do something wrong and create a problem or unnecessary expense for your employer, or even cause injury to a coworker.

Selective Listening

Are you guilty of allowing selective communication to be a barrier in your conversation with others? **Selective listening** means hearing only what you want to hear. It means "tuning out" someone who is trying to make a point or call attention to a problem or concern.

It is a common human characteristic to skip over the uncomfortable, the unpleasant, or the difficult and comprehend only part of a message. This may happen when you hear something that conflicts with your personal thoughts, beliefs, or convictions. Or you may be selective when you receive information that you don't want to hear or that is simply being presented at an inconvenient time. Selective listening is not an option in the workplace. You must pay careful attention to everything being said.

How do you spot an active listener? An active listener:

- Is genuinely interested in understanding what the sender is thinking and feeling, what the sender hopes to accomplish, and what the message means.

- Has a confident, positive attitude.

- Sets aside prejudices and listens with an open mind.

- Blocks out noise and distractions.

- "Listens" to nonverbal messages as well as verbal ones.

- Jots down the speaker's main points and questions to ask (when appropriate).

- Paraphrases and interprets what is being said.

- Uses body language, gestures, and verbal comments to show that he or she is listening.

ACTIVE LISTENING

You spend more time listening than speaking, reading, or writing. Yet listening remains one of the least understood and least studied parts of the communication process. Other people naturally expect you to listen to what they are saying, but listening is an art that needs to be practiced to be perfected.

If you want to improve your listening skills, your goal should be to become an "active listener." An active listener makes a conscious effort to hear not only the words that another person is saying but, more importantly, to try and understand the total message being sent.[4] Active listening requires concentration and determination on the part of the listener. Be deliberate with your listening and remind yourself constantly that your goal is to hear and understand what the other person is saying. With active listening, the receiver sends the speaker's message back to the speaker (sender) for verification. If a misunderstanding has occurred, it will be known immediately, and communication can be clarified before further misunderstandings occur.

There are other benefits to active listening. Sometimes a person needs to be heard and acknowledged before being willing to consider an alternative or soften a position. Active listening can clarify points of agreement so that the areas of disagreement are put in perspective and diminished rather than blown out of proportion. By preparing to listen, avoiding emotional responses, and separating fact from opinion, you become a better communicator and improve your relationships with others.

Prepare to Listen

"To listen well is as powerful a means of influence as to talk well and is as essential to all true conversation."

Your efficiency as a listener improves if you prepare yourself mentally and physically to listen. Block out miscellaneous thoughts that are running through your mind. Try to erase competing thoughts, such as what was said in the carpool or your plans for Saturday night. You cannot act on these thoughts now, so push them aside and prepare to listen. Focus on what is being said and block out what is not important at the time.

An active listener acts like a good listener. Sit or stand in a way that is comfortable. Face the speaker and be alert. Your body position defines whether you have a chance to be an active listener. Look directly at the speaker. A visual bond between speaker and listener is important for effective listening. Your eyes will complete the communication circuit that must be established between speaker and listener. When you focus attention on the speaker and what is being said, you reinforce what you are hearing. Active listening means accepting 100 percent responsibility for receiving the same message that the speaker sent, uncontaminated by your own thoughts or feelings.[5]

Marco was busily keying a report that was due at noon when he was called to a workgroup meeting in his supervisor's office. Marco's mind was still on the report, but he knew the information his supervisor was presenting was important. He deliberately thought, "I must stop worrying about that report. I must listen to what Ms. Frosch is saying."

When a speaker provides precise details such as dates, figures, major points, and deadlines, you may need to take written notes to supplement your careful listening. The processing of jotting down key points strengthens your listening skills.

on the job

Four employees are seated around a conference table discussing the requirements for the company's new webmaster position. This is a key role because management has decided to develop its websites internally instead of hiring outside agencies to create them. Mike feels strongly that the webmaster should have a background in technology and website design. Alexis stresses that the person must be creative and be able to project a forward-looking image for the company. Ed wants someone who works well with coworkers and the company's large client base. Nicole will make the final decision, but she feels it is important to consider the opinions of others who will work with the new webmaster. Nicole asks, "Mike, do I understand that you want the webmaster to have a degree in information technology or a related field?" Mike responds, "No, I just want the person to have hands-on experience building sites for companies similar to ours. I want to see sites that person has designed." Nicole turns to Ed. "Do I hear you saying that you want a 'people person' in this position?" Ed responds, "You've got that right. This person will work with every section head and will have to say no to some requests. I want someone who gets along well with others." Nicole says, "Alexis, how are we going to find out if an applicant is creative?" Alexis replies, "I think we should give the applicants an actual project that requires creativity and have them complete that project as part of the interview process."

Is Nicole demonstrating active listening? What benefits will the company derive from her eagerness to listen to her coworkers' ideas?

Avoid Emotional Responses

You cannot fully listen to points of view or process information when you are arguing mentally or judging what is being said before the person stops speaking. An open mind is a must for an active listener. Your mind should receive and listen to all that is being said. Control your emotional responses to the speaker's message. Sometimes words trigger emotional responses—positive or negative. Poor listeners spend time reacting to "red flag" words and frequently miss the message.

Separate Fact from Opinion

In many situations it is necessary to separate facts from the opinions of those who are speaking to you. This is called **critical listening**. A critical listener determines the accuracy of the message and identifies the main ideas and details being shared. This is done to separate facts from opinions.

A **fact** is information that can be proven. For example, "Senator Barack Obama was elected the 44th President of the United States of America" or "The invoice for the refrigerator is $1,090.99." An **opinion** is based on personal beliefs or feelings; for example, "That restaurant serves excellent food" or "The theater was too hot." These statements reflect what people *think* about what they have witnessed, heard, learned, or experienced. Opinions are not necessarily true.

Critical listening is important when people express their opinion as fact. When someone says, "Eli is the best candidate for the position," it is a personal opinion. While it may not be based on fact, it remains true that the person believes that Eli is the best candidate for the position. You must evaluate each message to decide what is fact and what is opinion.

checkpoint

1. Why is thinking ahead a barrier to listening?

   _____

   _____

   _____

2. Why is lack of attention a barrier to listening?

   _____

   _____

   _____

3. How can you prepare to listen?

   _____

   _____

   _____

4. What is critical listening?

_____

_____

5. Explain the difference between fact and opinion.

_____

_____

_____

applications

1. Identify situations in which it would be especially important for you to be a critical listener. List two situations from your workplace and two from your personal life.

_____

_____

_____

_____

2. Give examples from your own experience (at home, at school, or at work) of when your listening was blocked. What could be done about the problem in the future?

_____

_____

_____

_____

3. Do you consider yourself to be an active listener? Why or why not?

_____

_____

_____

_____

4. Write four words (or more) that could bring an emotional response from you when you are listening. Write or discuss why these are "red flag words" for you. Describe what you might do to keep from being side tracked when hearing these words.

_____

_____

_____

5 points to remember

Review the following points to determine what you remember from the chapter.

- The communication model includes the sender, the message, the receiver, and the feedback. All four elements must be in place for two-way communication to occur.
- The forms of communication are written, oral, and nonverbal communication.
- Common communication barriers include poor word choice, confusing messages, poor channel selection, interruptions and distractions, information overload, and stereotyping.
- Listening is the process by which you make sense of what you hear. Hearing alone is not listening because hearing only means that you recognize that a message is sent; you may or may not be translating the information and trying to achieve common understanding between you and the speaker.
- Common barriers to effective listening include distractions, selective listening, lack of attention, the mind moving too fast, or thinking about what you want to say.
- Good listening skills include preparing to listen and avoiding emotional responses.
- Active listeners concentrate on what is being said and listen with deliberate intention to understand the message. Active listening can clarify points of agreement and prevent disagreements.
- Critical listeners can separate fact from opinion. Facts are statements that can be proven. Opinions are based on personal beliefs or feelings.

How did you do? Did you remember the main points you studied in the chapter?

KEY terms

communication

written communication

oral communication

nonverbal communication

sender

receiver

message

tactile communication

personal space

colloquialism

jargon

gender-neutral language

information overload

stereotype

listening

selective listening

critical listening

fact

opinion

Want more activities? Go to **www.cengage.com/careerreadiness/masters** to get started.

CHAPTER *activities*

1. Initiate a conversation with a friend so that you can practice reading facial expressions and gestures. Describe the friend's facial expressions and gestures and what you interpreted them to mean.

   _____

   _____

   _____

   _____

   _____

   _____

2. Think of a situation when your personal space was being invaded. What did you do? Are you aware of having invaded someone else's personal space? What did that person do?

   _____

   _____

   _____

   _____

   _____

   _____

3. Think of a time when you have been an active listener. What was the situation? How did you benefit from active listening?

   _____

   _____

   _____

   _____

   _____

   _____

4. Identify the communication barrier that may occur from hearing the following statements.

   a. "I'm having good vibes about how to make megabucks on this deal."

      _____

      _____

      _____

      _____

      _____

   b. "The NSCA is doing what the NSAA has determined is appropriate."

      _____

      _____

      _____

      _____

      _____

   c. Brady said, "Please pick up the latest Grisham book for me at the library."

      _____

      _____

      _____

      _____

      _____

   d. "Meet me in 10 minutes to discuss the new school policy."

      _____

      _____

      _____

      _____

      _____

CRITICAL *thinking*

Shana, a long-time employee of the bank where you work, lives in your apartment complex. You have seen her in the lobby of the apartment building and at the bank, but you have never really met. The bank offices have been reorganized and you have been assigned to work in investment services with Shana. You are excited about the move and look forward to working with new people. As you enter the investment office on your first day, you recognize Shana. You immediately introduce yourself. She says that you look familiar, but immediately becomes distracted by an incoming e-mail message. You tell her that you are looking forward to working with her. She asks, "Where is your desk?" As you respond, her fax machine begins to print, and she doesn't hear your response. You say, "Would you like to have lunch with me?" She says, "What was that again?" You repeat the question but notice Shana's attention is again focused on her e-mail messages. She doesn't look at you and doesn't appear to be interested in talking to you. You go to your desk and get to work. You see Shana in the elevator after work. She says, "What happened to you this morning? We were talking, but when I looked up you were gone." Just as you are about to respond, the elevator door opens and four jovial people get in. They continue laughing and talking so that meaningful conversation with Shana is impossible.

1. What is Shana's problem? Is she an active listener? Does she have a listening problem or does she not want to talk with you?

   _____

   _____

   _____

2. What communication problems are evident in this case?

   _____

   _____

   _____

3. Assuming that you still want to establish rapport with Shana, what is your next step? How important is it to establish a good working relationship with Shana?

   _____

   _____

   _____

CASE 5.2 Drowning in Acronyms

Alex works in a federal government office. He has just been to a briefing where he was told, "You will be moving to another section and working with NCLB legislation, Title I, ELL data and FRD information. It will be your job, in part, to gather statistics on schools not meeting AYP." He left the briefing feeling completely bewildered by the acronyms, shortened words, and other forms of jargon. He spent so much time trying to figure out the jargon that he didn't really hear all that was said in the briefing. An hour later Ms. Lupo, his supervisor, stops by and asks, "Do you have the figures requested at the briefing?" Alex doesn't recall that any requests were made of him. He asks, "What figures?" Ms. Lupo replies, "Everyone was to determine the number of hours they anticipate spending on AYP data this week and give me that information today." Alex stares blankly at her. He doesn't know what AYP means.

1. What should Alex say to his supervisor at this point?

_____

_____

_____

_____

_____

_____

2. What steps should Alex take to remedy his "bewildered" state?

_____

_____

_____

_____

_____

_____

3. Have you had to deal with acronyms and jargon where you work? Give some examples and explain what you did to learn the meanings and deal with the special terms.

_____

_____

_____

_____

_____

Getting Your Message Across

Think About It: Lindsey and Rod were trying to solve a problem with the new collating equipment. It would work fine for a few minutes but then one or more sheets would get stuck and the equipment would flash an error message and shut down. Gunther, a new employee, was walking through the area and hesitated as he passed them. Gunther has considerable experience in working with this equipment, but he hesitated to offer advice. He didn't know Lindsey and Rod very well and wasn't sure they would be open to his suggestions. Lindsey noticed Gunther and said, "Hello, Gunther." Gunther said, "Hi" but then walked away. Lindsey said to Rod, "He sure isn't very friendly. I hear he's very intelligent, but I can't seem to get more than a word or two from him." Rod replied, "Maybe he thinks he's too good to talk with other employees. I'll bet he chats up a storm when management is around." Lindsey said, "Yes, I notice that he spends a lot of time in the supervisor's office."

What assumptions have Lindsey and Rod made about Gunther? Why does Gunther appear unfriendly and perhaps aloof? How might a meaningful conversation have helped this situation?

©Yuri Arcus 2009/Used under license from Shutterstock.com

objectives

After completing this chapter, you should be able to:

1. Describe three basic styles of communication.
2. Describe nonverbal indicators that accompany assertive messages.
3. Identify the rewards of assertive communication.
4. Use small talk and other conversation openers.
5. Demonstrate techniques used to keep a conversation moving.
6. Use the four questioning techniques—open, closed, probing, and rhetorical.

Communication Styles

Your communication style affects your ability to communicate with others. Have you had the experience of standing in a grocery store checkout line and had someone step ahead of you? How did you react? If you said nothing, you reacted in a passive style. If you became enraged and demanded the situation be corrected immediately, you reacted in an aggressive style. If you corrected the situation and protected your rights without infringing on the rights of others, you reacted in an assertive style. While each style has its proper place and use, assertive communication is usually the most effective. Your goal is to develop a style that will allow you to justly express yourself but not offend others.

on the job

During their lunch hour, Denise and Dominic are waiting in a line with the hope of getting tickets to a popular concert. As they near the ticket window, two young men crowd in line in front of them. Denise looks them in the eye and speaks to them in a calm, firm voice. She says, "Excuse me. We've been in line for a half hour, and now you've crowded in front of us. Please go to the back of the line and wait your turn." The two intruders exchange glances, turn, and go to the end of the line. Dominic is impressed with Denise's communication skills, as are the people behind them in line. Denise stood up for her rights and the rights of others without being defensive, pushy, critical, or judgmental. Did Denise and Dominic get concert tickets? Absolutely!

Why was Denise successful in getting the two men to go to the back of the line? What might have happened if she had been more confrontational?

PASSIVE COMMUNICATION

When you use **passive communication**, you allow your rights to be violated because you fail to express honest feelings. Passive communicators attempt to avoid confrontation at all costs. Assume you asked for a window seat on the plane but received a boarding pass for a center seat. You don't point out the error and simply sit where assigned. In this instance, you exhibited passive behavior. People who use passive style do not talk much and seldom question. They don't like to "rock the boat" and feel that it is safer not to react than to stand up and be noticed. The passive communicator will internalize discomfort rather than risk upsetting others. The result

"Self-expression must pass into communication for its fulfillment."

6.1 Communication Styles 115

is often resentment, depression, and low self-esteem. Typically, a passive communicator:

- Doesn't express honest feelings.
- Makes little or no eye contact.
- Lets others make decisions.
- Feels anxious, helpless, and manipulated.
- Apologizes frequently.

Do not, however, mistake good manners for passivity. Sometimes it is the kind thing to say, "That's okay, go ahead of me. I can see that you're in a hurry." The context makes the difference. You always have the option of being generous (for example, your good manners show when you give your seat on the bus to someone who is physically challenged), but that is not the same as letting yourself be taken advantage of in any given situation.

AGGRESSIVE COMMUNICATION

Aggressive communication is the opposite of passive communication. An aggressive communicator sends strong feelings in a vigorous manner without regard to the rights and feelings of others. For example, upon ordering a rare steak and receiving one that is well done, the aggressive communicator might say, "I ordered a rare steak, not a piece of shoe leather. Bring me what I ordered—and do it fast!" An aggressive communicator's voice is often loud, and exaggerated gestures accompany the message. The aggressive communicator is defensive, faultfinding, and judgmental. This style of communication definitely allows you to communicate your feelings, but steps on the rights and feelings of others in the process.

> Enid was having a bad day. She was already late for work, and the bus was running 10 minutes behind schedule. When the bus finally came, she said loudly to the driver, "Why can't you ever be on time? I'm going to be late for work and it's all your fault!"

Aggressive communication may even escalate to physical contact—finger pointing, nudging, or pushing—all of which are unacceptable behaviors. Typically, an aggressive communicator:

- Makes decisions for others.
- Makes others feel uncomfortable.
- Is brutally honest.
- Participates in a win–lose situation only when it's possible to win.
- Shows impatience.
- Glares or stares at others.
- Is direct and forceful.
- Humiliates others.

Aggressive communicators require that their needs be met *now*. The outcome is usually that the aggressive communicator's goals are achieved at the expense of others. Aggressive behavior is often embarrassing and offensive to others and may leave a lasting negative impression.

ASSERTIVE COMMUNICATION

Assertive communication is a more positive and effective communication style than the passive or aggressive style. **Assertive communication** is the ability to express one's feelings and assert one's rights while respecting the feelings and rights of others. Assertive communication is appropriately direct, open and honest, and clarifies one's needs to the other person.[1] For example, an assertive communicator who ordered a rare steak and was served one well done might say, "This isn't the rare steak that I ordered. Please bring me another steak prepared the way I requested." The statement would be spoken in a normal voice tone and without hostility.

Aggressive communication infringes on the rights of others. Assertive communication is more positive and effective.

Assertive communication is effective two-way communication. You have the right to express your feelings in your own words, without guilt or remorse, and others have the right to express theirs. However, the assertive communicator expresses ideas or feelings in the most thoughtful manner possible. "I" statements are appropriate because you want to express *your* feelings. When you use "I" statements, you do not attribute blame—rather, you focus on your needs, feelings, and requests, and you allow yourself to be honest and direct. You might say, "I need more time to review these proposals because they each require much study. May I have two more days?"

An assertive person is open to the viewpoints of others. When you receive feedback from others following an assertive remark, listen without interrupting and accept what the other person has to say, even if you do not agree or if the feedback is negative. An assertive communicator does not react to criticism by counter-attacking, feeling anxious, denying, or feeling inadequate. Typically, an assertive communicator:

- Is direct and self-respecting.
- Demonstrates a willingness to negotiate, listen, and compromise.
- Chooses to make decisions.
- Makes others feel valued and respected.
- Converts win–lose situations to win–win solutions.
- Feels confident and task oriented.
- Demonstrates a concern for the feelings and rights of others.

Keep these basic points in mind when speaking with others:

Be clear. **Don't use multi-syllable words to impress the listener. Use words that are common and easily understood by all.**

Be complete but brief. **Include all necessary information but don't overburden the listener with information they don't need.**

Use variety in your speaking. **Make statements, ask questions, and change the tone of your voice.**

Omit distracting words. **Avoid using trite and meaningless terms such as "you know," "like," and "uh."**

Look for feedback. **Check often to determine if your message has been understood. Look for both verbal and nonverbal feedback.**

COMMUNICATION POINTERS

Assertiveness is a valuable communication tool; however, it is not appropriate in all circumstances.

Tim was obviously upset about the new overtime procedure. He confronted Jayleen from the HR department and immediately began to tell her why the new procedure wasn't fair and wouldn't work. Rather than be assertive, Jayleen listened patiently until Tim finished. "The new procedure obviously upsets you," she said. "Can we schedule a time tomorrow when we can sit down and discuss this further?"

While Tim's style was aggressive, Jayleen focused on Tim's needs rather than asserting her own. By doing so, she diffused what could have been a confrontational situation.

Nonverbal Indicators

Assertive communication is not only what you say but also how you say it. In addition to stating your feelings and saying the right words, you must be conscious of the nonverbal messsages you send. Remember, nonverbal communication is very strong and may overshadow the verbal message. Here are some guidelines for the assertive communicator:

- Establish eye contact with the receiver of your message. Do not stare—just look comfortably into the receiver's eyes.
- Use appropriate gestures to support your message. Do not use threatening gestures or those that could be interpreted as aggressive.
- Stand or sit erect, but not stiff. Position yourself so that you and the receiver are on the same eye level.
- Lean or move slightly toward the receiver.

Four-Step Formula

In an online article titled "4 Steps to Assertive Communication," Dr. Tony Fiore, a licensed psychologist and anger management trainer, suggests that the following four-step formula may be helpful in developing assertive communication skills:[2]

I feel _____ when _____ because _____ I need _____.

In the article, Dr. Fiore uses the example of a woman who is too exhausted to host the dinner her family always expects her to host on Christmas. He explains how the woman would put the formula into practice by using these four steps:

Step 1: "I feel . . ." Start by expressing how you feel about the behavior. Stick to one of the basic emotions: "I feel . . . overwhelmed, angry, hurt, etc."

Step 2: "When . . ." What specifically bothers you about the behavior or situation? Example: "When the family expects me to do this every year."

Step 3: "Because . . ." How does the behavior affect you? Examples: "I feel pressured to do something I really can't do this year." "It makes me feel taken advantage of."

"The basic difference between being assertive and being aggressive is how our words and behavior affect the rights and well-being of others."

Step 4: "I need . . ." "I need" has nothing to do with being selfish. Instead, it means giving listeners a clear signal of what you want them to do differently, so they have an opportunity to change. Examples: "I need for the dinner to be rotated among the family." "If everyone will bring a dish, I'll cook the ham."

Dr. Fiore concludes by stating that although the formula may not always work, it works a high percentage of the time. You may need to try variations of the steps using your own words.

Rewards of Assertive Communication

Assertive communication has the potential to create positive dialogue, but it also requires practice and work. Is it worth devoting time and energy to learning this skill? Definitely. Figure 6-1 lists some rewards of mastering the art of assertive communication.

Passive communicators are usually unhappy because they cannot state what they think and feel. Aggressive communicators get their ideas, thoughts, and feelings heard, but they usually create more problems for themselves and others because of their aggressive tactics. Assertive communicators work hard to create mutually satisfying solutions.

ASSERTIVE COMMUNICATION

- Reduces the anxiety and stress caused by misunderstanding.
- Improves your self-esteem and self-confidence.
- Provides respect for your ideas and opinions.
- Motivates others to clearly state their ideas and opinions.
- Provides a sense of control.
- Provides the ability to say "no" when you mean "no" without feeling guilty.
- Protects you from being taken advantage of by others.
- Minimizes alienating others.
- Demonstrates respect for the feelings of others.

FIGURE 6-1 Some rewards of assertive communication.

Each of the following characteristics relates to one of the three communication styles. If the item relates to a passive communicator, label it *P*. Write *AG* before items characteristic of an aggressive communicator and *AS* before items characteristic of an assertive communicator.

_____ Doesn't like to make waves.

_____ Wastes time and energy overdirecting others.

_____ Trusts others but not self.

_____ Withdraws when feeling treated unfairly.

_____ Is brutally honest.

_____ Achieves goals, often at the expense of others.

_____ Feels motivated and understood.

_____ Doesn't express true feelings.

_____ Likes to monopolize the conversation.

_____ Respects the feelings of others.

checkpoint

1. What is passive communication? Why is passive communication generally not a good choice?

_____

_____

_____

_____

_____

2. What are the characteristics of an aggressive communicator?

_____

_____

_____

_____

_____

3. List the four key words (phrases) of the "4 Steps to Assertive Communication."

_____

_____

_____

_____

_____

4. List five rewards of using assertive communication.

_____

_____

_____

_____

_____

5. Explain why the assertive communicator must be conscious of nonverbal messsages.

_____

_____

_____

_____

_____

_____

applications

1. Four aggressive-style messages follow. Rewrite each using words an assertive communicator would use.

   a. "This financial report is totally inaccurate. Rewrite it—now!"

   _____

   _____

   _____

   _____

   _____

   b. "Give me my money back! This sweater shrank even though I followed the label directions for washing! Is the quality of all your merchandise this poor?"

   _____

   _____

   _____

   _____

   _____

   c. "Guys, I've about had it with your loud chatter. While you are reliving all the exciting plays of the football game, I can't focus on my work. So keep quiet or go someplace else!"

   _____

   _____

   _____

   _____

   _____

   d. "That dress doesn't look good on you. The color isn't right. Can you return it?"

   _____

   _____

   _____

   _____

   _____

   _____

2. Describe a conflict you witnessed or were part of at work or school that you feel may have been caused by different communication styles. What communication styles were used? How was the conflict resolved?

_____

_____

_____

_____

_____

_____

3. Your coworker Dustin frequently borrows pens, pencils, and paper clips from your desk without your permission. Using the four steps to assertive communication, what might you say to stop him from "borrowing" your things?

I feel _____

When _____

Because _____

I need _____

4. You want to take next Friday as a personal day to move into a new apartment. Friday is the only day that your friend Brad can help you move. Using the assertive style, what might you say to your supervisor to get the day off?

_____

_____

_____

_____

_____

_____

_____

5. List three communication pointers to keep in mind when talking with others.

_____

_____

_____

_____

_____

_____

Conversation Skills

Conversation is the two-way spoken exchange of thoughts, opinions, and feelings. A good conversationalist is a joy to be around. People who speak effortlessly and effectively with others are generally well liked, influential, and successful. The sharing and understanding that are essential in good communication will more likely occur in a comfortable environment. You can create a comfortable environment with a friendly smile, a positive attitude, and a genuine attempt to understand others.

Improving your conversation skills can enhance your leadership skills, reduce your anxiety when talking in workplace meetings or social settings, boost your confidence, and lead to improved interpersonal relationships. This section will help you develop skills that engage others in the conversation and keep it moving.

Reuben wanted to establish a good working rapport with a new coworker, Nils. "Good morning, Nils," Reuben said. "How was your weekend?" "Quiet," Nils replied. Reuben persisted. "Great. Did you see the final quarter of the Packers game on television?" Nils replied, "I don't like football." Reuben responded, "Sorry, I forget that not everyone is a football fanatic." Reuben did not give up; he pushed onward. "What sports do you enjoy?" Nils replied, "Oh, my sport is hockey. I grew up in northern Wisconsin where hockey is very popular, and I've never lost my passion for the game." Reuben thought, "Aha, I finally asked the right question!" He said, "That's amazing. I grew up in Milwaukee and played hockey in high school and later on a club team. Maybe we have played on competing teams." The conversation was off and running.

Why was it important for Reuben not to give up on the conversation? Why do you think some people are more difficult to engage in conversation than others?

BEGIN THE CONVERSATION

The biggest fear in America is said to be speaking in public. The second biggest fear is starting a conversation with a stranger. Fear of rejection or having nothing to say may cause you to back away from engaging someone in a conversation. However, you can overcome such fears as you learn the strategies described here: using small talk and icebreakers as conversation openers, avoiding unpleasant statements or questions, remembering the listener's name, and working to hold the listener's attention.

"In a conversation, remember that you're more interested in what you're saying than anyone else is."

Conversation Openers

If you want to become a good conversationalist, put some thought into what you say and how you say it. One way to start a conversation is to use small talk and icebreakers. **Small talk** is light, informal conversation that has no agenda. It is simply a way to acknowledge the person's presence and create a comfortable environment. Polite greetings such as "Good evening!" or "Hello, how are you?" are good for starters. Because people generally enjoy talking about themselves, getting people to talk about themselves can be a good conversation starter.

Icebreakers, which are often stated in the form of questions, are another way to get people to talk about themselves or about something that matters to them. **Icebreakers** are topics used to lessen tension or awkwardness at the beginning of a conversation. Figure 6-2 suggests some common icebreakers that encourage the other person to provide feedback. These are only suggestions. You must choose icebreakers that fit the context of the situation.

Icebreakers may not be the first thing you would say to initiate a conversation. Sometimes it is best to begin with a statement and follow-up with an icebreaker question as an invitation to continue the conversation. Some examples: "I was very impressed by that speaker. What do you think of the suggestions she gave?" "You're working hard on that treadmill. What other equipment do you like to use?" "I hear that our school is going to get a new teleconferencing center. Do you think our class will get to use it?"

Some topics should be avoided. These include personal questions about health, religion, politics, or money. If you are in doubt as to whether a question is too personal, put yourself in the other person's place. How would you feel if someone asked about your politics or financial situation?

COMMON ICEBREAKERS

SOCIAL SETTING	WORKPLACE SETTING
Have you see any good movies lately?	How long have you been with the firm?
How long have you lived in the area? or Where in the area do you live?	Have you heard Dr. X (the speaker) before?
What's your favorite website?	How often do you attend these seminars?
What cell phone service provider do you use?	What do you enjoy most about your new job?
Can you recommend a good restaurant nearby?	What is the most challenging part of your work?
What's your favorite team in the World Series?	Do you know someone who can help me learn to _____?
Where do (or did) you go to school?	What seminar do you recommend?

FIGURE 6-2 Common icebreakers that encourage feedback.

"Don't knock the weather; nine-tenths of the people couldn't start a conversation if it didn't change once in a while."

Keep It Positive

People enjoy talking with someone who is upbeat and positive and tend to avoid individuals who make a habit of speaking negatively. Avoid negative or unpleasant statements or questions like these examples when trying to start a conversation: "Don't you hate Monday mornings? It is so hard to get going" and "Did you hear that the Dallas plant is closing? Hundreds of people are going to be out of work. I suppose we are next." Although these comments may start a conversation, they most certainly are negative and unpleasant.

Remember Names

The ability to remember people's names is an important social skill. Remembering a person's name not only creates instant familiarity and connection to the other person, it subtly pays an effective compliment. It implies that the other person is important to you and that you have made the effort to remember the name. A sample conversation overheard at the Leland Cosmetics company picnic follows. Note that Alison stopped the conversation until she was certain that she knew Kailee's name.

davex83/iStockphoto.com

Conversation skills are important in any situation.

Alison: "Hello. I'm Alison Jensen. I live in your neighborhood."

Kailee: "Hi, Alison. I'm Kailee Riley. Where do you live?"

Alison: "Could you repeat your name again please?"

Kailee: "Kailee—spelled K-a-i-l-e-e Riley."

Alison: "Thanks, Kailee, that's a lovely name. I live at the corner of Imperial Drive and Hamilton Avenue."

Kailee: "That's just a block north of where I live."

Alison: "Small world isn't it? We live in the same neighborhood and work for the same company. What do you enjoy most about working at Leland Cosmetics?"

No one likes to be called by the wrong name or have their name mispronounced. If you get distracted or do not hear the person's name when you are introduced, ask for clarification immediately. Say, "I'm sorry. Could you please repeat your name?" Then say the name out loud to verify that you are heard it correctly. Don't go through the entire conversation pretending you know the person's name—this can lead to disaster. If someone you know joins the conversation and you need to make an introduction, you will be embarrassed. If this does happen, say "I'm sorry. I have forgotten your name. Please remind me."

State your name when you meet someone—even if you have met previously and think the person might remember you. Extend your hand and say, "Hi, Mark. I'm Grace Gillis. How are you?" If the person remembered your name, no problem—you simply reinforced what he or she already knew. One more point about names—if a new acquaintance introduces himself as Stephen, don't call him Steve. If he wanted you to call him Steve, he would have introduced himself in that way. Many people do not want others to take liberties with their name.

KEEP THE CONVERSATION MOVING

Okay, you initiated the conversation. How do you keep the conversation going? This can be done more easily if you can keep an open mind, hold the interest of your listener, avoid total disagreement with others, say "no" in a positive way, and encourage feedback.

Barring exceptional circumstances, there are some topics that will stop a conversation in its tracks—telling off-color jokes or mentioning salaries, personal misfortunes, religion, or politics. If you are unsure of the appropriateness of a topic, forget it. Negativism destroys the spirit of cooperation that can be built by good, positive conversation. Your goal is to keep the conversation moving.

Keep an Open Mind

A good conversationalist keeps an open mind. **Open-minded** means having or showing receptiveness to new and different ideas and the opinions of others. Open-minded people are curious and eager to hear original ideas and discuss new topics. A conversation is a free exchange of ideas. Others will not enjoy talking with you if you constantly pass judgment and dominate every conversation. Rather, be receptive to the ideas and thoughts of others. Avoid being a "conversation blocker" who must always have the last word.

Hold the Listener's Interest

The ability to listen is an important conversational skill. Others will be more willing to continue a conversation if they feel you are truly listening to what they say. Listening involves mentally participating in a conversation. Be sure to exhibit the traits of an active listener that were covered in Chapter 5.

> *Colin and Melinda, both new employees, were talking about the orientation meeting they attended. Colin, who initiated the conversation, was an active listener. He was genuinely interested in Melinda's responses to his questions. He paraphrased what she said to make sure his interpretation was correct. He watched for noverbal indicators that his message was being received. Colin was able to hold Melinda's interest, and Melinda was happy to continue the conversation.*

Another way to hold a listener's interest is to to make that person feel important. Ask for an opinion or seek advice. Use the person's name. Recognize the achievements of others. For example, you might say: "Tiesha, what a great idea! Can you explain it in more detail?" or "Let's hear what Myles thinks—he has extensive experience in this area." Avoid phrases that put listeners down or give them the impression that they aren't important or their ideas are unworthy. Statements such as "You may not understand this, but . . ." or "I'll try to simplify this for you" are *not* the way to sustain a dialogue.

Avoid Total Disagreement

A conversation is not a win or lose event. It should be an open exchange among the participants. If you strongly express an opposite viewpoint to the one being related, or if you contradict or interrupt the speaker, you are being rude. Even more unfortunate, you will usually stop the conversation *cold*. A mild remark is more effective and may eventually open the door for you to make your point without being offensive. Remarks such as "Do you really think so?" and "Tell me more" are more tactful than "That can't possibly be true."

Work to eliminate feelings of competitiveness in your conversation. If you have a conflicting view, listen carefully and wait your turn to share your viewpoint. Think of a conversation as an opportunity to learn something new or re-examine your opinion.

Say No in a Positive Way

Previous chapters have discussed the importance of being positive. However, there are times when you must say "no." It is essential to learn and practice how to say no in a positive way and still get your message across. In some circumstances you can say no by simply implying it. If a coworker asks you to answer his phone over the lunch hour, you might reply, "I'm having lunch with my sister today at the same time your lunch hour is scheduled." You didn't deny the request and you didn't say no, but your coworker got the message.

- Start the conversation with a smile.
- Make an extra effort to remember names.
- Ask questions—lots of them.
- Know what is happening in the world.
- Get excited about the interests and successes of others.
- Change the topic when the conversation has run its course.
- Pay only sincere compliments.
- Don't settle for "yes" or "no" responses. Ask a follow-up question.
- Use humor, when appropriate.
- Tell a brief story or an anecdote.
- Make everyone involved in the conversation feel important.

Why would each of the following comments not be said in a good conversation?

1. "You're wrong! I saw the accident so I know what really happened."
   _____

2. "Don't you hate these rainy days? It makes me want to 'veg out' in front of the television."
   _____

3. "Does your religion believe in absolution?"
   _____

4. "I totally disagree with your statements about the advantages of the merger."
   _____

5. "How much of a salary increase did you receive?"
   _____

You can also avoid being negative by indicating what you *can* or *will* do. If a client requests an appointment at 1:30 on Friday and that time is not available, rather than saying, "No, I'm sorry that isn't possible," offer an alternative, such as "We have time open at 12:30 and 3:30 on Friday. Would either of those times work for you?"

Another technique is to make the "no" part of your sentence relate to an object or situation rather than a person. If you say, "This wallpaper appears to be warped, and we cannot accept it for return," the listener will likely accept your statement. If you say, "You must have stored this paper in a damp place because it's warped. We won't take it back." Your sentence becomes accusatory, and your listener may resent the remark.

"Good discourse sinks differences and seeks agreements."

Encourage Feedback

How do you encourage feedback? You encourage feedback when you ask for it directly and give reinforcement to the listener who responds to your question. Suppose you ask your coworker Bethina how she likes the new health insurance plan. Bethina responds, "I think the new program is too expensive for workers with children." If you say, "Well, you're lucky you have insurance that will cover kids!" Bethina will probably end the conversation. To encourage Bethina to continue the conversation, you might say, "I understand it is more expensive for employees with families. Have you considered expressing your views to management?" This comment will likely encourage Bethina to continue the dialogue. Other verbal cues that will encourage further feedback and conversation are: "Can you give me an example?" or "I'm not sure I'm clear on your thoughts concerning . . ."

"Feedback is the breakfast of champions."

In some situations, you may want to specify the kind of feedback you want. If this is the situation, try to make your questions explicit. While you could say to a coworker, "Let me know if there is any way I can help," it would be better to be more specific and say, "Could you use some help rearranging your workstation?" or "When I pick up my son at day care, would it help if I pick up your daughter, too?"

ASK QUESTIONS

When used effectively, questions can be used to initiate and keep a conversation moving along. There are four types of questions: open questions, closed questions, probing questions, and rhetorical questions. Become familiar with these types of questions so you can ask questions that are appropriate for the situation.

Open questions. Open questions typically elicit longer answers and encourage others to participate in the conversation. They usually begin with the words "what," "why," or "how." An open question asks the receiver about his or her knowledge, feelings, thoughts, or opinions. "Tell me" and "describe" can also be used in open questions; for example, "Can you tell me what happened at the budget meeting?" and "How would you describe management's reaction to the reorganization?"

Closed questions. Closed questions require single word or very short answers and are used to test one's understanding of another person's comments. For example, "If I understand what you said, your company will not participate in the fundraising effort. Is that correct?" Closed questions can also be used to close a discussion or finalize a decision. For example, "Are we all agreed that this is the right decision?"

Probing questions. Probing questions are used in seeking more detail to help clarify or verify what has just been said. Examples are: "Can you give me an example of what you mean by 'technophobia'?" or "How will this new database help our salesforce?" Probing questions are used to (1) make sure you have the whole story and that you understand it; or (2) draw information from another person who you feel may be trying to avoid telling you the whole story.

The word "exactly" is often used in this questioning technique—"Who exactly did you mean when you said someone will get back to me?" Speak in a normal tone and don't emphasize the word "exactly." If your receiver is uncomfortable with the question, the best reply would be "I'm just trying to get information."

Rhetorical questions. Rhetorical questions aren't really questions, because they don't require an answer. For example, "Wasn't that a great book?" The purpose of a rhetorical question is to engage the listener—to draw the listener out. Using a rhetorical question is much better than telling your listener, "That is a great book." Another example: "Don't you love the vivid colors in this design?" The listener is likely to continue the conversation by talking about the colors he or she sees in the design. On the other hand, saying "I love the vivid colors in this design" doesn't encourage the listener to say anything in return.

Although you likely use all of the question types, you may not have realized you were using them. By deliberately applying an appropriate questioning technique, you can gain information, keep a conversation moving, avoid misunderstandings, and perhaps even improve relationships.

checkpoint

1. What is the purpose of an open question?

2. Why isn't a rhetorical question really a question?

3. Give two examples of how to encourage feedback from the listener.

_____

_____

_____

_____

_____

_____

_____

4. List two topics that will "stop" a conversation.

_____

_____

_____

_____

_____

_____

_____

5. List three "conversation energizers" to keep in mind when talking with others.

_____

_____

_____

_____

_____

_____

_____

applications

1. Describe someone whom you consider a good conversationalist. Identify the skills this person uses to engage others in conversation and keep the conversation moving.

_____

_____

_____

_____

_____

_____

2. Label each of these questions as open (*O*), closed (*C*), probing (*P*) or rhetorical (*R*).

_____ Why do you want to see that movie?

_____ How difficult is it to solve these Sudoku puzzles?

_____ How do you know the exact peak altitude of Mt. Hood?

_____ What happened in the third act of the play?

_____ Isn't this a wonderful evening?

_____ How far is it from Kansas City to St. Louis?

_____ Why exactly do you think he quit his job?

_____ Isn't *They Walk Among Us* the scariest movie you've ever seen?

_____ Don't you love the smell of steaks cooking on a grill?

_____ Are we all ready for lunch?

3. Assume you are seated on a flight headed to Boston. A nervous flyer is seated next to you. He appears to be shy, but you get the feeling he wants to talk to calm his nerves. List three questions (or a statement followed by a question) you could use to start a conversation.

_____

_____

_____

_____

_____

_____

_____

_____

4. Identify a classmate or a coworker you would like to meet. Using the techniques in this chapter, introduce yourself and start a conversation. Then answer these questions: Which techniques did you use? How effective were the techniques? What did you learn about the classmate or coworker?

_____

_____

_____

_____

_____

_____

_____

_____

6 points to remember

Review the following points to determine what you remember from the chapter.

- The three styles of communication are passive, aggressive, and assertive. The preferred style of communication is assertive because it allows you to state your rights without stepping on the rights of others.
- Being assertive requires sending the right nonverbal messages—appropriate eye contact, nonaggressive gestures, and erect posture.
- Passive communicators do not stand up for their rights, and they internalize discomfort rather than risk upsetting others.
- Aggressive communicators get what they want but ignore the rights of others and may alienate others.
- Small talk and icebreakers are effective techniques for starting a conversation.
- Continue a conversation by keeping an open mind, holding the interest of the listener, avoiding total disagreement, saying "no" in a positive way, and encouraging feedback.
- Questioning techniques are helpful in keeping a conversation going. Open questions, closed questions, probing questions, and rhetorical questions serve difference purposes in a conversation.

How did you do? Did you remember the main points you studied in the chapter?

KEY terms

passive communication

aggressive communication

assertive communication

conversation

small talk

icebreakers

open-minded

open questions

closed questions

probing questions

rhetorical questions

Want more activities? Go to **www.cengage.com/careerreadiness/masters** to get started.

CHAPTER *activities*

1. With a classmate as a partner, script a conversation for the following scenario. The conversation should include at least one icebreaker, one open question, and one probing question.

   You manage a workgroup in the human resources department of a large insurance company. Sarina, whom you are meeting for the first time, has just been transferred to your group. She will help plan the orientation meeting for 115 new insurance agents. You and Sarina and the rest of your team will work side by side for the next few weeks to complete this important assignment, and you want to make this a pleasant experience for everyone involved. Sarina has experience planning small-group meetings for the marketing department.

2. With a classmate as a partner, script a conversation for the following scenario. The conversation should include at least one icebreaker, one probing question, one closed question, and one rhetorical question.

   Jody and Warren are among 15 people at the backyard picnic at the home of mutual friends, Alice and Dennis Lenner. Although both Jody and Warren are employed at Advertising by Design, they work several floors apart and have never met. Jody, an accountant, decides to make the first attempt at conversation with Warren, a designer. Jody has seen several outstanding advertising pieces Warren has produced. Warren recalls attending a workshop Jody conducted on new accounting procedures.

3. Read the three situations and decide how a passive person, an aggressive person, and an assertive person would respond. Write your responses below the scenario.

   a. You are working on an important task with a deadline. Coworkers in the adjacent cubicles are celebrating a birthday, and you are having a difficult time concentrating on your work. What would you do?

   [passive] _____

   _____

   _____

   [aggressive] _____

   _____

   _____

   _____

   [assertive] _____

   _____

   _____

   b. You are an executive assistant in a small company. Your supervisor asks you to pick up his dry cleaning at Speedy Cleaners several blocks away. What do you do?

   [passive] _____

   _____

   _____

   [aggressive] _____

   _____

   _____

   [assertive] _____

   _____

   _____

c. It's Friday. Earlier today, a coworker borrowed your company laptop "for a few minutes" to complete some office work. She has had it for several hours, and it's time to leave. You want to take the laptop home to finish a report that is due Monday. What do you do?

[passive] _____

_____

_____

_____

_____

_____

_____

[aggressive] _____

_____

_____

_____

_____

_____

_____

_____

[assertive] _____

_____

_____

_____

_____

_____

_____

4. Write how to say "no" in a positive manner to the following requests.

a. "May I use your smartphone to find an Italian restaurant in this area?"

_____

_____

_____

_____

b. "Can you drop this package at the post office on your way home?"

_____

_____

_____

_____

c. "Will you proofread my research paper for me?"

_____

_____

_____

_____

d. "These shoes don't fit. Can I get my money back?"

_____

_____

_____

_____

e. "Will you give me a ride to the mall after class?"

_____

_____

_____

_____

CRITICAL *thinking*

Evan, a medical records clerk in a small hospital, takes his job very seriously. He recognizes that a mistake in a record could jeopardize a patient's health, the reputation of the hospital, and possibly the patient's life. Marina is the night shift emergency room nurse. On the chart of one of the emergency room patients, Marina reports that the patient's left eye was injured in a worksite accident. As Evan is gathering the records for the patient, he notes that the doctor and the ambulance driver had stated that the patient's *right* eye was injured. Evan catches Marina's mistake and confronts her in the hallway. He shakes the patient's medical file at her and yells, "How could you be so negligent? Don't you know right from left? Do you realize you put the patient in jeopardy with this type of error? They could have treated the wrong eye! Don't you care about your patients and this hospital?" This outburst takes place within earshot of a waiting room overflowing with concerned relatives and friends of patients.

1. What is Evan's style of communication in this incident? What characteristics of the style does Evan demonstrate?

   _____

   _____

   _____

2. Who does Evan embarrass by his style of communication? What damage may have been done because of where he chose to speak to Marina?

   _____

   _____

   _____

3. What words and nonverbal communication could Evan have used to send his message in an assertive communication style?

   _____

   _____

   _____

4. Assume that Marina is an assertive communicator. What might she say to Evan after his outburst?

   _____

   _____

   _____

CASE 6.2 Off to a Good Start

Cody was hired as an assistant accountant with Swift Financial Services. This is his first job, and he is eager to use his skills. Cody is shy, but he recognizes the importance of becoming acquainted with other members of the staff. As he walks from the parking lot, he greets others with a smile and a "hello." He introduces himself to coworkers as they head to the orientation meeting. Four other new staff members are introduced at the meeting, and Cody takes special note of their names and departments. After Cody is introduced, he says, "I'm pleased to be on the staff of Swift Financial Services, and I look forward to working with all of you. I hope you'll be patient with me as I have much to learn." Later in the orientation he asks, "What exactly is the procedure for calling a customer with a delinquent account?" As he leaves the meeting, he says to one of the new employees, "Hello Shantel, my name is Cody and I work in accounting. Am I remembering correctly that you work in the loan department? What are your job responsibilities?"

1. Is Cody's day off to a good start? Why or why not?

_____

_____

_____

_____

2. What good conversation skills did Cody use?

_____

_____

_____

_____

3. What types of questions did Cody ask? Are they good questions?

_____

_____

_____

_____

4. Do you think Cody will be successful in his new job? Why or why not?

_____

_____

_____

_____

chapter 7

Communicating with Coworkers and Supervisors

©Image Source/Getty Images

objectives

After completing this chapter, you should be able to:

1. Demonstrate the positive traits necessary for interacting with others.

2. Avoid the negative traits that prevent you from fitting in and getting along.

3. Recognize that gossip distracts workers, wastes time, and can be hurtful.

4. Describe an effective team and the qualities of a team player.

5. Recognize the characteristics of the three categories of supervisory leadership.

6. Understand supervisory and employee expectations.

7. Make proper and efficient use of e-mail, text messaging, and voicemail.

Think About It: Nina graduated with honors from a legal assistant program in a well-respected community college. Her excellent grades and successful internship experience helped her get a job in a prestigious legal firm. During her first weeks on the job, an attorney complimented Nina on her attention to detail and a senior partner told her that she had a great future in the legal field. At the end of her probationary period, Nina's supervisor called her in for an evaluation conference. She expected a good evaluation. Instead, Nina was told that she would remain on probation for six more months with no pay increase. Her supervisor said, "Your coworkers find you unpleasant and demanding, and it has been reported that you have been rude to clients." Nina was devastated. She thought her work was going well. Nina snapped at the supervisor and firmly stated, "I do quality work. I'm not here to be cheerful!" She stormed out of the supervisor's office and muttered something about being unfairly judged.

What should Nina do? Should she schedule a meeting with her supervisor? If so, what should she say? What might improve her chances of getting off probationary status?

7.1 Fitting In and Getting Along

7.2 Becoming a Team Player

7.3 Working with Your Supervisor

7.4 Communicating Electronically

Fitting In and Getting Along

Have you seen employment ads that say, "Must be a team player" or "Must have excellent interpersonal skills"? The ability to interact well with supervisors, coworkers, suppliers, customers, and others in a variety of circumstances is a critical skill in today's workplace. Organizations are concerned about the relationships among people because people are their most important resource. Good human relations skills improve communication, increase productivity, and make the work environment more pleasant.

You may spend several years working hard and studying to become technically competent. You may have special talents and abilities. Yet wherever you work, you will not be successful if you cannot fit in and get along with others. When workplace relationships are positive, even heavy workloads or tight schedules can seem less burdensome.

POSITIVE TRAITS TO ACQUIRE

"There is no personal charm so great as the charm of a cheerful temperament."

Getting along with other requires tolerance, respect, and courtesy. Other personal traits are also valued in the workplace. Consider them "value-added qualities" because they add value to your current skills and abilities. These characteristics include cheerfulness, a sense of humor, tact, empathy, dependability, resourcefulness, and a team spirit. This does not mean that you must be the most popular, dynamic, and charismatic person to be a success. Your goal is to develop positive characteristics that communicate to others that you want to fit in and get along.

Cheerfulness

Cheerfulness is a state of mind, or an "inner attitude." Like a positive attitude, cheerfulness is contagious. A cheerful person communicates a good spirit and dispels gloom. Think about the people you enjoy spending time with—chances are they are cheerful. A cheerful person has the power to energize others by helping them look at the bright side of life.

Remind yourself each day to be cheerful. Cheerfulness keeps you in a positive frame of mind, and your coworkers will enjoy working with you. You will be happier with yourself and more pleasant to others.

Sense of Humor

No matter what your age or situation, life is good when you can laugh freely and often. Life is also healthier. Research finds that humor can help you cope better with pain, enhance your immune system, reduce stress, and even help you live longer. Doctors and psychologists agree that laughter is an essential component of a healthy, happy life.[1]

Humor is healthy in the workplace as long as it contributes to your professional image. Workplace humor deals with how you handle yourself, not how you can elicit laughter. Direct your sense of humor toward amusing situations (not people). It is never acceptable to be crude, tell off-color jokes, poke fun at others, or put others down as individuals or groups.

Tact

A tactful person has the ability to say or do the right thing without hurting another person's feelings. **Tact** is sensitivity to what is appropriate in dealing with others, including the ability to speak or act without offending others. Put another way, tact is the ability to hammer home a point without hitting the other person on the head or to make your guests feel at home when you wish they *were* at home. Though humorous, this definition helps you realize the delicate nature of tact.

Have you ever had someone ask for your opinion? Perhaps the person had just completed a new spreadsheet to use in your office. Suppose you aren't impressed with the work. Components are missing and some data could be misinterpreted. If you find something honest but nonthreatening to say, then you demonstrate tact. If you bluntly state what is wrong, then you show a lack of tact.

Wanting to be tactful isn't enough. Tact requires good judgment, thought, and choosing your words carefully. It is not wise to react immediately when a response requires tact. Take some time to determine the best way to respond to the other person. Avoid using a confrontational tone, words, or gestures that cause the other person to become defensive or feel challenged.

> Heidi listened carefully as Anton showed her the spreadsheet he had developed for their workgroup, but she immediately saw some flaws in it. "Using a spreadsheet to show sales over time is a good idea, Anton. Might it be helpful to add a column showing projected sales? And possibly change the heading of the third column to Fiscal Year Budget?"

By wording her opinions as questions, Heidi recognized Anton's initiative in developing the spreadsheet and pointed out the problems in a nonthreatening manner.

Empathy

Another quality closely associated with tact is empathy. **Empathy** is the ability to look at situations through the eyes of others—to "walk in another's shoes." Empathy is the capacity to share and understand another's emotions and feelings. If you have friends who have suffered the loss of a loved one, you can understand their feelings of sadness if you have experienced the same loss. If you are sensitive to the feelings of others, you will try to make them feel at ease.

©track5/iStockphoto.com

There is always time for showing concern for others.

To form positive relationships with your coworkers:

- Focus on your work, not on what others are doing.
- If you have a problem with someone, talk with that person—not everyone else in the workplace.
- Don't use your coworkers as therapists.
- Treat others as you would like to be treated.
- Don't brag about your salary, promotion, children, or possessions.
- Avoid monopolizing shared equipment.
- Look for favorable qualities in others.
- Return items that you borrow.
- Don't manage your personal life at work. Pay bills, place online orders, and talk to friends on your own time.
- Be as good as your word. If you say you will do something, do it.
- Understand the limits of your authority and stay within your boundaries.

Empathy has two components—recognizing another's feelings (a perception skill) and responding to those feelings (a communication skill). Empathy requires a "you" orientation rather than an "I" orientation to establish a positive climate and be in a position to be helpful. You can express genuine empathy (1) after you listen to what the person is saying (verbally and nonverbally) and understand what happened, (2) recall or imagine how you would feel under similar circumstances, and (3) say something that indicates your sensitivity to what the person is feeling and sends the message that you are willing to talk and offer help.

> Estelle knew that her coworker Jacob was having a hard time with his son, who had been truant from school and arrested for possession of illegal substances. Estelle had experienced similar problems with one of her children. At one point, Jacob raised his voice at Estelle for a minor error. Estelle recognized that Jacob was upset with her because of his emotional state and the stress in his personal life. Later, in a private conversation, Estelle told Jacob that she had been through a similar situation and offered to be available if he wanted to talk.

The terms "empathy" and "sympathy" are often confused. Both terms relate to how you respond to another person's emotions. Many people use the terms interchangeably, but the difference is important. **Sympathy** involves identifying with the person and feeling sorry for another who is suffering but without having a true understanding of what the person is actually feeling. Empathy focuses on experiencing and sharing the pain of another with full understanding of the feelings involved. A sympathetic response is, "I can understand why that new policy makes you angry." An empathetic response is, "That new policy makes me angry, too."

"You never really understand a person until you consider things from his point of view ... until you climb inside of his skin and walk around in it."

Dependability

Just as you depend on others, they depend on you to get the work done effectively and efficiently. Consider it a huge compliment if someone describes you as being dependable. Demonstrate dependability by being as good as your word, meeting deadlines, and being at work every day and on time. If you promise to do something, do it. If you have a deadline, meet it. If a meeting starts at 1 p.m., be there ahead of time. Others will observe your actions and know that they can count on you. The dependability of one team member sets an example for an entire group. The reverse is also true. One person's unreliability can affect the productivity of an entire team.

Resourcefulness

Solutions to problems and situations that you encounter are not always obvious. Some situations may require you to be resourceful—to use creativity and ingenuity to resolve the problem or deal with the situation. A resourceful person is persistent in asking questions: "What is the real problem? What resources are available? Who else has information that might help us? Is there anything else we can try?" Resourceful people often try unconventional ways of solving problems. They experiment and improvise. They take risks. And, most important of all, a resourceful person never gives up.

Abby Brown, a sixth-grade teacher at Marine Elementary School in Minnesota, is a perfect example of a resourceful person who "thinks outside the box." Unlike children almost anywhere else, students in Ms. Brown's class do not have to sit and be still. Quite the contrary, they may stand and fidget all class long if they want. Her goal was to give students the flexibility they need to expend energy and, at the same time, to focus better on their work rather than focusing on how to keep still. With the help of a local ergonomic furniture company, Ms. Brown designed an adjustable-height school desk and stool that gives students the option to stand while they do their work. Each desk is equipped with a "swing bar" for active feet. She got the idea for the stand-up desks after 20 years of watching children struggle to contain themselves at small, hard desks and after reading research by Dr. James Levine, a professor of medicine at the Mayo Clinic.[2] Do the students like the new desks? The answer is a resounding "Yes!"

Team Spirit

It is not necessary to be on a formal team to exhibit "team spirit." You exhibit team spirit when you commit to company and department goals and cultivate positive relationships with others. "How may I help?" is a question that workers who exhibit a team spirit often ask. Of course, the best way to help others is to do your own work completely and efficiently. It is not productive to help others until your work is done. However, when your workload permits, offer to help a coworker.

> *Karen was walking to the mailroom with a letter that had to go out that day. As she passed Javier's workstation, she noticed several letters in his out basket. She knew that the mail cart had already collected the afternoon mail. "Javier, I'm on my way to the mailroom. Would you like me to take those letters?" she asked. "Oh, thank you!" he said. "I didn't have them ready in time for the last mail pickup."*

Many employers have programs designed to foster team spirit. Company sales conferences, picnics, and softball teams are examples. Participate enthusiastically in such events and use them as opportunities to get to know your coworkers in an informal, social setting. Doing so will help you interact with others on the job.

Ralph works in the claims department of a large insurance agency headquartered in Chicago. Property claim supervisors from the five regional offices meet monthly to review processing procedures and claim summaries. Emma Grace, Ralph's manager, tells him that these meetings are important; however, she is concerned about costs. She mentions switching to quarterly meetings but then retracts the statement because she thinks that the claims supervisors need to meet monthly. Determined to come up with a less costly option, Ralph returns to his desk and gets to work. He knows that travel costs represent the biggest expense for the monthly meetings. He researches teleconferencing and finds that the technology is affordable. Ralph likes the conference call option and discovers several software programs that are affordable and enable teams to easily capture, distribute, and collaboratively manage meeting information and action items online in real time. Ralph selects the software package that offers the best features at a reasonable cost. From accounting, he gets the cost figures for the monthly meetings. He compares those figures with the cost of the software and the conference call service. He finds that the travel savings alone would pay for the software. Ralph presents his research to Emma Grace, along with a recommendation to consider teleconferencing as a cost-effective alternative to face-to-face meetings.

How did Ralph exhibit resourcefulness? Why is it important to be able to "think outside the box"? Do you think Emma Grace was pleased with Ralph's efforts?

NEGATIVE TRAITS TO AVOID

"Resentment or grudges do no harm to the person against whom you hold these feelings but every day and every night of your life, they are eating at you."

The first part of this section covered positive traits that contribute to your ability to fit in and get along with others. Now let's look at negative traits you will want to avoid because they work against positive interaction. These traits include resentment, irritating habits, envy or jealousy, and self-pity.

Resentment

Nothing consumes a person more quickly than harboring resentment. **Resentment** is a feeling of displeasure, ill will, and deep anger over something you believe (correctly or incorrectly) to be a wrong or an insult to you. Complaining and whining are examples of resentment expressed openly. Those who complain because they resent others or are dissatisfied with a circumstance are not pleasant people to be around.

You know that cheerfulness is contagious; unfortunately, complaining is also contagious. Consider Glenn's reaction to Carlotta's promotion: "I am so angry. I should have been promoted instead of Carlotta. I am more qualified. Nobody listens to me. She didn't deserve the promotion." Glenn may openly voice his resentment until others begin to avoid him as they tire of hearing him express his feelings.

Holding resentment inside until it causes you mental anguish is unhealthy. If you feel the resentment is justified, deal with the situation in a positive way. If it is not justified, move on to something constructive. Focus on a part of your job that you enjoy or take a walk during a break. Figure 7-1 offers a winning formula for putting your thoughts and actions into proper perspective. Combining action with enjoyment will help overcome resentment and put the original cause in a better perspective.

Action + Enjoyment – Resentment = Proper Perspective

FIGURE 7-1 Winning formula for a proper perspective.

Irritating Habits

Like it or not, you may have irritating habits that you need to eliminate to fit in and get along. Many irritating habits are "little things," but in a busy work environment where many people are stressed, an irritating habit may put someone "over the edge." Unfortunately, most people are quick to identify the irritating habits of others but slow to recognize their own. Polly Gum Popper in the next cubicle has no idea how much you'd like to steal her pack of gum. You either put on earphones or tactfully address the issue with Polly.

Do you have any of the irritating habits listed in the Apply It! activity in this section? If you think not, ask a good friend if that is true or not. Your friend's response may surprise you. Many people are unaware that they have picked up an irritating behavior. To eliminate an undesirable habit, be aware that you practice it and then make a conscious effort to stop it.

Do you have any of these annoying habits? Place a check mark beside any habit you need to eliminate. Do you have other habits that are not on this list?

_____ Clearing your throat repeatedly.
_____ Popping or snapping your gum.
_____ Fiddling with your hair.
_____ Playing with your jewelry.
_____ Whispering when others are talking.
_____ Jiggling change or keys in your pocket.
_____ Tapping your fingers or a pen or pencil.
_____ Interrupting conversations.
_____ Repeating meaningless phrases ("you know," "like," etc.).

Envy and Jealousy

"Envy is counting another's blessings instead of your own."

The closely related feelings of envy and jealousy are two of life's most destructive emotions. Resentfully desiring something that someone else has is called envy. **Jealousy** is a feeling of rivalry toward one who you believe has an advantage over you. Unfortunately, feelings of envy and jealousy are common in today's highly competitive world. But if you want to fit in and get along, you need to control these traits. Whenever you feel these destructive emotions, think about this adage: "Every time you turn green with envy, you're ripe for trouble."

You may never eliminate these emotions, but you can work to accept the advantages enjoyed by others and express happiness over their accomplishments. If you can become a person who is pleased when you hear words of praise for someone else, you will know you have taken a giant step toward becoming a professional.

Self-Pity

"There are few human emotions as warm, comforting, and enveloping as self-pity. And nothing is more corrosive and destructive. There is only one answer: turn away from it and move on."

Self-pity is feeling sorry for yourself without looking at the good things in your life. Although it is normal now and then to feel sorry for yourself, continually talking about your problems and dwelling on them causes others to avoid you. Your coworkers would soon tire of hearing a "poor me" monologue such as: "I'm so tired. I work here all day. Then I go home and meet the challenges of my house and family. The next morning, I get up and start all over again. My neighbor stays home all day and has time to shop and play golf. I'll never have that kind of luxury." This kind of self-pitying talk is exhausting to you and to those around you.

Self-pity is not a productive behavior. "Pity parties" can result when this trait takes over. The bad thing about a pity party is that no one else wants to attend. Recognize self-pity for what it is, then turn your thoughts to the things in your life that are working well, and move forward.

WORKPLACE GRAPEVINE

Gossip spread by the company grapevine or rumor mill is a form of communication that must be considered as you study fitting in and getting along. There is good news and bad news about the workplace grapevine. The bad news is that it is impossible to dismantle, discourage, or eliminate it. The good news is that this informal communication network usually contains some accurate information.

Gossip distracts workers, wastes valuable work time, causes anxiety, and can result in hurtful rumors. Gossip tends to surface when people are curious about a situation and the facts are not available. When this happens, speculation begins and the informal communication network known as the "grapevine" goes into action. But even accurate information can change as it moves from person to person. The receiver may not hear the whole message or be confused by a poor word choice, forget part of the message before passing it along, misinterpret what was said—or someone along the way may deliberately sabotage the message.

The worst type of gossip is gossip that hurts someone. When someone starts malicious gossip about an individual, it is wise to refuse to listen. The more an employee gossips, the less coworkers will confide in that person. Eventually, the gossiper develops a reputation as someone who cannot be trusted. Don't let gossip tarnish your professional reputation.

Don't speak evil of someone if you don't know for certain, and if you do know, ask yourself, why am I telling it?

checkpoint

1. List three positive traits needed to get along with others.

   _____

   _____

   _____

   _____

2. List three negative traits to avoid if you want to get along with others.

   _____

   _____

   _____

   _____

3. Why is self-pity a nonproductive state of mind?

   _____

   _____

   _____

   _____

4. Why should feelings of resentment not be openly expressed?

   _____

   _____

   _____

   _____

5. Why is gossip so popular? Why is it dangerous?

   _____

   _____

   _____

   _____

applications

1. List irritating habits of others that bother you. Do you have some habits that may be irritating to others? What are they?

_____

_____

_____

_____

2. Have you personally witnessed a negative situation that was lightened with humor? What was the situation? What was the outcome?

_____

_____

_____

_____

3. Describe a situation where you "thought outside the box" and came up with a creative solution to a problem. How did others react to your solution?

_____

_____

_____

_____

4. Explain why the traits of envy and jealousy may be considered the most dangerous of all human emotions.

_____

_____

_____

5. Give an example of information you heard through the grapevine. How accurate was the information? What action, if any, did you take?

_____

_____

_____

_____

Becoming a Team Player

There will be times in your life when you will be a member of an organized team. In your leisure time, you may play soccer or be on a volleyball team. At work, you may be part of a team charged with releasing a new product or updating a procedures manual. Businesses have recognized the benefits that come from having employees work together in formal or informal teams, and teams are now a common part of today's workplace. A **team** is an identifiable group of people who are committed to a common purpose for which they hold themselves accountable.

Not all groups are teams, but all teams are groups. The difference between a *team* and a *group* is that team members depend on each other for the team's overall performance. According to Patricia Fripp, sales trainer and author, a team is more than a group of people who work at the same time in the same place. A real team is a group of individuals who are committed to working together to achieve common goals. Most likely they are not all equal in experience, talent, or education, but they are equal in one vitally important way, their commitment to the good of the organization.[3]

Teamwork refers to people working together cooperatively to accomplish established team goals and objectives. For example, members of a football team play various positions but come together with the common goal of winning the game.

Workers who are part of a team typically find their work more rewarding and stimulating than working alone. Employers have recognized that teams are a good way to improve productivity and generate new ideas. Figure 7-2 lists some advantages and disadvantages of working in teams.

> "Never doubt that a small group of thoughtful, committed citizens can change the world."

TEAMS IN THE WORKPLACE

ADVANTAGES	DISADVANTAGES
Provides for a larger pool of ideas.	Some individuals are not compatible with teamwork.
Results in more work being accomplished in less time and in better quality products.	Team commitments may overshadow personal desires.
Interaction among team members enhances the knowledge of the whole team.	Management may recognize group achievement rather than individual achievement.
The potential exists for greater acceptance and understanding of team-made decisions.	Workers must be selected to fit the team as well as have the job skills required.
Less experienced workers have the opportunity to learn from more experienced workers.	Needless meetings may result in wasted time.
Helps all workers grow by exposing them to more viewpoints.	"Free-riding" on teams may occur.
Team commitment may stimulate performance, motivation, and attendance.	One person's negativity can demoralize an entire team.

FIGURE 7-2 Advantages and disadvantages of teams in the workplace.

WHAT MAKES A TEAM EFFECTIVE?

The purpose of a team is to accomplish goals that would be difficult or impossible for individuals working alone. However, this does not mean that all teams are effective. People working together with a true sense of team spirit can achieve powerful results, but effective teams don't just happen. Successful teams require a deliberate effort on the part of a good team leader and cooperation from each team member. The following discussion will help you understand how an effective team comes together.

Group Ownership and Understanding

Members of an effective team are committed to their mission, clearly understand the team's goals, and acknowledge that these goals are best accomplished with mutual support. Team members understand the contribution each person makes to the group as a whole. They don't waste time struggling over "turf" or attempting personal gain at the expense of others. Members are aware that they are on the team to apply their unique talents, knowledge, and creativity to team objectives. They feel a sense of ownership for their individual jobs within the group.

Members of an effective team focus their combined energy on completing tasks and learning from any setbacks along the way to success. They focus on the positive and take the negative in stride, not allowing it to get them or their team members down.

Open Communication

Effective teams work together in an atmosphere of open and honest communication that increases trust, decreases problems, and builds healthy relationships. Members are encouraged to express their ideas, thoughts, opinions, disagreements, and feelings. Team members recognize that differences are a normal part of human interaction and that opinions will differ at times. Team members make an effort to understand each other's point of view. There is no game playing—everyone is encouraged to be open, honest, direct, and respectful.

Clear Leadership

People working together with a true sense of team spirit can achieve powerful results.

©Stockbyte/Getty Images

Teamwork exists in a controlled environment. Team members know what boundaries exist and who has the final authority. Team members know and accept the leader's role. An effective leader will "walk the talk" and model the role of a good team player. The leader sets high standards of performance and is respected based on active, willing participation on the team. A good leader recognizes that some competition can be healthy and positive if handled properly. A good leader can be trusted to come up with a win-win outcome if there are differences of opinion or conflicts within the team about the best way to accomplish a goal.

Cassy joins Clyborn Interiors after designing kitchens for another company for several years. Clyborn's goal is to design high-quality, functional, eye-appealing kitchens for commercial and residential clients. Cassy has always worked alone, but is told that the work at Clyborn is accomplished through teams. Cassy is assigned to work on a team designing residential kitchens. The team includes workers with different skill sets—a cabinetry specialist, a flooring and countertop expert, and an appliance expert. Lighting, window covering, and construction specialists join the team as needed. Franco, the team leader, has worked in residential and commercial kitchen design for many years. The first week on the job is fascinating and satisfying to Cassy. Franco presents the kitchen specifications of a new client. As a team, they discuss the client's requirements, the space, the budget, and deadlines. The team then moves on to the specifics of the project, with team members offering their suggestions. As the designer, Cassy captures their suggestions in sketches during the meeting. There are conflicts at times—but they work through the problems as a team. Franco facilitates the discussion and the team is happy with the results. Franco reminds them several times during the day-long meeting of the goal for the project.

Why do you think Cassy was pleased with her new position at Clyborn? What characteristics of an effective team do you see at Clyborn?

WHAT IS A TEAM PLAYER?

A **team player** is someone who emphasizes group accomplishments and cooperation rather than individual achievement. What are the characteristics of a good team player? Cheerfulness, a sense of humor, tact, empathy, dependability, and resourcefulness are important when interacting with all coworkers, including members of your team. Let's look at other behaviors that a team player exhibits.

"To reach your goals you need to become a team player."

Committed to a Common Goal

Team players believe in the importance of what they do, know that the team needs their contributions, and are committed to a common goal. Whether you are an accountant, a computer salesperson, or a football tight end, you must do your job well if the team is to succeed. Imagine that you are a member of a bucket brigade trying to put out a fire. Long lines of people pass buckets of water from a stream at one end of the line to the fire on the other end. Each person in the brigade is an important element in putting out the fire, and a break in the line would create problems. So it is in the workplace. Everyone on a team has an important role to play to achieve the team's goals. Reaching those goals creates positive energy on a team and pushes the team forward to do even better.

Shares Information, Ideas, and Praise

Teamwork requires sharing. Team players don't hoard information; they share freely what they know. When sharing your thoughts and ideas, think about what you are going to say and use good judgment in deciding when to speak up and when to listen. Others may have a different perspective or will have noticed details that you may have overlooked. Be willing to consider a new direction even when it goes against a recommendation you made. If the team makes a decision that overrules or rejects your idea, accept and support your teammates' decision without any feelings of ill will.

Team players do not perceive their teammates as competitors but as partners who complete the whole team. Praise the people on your team and be willing to share the glory for your work, ideas, and contributions.

Cooperates and Supports

Cooperation is the foundation of an effective team. Let other members of the team know that you support them and have genuine concern for them. A good team player thinks in terms of "we" and "our" rather than "I" and "my." You can support others by encouraging them and helping them complete their tasks when necessary.

> *Deveron finished his work just before quitting time. "Whew," he said, "That's a big job done!" Then he noticed that Inga across the aisle had papers spread out all over her workstation. "Gee, Inga, it looks like you're still working on your end of our big project. Is there anything I can do to help?"*

Are you a good team player? Circle your response to the following statements.

1. I enjoy learning from my coworkers.	Yes	No
2. I am not afraid to share what I know.	Yes	No
3. I listen before I respond to another's opinion.	Yes	No
4. I listen to my coworkers' ideas.	Yes	No
5. I ask my coworkers for their opinions.	Yes	No
6. I recognize my coworkers for work well done.	Yes	No
7. I can accept new ideas and changes.	Yes	No
8. I focus on ideas, not on who suggests the idea.	Yes	No

Scoring: If you circled yes 6 or more times, you are a good candidate for teamwork. If you circled yes 4 or 5 times, you are on your way to being a team player. If you circled yes 3 or fewer times, you have some work to do.

Avoid saying or doing anything that would undermine the group. Although you may not always agree with the group decisions or with the team leader, you need not share those opinions with others outside the team.

Embraces Change

Flexibility and adaptability are key characteristics of a good team player. The workplace is constantly changing and workers must adapt. This is especially true when the workers are members of a team. If you are rigid in your approach to new concepts or ideas, your teammates will be negatively affected because they, too, must adapt. Retain your self-confidence and don't be threatened by new ideas. Accept changes when they are best for the team and let your flexibility be an example to others.

WHAT IS A VIRTUAL TEAM?

Today's technology has brought about a new kind of team—the virtual team. A **virtual team** is a group of people physically separated by time and/or space and whose members primarily interact electronically in cyberspace. Examples of virtual teams include individuals working at different geographic locations and a team whose members work (or *telecommute*) from home.

More and more companies and organizations are using virtual teams to cut travel, relocation, real estate, and other business costs. If you work on a virtual team, you will likely use special software called *groupware*. Because virtual teams must share information, they often use a password-protected website to store and distribute document files, schedules, flowcharts, and other items.

Not everyone can perform well in a virtual team environment. The members of a virtual team must be self-motivated and able to work independently.

checkpoint

1. What is the difference between a group and a team?

   _____

   _____

   _____

   _____

2. List three characteristics of an effective team.

   _____

   _____

   _____

   _____

3. What are three advantages of teams in the workplace?

_____

_____

_____

4. What are three characteristics of a good team player?

_____

_____

_____

5. How can you show support to other team members?

_____

_____

_____

applications

1. Compare the work of an athletic team to a team in a workplace setting. What are the similarities? What are the differences?

_____

_____

_____

2. Describe a disagreement you have experienced while on a team. What were the causes? How was the disagreement resolved?

_____

_____

_____

3. Why are teams necessary in today's work environment? Why are some teams successful while others are not?

_____

_____

_____

4. Would you prefer to work in a team environment or on your own? Why?

_____

_____

5. Why might a virtual team require a different kind of leadership than a face-to-face team?

_____

_____

Working with Your Supervisor

So far, this chapter has focused on your relationship with your coworkers. In this section, the emphasis shifts to your relationship with your supervisor. A supervisor may be called a *team leader, facilitator, coordinator,* or numerous other titles. A **supervisor** is an employee whose key responsibility is to ensure that the employees being supervised—sometimes called the supervisor's *direct reports* or *subordinates*—produce the assigned amount of work on time and within acceptable levels of quality.

Your on-the-job success may hinge on your ability to establish a good working relationship with your supervisor. A good working relationship does not mean "apple-polishing" (conniving or manipulating to ensure you are in good standing with the supervisor). Your relationship with your supervisor should be one of mutual respect.

Your on-the-job success may hinge on your ability to establish a good working relationship with your supervisor.

HOW DO YOU VIEW YOUR SUPERVISOR?

Supervisors are human, too. They have the same types of feelings you do. Like everyone else, they have strengths and weaknesses, good and bad days, hopes and fears, and irritating habits. They are skilled at some things and not others. But supervisors have a job to do—they are assigned the task of overseeing others as they strive to meet company goals.

As an employee, you will find it helpful to get to know and understand your supervisor. What are that person's likes and dislikes, hot buttons, and pet projects? What is his or her leadership style? You want this information so you can interact better with that person—not so you can be friends or pals. Your goal is to understand, respect, and respond positively to your supervisor.

"If your actions inspire others to dream more, learn more, do more and become more, you are a leader."

LEADERSHIP STYLES

The method a supervisor uses to manage and communicate with people who directly report to him or her is called a **leadership style**. Three basic leadership styles are laissez-faire, democratic or participatory, and autocratic. Each style has advantages and disadvantages. A supervisor may use a mixture of styles to accomplish the goals of the organization. Nevertheless, there will always be a primary, underlying style. The supervisor's style will probably not change. Simply stated, your job is to adapt to the supervisor's style or find a new department or workplace.

The Laissez-Faire Leader

Laissez-faire is a French phrase meaning "to allow to do; to let someone do something on their own." A **laissez-faire leader** gives responsibility to employees to carry out their duties without a great deal of direction or close supervision. The laissez-faire leader provides information, ideas, and guidance when asked, but exercises a "hands-off" policy when dealing with employees. The laissez-faire supervisor sets goals and lets individuals determine how to reach the goals.

The characteristics of this leadership style are shown in Figure 7-3. The laissez-faire leadership style works well in organizations that require creativity from its employees. For example, employees in advertising agencies, architectural firms, and fashion design houses work best in a free-thinking, open environment.

If you are a creative, self-confident, assertive person who can set and achieve your own goals, you will do well working for a laissez-faire leader. Even in this environment, you must check in with your supervisor periodically to be sure that you are meeting expectations. It is often necessary to earn the freedom of working in this environment by showing that you have the initiative and drive that will enable you to reach the goals the organization has set for your role.

CHARACTERISTICS OF LAISSEZ-FAIRE LEADERS

1. Lets employees make independent decisions.
2. Encourages initiative and creativity.
3. Lets employees work independently.
4. Avoids providing specific directions.
5. Provides only general guidance on how to do a job.

FIGURE 7-3 Characteristics of laissez-faire leaders.

The Democratic Leader

A **democratic leader** encourages employees to participate in the management process. This type of leader will seek your ideas and thoughts and give you an opportunity to use your problem-solving abilities. A democratic leader recognizes that everyone has good ideas, seeks the input of all workers, and exercises only a moderate degree of control over employees. The democratic leader has confidence in the employees, and employees have confidence in their supervisor. Those who work with a democratic leader feel engaged in their work. Under democratic leadership, committees and meetings are part of the work environment. *Participatory leadership* is another name for this style of leadership.

The democratic supervisor may suggest specific policies, procedures, tasks, and roles but allow employees to participate in these decisions. Although the democratic leader readily accepts input, he or she still makes the final decisions and accepts responsibility for the decisions. One drawback of this leadership style is the time needed for this collaborative effort. When you ask people for their opinions, it takes time for them to explain what they think and for others to understand what they are saying. When a business need is urgent, the democratic leader may need to modify that style.

If you like the idea of sharing your thoughts and ideas, participating in the decision-making process (what to do and how to do it), and expressing your opinions, you will enjoy working with a democratic supervisor.

The Autocratic Leader

An **autocratic leader** is an "in charge" person who exercises unlimited power or authority. He or she develops policies and procedures, defines and assigns tasks, and, in general, dictates how work will be accomplished. Autocratic leadership is associated with government offices and the military. There is no question about who the leader is and who the followers are.

If you work for an autocratic leader, you will be told what to do, when to do it, and how to do it. Your goals will be established for you. Your thoughts, opinions, and ideas will usually not be requested. The autocratic supervisor usually does not delegate authority. In other words, the autocratic supervisor does not totally entrust an activity, decision, or responsibility to an employee.

> *Marcus, the supervisor of 15 quality control technicians in an assembly plant, is an autocratic leader. He refers to the technicians as "his" technicians. He assumes responsibility for the job that each technician completes. He gives very specific instructions and has strict rules about the number of minutes allowed for lunch and breaks, the order for checking components, and the procedures for approving finished products. Lester likes working for Marcus because he knows what Marcus expects of him and how Marcus will evaluate his work. Lester does not care to be involved in decision-making activities at the plant.*

Missy and Jared are coworkers at Awards Unlimited, a company that designs and sells corporate recognition items such as trophies and plaques. Missy is the manager in charge of design and production. Jared manages the sales and marketing departments. Eduardo Sanchez, the owner, feels confident that the company is in good hands with Missy and Jared. He is away most of the time researching new markets. Missy enjoys her work. She likes the freedom to select the design equipment and raw materials. As long as she can justify her decisions to Mr. Sanchez, no questions are asked. Jared works long hours, but he enjoys the responsibility he has for making sales and marketing decisions. He meets with Mr. Sanchez periodically, and they talk about market fluctuations and how best to meet customer needs. Mr. Sanchez is very complimentary of the work of Missy and Jared and pleased with their initiative and ability to work without close supervision.

What kind of leadership style is at work in this scenario? How well is it working? What leadership style do you think Missy and Jared use with employees who report to them?

If you feel comfortable taking directions and prefer specific job instructions, you will enjoy working for an autocratic supervisor. Perhaps, like Lester, you prefer not to be responsible for the challenging tasks of setting goals, planning the work, and making decisions. On the other hand, you will need to be patient, cooperative, accepting, and reliable to function under an autocratic supervisor. You must also follow directions carefully and adhere strictly to the rules set down by your supervisor. An advantage of working for this type of leader is that you always know where your job begins and ends.

WHAT YOUR SUPERVISOR EXPECTS OF YOU

Relationships between supervisors and employees are better when each meets the other's expectations. Supervisors have the right to expect employees to be accountable for their work, present and on time, loyal and enthusiastic, and adaptable and open to changes in the workplace. If you understand these expectations, your chances of getting along with the supervisor will be improved.

Accountability

Your supervisor will hold you accountable for your assigned tasks and expect you to exhibit a strong work ethic. Whatever your work assignment, you should do it with accuracy, efficiency, and dedication—and complete it in a timely manner. You will be expected to do your job to the best of your ability. If you make mistakes, own up to them, correct them when possible, and don't repeat the same mistakes. Good job performance remains the most effective strategy for building a positive relationship with your supervisor.

Being accountable also includes checking in with your supervisor frequently, attending all meetings, observing the rules and regulations of the organization, asking questions about tasks you don't understand, and being alert for better ways of doing your job and solving problems.

Dependability

One of the highest compliments a supervisor can give an employee is to describe that person as dependable. You will be expected to be on the job every day and on time. Your absence can disrupt the work of others and frustrate your coworkers who have to fill in for you. Chronic absenteeism and tardiness tell your supervisor that you do not take your work seriously. By being at work and on time and completing your assignments on time, you demonstrate that you are dependable, conscientious, and professional.

Loyalty

When you are loyal, you demonstrate your allegiance and commitment to your supervisor and to the company. Make an effort to speak well of your supervisor to your coworkers and people outside the workplace. Never "bad mouth" your supervisor, the company, or its products or services, even if you hear others doing these things. If you having nothing good to say about your supervisor, be professional and say nothing. If you disagree with your supervisor, say so diplomatically, but never when others might overhear your comments.

Enthusiasm

Many supervisors believe that the best employees are those who show enthusiasm for their work. All jobs have some unpleasant aspects. Do not dwell on the tasks you dislike; instead, focus your thoughts on what you enjoy most about your job. When you are asked about your work responsibilities, describe the aspects of your job that you like. By focusing on and sharing the positive parts of your work, you will become a more productive and successful employee.

"Fear of change is always a brake on progress."

Adaptability

Change is inevitable in today's workplace. Equipment and technology that you use today may be obsolete tomorrow. Your positive attitude, coupled with your adaptability, will help you adjust more easily to changes that will undoubtedly come along. Your supervisor will expect you to accept changes and be open to upgrading your skills as jobs are redesigned. For example, you may be given the opportunity for on-the-job retraining or to attend an off-site workshop. Taking advantage of these opportunities tells your supervisor that you are committed to your job and to continued professional development.

SPECIAL SITUATIONS

Situations will arise when you must make an extra effort to communicate with your supervisor. For example, you may need to communicate an idea you have for making things better or discuss possible solutions to a troublesome problem. Thinking through these situations beforehand will help you communicate with your supervisor effectively.

Sharing Your Ideas

With some on-the-job experience, you will have ideas that are worthy of sharing. Don't hesitate to share your ideas with your supervisor because you fear your idea may be rejected or "shot down." You owe it to yourself and to the organization to share your thoughts.

To form a positive relationship with your supervisor:

- Keep your supervisor informed of the progress of your work.
- Be aware of your supervisor's expectations, strengths, weaknesses, and leadership style.
- Do not try to change your supervisor. Try to adapt to his or her leadership style.
- Know your supervisor's goals and understand how your job contributes to meeting those goals.
- Be sure that your priorities are in agreement with those of your supervisor.
- Ask for feedback on your job performance.
- Be honest about problems and admit your mistakes.
- Avoid wasting your supervisor's time with things you can handle yourself.
- Be flexible and open to new technologies and changing priorities.

RELATIONSHIP BUILDERS

You work for three professors in the Social Science Department of a large university. Your responsibilities include preparing multimedia presentations for professors to use in their classes. The presentations that you create are time consuming, as they require graphics, sound, and text that you must pull from a variety of sources. Professors Fernandez and Atkinson are considerate of your time and give plenty of notice when they need a presentation. Professor Krey, however, often waits until Friday afternoon to give you instructions for a presentation she needs for class on Monday. You are happy to do the work, but you need more preparation time. You decide to take this concern to Professor Krey.

1. How will you prepare for the conversation?
2. What will your main points be?
3. What result would you like from this conversation?

"A small idea is the birthplace of great accomplishments."

A good supervisor will encourage you to voice your opinions and share your creativity. Figure 7-4 shows the steps to take as you prepare to communicate your ideas to your supervisor. By following the steps, you will demonstrate that you are creative and willing to take the initiative to improve the organization.

SHARING IDEAS WITH YOUR SUPERVISOR

1. Plan the conversation. Research all aspects of your idea. Verify that it is compatible with company policy.
2. Arrange a time to talk with your supervisor. Don't share your idea on the spur of the moment or in a hallway conversation. Set up a meeting at your supervisor's convenience.
3. Support your thoughts with notes. Let your supervisor know that you considered the new concept carefully. Be brief and focus on the key points. Don't oversell the idea.
4. Close with a positive statement. For example, you might say: "Please consider this plan and let me know what you think. I hope that you can support it."
5. Be prepared to leave a brief written summary of your idea. Leave with a friendly smile, and say sincerely, "I look forward to hearing from you. Thanks so much for listening."

FIGURE 7-4 Steps for presenting ideas to your supervisor.

Calling Attention to Problems—and Alternative Solutions

Supervisors don't like surprises and want to be made aware of problems as they arise. However, exercise some judgment about taking problems to your supervisor that may not be appropriate or may not require a supervisor's attention. Generally, the problems you bring to your supervisor should be work-related. However, if you are having a significant personal problem that could affect your work, keep your supervisor informed. Follow the steps

1. Do your homework before approaching your supervisor. The facts you present should be specific, documented, and accurate.
2. Establish a suitable setting. Your goal is to share the problem with your supervisor, not the entire workforce. Step into a private office or quiet area.
3. State the problem in your own words. Be succinct and use terms that accurately describe your concerns and feelings.
4. State the facts of the problem clearly and precisely. You will lose credibility by stating generalizations, half-truths, or innuendoes. Avoid phrases like "I assume . . ." or "Rumor has it that . . ."
5. Check to make sure that your supervisor has understood you. Ask whether you have stated the problem clearly. This step lets your supervisor ask questions or clarify information.
6. Be prepared with some suggestions on how to solve the problem. If you have no possible solutions in mind, you are not ready to communicate with the supervisor.
7. Indicate the solution you think is best, but do not push for it. There may be options you haven't considered.
8. Thank your supervisor for the time and attention. If appropriate, request a follow-up to the conversation.

FIGURE 7-5 Steps for bringing problems to your supervisor.

in Figure 7-5 to organize your thoughts so that you will take a minimum amount of your supervisor's time. Ideally, you will be able to suggest possible solutions to the problem.

WHAT TO EXPECT OF YOUR SUPERVISOR

When you accept a job, you do so with certain expectations of the company. You expect the company to pay you a fair wage for an honest day's work. You also expect the company to provide a safe, clean, and healthy work environment. The Occupational Safety and Health Administration (OSHA) is a federal agency that sets and enforces standards for the work environment. For example, employers must keep records of work-related injuries or illness and provide constant examinations of workplace conditions to ensure compliance with OSHA regulations.

"An ounce of performance is worth a pound of promises."

As an employee, you also have the right to expect certain things of your supervisor. Let's look at some of these expectations. If all of these expectations are met, you are most fortunate and you should, in return, remain loyal to your supervisor and to the company.

Clear Performance Expectations

Your supervisor has the responsibility to talk with you about your position and communicate clearly and in detail what is expected of you. Ideally, you will be given a written job description. A **job description** typically identifies (1) the specific duties and responsibilities of your job, (2) the skills and competencies required, (3) the equipment and tools to be used, (4) the outcomes and contributions to the organization your position is to achieve,

(5) reporting information (who your supervisor is), and (6) the relationship of your position to other positions in the company. You should be given an opportunity to ask questions about any part of the job description and your responsibilities.

Proper Materials and Equipment

You have the right to expect to have the proper materials and equipment to do your job efficiently. Communicate any concerns you have about these items to your supervisor immediately. Keep your supervisor informed about any safety issues or equipment problems that hamper your ability to do your work.

> *Nadia had been on the job only a few days when she discovered that her printer wasn't working properly. Documents created in her word processing program printed without a problem, but e-mail messages printed with irregular spacing and strange characters. Nadia knew she could not do her job properly if her printer continued in this manner and alerted her supervisor at the first opportunity—after asking her supervisor if it was a good time to talk, of course.*

Performance Evaluations

You have the right to a fair and honest evaluation by your supervisor on a regular schedule. This may be done on a formal basis (annual performance evaluation) or informally (periodic discussions with your supervisor). You have the right to know if you are meeting your supervisor's expectations and, if not, what you need to do to improve your performance. If you have questions, you need not wait for a formal performance evaluation. You can ask your supervisor for a convenient time to talk about your job performance. Doing so communicates your sincere desire to do your job well and your willingness to accept suggestions for improvement.

You may be asking yourself, "Why should I want to receive criticism?" The truth is that you need to hear justified criticism along with recommendations for improvement. Constructive criticism should not be viewed as negative. Rather, constructive criticism is a necessary step on the road to self-improvement. No matter how talented or skilled you become, improvement is always possible.

Recognition

You have the right to be recognized for your strengths and contributions to meeting company goals. This doesn't mean that you should expect daily recognition or frequent pay increases. It means that your supervisor should recognize your contributions (big and small). This is often accomplished by an occasional "pat on the back" in the form of a personal comment or a written note. If you receive a compliment from your supervisor, your first words should be "Thank you." Say "thank you" with sincerity and eye contact. If appropriate, acknowledge the contribution of coworkers who also should share the compliment or praise.

checkpoint

1. Which leadership style would you prefer to be the dominant style of your supervisor? Why?

   _____

   _____

   _____

   _____

   _____

2. List three expectations supervisors have of employees.

   _____

   _____

   _____

   _____

   _____

3. List three expectations you should have of your supervisor.

   _____

   _____

   _____

   _____

   _____

4. What types of recognition should an employee anticipate?

   _____

   _____

   _____

   _____

   _____

5. Why is constructive criticism valuable to your work performance?

   _____

   _____

   _____

   _____

   _____

applications

1. The following phrases describe characteristics of leadership styles. Identify which style is being described by labeling it *A* for autocratic, *LF* for laissez-faire, or *D* for democratic. As you read the statements, think about whether some of these phrases might apply to more than one style.

_____ a. Frequent committee meetings are called.

_____ b. Decisions are made by the group.

_____ c. Decisions are made by the supervisor.

_____ d. Workers are encouraged to be creative.

_____ e. Supervisor may often be absent from the workplace.

_____ f. Original work is encouraged.

_____ g. Everyone's work is valued.

_____ h. Authority is not delegated.

_____ i. Specific instructions are not given.

_____ j. Workers are cooperative and productive.

2. Have you had the opportunity to use one of the leadership styles? What was the situation? Which style did you use? How did it work for you?

_____

_____

_____

3. Describe a situation where you received deserved criticism. What were your feelings? What changes did you make because of the criticism?

_____

_____

_____

4. Describe the forms of performance evaluation you receive at school or work. Which form do you feel is most effective? Why?

_____

_____

_____

5. Describe a situation at school or work that required you to adapt to a change. How did the change affect you? How did you react to the change? How would you rate your ability to adapt to future changes?

_____

_____

Communicating Electronically

Technology continues to have a major impact on the way we communicate with others. E-mail was once a "new" technology used by only a few. Today, it is an essential communication tool in the workplace and at home. Rapidly changing technologies, falling prices, and the increased use of wireless technology allow us to send text, images, and sound from virtually anywhere.

Because advances in technology have enabled workers to communicate more easily and quickly, the influence on the workplace has been positive. However, the technology also presents challenges to interpersonal communication as people adapt to the evolving technologies and learn how to use them effectively. No matter how high tech the world becomes, do not forget that ultimately you are communicating with human beings.[4] All electronic communication must be used correctly and carefully.

Chances are that you use one or more of the most popular forms of electronic communication: electronic mail, voicemail, and text messaging. This section discusses the proper use of these technologies.

E-MAIL

People in all lines of work depend on e-mail to stay in touch.

Electronic mail (e-mail) is one of the most common and efficient technological advances of modern times. This is especially true since the proliferation of the Internet in the early 1980s. **E-mail** is a system for sending and receiving messages electronically over a computer network. The joke in many workplaces is that even people who are within sight of one another send e-mail messages instead of speaking face to face. People in all lines of work depend on e-mail to stay in touch. Even President Barack Obama has been photographed checking e-mail on his Blackberry.[5]

Proper Use of E-Mail

E-mail has its limitations and challenges. Employees often show poor judgment about using this popular workflow tool. For example, because e-mail is fast, informal, and readily available, people often do not take care in writing e-mails. This can be especially troublesome in the workplace. Some guidelines for the proper use of e-mail follow.

Organize your thoughts. Before you key anything, think about these questions: Why am I writing this? What exactly do I want to happen because of the message? Will the reader understand this? If you can't answer these questions, you are not ready to send the message. Typically, you send an e-mail message to provide information, request information, or request some type of action.

Use the subject line effectively. Everyone gets a lot of mail. To make sure your message is read, include a subject line that clearly describes the content. Ideally, the subject line should provide information or ask a question. Examples are: "Friday dinner meeting canceled." or "Is the budget set?" At the very least, it should clearly identify the subject of the e-mail. For example, "Budget meeting summary."

Keep the message brief and to the point. How would you feel if you checked your e-mail at 4:57 p.m. only to find a three-page message in your mailbox? You probably won't be too excited about reading it. The messages you send should be brief, clear, and to the point. Avoid the tendency to ramble on. A good visual trick is to keep the body of your text brief enough so that it fits onto one screen with no scrolling necessary. E-mails longer than one screen are often filed rather than read. If your message includes a request, be clear about what you will need.

Be conscious of the tone. Could someone misinterpret your message? Never write an e-mail message when you are angry, and never use sarcasm. Angry or sarcastic messages can come back to haunt you.

Be informal, not sloppy. Although your e-mail messages need not look like formal documents, ignoring the rules of grammar, spelling, and punctuation gives a bad impression of you and your company. Most e-mail programs have spell-check and grammar-check features—use them. Use active voice rather than passive voice whenever possible. Active voice tends to sound more personal and less formal; therefore, it is most appropriate for e-mail messages. For example, "We will meet about the move to the third floor on Thursday" (active voice) is more appropriate—and shorter—than "The meeting about the move to the third floor will be held on Thursday" (passive voice).

Use short paragraphs and blank lines between each paragraph. Although e-mail correspondence is less formal, you need to be conscious of how to make your message more "readable." Use short paragraphs with blank lines between paragraphs. Number your points or use bullets to mark each point as separate to keep the message clear.

Proofread the message before hitting "Send." Don't be the person who regrets having sent an e-mail. Take the time *before* you send it to read the message aloud. This gives you the opportunity to verify that you have communicated what you want to say. A poorly chosen word, clumsy phrasing, or a misspelled word can change your intended meaning.

Make sure attachments are attached. No one likes to get an e-mail message that says "Attached is . . ." only to find no file attached. It is a good practice to attach the file as soon as you key the words "attached is" in the message.

Include a signature block. A signature block at the bottom of a message identifies the sender and provides contact information the recipient may need. Typically, a signature block includes your name, address, and phone number, but can also include a fax number and your organization's website address. You can add a logo or an image of your handwritten signature. A signature block can be added automatically to outgoing messages, or you can insert it manually.

Do not send inappropriate messages. E-mail is not confidential. Never send something you wouldn't want circulated throughout your workplace or even beyond. Your recipient has both a printer and a "forward" button and may be all too eager to share your communication with others. Never send a message that includes slanderous, offensive, obscene, sexist, or racially discriminating remarks.

Do not include usernames, passwords, credit card information, or social security numbers. This is sensitive information that must be kept personal. E-mail is not encrypted, meaning that your e-mail is "open" and could possibly be read by an unintended person as it is transmitted to your reader.

E-Mail Etiquette

Although there are no standard rules of etiquette that apply to e-mail, there are certain expectations of those who use it. Using proper e-mail etiquette shows that you are a professional who respects those with whom you correspond. Keep these behaviors in mind as you work with e-mail.

Respond quickly. People expect a quick response to e-mail. In general, try to reply within 24 hours, and preferably on the same workday. If the sender asks you to provide information and you cannot do so within 24 hours, acknowledge receipt of the request and indicate when you will send a response.

Be considerate. Use "please" and "thank you" just as you would in a face-to-face conversation. Resist the temptation to start the message without a greeting, but keep the greeting professional. Use a salutation such as "Tracy" or "Hello, Tracy."

Consider file size. Do not attach unnecessary files to an e-mail. Compress your attachments whenever possible. Huge attachments can bring down a recipient's e-mail system.

- Do not use e-mail to criticize or belittle others.
- Avoid the use of smiley faces and other emoticons.
- Avoid unusual fonts, color, and highlighting (including bold and italics) that may not look the same on a different e-mail system.
- Don't write in all capital letters or use multiple punctuation marks at the end of a sentence. That is considered shouting.
- Don't annoy others with pointless messages.
- Don't reply to spam. By replying or unsubscribing, you are confirming that your e-mail address is "live."
- Include a signature block at the end of your e-mail message to identify yourself and provide contact information.
- Schedule blocks of time to read and send e-mail.
- Never send sensitive information (passwords, credit card numbers, etc.) in e-mail.
- Think before you press "Send." E-mails are not private. Even e-mails that have been erased can be retrieved.

"Diamonds are forever. E-mail comes close."

Be sparing with group e-mail. Send group e-mail only when it's useful to every participant. No one wants to get unnecessary e-mail.

Do not send chain letters, virus warnings, or junk mail. These items may actually contain a virus. If a steady stream of jokes from a friend annoys you, be honest and ask to be removed from the list. Always check a reputable antivirus website or ask your IT department if a reported virus is "real" before sending out a virus alarm.

Avoid using the "high priority," "urgent," and "important" flags. Use these flags only when absolutely necessary or they will lose their significance.

Avoid using abbreviations and emoticons. Abbreviations such as BTW (by the way) and LOL (laugh out loud or lots of love) that you use when sending text messages can be misinterpreted and are not appropriate for business e-mail or e-mail to your instructor. Smiley faces and other emoticons are also not appropriate for business e-mails.

TEXT MESSAGING AND VOICEMAIL

Text messaging and voicemail are two other forms of widely used electronic communication. Text messaging is used for keying short messages from mobile phones and some personal digital assistants (PDAs). Voicemail is used to manage telephone messages electronically. Both technologies are discussed here, along with techniques for their proper use.

Chun, a quality control worker for Rayburn Foods, is discouraged and ready for a change. He sends an e-mail to his friend Turner, who also works at Rayburn, in which he voices frustration with his supervisor's management style. According to Chun, his supervisor fails to recognize the good work of the quality control team, is frequently absent, plays favorites, and despite repeated requests from Chun and others, hasn't corrected two safety violations. Chun tells Turner that he would like to transfer to the sales department where Turner works. As Turner reads Chun's e-mail about his supervisor's shortcomings, he is reminded of the good relationship he has with his supervisor. Turner respects his supervisor and knows that his supervisor respects him. He thinks Chun would be a welcome addition to the sales department so he forwards Chun's e-mail to his supervisor, along with a comment about Chun's strong work ethic and skills.

Do you see any problems resulting from forwarding Chun's e-mail? How well did Chun handle this situation? How well did Turner handle it?

Text Messaging

Text messaging (or *texting*) is a term for sending short text messages (160 characters or fewer, including spaces) from a mobile device to a cell phone, PDA, or pager. For example, you might send a text message to confirm an appointment or let your supervisor know you're running late. Because the space for texting is limited, users have developed "shorthand" for their messages. The abbreviated language used for text messaging is sometimes called *text speak*. Figure 7-6 shows a few of the many commonly used texting abbreviations.

ABBREVIATION		TRANSLATION	
BC	because	NRN	no reply necessary
BTW	by the way	QQ	quick question
DNBL8	do not be late	SIT	stay in touch
G2G	got to go	TIA	thanks in advance
GMTA	great minds think alike	WIIFM	what's in it for me?
JMO	just my opinion	WTG	way to go!

FIGURE 7-6 Examples of common texting abbreviations.

Although texting is quick and easy, you should follow these guidelines for proper use.

Keep your messages brief. Become familiar with "text speak" so you can keep your message short. Since not everyone may understand all the shortcuts you use, stick to the most common ones.

Be patient. You may not receive an instant response.

Remember that text messages are not private. Do not send anything you wouldn't like read by others.

Text at appropriate times. Texting during business meetings is rude and inappropriate. Don't send or receive messages in class or at weddings, funerals, or religious services. Do not endanger your passengers, yourself, and others by texting while driving.

Voicemail

Voicemail is a centralized electronic system of managing telephone messages for a large group of people. Used broadly, the term *voicemail* refers to any system of sending, receiving, and storing voice messages, including answering machines. Voice messaging systems are widely used in homes and offices. The systems permit you to record a message to be heard by callers when you aren't available to answer your phone. You can listen to messages and return calls when it is convenient, and you can store them and listen to them a second time.

Like e-mail and text messaging, voicemail requires proper use to be effective in the workplace. Some guidelines for proper use follow.

Record a clear, concise, and professional message. This sample message encourages the caller to feel comfortable leaving a message and provides an alternative person to speak with:

> *Hello. This is Lee Wagner in the marketing department. Today is Wednesday, June 5. I will be out of the office until Monday, June 10.*

I will check my voicemail and return calls between 5 p.m. and 7 p.m. If you leave your name and a number, I'll call you at that time. If you require immediate assistance, please press 0 and my assistant Janet will help you. Thank you.

Leave clear, succinct, and professional messages for others. These messages represent you and your organization, so word them carefully. Speak slowly and clearly and don't leave a rambling message. The elements of a good voice message include your name (pronounced clearly and spelled, if necessary), your company or organization, the date, and the purpose of your call. If you are returning a call, like the example below, explain what the caller should do if immediate assistance is needed and when the caller can expect a response.

Hello. This is Amanda Tewell (T-e-w-e-l–l), media coordinator for Lyons Pharmaceuticals. Today is Wednesday, May 5. I'm returning your call. I'm about to board a plane and won't be taking calls until I land in Miami, which should be about 5 p.m. If you require assistance before then, my assistant Jim Woodford, at 402-555-3423, will be happy to help you.

Repeat your contact information. It is a good practice to repeat the contact information and to spell your name, if necessary.

Hello. This is Sue Dali (that's spelled D-a-l-i), at 412-555-6622. I would like to speak with you about the computer and monitor you advertised in yesterday's Pittsburgh Post-Gazette. Please call me as soon as possible. Again, this is Sue Dali at 412-555-6622.

APPLY IT!

Assume that you work in the research department of Leland Graphics. Your direct phone line is 513-555-3441. Wesley Adams, your assistant, can be reached by pressing zero. What voicemail message would you leave in each of these situations?

1. You will be on vacation for the next two weeks. You will not be accessing voicemail while you are away.

2. The offices of Leland Graphics will be closed for renovation Monday through Wednesday of next week. Offices will reopen on Thursday at 8 a.m. All calls will be returned at that time.

3. You want to cancel your dentist appointment with Dr. Gale for 9 a.m. tomorrow. You don't want to reschedule at this time.

4. You need information from Caleb, a coworker. You must have sales figures for the Waterman account by 5 p.m. today.

Re-record your message if you don't feel you have communicated clearly. Many systems give you the option of listening to your message and recording it over if necessary. It is better to re-record a message than hang up and wish you had been clearer.

After an absence (momentary or longer), check your messages. This should become a habit. Put a note by your phone that says "Check phone messages!" If someone has left a message, he or she is waiting for a response. Not returning calls in a timely fashion is rude and unprofessional.

checkpoint

1. List four guidelines for the proper use of e-mail.

_____

_____

_____

_____

2. List four rules of e-mail etiquette.

_____

_____

_____

_____

3. List five guidelines for text messages.

_____

_____

_____

_____

4. Why do you think some people are not concerned with privacy when sending e-mail? How concerned with privacy are you when sending e-mail?

_____

_____

_____

5. What information should you include in a voicemail message you leave on someone else's service?

_____

_____

_____

applications

1. Compose an appropriate e-mail message to your instructor. Include a subject line. Assume that you will have surgery in Palms Hospital on Monday of next week to correct a bone spur in your right arm. You expect to remain in the hospital overnight and then recuperate at home the following week. You will miss class during that time. You would like to have your assignments in advance, if possible.

_____

_____

_____

2. Should companies regulate use of e-mail? Should they allow unlimited access to the Internet? Why or why not?

_____

_____

_____

3. Give examples of inappropriate use of e-mail you have witnessed. How much attention do you think people give to the e-mails they send?

_____

_____

_____

_____

4. You are the booking agent for the Funky Chicks jazz combo. You return a call to Frank Dixon but reach his voicemail. You understand that he wants to book the Funky Chicks for a party on August 15. You would appreciate a return call at his earliest convenience. You need additional information before you can schedule the band. What message would you leave on Frank Dixon's voicemail?

_____

_____

_____

5. How much thought did you give to the message on your home phone or personal cell phone? Do personal "not available" messages warrant more or less thought than those you would record in the workplace? Why?

_____

_____

_____

_____

7 points to remember

Review the following points to determine what you remember from the chapter.

- The following traits are essential to fit in and get along in the workplace: cheerfulness, a sense of humor, tact, empathy, dependability, resourcefulness, and team spirit. Negative traits to avoid include resentment, irritating habits, envy, jealousy, and self-pity.

- Gossip is a form of workplace communication. Verify the accuracy of the information and do not pass along information that may be hurtful to another.

- Characteristics of an effective team are group understanding, open communication, and clear leadership.

- Team players know their role and embrace team goals. They share information, support each other, and are flexible.

- Members of a virtual team interact electronically for the most part.

- Know your supervisor's leadership style (laissez-faire, democratic, or autocratic) and the characteristics of that style.

- Supervisors expect employees to be accountable, dependable, loyal, enthusiastic, and adaptable.

- Employees expect supervisors to provide clear expectations for the work, appropriate equipment and materials, fair performance evaluations, and recognition when deserved.

- E-mail, text messaging, and voicemail are essential communication tools. Use appropriate etiquette when using these tools to ensure their effective and proper use.

How did you do? Did you remember the main points you studied in the chapter?

KEY terms

tact

empathy

sympathy

resentment

jealousy

self-pity

team

teamwork

team player

virtual team

supervisor

leadership style

laissez-faire leader

democratic leader

autocratic leader

job description

e-mail

text messaging

voicemail

Want more activities? Go to **www.cengage. com/careerreadiness/masters** to get started.

CHAPTER *activities*

1. Review the qualities in Section 7.1 for fitting in and getting along at work. Also, review the qualities of a team player. Identify the qualities that you possess. Identify the qualities that need improvement and explain how you plan to improve.

   _____

   _____

   _____

2. Divide into groups of three to five students and appoint a discussion leader. Then discuss the following.

   a. Identify teams in which you have participated at school, in your free time, or at work. Identify characteristics that made each team either "effective" or "ineffective."

      _____

      _____

   b. Which team appeared to be the most effective? Why?

      _____

      _____

      _____

   c. Which team appeared to be the least effective? Why?

      _____

      _____

   d. How effective was your group in appointing a leader and carrying out the work of the group?

      _____

      _____

      _____

3. During the next week, evaluate how well you manage your personal e-mail. Begin by noting the number of e-mails you send and receive each day. How many are jokes and chain letters? How many are news alerts or product announcements? How do you decide which messages to keep and which messages to delete? Do you make a conscious attempt to keep your mailbox organized? At the end of the week, answer the following:

   a. Explain why you feel you do (or do not) manage your e-mail effectively.

      _____

      _____

      _____

   b. What changes do you plan to make as a result of your analysis?

      _____

      _____

      _____

4. You work in the billing department of a large medical center. Suppose you think your supervisor is moving the department in the wrong direction. Rather than implementing new technologies that would make your job easier and reduce the time to send statements and process payments, your supervisor prefers to maintain the status quo. Explain how you would approach your supervisor and what your main points would be.

   _____

   _____

   _____

CRITICAL *thinking*

CASE 7.1   Community Service is a Good Thing

The employees in the investment department of Equity Bank support the local food pantry with contributions of time and money. Nathan and Aretha, employees in the loan department, decide to find a similar community service project for their department. They identify three local charities that could use their support—a homeless shelter, a soup kitchen, and a shelter for abused women and children. After deliberating the pros and cons of each, they decide to support the Gulfport Shelter for Abused Women and Children. The family room and kitchen need painting, the children need games and toys, and the yard is dangerously overgrown.

Nathan and Aretha devise a plan to enable the loan department to help the shelter with contributions of time and money. First, they would seek volunteers willing to paint and weed. Next, they would hold a fundraiser to pay for games and toys for the children. They would continue to support the shelter as needed. Nathan and Aretha are ready to present their idea to Ms. Doria, the loan department supervisor. They plan to ask her to support their idea by recommending that the loan department support the Gulfport Shelter.

1. How did Nathan and Aretha prepare for the conversation with their supervisor?

   _____

   _____

   _____

2. What should Nathan and Aretha say to their supervisor to gain her support for a community project for the loan department?

   _____

   _____

3. What qualities are Nathan and Aretha demonstrating that supervisors expect? Explain how each quality is being demonstrated.

   _____

   _____

   _____

4. How should Nathan and Aretha conclude the conversation with their supervisor?

   _____

   _____

CASE 7.2   All Aspects of the Job are Important

Sheena is an office assistant at Hanson Motors. She considers herself a "people person" and enjoys talking with customers. Sheena's e-mail address appears as a link on the new Hanson Motors website as the person to e-mail with questions about the dealer's services. Sheena's job description includes other responsibilities, which she enjoys. But she does not enjoy being the website contact person. In fact, she considers the 20 or 30 queries each day to be a nuisance because they interfere with her other duties.

To maintain customer satisfaction, Hanson Motors conducts a monthly survey. The survey feedback is good in all areas except website assistance. Customers say that the wait time for replies is too long and that messages are confusing and brusque. The manager of Hanson Motors reviews the e-mail responses Sheena sent. He is both surprised and concerned about Sheena's lackluster performance in this area of her responsibilities. Sheena completes her other duties extremely well and has been praised repeatedly by her supervisor and coworkers.

1. What is the real problem here? Is it solely one of Sheena's making?

_____

_____

_____

_____

2. If you were the manager, what would you say to Sheena?

_____

_____

_____

_____

3. What rules of e-mail etiquette would you reinforce with Sheena?

_____

_____

_____

_____

4. Would you consider reassigning the e-mail response duties to someone else? Why or why not?

_____

_____

_____

_____

chapter 8

Managing Conflict

BananaStock/Jupiter Images

Emil works in the design center of Lloyds, a local furniture store. Emil entered the interior design program at a community college and moved into part-time sales at the store while in school. After graduating with an associate's degree, he began full-time work in the design center. Emil has a flare for design. He attends design shows and asks questions of more experienced designers. He enjoys helping the store prepare show homes. Home-builders like his work and seek him out to put the finishing touches on their most prestigious homes. Miranda is very pleased with Emil's work but is concerned about his long hours. She hires a new designer, Nila, to assist with the workload. Nila has 15 years of experience and a four-year degree in interior design. Miranda takes Nila to a show home Emil is decorating. Nila is very critical of what she sees. She tells Miranda that the color palette is too bold and that the interior design doesn't match the style of the home. Miranda recognizes that Nila and Emil have different approaches and sees potential conflicts between the two designers.

Why would Nila, a new employee, make negative comments about Emil's design work? What potential conflict do you see among Miranda, Emil, and Nila?

objectives

After completing this chapter, you should be able to:

1. Identify the four types of conflict.
2. Explain how conflict can bring about positive results.
3. Describe methods of preventing conflict.
4. Describe the five phases of a conflict.
5. Identify ways to resolve conflict.
6. Respond appropriately to conflict.
7. Describe the six steps of problem solving.

8.1 What Is Conflict?

8.2 How Is Conflict Resolved?

What Is Conflict?

Conflict experiences begin at a very young age. As a child, you had conflicts or squabbles with a sibling or friends over toys or other possessions. As life goes on, the potential for conflict increases as you interact with others in your personal life and in the workplace. You read and hear about conflict daily—conflict between individuals, countries, and labor and management. In this chapter, **conflict** refers to a difference of opinion caused by opposing attitudes, behaviors, ideas, needs, wants, or goals. Conflict is usually associated with negative thoughts or unpleasant situations and, if ignored, can be destructive, as shown in Figure 8-1. However, when managed properly, some conflict can be positive.

Everyone has likes and dislikes, ideas, habits, flaws, and needs. These personal differences can lead to conflict. Conflict in the workplace is serious as it has the potential to decrease productivity, increase employee stress, undermine morale, hamper performance, increase turnover rate and absenteeism, and lead to irresponsible behavior. Conflict in your personal life can lead to stress, loss of self-esteem, depression, and general unhappiness.

This section presents the types of conflict and suggests ways to prevent it. Section 8.2 discusses the phases of conflict and suggests techniques you can use to resolve conflict.

THE NEGATIVE SIDE OF CONFLICT

Conflict is destructive when:

- The resolution of the conflict ends with a winner and a loser.
- It keeps you from doing your work or feeling good about yourself or others.
- It undermines morale.
- The individuals involved act aggressively.
- It is harmful to an individual's emotional or physical well-being.
- It increases absenteeism and turnover rate.

FIGURE 8-1 Conflict, if ignored, can be destructive.

"The people to fear are not those who disagree with you, but those who disagree with you and are too cowardly to let you know."

TYPES OF CONFLICT

Conflict in the workplace can be traced to poor communication, conflicting goals, confusion about job responsibilities, and poor leadership. Some conflict is inevitable—for example, when two individuals cannot get along. Other conflicts can be avoided—for example, when you politely excuse yourself from an emotional conversation. Sometimes conflict is out in the open for all to see. At other times, it's hidden below the surface just waiting to happen. You will be better able to deal with conflict if you understand the four basic types of conflict: simple conflict, false conflict, ego conflict, and values and beliefs conflict.

Simple Conflict

Simple conflict is usually over a fact or piece of information. Simple conflict is seldom serious and usually easily resolved.

Sarina and Jack were discussing last year's sales. Sarina said their department brought in $1.4 million in sales. Jack said that was *incorrect—the department brought in $1.2 million. Sarina was sure her figure was correct, and Jack was sure his figure was correct. When Sarina and Jack checked last year's annual report, they found they were both wrong—the actual sales were $1.8 million.*

Conflict over facts or data can be resolved by consulting a source that both parties involved in the conflict consider to be reliable. If you are right, don't gloat. If you are wrong, simply say, "Well, you were right. That's a fact I won't forget." Do not allow a simple conflict to harm your personal or professional relationships.

False Conflict

You may think a conflict exists when in reality it does not. This is called **false conflict.** The following conflict between employees should not have happened—it was a false conflict.

Mike pulls into an executive parking space. Seeing Mike park the car, Lionel says to a friend, "Who does Mike think he is parking in an executive space? He's so arrogant." Lionel sees Mike at the break and confronts him about thinking he is "too good" to park in staff parking. Mike is offended at Lionel's aggressive remarks and tries to explain, but Lionel won't let him get a word in. Toby, a company executive, overhears the exchange and says, "Mike, thanks for parking my car this morning. You saved me from being late to the board meeting."

The first step when you feel you are faced with what appears to be a conflict is to determine whether the conflict exists—is it real? Make it a practice not to jump to conclusions, because you may not have all the information. Getting upset over a false conflict is wasted energy. In the previous example, Lionel didn't have all of the information, and the situation was certainly not worth attacking the character of a coworker.

Ego Conflict

Conflict involving egos is probably the most damaging to relationships. **Ego** is your consciousness of your own identity and self-worth. In an **ego conflict**, the individuals view "winning" or "losing" the conflict as a measure of their expertise and personal worth. This type of conflict, which often results from personality clashes or conflicting ideas, is all too common. Ego conflict escalates when one or both parties introduce personal or judgmental statements.

Aaron, Paul, and Tamara are meeting to determine how to streamline production costs. Aaron believes strongly in his plan. Paul and Tamara feel just as passionately that their plan is better. After a few heated exchanges, Aaron says, "How can you think your plan will work when it's obvious you haven't thought it through? It's a dumb idea—plain and simple." Paul and Tamara are livid at Aaron's outburst. "This meeting is over," Paul announces, and he and Tamara leave the room.

Once your ego (and therefore, your emotions) becomes involved in a conflict, you jeopardize your ability to behave in a rational manner. Be careful to separate the content of a conflict from your potential ego involvement. Even well-intentioned people can become involved in ego conflict. The key is to focus on the issue and construct a response that won't put the other person's defenses on alert.

on the job

Heather and Ivory work in the same marketing office and report to the same supervisor, Dawn. They are coworkers and good friends. Ivory notices that Heather has been in and out of Dawn's office several times during the morning. At lunch, Ivory hears through the grapevine that Heather will represent the office at a meeting in San Francisco next month. Ivory is furious. Only last week she told Heather that she hoped to be the one selected to attend the meeting. She decides that Heather has been trying to persuade Dawn to send her to San Francisco. "Heather hasn't said a word to me about going," Ivory thinks. "Some friend she is, going behind my back to get an assignment I wanted." Ivory ignores Heather for the rest of the day and leaves without saying good-bye. Ivory's behavior puzzles Heather, but she says nothing. The next day Heather and Ivory do their best to avoid each other. Dawn calls Ivory into her office and asks if she would be willing to attend the San Francisco meeting. Ivory is elated but also confused. "I'll be happy to go, but I heard you were sending Heather," she says. Dawn responds, "I'm sending both of you. Sorry I was so busy yesterday that I didn't get to talk with you about the trip."

What was the perceived conflict? Who jumped to conclusions? What could Ivory have done to avoid a day where she was confused and upset? How should Ivory approach Heather and explain her behavior on the previous day?

Values and Beliefs Conflict

A **values and beliefs conflict** occurs when people differ in their feelings about an aspect of life, and those differences are brought into focus on a particular issue. For example, one employee may believe that society has a responsibility to maintain a welfare system to take care of people whose basic needs are not being met. A coworker may believe that people are responsible for taking care of themselves and that welfare programs should not exist. You can probably think of many other topics that can quickly lead to a values and beliefs conflict.

Can values and beliefs conflicts be resolved? Probably not. Your own values and beliefs may change over your lifetime, but you know from experience that they do not change quickly, and you cannot expect to change the values or beliefs of others. If a controversial subject on which you and a coworker have conflicting views arises in a discussion, respect the other person's opinion, agree to disagree, and end the conversation quickly and graciously. A far better solution in the workplace is to avoid discussing topics that can lead to a conflict among values and beliefs. Prevent conflicts before they start. This topic is covered in more detail in the Section 8.2, "How Is Conflict Resolved?"

CAN CONFLICT BE A GOOD THING?

Although it is certain that you will experience conflict in your life, the good news is that conflict is not necessarily a bad thing. Conflict can be healthy when effectively managed. Healthy conflict can lead to growth and innovation, new ways of thinking, and additional management options.[1] In addition, conflict forces you to make a choice, and making a choice can help you test the merits of conflicting ideas, attitudes, behaviors, needs, or goals. Conflict can be a positive force when the people involved have a positive learning experience from the event. Figure 8-2 identifies some of the positive results of conflict.

CONFLICT CAN BRING POSITIVE RESULTS
Conflict is positive when it:
• Is the means to effect change.
• Leads to new ways of thinking and behaving.
• Brings problems to the surface.
• Helps people recognize and benefit from diversity.
• Motivates people to participate.
• Forces people to make choices.
• Supports good decision making.
• Builds cooperation among people through learning more about each other.
• Clarifies important issues.

FIGURE 8-2 Some positive results of conflict.

Decide whether the following may result in (S) simple conflict, (E) ego conflict, (VB) values and beliefs conflict, or (F) false conflict.

_____1. Abby insists that Veterans Day is celebrated in October. Tim says it is in November.

_____2. Mardi believes the best way to educate children is by home schooling. Sally believes it is best to send children to public school.

_____3. Eric says to Ben, "Based on my experience with computers, I know your idea won't work."

_____4. Armand says that Zion National Park is in Utah. Todd says it is in Arizona.

_____5. Joy wants to get an apartment with Robert. Robert wants the two of them to get married first.

_____6. Huey says, "Please bring me a cup of coffee—black, no sugar." Joel replies, "I have a college degree, and I didn't earn it to make coffee for you."

_____7. Cheryl tells Dan that she plans to take a night course at the local community college. "What are you trying to do," Dan asks, "show off for the new boss?" She is actually taking an exercise class.

CAN CONFLICT BE PREVENTED?

While some conflict will never be eliminated, there are ways to prevent it. There is a difference between *preventing* conflict and *avoiding* conflict. When you avoid conflict, you withdraw from the situation or fail to admit that conflict exists. When you prevent conflict, you consciously take steps to remedy a situation before it becomes a conflict. For example, there is a difference between *preventing* damage to your laptop by carrying it in a padded case and *avoiding* the situation entirely by not taking your laptop with you. The same principle applies to conflict. The following practices will help you prevent conflict.

Build constructive relationships. Think of people you know who seldom find themselves in conflicting situations. Perhaps a coworker or a supervisor or a family member or friend comes to mind. Chances are they have a positive attitude and good relationship skills. Building constructive relationships with coworkers, family, and friends can keep the number of unpleasant conflicts at a minimum.

Discuss problems before they escalate to a conflict. Beware of the advance warning signs of a potential conflict—someone showing defensive or uneasy body language, strongly disagreeing with you regardless of the issue, demonstrating a lack of respect toward you, or encouraging you to argue in defense of your values and beliefs. Rather than being drawn into an argument, talk with the person rationally. Try to identify the problem before it becomes a conflict.

Watch your language when you are annoyed. When you are angry, do not make "blaming statements" such as "*You* make me so angry when *you* waste time and don't do *your* share of the work." Such statements put the receiver of the message on the defensive. Instead, say, "*I* feel angry when *I* have no choice but to work late to get these invoices processed on time." When you say *I* (not *you*), the conversation is about your feelings, not the other person's perceived errors or failures. Your statement gives a reason for your feelings that helps the other person understand your point of view. Hopefully, with new insight, the other person will change his or her behavior.

Stop and think before you react. Thomas Jefferson advised that before you speak when angry, count to 10 (or to 100 when very angry). This is good advice. Try to think ahead and predict the consequences of your words and actions. Ask yourself questions such as these: "Will my comment result in a conflict or escalate a conflict?" "Will my words hurt someone's feelings?" "Will my words put me in an embarrassing situation the next time I see this person?" These questions may sound easy but in a moment of anger, it is difficult to take the time to ask—and answer—them. Once you are relaxed and more in control, you can respond more appropriately.

checkpoint

1. What are the four types of conflict?

_____

_____

_____

_____

_____

_____

2. Why can ego conflict damage relationships?

_____

_____

_____

_____

_____

_____

3. How can conflict bring about positive results?

_____

_____

_____

_____

_____

_____

4. Why is "I" a better word to use than "you" when you are angry?

_____

_____

_____

_____

_____

5. What are four ways of preventing conflict?

_____

_____

_____

_____

_____

applications

1. Do you believe the statement "Conflict is inevitable?" Why or why not?

   _____

   _____

   _____

   _____

2. Identify several consequences that might result from conflict in the workplace.

   _____

   _____

   _____

   _____

   _____

3. List two conflicts from the news, your workplace, or from experiences with friends. Briefly describe each conflict and identify the type of conflict. Some situations may involve more than one type of conflict.

   _____

   _____

   _____

   _____

   _____

4. Review the positive results of conflict listed in Figure 8-2 on page 179. Select two of the results. In each case, explain how or why conflict could have that positive result. For example, how might conflict lead to new ways of thinking and behaving?

   _____

   _____

   _____

   _____

5. Give an example of when you were able to avoid "blaming statements" when faced with conflict. Why is it important to avoid such statements?

   _____

   _____

   _____

   _____

How Is Conflict Resolved?

Conflict among coworkers is very destructive because it can ruin the morale of the people involved, divert energy from the tasks to be done, reduce the cooperative spirit of the work team, increase stress, and disrupt communication. Conflict occurs in all workplaces, and it is worth your time to study how conflict can be resolved. You may not be able to control where and when conflict occurs, but you can control how you respond to it. To respond appropriately, it is helpful to understand that conflict involves phases—that conflicts have a beginning and ending. This knowledge helps you better understand the dynamics of any conflict. You can then take appropriate action to resolve the conflict.

"A good manager doesn't try to eliminate conflict; he [sic] tries to keep it from wasting the energies of his [sic] people. If you're the boss and your people fight you openly when they think you are wrong—that's healthy."

PHASES OF CONFLICT

Conflict begins when individuals have differences or perceived differences. Conflict ends when the individuals make adjustments that resolve the conflict and lead to new understanding. Conflicts go through phases, which include "spark," "fanning the flames," "taking sides," "showdown," and "resolution and adjustment."

Spark

The first phase of conflict typically involves a "spark" or triggering incident that brings a difference (or a perceived difference) to the surface. The incident could be a simple misunderstanding that escalates into something more. Or it could be a spontaneous (and very public) confrontation.

> *Jasmine does not consider herself to be a "political animal" and has long been annoyed by coworkers who discuss politics in the office and circulate political cartoons. Unaware of Jasmine's strong feelings about politics, Eugene says, "I've got a great political cartoon to show you. You'll laugh out loud when you read it!" Those seemingly harmless comments served as the spark that ignited a conflict.*

Fanning the Flames

Fanning the flames is the next phase of a conflict. In this phase, the conflict increases in intensity—it "heats up." The parties involved typically try to "score points" through using persuasion or statements that try to prove their case. Perhaps you have overheard an exchange similar to the following: "My plan will save the company money." "Well, my plan doubles our output in two years." "That's nothing. My plan will improve our safety record." And the scorekeeping continues. Conflict can arise over the slightest thing and can escalate into a major confrontation.

Taking Sides

Workplace conflict may begin with two individuals, but it doesn't take long for others to become involved. It's natural for others to take sides in a conflict. Taking sides is harmful and can split the workforce into "camps" that are for or against one side or the other of the issue. Taking sides undermines teamwork, decreases productivity, and can cause tension and stress. When you see people taking sides in a workplace conflict, try to remain neutral and be part of the solution rather than part of the problem.

Showdown

The most volatile phase of conflict is the showdown. Those involved in the original conflict may decide that they "just can't take it anymore" and confront the "opposition." In some cases, this confrontation can be a constructive experience because it finally gets the main issue out in the open, where both parties can face the reality of the situation. Unfortunately, the reverse is often true. A confrontation can be destructive because the people involved threaten each other verbally or physically or react in some other negative manner.

A showdown can also end with a standoff or stalemate. Perhaps you have witnessed a showdown where a shouting match continued until a deadlock was reached where neither side would budge and nothing was resolved.

Lucas and Jeremy have been in conflict for several days over Lucas's refusal to help Jeremy with a work-related project on Saturday morning. Lucas considers Saturday a day for recreation, rest, and family. Jeremy was aware of Lucas's feelings, but he couldn't understand why Lucas was unwilling to make an exception and work one Saturday to complete a project with a deadline. The tension between Lucas and Jeremy was building and affecting their ability to work together. Finally, Lucas said, "We've got to talk about the hostility that's brewing between us." Jeremy agreed. They talked through their lunch hour about the incident that caused the conflict. Jeremy explained that he didn't understand why Lucas couldn't make an exception on one Saturday. Lucas explained how important Saturday was to him and his family. Jeremy promised to respect Lucas's priorities, and Lucas agreed to consider Jeremy's feelings about wanting to get the work done. Both Lucas and Jeremy decided that working late one or two weeknights would get the work done without creating a conflict for either of them.

What lessons did Lucas and Jeremy learn through this experience? What factors contributed to the positive outcome? What other solutions might have been possible?

Resolution and Adjustment

Once the main issues are out in the open, the parties can propose solutions and, hopefully, come to a decision that is agreeable to all. This is called **resolution**. After the conflict has been resolved, the decision must be implemented. **Adjustment** refers to the measures that are necessary to put into action the settlement agreed upon by the parties. Typically, those actions involve changes in the behavior of one or both parties.

The adjustments made determine how well the conflict is settled. If only one side adjusts, the conflict may start all over again. The goal is to make adjustments that settle the conflict in a constructive manner. An open and honest discussion of the underlying cause of the conflict and related issues will ideally lead to a resolution that is agreeable to both sides.

RESOLVING CONFLICT

Conflict is not necessarily a bad thing. Resolved effectively, conflict can lead to personal and professional growth. Resolving conflict is a process that takes time, thought, and cooperation from all involved. The term **Conflict resolution** refers to managing conflict by defining and resolving issues between individuals, groups, or organizations. In many cases, effective conflict resolution skills can make the difference between positive and negative outcomes from conflict.

You have a choice when faced with conflict. You can confront the conflict head on and try to resolve it or you can use other techniques that may be viewed as either positive or negative. Techniques such as avoidance, accommodation, delay, and confrontation may postpone or temporarily help the situation, but they will not resolve the conflict completely.

Avoidance

A common response to what might be a conflict is to avoid it. Someone might think, "Perhaps if I don't bring it up, it will blow over." But, generally, all that happens is that feelings get pent up, views go unexpressed, and the conflict festers until it becomes too big to ignore. Like an illness that may well have been cured if treated early, the conflict grows and spreads until it kills the relationship. Because needs and concerns go unexpressed, people are often confused, wondering what went wrong in a relationship.[2]

Another way to avoid conflict is to pretend it doesn't exist. You choose to remove yourself physically and emotionally from the situation. You avoid the person involved in the conflict or walk away when the conflict surfaces. Avoidance is used when it is simply not worth the effort to face the situation (or it doesn't appear to be worth the effort). Avoidance does not resolve conflict. In fact, avoiding the situation may actually escalate the problem. Productive work is very difficult in an environment where a conflict is ignored. The conflict needs to be faced, and a suitable adjustment needs to be determined.

Accommodation

Accommodation means giving in to others to the extent that you compromise yourself. You play down the differences and concentrate on areas of agreement. Perhaps you know that you could argue more but don't want to face the struggle. This technique may work for you if the issue is more important to others than to you. It is a goodwill gesture on your part.

> *Andrea tells Mary, a coworker, that she was disappointed in her because she declined to be the department representative for the United Way drive. Andrea has represented the department for two consecutive years and feels that it is someone else's turn to do this job. She tries to put a "guilt trip" on Mary by telling her she should consider this task her civic responsibility. Mary doesn't want an argument. She gives in and reluctantly agrees to take the job even though she really doesn't want the responsibility.*

"An apology is the superglue of life. It can repair just about anything."

Mary resolved the conflict through accommodation, but will the conflict flare up again? Probably. The conflict will come up again because the underlying issue was not resolved and neither person is happy with the solution. Mary feels stuck with a job she doesn't want, and Andrea is annoyed with Mary's lack of enthusiasm for taking on the assignment.

Resolving conflict takes time, thought, and cooperation from all involved.

Digital Vision/Getty Images

Delay

Another technique for handling conflict is to delay resolution. You may settle a small part of the conflict but not handle the critical issues. The excuse used is that you are temporarily defusing (or neutralizing) the situation.

Alan and Julio work in a print shop and know the importance of getting orders out on time. This evening, Julio is eager to leave to see his son play football. But the press breaks down and will take a couple of hours to repair. Everyone must work late to get a large order out on time. Julio says, "I've worked my share of the overtime. I'm going to leave at 5 p.m." Alan replies, "But I can't do this job alone. You have to stick it out and help." Some unkind remarks fly back and forth between Alan and Julio. The supervisor, Jeff, overhears the conflict. He diffuses the situation by saying that he will help Alan and tells Julio that he may leave at 5 p.m. The immediate conflict is resolved, but the underlying conflict between Alan and Julio still needs attention.

This technique is not entirely negative. Sometimes postponing a discussion over a conflict is a good thing. It provides an immediate solution and at the same time allows people time to cool down. The next time the conflict arises, perhaps they can reach a reasonable compromise or solution.

Identify the technique (avoidance, accommodation, delay, or confrontation) that was used to resolve the conflict in each of these situations.

1. Betsy's supervisor asks her to assume the responsibility of picking up and sorting the mail for her department. Betsy feels the mail duties should be shared by both administrative assistants—that it should not be her responsibility alone. Rather than try to justify her position, she unenthusiastically tells her supervisor she will accept the task.

2. Robert and Eve argued loudly over how much money to spend for computer upgrades during the upcoming fiscal year. Finally, Eve said, "Let's forget this for now and discuss it next week."

3. Anisa and Rubin were assigned to work on a marketing brochure for a car rental agency. They could not agree on the design or content. After a heated discussion, they both walked away and avoided each other for the rest of the day. The agency director wants the brochure finalized this week.

4. Several coworkers tell Brad that a rumor is going around that he is quitting his job. Brad likes his work and has no intention of leaving. He thinks Sylvan started the rumor. He storms into Sylvan's cubicle and demands to know why he started the rumor.

5. The employees of an upscale retail store are concerned. Their hours have been cut, salaries have been frozen, vacant positions are not being filled, and inventory is low. The signs are that the store is in big trouble, and rumors are flying. The employees want to know what is happening. They select two representatives to talk with the general manager and demand to know the store's financial condition and management's plans for the future.

Confrontation

The most effective way to resolve conflict is through a combination of confrontation and problem solving. The word *confrontation* sounds negative, but it can actually be very positive. When used effectively, confrontation can result in a win–win situation. Confrontation in this case refers to confronting the *issues*, not personal confrontation. It requires that the parties exchange ideas and actively work through their differences until they reach a resolution everyone can agree on.

The key to managing confrontation is to redirect the emotional energy generated by the conflict toward a constructive solution. If you are involved in a conflict, or if you are trying to resolve a conflict, work to establish the correct frame of mind among the parties involved. Conflicts can be resolved only when both parties:

- Agree to cooperate.
- Believe the problem has a solution.

- Recognize that a difference of opinion is not a personal attack.
- Respect the opinions of all involved.
- Make an effort to be patient.

Once these attitudes are in place, you are ready to use a problem-solving technique to resolve the conflict.

PROBLEM-SOLVING TECHNIQUE

No matter where you work, you will be faced with problems resulting from conflict. You will need to solve similar problems in your personal life. Figure 8-3 shows a six-step problem-solving technique that can help individuals and groups solve conflicts.

By answering the six questions in Figure 8-3, you will be equipped to begin to solve the conflicts you face at work and in your personal life. One reason for the success of the six-step method is the mental attitude you must adopt if you are to follow the first three steps. You cannot answer the first three questions (What is conflict? What are the facts? What is the overall objective?) until you detach yourself emotionally from the situation. When you can put aside your emotions temporarily and put your mature self in charge, you will find it easier to identify solutions and resolve the conflict.

SIX-STEP PROBLEM SOLVING

Ask yourself:
1. What is the conflict?
2. What are the facts?
3. What is the overall objective?
4. What are some possible solutions?
5. What is the best solution?
6. Did the solution work?

FIGURE 8-3 Use the six-step problem-solving technique to resolve conflict.

What Is the Conflict?

A problem well stated is half solved.

This question may sound simple, but as you begin to define and describe the exact conflict, you may change your mind. You may know something is wrong—you are in conflict with another person—but you cannot describe the true conflict. As you try to state the conflict in specific terms, take care to be nonjudgmental and objective and to consider the feelings of everyone involved.

The following situation with Peter and Estelle demonstrates the first step of problem solving.

Peter and Estelle are talking about moving when the lease on their apartment ends. Estelle says, "Let's buy a house." Peter agrees, "Yes, I think the market is right." Estelle replies, "I think we should get a small, 'starter' ranch house. Let's ask a realtor to show us ranch houses." Peter responds in a harsh voice, "What do you mean a small ranch house? You know I want a two-story house with an attic and a basement for storage."

What is the conflict? Peter and Estelle do not agree on the type of house that they want to buy. There is no right or wrong in the statement of the problem, and no attempt at a solution is made.

What Are the Facts?

Don't just think about the answer to this section question, write it down. Take care to record the facts—not opinions or value judgments. Each fact listed must relate to the problem. Drop any "ifs" or "shoulds." The facts in Peter and Estelle's conflict scenario are:

1. They agree it is a good time to buy a house.
2. Estelle wants a small ranch house.
3. Peter wants a two-story house with an attic and a basement for storage.
4. Peter and Estelle need to discuss what they want in a house.

What Is the Overall Objective?

The answer to this question can be difficult, but it must be considered. Perhaps you have never tried to identify the main objective involved in a conflict. But it is helpful to write down the desired objective, or outcome. Peter and Estelle's objective is not hard to see: they want to find a home that is pleasing to both of them.

What Are Possible Solutions?

As you answer this question, write down all possible solutions. Be creative, and think of as many ideas as you can. No idea is too absurd or silly. In essence, you want to "think outside the box." This process is called brainstorming. **Brainstorming** is typically a group technique used to generate a large number of ideas or solutions to a problem, but individuals can also brainstorm effectively.

Write down the extreme solutions first. The extremes for Peter and Estelle might be as ridiculous as buying two houses or getting a divorce so each of them can live in the house of his or her choice. After writing down the extreme solutions, devote your attention to realistic possibilities to solve the conflict. The possibilities for Peter and Estelle's conflict might include:

1. Look for a ranch house with a basement and yard large enough for a storage shed.
2. Look for a split-level house with a basement and a yard large enough for a storage shed.
3. Design a new home with features they both like.
4. Renew the lease on their apartment.

Brainstorming can be an effective way for a group or individual to generate lots of ideas.

- Clearly identify the problem or issue.
- Set a time limit (30 minutes, for example).
- Collect as many ideas as possible without criticizing or judging the ideas. There should be no discussion—just free-flowing ideas. No idea is silly or ridiculous.
- Letter each idea and write it on a board or flipchart for all to see.
- When time is up, each participant ranks the ideas in numeric order: 1 for the best idea, 2 for the next best idea, and so on.
- As a group (or an individual), agree on the five ideas with the highest ranking.
- Write down criteria for judging the top five ideas; assign a point value between 0 and 5 to each criterion.
- Give each of the top five ideas a score of 0 to 5, depending on how well it meets each criterion. Once all the ideas are scored for each criterion, add up the scores for each idea.
- The idea with the highest score should best solve your problem.

"STRETCH" YOUR MIND

What Is the Best Solution?

The fifth question is best answered by considering all the facts you listed in response to question two and then selecting the best possible solution. Consider and compare the pros and cons of each solution. Be as objective as possible. The best solution must improve the situation and must help, not hinder, reaching the overall objective. What is the best solution for Peter and Estelle? It could be 1, 2, 3, or 4—or a combination of a couple of the solutions. Peter and Estelle (the ones involved in the conflict) are the only ones who can make the final decision about their future home.

Did the Solution Work?

In this final step, the conflicting parties review the solution after giving it an opportunity to work. Ideally, you will find that the outcome proved to be effective for both parties. But that may not always be true. You may find that the solution has weaknesses. If so, both parties must be willing to revise their decisions and agree to make changes—just as they agreed to the original solution.

An individual or group involved in a conflict may decide not to participate in a solution. If this situation occurs, try to return to the first step of the problem-solving technique, and try again to get everyone to participate in finding a solution. If everyone involved cannot accept a solution after the second attempt to move through the problem-solving steps, both sides will have to adjust to functioning with the conflict unresolved. Living with a conflict in place is not a pleasant situation. After a period of time, try again.

checkpoint

1. Why is conflict among coworkers destructive?

_____

_____

_____

_____

_____

2. Why is it important to list all possible solutions to a conflict, including those that might be considered unreasonable?

_____

_____

_____

_____

_____

3. Who needs to select the best solution to a given problem?

_____

_____

_____

_____

_____

_____

4. Define brainstorming and explain why it is a useful process when problem solving.

_____

_____

_____

_____

_____

_____

5. Why is the last step of the problem-solving technique necessary?

_____

_____

_____

_____

_____

applications

1. Describe a situation when the conflict you were involved in was a positive rather than a negative experience. How was the conflict handled? How was it resolved? Why do you feel it was a positive experience?

_____

_____

_____

_____

2. Find a news article that describes a conflict between two or more persons or groups. Describe the conflict briefly. How would you solve the conflict? Base your solution on the facts and good judgment.

   a. Describe the situation.

_____

_____

b. What is the conflict?

_____

_____

_____

c. What are the facts?

_____

_____

_____

d. What is a desirable outcome?

_____

_____

_____

e. What are some possible solutions to the conflict?

_____

_____

_____

f. What is the best possible solution to the conflict?

_____

_____

_____

3. Assume that you are walking down the street and see a neighbor coming the other way. In the past, you have confronted this neighbor about a noisy dog that barks at all hours of the night. Thus far, he has done nothing to remedy the problem.

a. What will you do as the neighbor approaches?

_____

_____

b. What is the rationale behind your decision?

_____

_____

4. Brainstorm ideas with classmates to solve Miranda's dilemma in the Think About It scenario at the beginning of this chapter. What might she do to get Emil and Nila to work harmoniously in the design center?

_____

_____

_____

points to remember

Review the following points to determine what you remember from the chapter.

* Conflict is inevitable and refers to differences in opinions caused by opposing attitudes, behaviors, ideas, needs, desires, or goals. Four basic types of conflict are simple conflict, false conflict, ego conflict, and values and beliefs conflict.

* Conflict in the workplace is serious as it has the potential to decrease productivity, increase stress, undermine morale, hamper performance, increase turnover rate and absenteeism, and lead to irresponsible behavior. Conflict in your personal life can lead to stress, loss of self-esteem, depression, and general unhappiness.

* Conflict can be a positive force when the people involved have a positive learning experience because of the event.

* While conflict may never be eliminated, it can be prevented by building constructive relationships, discussing problems before they escalate to a confrontation, watching your language when you are angry, and stopping to think before you react.

* The five phases of conflict are the spark that ignites the conflict, fanning the flames, taking sides, a showdown, and finally, resolution and adjustment.

* Adjustment techniques such as avoidance, delaying action, accommodating, and confronting may help, but they will not resolve it completely.

* The most effective way to deal with conflict is to answer the questions in the problem-solving method: What is the conflict? What are the facts? What is the overall objective? What are some possible solutions? What is the best solution? Did it work?

How did you do? Did you remember the main points you studied in this chapter?

KEY terms

conflict

simple conflict

false conflict

ego

ego conflict

values and beliefs conflict

resolution

adjustment

conflict resolution

brainstorming

Want more activities? Go to **www.cengage.com/careerreadiness/masters** to get started.

CHAPTER *activities*

1. Role play the following discussion with a classmate to get the full impact of the situation. Then answer the questions.

   Paul: "The paint smell in this room is awful. I have a headache from the odor, and I can't concentrate on my work. I'd open a window, but they are stuck. You've got to do something."

   Zach: "You're kidding, right? What does the smell of fresh paint have to do with your headache? No one else is complaining. Besides, the walls need painting."

   Paul: "I just told you. The smell of the paint makes my head throb and my eyes water. Are you blind? Can't you see how red my eyes are? I'm going to stop at a clinic on my way home. Maybe I should also call my lawyer. I can't believe it's legal to require people to work in a toxic environment."

   Zach: "You complain too much. You probably have a sinus infection, and that's what is causing your headache. Take an aspirin and forget about it."

   Paul: "So now you're a doctor!"

   Zach: "Whoa! I don't need that kind of attitude. You're making a big deal out of nothing."

   Paul: "I'm not showing attitude and I'm not making a big deal out of nothing. To me, the paint smell *is* a big deal. I just want you to do something about the smell so that I can do my job."

   Zach: "That does it. I've heard enough. Get back to work."

   a. What is the conflict?

   _____

   _____

   b. What are the facts?

   _____

   _____

   c. What additional conflicts may result from this disagreement?

   _____

   _____

   d. What are some possible solutions?

   _____

   _____

   e. What is the best solution (based on the facts)?

   _____

   _____

2. Recall a resolved conflict in which you've been involved. Describe the conflict as it progressed through the five stages.

   Spark:

   _____

   _____

   Fanning the flames:

   _____

   _____

   Taking sides:

   _____

   _____

   Showdown:

   _____

   _____

   Resolution/adjustment:

   _____

   _____

CRITICAL thinking

Donna and John, product managers at Werner Industries, share an administrative assistant, Blake. They both are responsible for an important company event this week. Donna will hold a press conference to introduce a new product. She expects preparing for her press conference to be Blake's number one priority for the week. This includes developing a multimedia presentation, faxing advance press releases, assembling handout packets, and arranging for the room and audiovisual equipment. John will conduct the monthly managers' luncheon meeting. He expects Blake to make preparing for the meeting his number one priority. This includes finalizing and transmitting the agenda, preparing support materials, ordering lunch, and setting up the audiovisual equipment needed.

Blake comes to work on Monday expecting to continue to work on two projects he started last week. But then Donna and John each meet with him separately to describe the week's priority from their point of view. Blake feels overwhelmed and at a loss as to what to do first. He loses control and shouts, "This isn't fair. I can't do everything." and storms down the hall.

1. What is the conflict?

_____

_____

2. What are the facts?

_____

_____

3. What is the objective or the desired outcome?

_____

_____

4. What are some possible solutions?

_____

_____

5. What in your opinion is the best solution?

_____

_____

_____

CASE 8.2 Balancing Responsibilities

Tabitha, a part-time employee in a real estate office, manages the office from 11:30 a.m. to 3:30 p.m. every day. Tabitha and her husband Cal have two sons who attend afternoon preschool. Tabitha made it clear in her employment interview that she needed to leave promptly at 3:30 to pick up her sons. The interview team assured Tabitha that her responsibilities would end at 3:30 each day. The realtors agreed that on alternate days they would take responsibility for the office from 3:30 until closing at 6:00. The realtors were late getting back to the office several times, and Tabitha had to call Cal to pick up the boys.

Yesterday afternoon, the agent who was to relieve Tabitha didn't show, and Cal was out of town. Tabitha tried to reach the other realtors, but all were with clients and couldn't come into the office. Tabitha locked the office, left a note on the door, picked up the boys, and brought them back to the office. The office was unattended for 45 minutes. Unfortunately, an important client called during that time. He reportedly called the owner, Sam Bartu, and asked why no one was answering the phone. At 5:15 p.m. Erin, one of the agents, returned and saw Tabitha's sons. She said, "Why are your children here? I have important clients coming over in a few minutes. You'll have to take them home." Tabitha left to take the children home, which meant that Erin was alone there to tend the office. The following day Tabitha was called in to see Mr. Bartu. He asked, "Why did you leave the phone unattended? Why were your children in the office? Why did you go home when Erin had important clients coming in and wouldn't be available to answer the phone?"

1. What is the problem?

_____

_____

_____

_____

_____

_____

2. What are the facts?

_____

_____

_____

_____

_____

_____

3. What is the desirable outcome?

_____

_____

_____

_____

_____

_____

4. What are some possible solutions?

_____

_____

_____

_____

_____

_____

5. What in your opinion is the best solution?

_____

_____

_____

_____

_____

_____

6. What follow-up steps would be appropriate?

_____

_____

_____

_____

_____

_____

Meeting Essentials

Digital Vision/Getty Images

Think About It: Henry is about to begin the monthly staff meeting. "Let's all quiet down," Henry says. "What do you want to talk about today? We need to get out of here by 3:30. Caroline, you said you had something to discuss." "Uh, yes," she says, "The marketing staff has new software. Why are they getting special treatment when we haven't been able to get the software we need?" Henry replies, "Talk to Glenn about that. He wasn't able to attend our meeting today." Dale says, "The elevators in this building aren't working again. Will they ever work properly? I walked up six flights today." Henry responds, "Has anyone else had problems with the elevators?" "I have," Alice says, "but I think it is healthy to take the stairs. Dale, you could use the exercise!" "Okay," Henry says, "I'll look into the elevator situation." Chang says, "My section has been without a support person for two months. HR keeps putting me off and blaming it on a hiring freeze." Henry asks, "What hiring freeze? I'll call HR to see what I can find out." Mitch asks, "How do I get a key to the data center so I can work next Saturday?" Henry replies, "I'll check into that." Maria asks, "When is the paperwork for merit raises due? I have several names that I want to submit." Evan says, "Yes, I want that information too." Henry replies, "I'll find out and get back to you. Oops, time's up. Thanks for coming."

Was this meeting effective? What is lacking in this meeting? What follow-up will be necessary?

objectives

After completing this chapter, you should be able to:

1. Describe the categories and frequency of meetings.
2. Explain the styles of meetings.
3. Describe common types of electronic meetings.
4. Understand the importance of being a good meeting participant.
5. Plan, conduct, close, and follow up a meeting.
6. Identify the special requirements of formal meetings.

9.1 Meeting Basics
9.2 Planning and Conducting Meetings

Meeting Basics

eetings are an important part of the communication network in the workplace. Meetings are a common way for employees to share information, discuss problems, and make decisions. Managers often prefer meetings because open communication encourages discussion and yields feedback that helps in decision making.[1] A **meeting** is a formal (or informal) assembly of two or more individuals who come together to discuss one or more topics. Meetings are often held to share information, assign tasks, discuss issues, make decisions, solve problems, and plan for the future. You will participate in meetings throughout your career. At times, you may be the person responsible for planning and conducting the meeting.

Meetings can be very productive or they can be a waste of valuable time. According to Bob Hagerty, CEO of Polycom Inc., "Unsuccessful meetings can be a disaster—they're unpleasant to be in, they're ineffective, they're a waste of time, and they create a huge productivity hole."[2] Productive meetings do not just happen. Rather, they are carefully planned and executed. This chapter discusses various types of meetings and explains how to participate effectively in meetings.

"The interaction of many minds is usually more illuminating than the intuition of one."

TYPES OF MEETINGS

Meetings have different purposes and are referred to by different names. It will be helpful to become familiar with various types of meetings and their purposes.

Staff or Team Meetings

Meetings that are typically called by a team leader or manager for those who report to that manager either directly or indirectly are called **staff meetings** or **team meetings**. These meetings are often held on a regular basis to keep the lines of communication open within the team or work unit. Staff meetings encourage two-way communication and are often used to pull together information for decision making, communicate problems or solutions, and provide focus for the team.

The number of people attending these meetings varies greatly. For example, a team meeting could involve a team leader and four team members, while a staff meeting could involve a whole department or an organization's entire workforce.

> *Zoe, the team leader of the Lancaster County Planning Unit (a division of county government), wanted help in deciding how to inform local contractors of the new zoning law for street paving. She put the question on the agenda for a staff meeting and received helpful input (based on the experience of staff) on the best way to provide information to contractors.*

Status Meetings

The word "status" means *standing* or *condition*. A **status meeting** provides current information about something that is ongoing. For example, a status meeting may be called to keep staff up to date on the development of a new product line or intended revisions to the bonus pay plan. A status meeting is typically called and led by a team leader, supervisor, line leader, or some other person in charge. This type of meeting generally involves one-way communication, unless there are questions from the participants.

One-on-One Meetings

The most frequent workplace meetings are **one-on-one meetings**. These meetings can take place between coworkers, supervisors and their direct reports, employees and suppliers, or other combinations.

One-on-one meetings may be informal or formal. For example, you may be asked to help a coworker learn a new database program. In this case, you would arrange a time to meet with that person to share your knowledge. The meeting between you and your coworker would be an informal one-on-one meeting. A yearly performance appraisal (judgment of how well someone is performing on the job) with your supervisor is an example of a formal one-on-one meeting. One-on-one meetings can take place electronically as well as in person.

Management Meetings

Meetings at which management or administrative staff from various levels in the organization gather to report on their areas of responsibility and learn about new policies, procedures, and challenges are called **management meetings**. These meetings are usually held on a regular basis. The size of the organization and the number of management levels in the organization affect how many individuals attend such a meeting.

> *At the monthly meeting of the 12 department managers of Gilmans Department Store, Lily (cosmetics) reported that perfume sample cards would be placed at each customer checkout station beginning next Monday. She asked all managers to encourage their sales associates to invite customers to take a sample. Maurice (shoes) reported a 15 percent drop in sales over the last month. He attributed the decline to winter storms causing travel problems. He expects sales to pick up when the new spring styles arrive.*

Board Meetings

Meetings held for administrative purposes are called **board meetings**. These formal meetings involve members of boards of directors of corporations or organizations or elected officials of a government entity, such as a school board. A **board of directors** is an elected or appointed body that oversees the activities of a company or organization. The body may have a different name, such as *board of trustees* or *board of governors*. Often, it is simply referred to as *the board*.

What type of meeting (staff/team, status, one-on-one, management, board, or ad hoc) would be appropriate in the following situations?

_____ The regular monthly meeting of the accounting staff.

_____ The meeting of a group specifically appointed to discuss bonus pay.

_____ The quarterly meeting of the policymakers of Bethke Corporation.

_____ A hallway encounter with a supervisor.

_____ A meeting of the regional vice presidents of Jacobi Distributors.

_____ A meeting of all employees to learn the details of the merger with Swanson Brothers.

Meetings are typically held at definite intervals (monthly, quarterly, etc.) to consider policy issues and discuss major problems. An officer of the company or organization usually calls the meeting. Old business (items that were discussed at a previous meeting) and new business (topics or discussions that are on the agenda for the first time) are discussed, and reports are given.

Ad Hoc Meetings

Ad hoc is a Latin phrase which means "for this purpose." **Ad hoc meetings** are called to address a specific issue or situation. Once the task is complete, the committee disbands. Typically, you would be assigned to an ad hoc committee on a temporary basis. The committee may meet only one time or several times, depending on its purpose. The individual who called for the formation of the committee (or who was elected by the members of the committee) appoints the meeting leader.

> *The school board of Tryon County had been discussing the health curriculum for about 30 minutes. There were additional issues on the agenda that needed to be addressed, so the chairperson appointed an ad hoc committee to review the health curriculum suggestions and asked the committee to present its recommendations to the full school board at the next meeting. The board continued discussing the other issues on the agenda.*

FREQUENCY OF MEETINGS

The frequency of meetings varies depending on the nature and type of meeting. You may attend a one-time-only meeting, while other meetings may be scheduled weekly, biweekly, monthly, or quarterly. For example, a meeting to alert the staff to changes in the amount employees must pay toward health insurance would likely take place only once. On the other hand, a meeting of all department managers may be held on the first Thursday of each month.

One-Time Meetings

"No grand idea was ever born in a conference, but a lot of foolish ideas have died there."

One-time meetings can be held for several hours, an entire day, or span several days. These meetings may involve a few individuals or an entire global workforce. For example, a network administrator may call a one-day meeting to train all account representatives in the use of software that will enable them to access the company's databases while traveling. Or, the company president may call a meeting of the entire workforce to inform them of a pending merger. The president's meeting could include members of the workforce throughout the United States or in any other location where an electronic connection is available.

Recurring Meetings

Recurring meetings are held periodically—every week, twice a month, once a month, every year, and so on. Examples are a department meeting every Friday at 10 a.m. the monthly chamber of commerce meeting, or the yearly meeting (called a *conference*) of the Association for Career and Technical Education. Weekly and monthly meetings are scheduled when management determines that it is important for participants to come together on a recurring basis. A recurring meeting can be ongoing for the near future (a weekly team meeting, for example) or have an ending date (six weekly staff development meetings, for example).

Large organizations such as the American Medical Association, the Texas Bankers Association, and the National Organization for Women typically hold regional meetings and assemble once a year at a *conference* or *summit*. These meetings usually include lectures and events that continue over several days, such as workshops and seminars.

Series Meetings

"The time to stop talking is when the other person nods his head affirmatively but says nothing."

This type of meeting is similar to a recurring meeting, but the details differ at each meeting. One example of a series meeting is a monthly brown bag lunch to discuss a topic of particular interest to employees. **Series meetings** are held at the same time each month but the topic discussed varies. Series meetings are popular because they encourage individual input in an informal setting, build team spirit, and strengthen the knowledge base of employees.

MEETING STYLES

Meetings may be categorized according to the style or manner in which they are conducted—informal meetings and formal meetings.

Informal Meetings

Staff meetings, team meetings, and status meetings will generally be held in an informal or relaxed setting. For example, a team leader may hold weekly staff meetings in a conference room or a lead production supervisor may

meet with direct reports at a workstation. These meetings are sometimes held in conjunction with breakfast or lunch to make the best use of workers' time.

Do not let the word "informal" fool you. Although informal meetings lack the more rigid structure of a formal meeting, they play an important role in the overall operation of the organization. Informal meetings provide an opportunity to exchange information and to identify and solve problems. They also serve as a forum for decision making *by consensus* (agreement of most participants). Like formal meetings, informal meetings require planning, an agenda, and follow-up. An **agenda** is a list of topics to be addressed at the meeting. Agendas are discussed in more detail in Section 9.2. Follow-up usually involves the need to take action and/or send a meeting summary to all participants.

Team meetings are common in the workplace.

Impromptu Meetings. *Impromptu meetings* typically occur when people meet spontaneously and have a conversation about business matters. Impromptu conversations provide an opportunity to network and exchange information. The setting may be a hallway, lunch or break room, elevator, stairway, or even a restroom. In other words, impromptu meetings could take place anywhere. For example, workers at a company with an onsite fitness center may bounce ideas around while running on the treadmill or pumping iron. In the On the Job scenario in this section, Lee and Paula engage in an impromptu meeting when they meet in a hallway and discuss training administrative assistants in the use of presentation software.

Stand-Up Meetings. An informal team meeting held daily to provide a status update to the team members is called a *stand-up meeting*. Some teams meet daily around a workstation or form a circle in an open area. Making commitments to each other as a team is the most important goal of daily stand-ups. Although participants report on their progress and status, this is secondary to team members publicly committing to each other and identifying obstacles that prevent them from meeting their commitments.[3] Meetings are usually held at the same time and place every workday and are typically short (5 to 15 minutes). They are held standing up to remind the participants to keep to the point.

Bethany holds stand-up meetings each morning with the six members of her group. She gives each person an opportunity to talk about his or her progress since the last stand-up meeting and identify any problems. Although the meetings last only 10 minutes, they allow team members to make a daily commitment to each other and coordinate efforts.

Lee sees Paula coming down the hall and moves quickly to speak with her. "Hi, Paula, glad I caught you. Do you have a minute to talk?" Paula replies, "I'm on my way to lunch, but I have a few moments." Lee says, "Thanks. I know you have experience using presentation software." Paula replies, "You've got that right. I prepare two or three presentations a week. And I just finished an advanced class in PowerPoint at the local community college." Lee says, "Let me get right to the point. Would you be willing to train the administrative assistants in my area on the use of presentation software? They're willing to stay after work or come in a few Saturdays. They're eager to get some pointers but don't feel like they have time to take a formal class. I've talked with your supervisor, and she is supportive of the idea. My budget will allow me to offer you $30 per hour. Are you interested?" Paula replies, "I appreciate your confidence in me. Let me think about it and get back to you. Meanwhile, please verify that the assistants are willing to come in on Saturdays. I need to get home to my children and can't stay late after work."

What type of meeting has just been held? What follow-up will be necessary on Paula's part? What follow-up will be required of Lee? Is this type of meeting appropriate for the topic discussed? Why or why not?

Formal Meetings

When you attend a formal meeting, you participate in a structured event. A formal meeting requires extensive planning and has a predetermined list of topics that will be discussed, along with a set of objectives to be achieved at the meeting. Formal meetings are typical for public meetings (a city council meeting, for example), board meetings of elected officials, corporate officer meetings, stockholder meetings, union meetings, and other large-scale meetings. By law, public meetings and some private meetings must be publicly announced before the meeting.

A formal meeting follows an established set of rules. The agenda is often distributed or posted before the meeting. In some cases (for example, a chamber of commerce meeting), the agenda must be posted a certain number of days before the meeting. Formal meetings are usually tightly controlled so that they start and end on time. A senior executive or board chair often presides over the meeting.

Minutes, the written record of what takes place at the meeting, are distributed to participants and in some situations made available to the public. Minutes can be transmitted electronically very quickly to all constituencies. Minutes typically include the name of the organization, date and time of meeting, who called it to order, who attended and if there is a *quorum* (the legal number of participants needed to conduct business), all motions made, votes taken, any conflicts of interest, when the meeting ended, and who developed the minutes. The minutes provide input for future meetings.

ELECTRONIC MEETINGS

Not all meetings are held face to face with participants in the same room. Electronic meetings have gained prominence as a means of saving time, reducing travel costs, and improving collaboration among employees who do not work in the same location. Technology makes it possible for individuals at various locations to meet as though they were in the same room. For example, in Chapter 7 you learned that virtual teams use special software called *groupware* to work collectively from remote locations. A member of a virtual team will use groupware to attend electronic meetings, with each person able to see and display information received from and sent to others. Several common types of electronic meetings are discussed here.

Voice and Video Chat

Voice and video chatting is a popular form of communication via the Internet. This means of communicating is made possible through chat software. Voice and video chat enables people connected electronically throughout the world to have an actual conversation with someone or even chat face to face almost free of charge. A video of the person with whom you are speaking can appear on your computer screen in a chat box that can be enlarged so you can see the person's expressions and gestures.

Joel, who works for an international investment company, has been transferred from the Charlotte office to the company headquarters in Amsterdam. He speaks daily via voice and video chat with branch offices in New York, London, Hong Kong, and Mumbai. Joel holds one-on-one meetings with staff and other managers via the Internet.

Teleconferencing

Teleconferencing enables two or more people to hold a meeting via a telephone or a network connection. A teleconference is more sophisticated than a two-way phone conversation. At its simplest, a teleconference can be an audio conference with parties at one or both ends of the conference sharing a speakerphone. A speakerphone has a built-in speaker that enables a person or group to talk without using the receiver.

Lara, Enid, and Marcello gather in a conference room in Atlanta. A speakerphone sits in the middle of the conference room table. A conference call has been arranged for 10 a.m. to discuss a new advertising campaign. Corine (in the Cleveland office) and Eugene (working from home in Nashville) call a special number to connect to the conference.

The speakerphone enables Lara, Enid, and Marcello to hear and respond to all comments made by Corine and Eugene, and Corine and Eugene can hear and respond to their colleagues in Atlanta.

With considerably more equipment and special arrangements, a teleconference can become a videoconference with enhanced capabilities.

Videoconferencing

Videoconferencing (also known as a *video teleconferencing*) brings people at different sites together for a meeting where they can see still or real-time video images of each other. A simple conversation between two people in private offices is called a *point-to-point* video conference. Each participant has a computer with an attached video camera, microphone, and speakers. As the two participants speak to one another, their voices are transmitted to the other person's speakers, and whatever images appear in front of one participant's video camera appear in a window on the other person's monitor.

A videoconference brings people at different sites together for a meeting.

A videoconference that involves several sites with people in *virtual conference rooms* at different sites throughout the country or around the world is known as a *multipoint* video conference. A video conference requires special telecommunication arrangements and a special room at each end. For example, the board of directors of an international company headquartered in Los Angeles might meet with top management assembled in regional offices in Miami, Chicago, Beijing, and Paris. Once a videoconference is established, the technology enables the group to see each other on a large screen and share applications, documents, and a common whiteboard. Many analysts believe that videoconferencing is one of the fastest-growing segments of the computer industry.

Image Source/Getty Images

Web Conferencing

Web conferencing is used to conduct live meetings or presentations over the Internet. In a web conference, each participant sits at his or her own computer and is connected to other participants via the Internet. The use of webcams and headsets or other microphones for both visual and audio communication enhances communication. Participants can use an application on each person's computer or a web-based application where the attendees simply enter a URL (website address) to join the conference. Many web-conferencing applications allow screen sharing, document sharing, and comment sharing.

A **webinar** (short for *web-based seminar*) is a specific type of web conference that refers to a lecture, presentation, workshop, or seminar transmitted over the Web. A key feature of a webinar is its interactive or collaborative elements. Assume, for example, that you are to take part in a nationwide webinar to introduce a new software package. After the initial presentation, you might participate in a question and answer session that allows full participation between the audience (that's you) and the presenter. Whereas web conferences are run more as small group meetings, webinars tend to be conducted by a lead presenter who distributes presentation materials electronically to all attendees, encourages questions, and may ask attendees to answer on-the-spot survey questions with real-time results.

PARTICIPATING IN MEETINGS

Now that you are familiar with the types, frequencies, and styles of meetings, it is time to focus on what you need to do to participate effectively in meetings. As Nancy Knowlton, Co-CEO of SMART Technologies, Inc. says:

> *"Meetings are a huge investment of time, and the number one expense that most companies have is their people. When people make good use of their time, there is a terrific return on investment. But when people don't make good use of their time in meetings—they don't achieve their objectives, there's useless chatter or they're cycling around on the same topic—that's a prescription for no return on investment."*[4]

Your responsibilities involve a great deal more than simply "showing up." You would be wise to remember the three "BPs" of participating in meetings—**B**e **P**resent, **B**e **P**repared, and **B**e **P**articipatory.

Be Present

To be present means that you consider the meeting a serious commitment. It means that you should be on time or early. When you are late, you waste the time of other participants who must either wait for you to arrive or wait while someone fills you in on what the group discussed before you arrived. Being late is rude, annoying, and inconsiderate.

If you are scheduled to attend a meeting and cannot be present for a good reason (medical appointment, previously scheduled meeting, etc.), contact the meeting leader and explain why you will be unable to attend. Ask to receive any handouts and a meeting summary. If you cannot be present physically, check into being connected electronically.

Be Prepared

Whether the meeting is informal or formal, get ready for it by assembling the items that you need to bring to the meeting and preparing yourself mentally. You do not want to be someone who simply arrives at a meeting without any forethought as to what to bring. But what should you bring? Take a notepad and pen or pencil to jot down assignments you may receive or to record key points to refer to later. In some workplaces, you may be encouraged to bring your laptop for note-taking or reference purposes. You will also need your printed or electronic calendar to check your availability for future events and record the dates. If you are asked to share information at the meeting, be sure to bring copies for all participants. Finally, bring the agenda and/or any support materials you received before the meeting.

How should you prepare yourself mentally for the meeting? Begin by reviewing the agenda. It is always helpful to know in advance the purpose of a meeting and the topics to be discussed. If you received a summary or minutes from a previous meeting, review the document before going to the current meeting. Finally, remind yourself why you are attending.

Be Participatory

To participate means to contribute or take part—to become involved. Be an active listener—pay careful attention to what is said and make eye contact with the person leading the meeting and each person who speaks. Avoid distracting or annoying the other people at the meeting by participating in side conversations.

Direct your full attention to the items on the agenda. Taking notes during a meeting is essential. As the meeting unfolds, write down questions or comments as you think of them. This is your chance to get answers and express your opinions. You may find it helpful to write comments on the agenda. If your comments are directly related to one of the topics of the meeting, wait for an opening and ask your questions or share your ideas with everyone. If your comments are only indirectly related to the meeting agenda items, keep them to yourself and address them with the appropriate person after the meeting.

FOLLOWING UP

Your responsibility as a meeting participant does not end when the meeting adjourns. Review your notes to make sure you understand the key information presented at the meeting. Also note any actions you agreed to take.

Jane reviewed her notes at the end of the committee meeting. She promised to do three things: contact the retirement office to get the names and addresses of recently retired employees, reserve the pavilion at the city park for July 28, and draft a survey to send to employees asking what activities they would like available at this year's picnic. By the end of the workday on Wednesday, Jane had completed her follow-up actions.

Review these tips before you attend a meeting:

- Be alert; look confident and interested.
- Be courteous to other participants and to the leader.
- Be respectful of the thoughts, ideas, and opinions of others.
- Be willing to share your ideas.
- Don't interrupt the comments of others.
- Don't monopolize the discussion— others have important ideas too.
- Don't make critical remarks about the thoughts and opinions of others.
- Don't be defensive if others don't agree with your ideas.

Tuesday, January 28
3 p.m. in the Cafeteria
Agenda

1. Purpose of Meeting
2. Picnic Theme Selection   *Hawaiian Luau*
3. Date/Time/Picnic Site   *5/23 at 2 p.m. In city park pavilion, will park office to reserve pavilion*

4. Entertainment and Activities   *To be determined*
5. Food   *Roast pig, chicken, and lasagna*
6. Special Invitations   *Call relevant office for recent list of retirees and their addresses*

7. Other   *Draft employee survey on what they want for activities*
8. Next Meeting   *2/12 at 3 p.m. in the cafeteria*

FIGURE 9-1   Follow-up notes written on a meeting agenda.

Figure 9-1 shows how Jane's agenda with her handwritten notes might look after the meeting.

After many meetings, a summary (or, in the case of a formal meeting, the minutes of the meeting) will be distributed. Review the summary or minutes carefully for accuracy, and be sure you understand any actions required of you. If you must take action, set a deadline for completing the action. Keep a record of your follow-up actions and be prepared to report on them at future meetings. If you find an error in the summary or minutes, contact the author and report suggested changes. If another meeting is scheduled, record it on your calendar.

If you participate in an impromptu or stand-up meeting, no summary or minutes will be distributed, but some follow-up will likely be needed. You must rely on yourself to take any actions necessary. In the case of the On the Job hallway conversation between Lee and Paula, Lee would be wise to acknowledge in an e-mail the points agreed upon during their conversation.

"History is written by people who attend meetings, stay until the end, and review the minutes."

checkpoint

1. Why are meetings held? What topics might be discussed at a staff or team meeting?

   _____

   _____

   _____

2. What is the purpose of an ad hoc meeting?

   _____

   _____

   _____

3. What is the difference between a formal and an informal meeting?

_____

_____

_____

4. Why are more workplaces holding electronic meetings?

_____

_____

_____

5. What are the three "BPs" of participating in meetings?

_____

_____

_____

applications

1. Summarize a meeting you recently attended. What type of meeting was it? What was the style of the meeting? What information did you receive before the meeting? What follow-up information did you receive?

_____

_____

_____

2. Why is it important for a city council meeting to be formal? Why is it important to give advance public notice of a city council meeting?

_____

_____

_____

3. Describe an impromptu meeting you have attended at work or at school. What was the purpose? What are the advantages and disadvantages of impromptu meetings?

_____

_____

_____

4. Describe a formal meeting in which you have been involved. How did you prepare for the meeting?

_____

_____

_____

Planning and Conducting Meetings

At some point in your career, you will be responsible for planning and conducting a meeting. Some of the meetings will be informal or small-group meetings. Others may be more formal and involve a larger group. For example, you may call a meeting of your team to bring them up to date on a new procedure. Or, you may be appointed chair of a committee charged with meeting several times to plan an off-site workshop for your department.

Conducting meetings carries with it the responsibility for using people's time to the advantage of the organization. Time—your time and that of those who participate in meetings—is a valuable resource that must be used wisely. Unfortunately, not all meetings are worthwhile experiences. Too many unnecessary or poorly planned meetings are held. These meetings waste everyone's time and accomplish nothing.

This section presents the basics of conducting meetings. It explains how to plan a meeting, determine the participants (including people at remote locations), prepare an agenda, keep the meeting on track, finalize decisions, assign follow-up actions, and summarize a meeting. These actions are important for all meetings—even one-on-one meetings with coworkers. If the thought of conducting a meeting gives you butterflies, the best thing you can do to rid yourself of those butterflies is to plan ahead.

"If you have no confidence in self you are twice defeated in the race of life. With confidence you have won even before you have started."

Controversy is brewing over which employees will be allowed to park in the newly paved parking lot next to the building. The lot has a capacity of 40 cars. On a typical workday about 60 parking spaces are needed. Todd is executive assistant to the company president, Marlene McCall. Ms. McCall asks Todd to get employee input on how to solve the parking problem. She wants two or three suggestions on her desk in ten working days. Todd knows the value of people's time. He conducts an e-mail survey to give everyone an opportunity to state an opinion. This will require just a few moments of their time and save the time and expense of a company-wide meeting. After the surveys are returned, he compiles a list of the suggestions. He eliminates ideas that obviously won't work and lists the others that have potential. Then Todd invites a representative from human resources, sales, marketing, administrative support, and manufacturing to attend a meeting. The purpose of the meeting is to select and fine-tune the two or three ideas that are most realistic. After the meeting, Todd gives these suggestions to Ms. McCall.

What do you think of Todd's decision to use an e-mail survey as a meeting alternative? Why did Todd meet in person with representatives from different areas of the company to select the two or three suggestions to pass along to Ms. McCall?

PLAN THE MEETING

Meetings that produce results begin with planning. A plan is typically any procedure used to reach an objective. You must know where you want to go before you can determine how to get there. After the purpose and objectives of the meeting are apparent, questions about who will attend, where (and when) the meeting will be held, what electronic connections will be needed, and so on will be easier to answer. Planning a meeting has several steps.

Clearly Identify Objectives

Meetings should have one or more clearly identified objectives. As Stephen Covey says in *Seven Habits of Highly Effective People,* "Begin with the end in mind."[5] Review the objectives carefully to confirm that a meeting is the best way to accomplish the goals. A fundamental rule to remember is this: hold meetings only when necessary. Meetings are expensive when you take participants' time into account. Make sure that a meeting is the best way to accomplish your objectives.

The purpose of the meeting will determine the focus of the meeting, the meeting agenda, and the participants.

"Planning is bringing the future into the present so that you can do something about it now."

> *Arunesh leads the marketing team at Gateway Florists. He plans to hold a meeting with a small group before beginning work on a brochure to showcase flower arrangements for Valentine's Day. Arunesh determines that there are four goals for the first meeting: (1) convey the objectives, proposed budget, and timeline for the brochure; (2) assign responsibilities for portions of the brochure; (3) determine which arrangements to include in the brochure; and (4) get a commitment from each participant about their responsibilities for the brochure.*

Determine the Participants

The purpose of the meeting determines who should attend. In some instances, you may need to determine how to connect participants at remote locations electronically.

> *Arunesh reviews the workload of his team of designers and copyeditors. He selects four team members whose schedules permit a new assignment, including a creative designer with special expertise in theme design.*

Determine Time, Place, and Equipment Needed

The time and place of the meeting may depend on the availability of the participants. Think ahead and arrange for any equipment you may need.

> *Arunesh is ready to get down to the specifics of the meeting. He checks the work schedules of the participants and finds they are all available on Thursday afternoon. He reserves the conference room for that time. He decides to run his presentation from his computer and arranges to have a video projector in the room.*

An agenda serves as your outline as you conduct the meeting. It also makes the meeting more productive for everyone because it serves as a checklist to ensure that all the topics are covered. While the agenda for a one-on-one meeting may be a mental list or a few notes jotted on a slip of paper, you still need an agenda.

Arunesh develops the agenda on Friday morning. This helps him think through the meeting and decide on the order in which topics should be discussed and how much time to spend on each topic. He reviews the overall meeting objectives and identifies what the group needs to discuss to accomplish the objectives. On Friday afternoon, Arunesh sends an e-mail to participants asking them to attend a meeting next Thursday from 2:30 p.m. to 3:30 p.m. in the conference room. He explains that the purpose of the meeting is to discuss the Valentine's Day brochure and asks them to look at the attached agenda before the meeting.

An agenda for a formal meeting will be more formal in appearance and include more detail—for example, how much time will be spent on each topic and who will present topics at the meeting.

CONDUCT THE MEETING

Conducting a meeting takes forethought, attention to detail, and good leadership skills. As meeting leader, you should encourage active participation, keep everyone focused on the current topic, and maintain order.

On the day of the meeting, Arunesh is prepared. The conference room is arranged so that everyone can see the pull-down screen, and his computer is connected to the video projector. The meeting objectives are written on the whiteboard, and the agenda is displayed on the screen. Refreshments are available—always a nice touch to make people feel comfortable.

Some guidelines for conducting a meeting follow.

Start On Time

Meetings should start and end on time. Starting and stopping on time shows a respect for everyone's time—including your own. Soon your coworkers will realize that they don't want to be late for your meetings. Welcome the participants and thank them for attending the meeting. Review the agenda, covering the highlights and announcing the anticipated outcomes of the meeting. A formal meeting would include additional opening items such as a roll call, approval of the minutes of the previous meeting, and approval of the agenda for the current meeting. These steps are not typical of an informal meeting.

Enlist the Help of Others

In the online article "How to Run an Effective Meeting," Cyrus Farivar states that meetings run more smoothly when the organizer enlists others to help handle the details. The leader is then able to focus full attention on running the meeting. Involving others is also a good way to engage coworkers who might otherwise stare out the window or pass the time by twiddling with their Blackberry. He suggests the following assignments:

- *Timekeeper:* Makes sure the meeting starts and stops on schedule, reminds facilitator when agenda items are going over their allotted time.
- *Note Taker:* Records actions taken at the meeting and distributes minutes as needed. Minutes should focus on three categories of information: decisions reached, action items that people need to follow up on, and open issues. Be sure to tell participants at the beginning of the meeting if minutes will be distributed.
- *Whiteboard Wrangler:* Writes ideas on the whiteboard during brainstorming sessions, makes sure every idea is recorded, whether or not it seems promising at first glance.[6]

Discuss the Agenda Items

"Talent wins games, but teamwork and intelligence wins championships."

As the leader of the meeting, it is your responsibility to guide the discussion so that the agenda items are covered and the objectives are met. Items should be discussed in the order they appear on the agenda. Open the discussion of the first agenda item. Then move on to the remaining items.

Encourage everyone to contribute. Give everyone who wishes to speak or ask a question the opportunity to do so. If someone isn't contributing, encourage them to speak up. You might say, "Sheila, we haven't heard from you for a while. You always have good ideas. What do you think?" Keep your own comments to a minimum. Your job is to direct the discussion and encourage others to share their ideas and concerns. Including others is especially challenging when some attendees participate electronically from remote sites.

Allow only one person to speak at a time. Do not let a participant dominate the meeting by doing all the talking. This may require a little tact, but it can be accomplished.

Arunesh opened the discussion about which flower arrangements to include in the Valentine's Day brochure. Fritz and Pat speak out at the same time. Arunesh says, "Pat, please continue. Fritz, please hold that thought for a moment." Later Arunesh says, "Fritz, we have

Image Source/Getty Images

Conducting a meeting takes forethought, attention to detail, and good leadership skills.

heard several thoughts from you. You always have great ideas, but let's give others a chance to make suggestions."

Keep the discussion on track. As meeting leader, keep your comments to a minimum, but do not hesitate to clarify statements made by others. At times, a comment that isn't relevant to the topic being discussed will come up. Immediately get the meeting back on track.

Arunesh says, "Pat, we can discuss the St. Patrick's Day brochure at another meeting. Our time is limited so let's get back to the topic at hand."

Maintain order. Even in a small group meeting, it is possible for attendees to lose their focus and begin talking among themselves. These private conversations interfere with the meeting and distract others.

A secondary conversation develops between Alvin and Gabby. Arunesh interrupts and says, "Alvin and Gabby, please share your thoughts with all of us when Pat has finished talking."

CLOSE THE MEETING

Meetings should not just "end." It is important to give thought to the final moments of a meeting. Allow time to summarize actions taken and responsibilities assigned. Evaluate the meeting and decide if a follow-up meeting is needed.

Summarize Actions and Responsibilities

To provide better understanding for all participants, it is useful to summarize the meeting before everyone leaves. People may hear the same things but interpret them differently.

At the close of the meeting, Arunesh reviews the agreed-upon actions and confirms each person's assignments and deadlines. He sets the time for the next meeting and gets a commitment from each person to attend. After checking with Nadine (the assigned note taker), Arunesh tells participants that Nadine will e-mail a summary of the meeting within 24 hours.

Ask for Evaluation Feedback

Set aside the last five minutes to evaluate the meeting. In a small, informal meeting such as the one Arunesh had with members of the marketing staff, he could simply pose a few questions: "Was this meeting worth your time?

Do you feel we made progress? What could have been done to improve the meeting?" In a meeting with many participants, you might ask them to complete a quick survey by responding to a few questions about the meeting. Remember, your goal is to make the next meeting even better than this one. Do not take criticism personally. Refer to your notes or survey results before planning this next meeting.

Finally, conclude the meeting at the stated time. A meeting that runs late may affect other commitments made previously by the participants. There is also a point at which no further discussion is meaningful. Perhaps you've heard the saying that "the mind can absorb only what the seat can endure." Always close on a positive note. Thank the participants again for their time and input.

FOLLOW-UP ACTIVITIES

Follow-up activities after a meeting include sending participants a summary or minutes of the meeting and evaluating the effectiveness of the meeting. The meeting leader also needs to follow up with participants regularly to make sure items requiring action are underway.

Distribute a Summary or Minutes

It is important to e-mail a meeting summary or minutes promptly—ideally within 24 hours. Many people wait for the summary before they tackle their assigned duties.

> *Arunesh reviews the meeting summary that Nadine prepared. He recommends two minor changes and reminds Nadine to e-mail the summary to all participants within 24 hours of the meeting. The summary lists the topics discussed, assignments accepted by each participant, and the deadlines. It also lists the date and time of the next meeting and thanks the attendees for their participation and commitment to the project. He wants everyone to receive the summary while the meeting is still fresh in their minds.*

Evaluate the Effectiveness

Review the feedback you received at the end of the meeting. Then ask yourself: "Was the meeting successful? Did it accomplish my objectives? Did the attendees seem engaged and willing to participate? Is there anything I should do differently next time?" Do not skip this important step—it helps you grow as a meeting planner and can make future meetings even more effective.

Verify That Assigned Duties are Underway

Do not assume that the assigned actions are in progress. Instead, check with each individual and ask for an update. By doing so, you indicate that you are "on top of things" and foster a sense of accountability that makes it "not okay" to show up at the next meeting with action items incomplete.

checkpoint

1. What should a leader consider when planning a meeting?

_____

_____

_____

_____

_____

_____

2. Why is it important for a meeting to begin and end on time?

_____

_____

_____

_____

_____

_____

3. What are the primary responsibilities of a meeting leader?

_____

_____

_____

_____

_____

_____

4. Why is it important to ask participants to evaluate a meeting?

_____

_____

_____

_____

_____

5. Why is it important to send a meeting summary promptly after a
meeting?

_____

_____

_____

_____

applications

1. What are some behaviors and skills required of someone who conducts an effective meeting? With these characteristics in mind, identify someone you feel runs effective meetings. Why did you select this person?

_____

_____

_____

_____

_____

2. Describe a meeting you conducted (or that was conducted by someone else) where one person dominated the meeting. What were the circumstances? What did you (or the meeting leader) say or do to give others the opportunity to speak?

_____

_____

_____

_____

_____

3. Make a list of three groups to which you belong that hold meetings (such as a school club, a civic organization, a group at work, or a professional organization). Categorize each meeting by type, frequency, and style. How effective are the meetings?

_____

_____

_____

_____

_____

4. Why is follow-up to a meeting important regardless of the type of meeting? What follow-up actions should a participant take? What follow-up actions should a meeting leader take?

_____

_____

_____

_____

_____

9 points to remember

Review the following points to determine what you remember from the chapter.

- Meetings have different purposes and are categorized as follows: status, staff or team, management, one-on-one, board, and ad hoc meetings.

- The frequency of meetings depends on the nature and type of meeting. Three types of meeting frequency are one-time, recurring, and series. Meetings are categorized by the style or manner in which they are conducted (informal and formal).

- Planning a formal meeting requires sending an agenda before the meeting, conducting the meeting, and distributing minutes as a record of the meeting.

- Electronic meetings save time, reduce travel costs, and allow staff in remote locations to participate. Electronic meetings include voice and video chatting, teleconferencing, videoconferencing, and web conferencing.

- Your responsibilities as a meeting participant include being present, being prepared, being participatory, and following up on any actions assigned to you.

- Conducting a meeting takes forethought and attention to detail. Guidelines for conducting a meeting include: start on time, stick to the agenda, encourage all participants to share ideas, allow only one person to speak at a time, maintain order, keep the discussion on track, summarize actions taken and assignments given, and evaluate the meeting.

- Send participants a summary within 24 hours. Review the meeting feedback and consider it as you plan future meetings.

How did you do? Did you remember the main points you studied in the chapter?

KEY terms

meeting

staff meeting

status meeting

one-on-one meeting

management meeting

board meeting

board of directors

ad hoc meeting

recurring meeting

series meeting

agenda

minutes

voice and video chatting

teleconferencing

videoconferencing

web conferencing

webinar

Want more activities? Go to **www.cengage. com/careerreadiness/masters** to get started.

CHAPTER activities

1. Observe a community, company, or organization meeting and summarize your thoughts about the meeting. (If you can't attend a "live" meeting, watch one on your community access cable channel.) Was there a public notice of the meeting? Was there an agenda? Did the meeting begin on time? Were the objectives of the meeting obvious? Did the leader cover the agenda items in the order listed? Was there an opportunity for everyone to speak? Was there time for questions? Were any comments made that were not relevant to the discussion items? Did the meeting end on time? Was the meeting a benefit to the community, company, or organization?

   _____

   _____

   _____

   _____

2. For each meeting category, describe a meeting in which you participated or observed. Identify the setting, the group that met, and the goals of the meeting.

   Staff or team meeting

   _____

   _____

   _____

   Status meeting

   _____

   _____

   _____

   _____

One-on-one meeting

_____

_____

_____

Ad hoc meeting

_____

_____

_____

3. Assume you are responsible for planning and conducting a meeting of your class. The purpose is to decide how to distribute the $1,000 your class raised recently. The money will be given to three local charities, which the class must determine. Three volunteers are needed. Each volunteer will contact one of the charities chosen and donate the funds determined by the class. A fourth volunteer is needed to take digital photos of the three charities in operation and prepare a display for the school's community service board. List the topics you will include on the agenda for the meeting.

   _____

   _____

   _____

4. Find examples of at least two agendas. Search the Internet or use examples from community organizations or organizations to which you belong. Share the samples with your classmates. Do all the agendas share certain elements? You may want to collect agenda styles for future use.

   _____

   _____

   _____

CRITICAL *thinking*

CASE 9.1 How to Tell the Tellers

Lori supervises six tellers at Columbia Bank. She isn't comfortable leading a meeting; in fact, she avoids calling meetings. Lori must inform the tellers that they each must work one Saturday per month. She decides to send an e-mail message to inform them of this new requirement. Unfortunately, Lori's e-mail message is confusing, and the tellers have many questions. Who determines which teller will work on which Saturday? Will they get paid overtime? When does this policy start? Inaccurate rumors are soon spreading through the grapevine.

On another matter, several counterfeit $20 bills have been found in the teller drawers. Lori must ask the tellers to watch for counterfeit $20 bills and show them a simple test to spot bad bills. She decides to pass along this information in impromptu meetings with individual tellers. At the end of the day, she can't remember which tellers she talked with and whom she has to approach tomorrow. The next day several more bad bills are found in teller drawers. Some tellers said, "You didn't tell us to look for bad $20 bills." Other tellers counter with "Well, she told me about the bills."

On yet another matter, top management agrees with Lori that the jackets tellers have been issued are outdated and should be replaced. Lori must get suggestions from the tellers about the color and style of the new jackets. Lori thinks to herself, "Well, I'll have to ask them individually. Either that or I'll send out another e-mail."

1. Is Lori communicating effectively with the tellers through her use of e-mail and stand-up meetings? Why or why not?

   _____

   _____

2. How do you think the tellers feel about Lori's ability to communicate information to them?

   _____

   _____

3. Assume that Lori gives in and decides to have a meeting to address the recent issues. Develop an agenda for Lori to use. The meeting is set for tomorrow at 8 a.m. in the bank's conference room. It will last 45 minutes.

   _____

   _____

4. Should Lori distribute the agenda ahead of time? Why or why not?

   _____

   _____

CASE 9.2 Missing Agenda

Cliff opened the weekly staff meeting with the comment, "Let's get this meeting started. This will be a short meeting so we don't need an agenda. Where is Addie?" Eric responds, "She's on a conference call—she'll be about 15 minutes late." Cliff says, "I guess that's okay. We need to talk about the new plant opening in Detroit. Does anyone want to transfer? Um, I don't see any hands. Well, like it or not, several of you will be transferred. [Grumbling is heard in the background.] You also need to know that the plant cafeteria will be closed all next week. Sorry about that. All the serving line equipment is being replaced and a new oven is being installed. The cafeteria may reopen the following week—or maybe the week after that." [Harry and Deon are talking in the back of the room.] Cliff says, "You guys in the back—knock it off. I'm talking." Addie walks into the room. Cliff says, "Well, Addie. It's about time." Addie replies angrily, "So, what, if anything, have I missed?" Cliff says, "If you want a transfer to Detroit, see me. And the cafeteria is closing next week." Addie says, "Why would anyone want to transfer to Detroit? Why is the cafeteria closing?" Cliff replies, "See Eric after the meeting—he can fill you in."

Cliff continues, "Okay, moving to a new topic. We need volunteers to move to the packing section next week. Do any of you want to volunteer?" Leon says, "I'm certainly not going to volunteer. The people in packing aren't very friendly. I don't want to work there." Cliff says, "I repeat—do I have any volunteers?" Yolanda says, "I'll go, but I have a few questions. Are their hours any different? Is the hourly rate the same?" Cliff says, "Thanks for volunteering, Yolanda. I'll get the answers to your questions as soon as I get a free moment. That's it. Get back to work, everybody!"

1. Was Cliff correct when he said an agenda was not necessary for this meeting? Why or why not?

_____

_____

_____

2. What rules of conducting a meeting did Cliff fail to follow?

_____

_____

3. Was this meeting necessary? Why or why not? What information was actually communicated?

_____

_____

4. What follow-up actions are needed as a result of the meeting?

_____

_____

Workplace Focus

Michael Hu is a financial analyst for the Health Alliance of Greater Cincinnati. Michael supports hospital finance staff by using software tools to collect, maintain, and analyze data.

For Michael, preparation is key to being successful and reducing on-the-job stress. "Everyone has his or her own work and organizational style. Figure out the approach that works best for you and tackle projects with your own customized plan. Calendars and task lists can help prioritize your work and increase efficiency. If you let it, working with a diverse team can teach you new methods and approaches to work and life. Encourage and embrace a diverse environment to become a better team member and individual."

"Client satisfaction should always be your top responsibility," advises Michael. "Their satisfaction or dissatisfaction correlates directly to your job proficiency and the organization's image. I take a personal stake in my work and our clients' satisfaction, and that motivates me to excel even more."

Michael balances hard work with post-work recreation. "Having activities you look forward to outside of work lets you unwind and is very healthy for your sanity. In my case, I schedule evening rock climbing or cycling two or three times a week. By planning ahead, I can flow from work to play and focus on the exercise at hand."

Applying Critical Work Skills

killerb10/iStockphoto.com

Think About It: Sonya arrives at Topco Electric a few minutes early. She hangs up her coat, pours herself a cup of coffee, logs on to her computer, and uses the first few minutes of her morning to plan the day. She views her To Do list and organizes the

What do you think about Sonya's system of organizing her day? Does she use her time well? How does Sonya's early morning planning help her to avoid stress?

items in the order of importance. She reviews her e-mail to see if additional items should be added to today's priorities. An e-mail from Helen, her supervisor, requires her to make two phone calls.

Sonya adds the calls to her To Do list. She checks her electronic calendar to see what meetings or appointments are scheduled for today, pulls documents that she will need for the meetings, and finds the telephone numbers needed for today's work. She organizes her desk and checks to make sure that the copier, printer, and fax machines are loaded with paper. Many interruptions take her in different directions during the day, but she takes each interruption in stride, deals with it, and then returns to her planned list of tasks. She checks off each task as she completes it. At the end of the day, Sonya straightens up her workspace and takes a final look at the To Do list. She moves any incomplete or delayed tasks to her list for the next day.

10.1 Self-Management Tools

10.2 Efficient Work Habits

10.3 Public Speaking

objectives

After completing this chapter, you should be able to:

1. Develop and apply time-management skills.
2. Understand the importance of balancing life and work.
3. Practice techniques for reducing stress and anger.
4. Develop skills for effective decision making.
5. Take steps to develop your creativity.
6. Use technology effectively and safely.
7. Develop the skills necessary to speak before a group.

Self-Management Tools

Preparing for a job and a career includes developing self-management skills that enable you to complete tasks independently and take an active role in monitoring and reinforcing your own behavior. These value-added skills tell your employer that you have efficient work habits.

If you have good self-management skills, your life and work are well organized. This means that your behavior is disciplined and directed toward clearly defined goals. You have the motivation and the ability to be orderly, efficient, and systematic in your work life and personal life. This section will help you manage your time, balance life and work, and manage stress and anger.

TIME MANAGEMENT

Many people spend their days in a frenzy of activity but achieve very little because they are concentrating on "being busy" rather than focusing on getting results. If you were to ask supervisors and managers to identify the most important efficiency factor, most would choose time management. **Time management** refers to planning and using the hours and minutes of a workday in the most effective and efficient manner possible to complete specific assignments, projects, and goals.

"There are a million ways to lose a work day, but not even a single way to get it back."

Time is a valuable resource that you must learn to use wisely. You may know how to manage money. What is so different about managing time? Money lost can be earned back; however, time once spent is gone forever. Time management requires practice; and with practice, you can improve your skill. Some time-management techniques follow.

Get Organized

Disorganization can be a major time waster and lead to inefficiency, thereby reducing productivity and increasing costs. Searching for the paper you just had in your hands, shifting from one project to another, and missing deadlines are all signs of a disorganized person.

The ability to organize is a key factor in time management. Start by organizing your workspace so that you can work efficiently and productively. Everything you use on a daily basis should be nearby. Place your telephone, computer components, and reference materials within easy reach. Eliminate clutter from your workstation surface area. Put materials and supplies that you use infrequently close by in a drawer, on a shelf, or in a supply cabinet. Everything at your workstation should have a place and be in its place.

Analyze How You Spend Your Time

How do you spend your time? Keep a written record of what you do and how much time is used so you can determine whether you are using your time effectively. First, create a time-use log by listing time intervals (15-minute intervals seem to work best) down the left side of a sheet of paper. Record all activities in the log—time spent returning telephone calls, reading and responding to e-mails, attending meetings, etc. Don't forget to record lunch and break time. You may opt to keep the log for a day, a week, or longer. The longer you keep the log, the more representative it will be of how you spend your time.

When your log is complete, analyze the results. Ask yourself these questions:

1. During what time of the day was I most productive? When was I least productive?

2. What caused me to lose or waste time?

3. Are certain times during the day peak or slack work periods?

Everyone has a "best time." If you are a morning person and do your best work before lunch, try to manage your schedule to keep mornings free for the most important work. If you find that you tend to waste time about 3:00 each afternoon, you might schedule your afternoon break at that time. Once you have identified your peak and slack work periods, you can plan ahead. To accommodate a peak period, think ahead to tasks you can complete before the peak period hits so you can focus on the most important work during that time. Use slack periods to catch up on tasks that do not have deadlines but must be done.

Prioritize Your To Do List

Take five or ten minutes at the beginning or end of the workday to do your planning. Creating a To Do list (either on the computer or by hand) is an excellent way to organize your time, tackle the right things first, and ensure that you don't forget any essential tasks.

Making the list is an essential first step; prioritizing the To Do list is also important. Focusing on the task at hand and putting other tasks at the margin of your concern is essential if you're going to work productively. Without prioritizing, you may work very hard, but you won't achieve the necessary results because you are not completing the tasks in priority order. Unfortunately, people tend to complete first

TO DO LIST
MONDAY, MARCH 23

Priority	Item	Completed X = done F = forwarded
A-3	Order office supplies before 10:30 a.m.	
A-1	Call service company to repair laser printer.	
B-2	Make plane reservation for trip to New Orleans next month.	
B-3	Arrange for car rental in New Orleans.	
C-1	Archive last year's copies of sales agreements with vendors.	
A-2	Key agenda for tomorrow's staff meeting; e-mail team the agenda and reminder about tomorrow's 1 p.m. meeting in Conference Room A	
A-2	Key expense reimbursement documents for Ellis and Cathy and submit them to accounting.	
B-1	Reserve conference room for next month's staff meeting.	

FIGURE 10-1 Sample To Do list at the beginning of the workday.

the tasks they enjoy or that seem the easiest, but these tasks may not be the most important ones. Your goal should be to work smarter, not harder.

There are many styles of To Do lists so find the one that best works for you. Create your own or download a template from sites such as Mindtools. com. Figure 10-1 shows a sample To Do list. Notice that tasks have been assigned a priority of A, B, or C. The A-level tasks are those that need immediate attention or completion. Tackle B-level tasks after the A-level ones are completed. C-level tasks have no specific deadline and are completed last. You may find it helpful to further prioritize the list by assigning 1, 2, 3 etc. within each priority level. For example, calling the service company to repair the laser printer is identified as the A-level task to complete first because the printer being out of service affects everyone in the department.

To determine the priority of the tasks, ask yourself:

- How important is this task? If you have too many A tasks, decide which is most important. Determine the difference between "important" and "urgent."
- Is there a deadline? What will happen if this task isn't completed on time?
- Do I need input from others to complete this task?
- Can the task be broken down into manageable chunks?
- How much time will it take to complete this task? You cannot use time wisely unless you can predict how much time you need to complete a given task.

If you keep your To Do list on the computer, consider organizing the list with the most important tasks at the top, preferably in red font. If necessary, discuss your priorities with your supervisor. Once you have set your priorities, keep the list accessible and check it frequently. Follow through by completing the tasks in priority order and checking them off as you go.

Develop a Workable Schedule

After you prioritize the items on your To Do list, the next step is to schedule each item. Consider this your action plan. **Scheduling** is the process by which you plan the use of your time and set deadlines for completing tasks. It is best to schedule on a regular basis—at the beginning of the week, for example. When you schedule effectively, you reduce stress and maximize your efficiency.

Alicia must complete an important project by Friday morning. On Monday morning, she schedules a two-hour block of time each day (Monday through Thursday) to work on the project. By Thursday morning, she notes that the project is almost finished. She'll make her deadline with time to spare!

Using a printed schedule (kept on the computer or in a daily, weekly, or monthly planner) to plan and monitor your activities helps you make the best use of your time. Check off each task as you complete it. However, do not become a slave to the schedule. Unexpected demands will occasionally take your time.

Control Large Projects

It is sometimes difficult to start working on a large project—even though that project may be important. For example, you may put off gathering the tax information needed by the person who prepares your taxes. Rather than trying to do all the work at once, divide the large project into smaller tasks and begin with a simple task to get the momentum going. Day one, call the tax preparer and set up an appointment. Day two, pull together your income statements. Day three, list your expenses and divide them by categories, and so on. Soon you will have organized the information and be ready to meet with the tax preparer.

Watch Out for Time Wasters

If you are aware of events in your day that are not productive, you may be able to gain additional minutes or hours by eliminating these time wasters. Check out the following time wasters.

"We all have our 'good old days' tucked away inside our hearts, and we return to them in daydreams like cats to favorite armchairs."

Visitors. Coworkers who drop by to chat can be one of the worst time wasters. If you have a door that you can close, do so. Others will get the message that you are busy. If you work in an open area, you might tell colleagues in a friendly tone of voice, "I really must get back to work. Maybe we could discuss this at lunch."

Phone calls. Phone calls can interrupt your work. Try setting aside a time each day to make and return phone calls.

Leaving your workstation. Leaving your work area often leads to unplanned conversations with coworkers that distract you from your intended destination and waste time, especially when workers want to talk about the latest reality TV show. Be ready with a response for those who just want to talk.

Daydreaming. It happens to everyone now and then. Your mind wanders to something else—to something more enjoyable or to a nagging problem. This causes you to lose concentration and your productivity slips. When this occurs, take appropriate action. If you are daydreaming about what you plan to do later, force yourself to regain focus on the task. If the daydreaming involves a problem, take an action step toward resolving the problem.

E-mail and Internet. E-mail can be a classic time waster. Responding to e-mails the moment they arrive decreases your efficiency and causes you to lose your concentration. Set a time each day to read and send e-mail rather than interrupting your work each time a message arrives. Surfing the Internet can also use up significant chunks of work time. Confine your surfing to job-related tasks and do your personal surfing on your own time.

Misplaced items. How often do you waste time looking for a misplaced key, a folder, or a cell phone? Items that you frequently misplace should have a specific "place" and be in that place when they are not being used.

False starts. Avoid false starts by having an overall understanding of each task and assignment. Make sure you completely understand what you are to do and how to do it. Assemble all the information and supplies you will need before beginning your task.

Stop Procrastinating

Procrastinating or delaying an action to a later time is a major drain on productivity. Perhaps you have already learned from experience that putting things off provides only a temporary feeling of relief. Everyone procrastinates at one time or another. The key is to recognize when you are procrastinating and take action to remedy the situation. The causes of procrastination vary—disorganization (the scope of a project has you feeling overwhelmed), fear (what if you don't do a good job or what if you don't meet your deadline?), or lack of enthusiasm for the task (purging files, for example). Try these techniques for dealing with procrastination.

©Andresr, 2009/Used under license from Shutterstock.com

Where is my cell phone? Hunting for misplaced items is a waste of valuable time.

Make promises to others. You may find it easier to do unpleasant assignments by assuring others that the work will be done. You may be willing to disappoint yourself by procrastinating, but you won't let others down or be embarrassed by not meeting a goal or deadline. For example, you announce to your team that the vacation schedule will be posted on a specific day. You don't want to disappoint them, so you make an extra effort to post the schedule on time.

Attack the task. Attack the task and prove to yourself that it was not as difficult as you had feared. The next time you catch yourself saying, "I don't want to do this now—I can do this later," push away the negative feelings and just do it!

Evan had procrastinated all day about keying the minutes from a long meeting held earlier in the week, but he knew he was running out of time. First, he made a conscious decision to begin. He referred to his notes and handout materials from the meeting. When he was sure he had all the materials needed, he keyed the minutes. Much to his surprise, the dreaded task was not as bad as he had anticipated.

Make a contract with yourself. Agree to reward yourself with an activity you like or an item you want after you accomplish the task. The flip side of this agreement is that you must accept a "punishment" if you don't accomplish the task (no chocolate for a week, for example).

Kicking the procrastination habit may take some time. However, the satisfaction of knowing you can complete difficult or dreaded tasks will provide a great sense of accomplishment and may motivate you to ignore future temptations to procrastinate.

Take Care When Multitasking

Quite simply, **multitasking** is attempting to do more than one task at a time. It has become common practice to check or send text messages while at a ballgame or to read e-mail while talking on the phone. But is multitasking a skill you want to acquire? Maybe, or maybe not.

Advocates of multitasking would lead us to believe that doing two things at once allows us to accomplish more. However, not everyone is an advocate for multitasking, nor is multitasking always appropriate. Studies show that negative consequences can occur when someone attempts two activities that require creativity or analytical ability. Dr. David Meyer, director of the Brain, Cognition and Action Laboratory at the University of Michigan, says, "The bottom line is that you can't simultaneously be thinking about your tax return and writing a report, just as you can't talk to yourself about two things at once."[1] Each time you switch your attention, you lose focus. However, multitasking may produce positive results for simple, routine tasks that do not require a good deal of concentration.

> *Cynthia was able to multitask while waiting for her computer to finish backing up her files. Once she started the backup function, no action other than monitoring was needed until the backup was complete. During that time, she was able to file hard copy documents.*

Deacon is the assistant manager of a supermarket. His goal is to manage one of the large stores in the chain within three years. He works extremely hard and tries to learn everything he can by observing others, asking questions, and searching the Internet for articles on management. After one year, he is recognized as the "employee of the year." He is thrilled. In his eagerness to continue to climb the success ladder, he puts in voluntary overtime, offers to help coworkers in all departments, provides special services for customers, and designs a "green" program for disposing of cartons and pallets. Deacon ignores the fact that he hasn't taken any vacation time in the last year. Some nights he is unable to sleep because he is thinking about work. He is losing weight, feels tense, and his stomach is frequently upset. His friends and family are concerned about him.

What could be causing Deacon's physical symptoms? If you were Deacon's friend, what advice would you offer?

Dr. Fortgang recommends this exercise to determine what matters most to you. Think very carefully before answering each question:

1. If my life could focus on one thing and one thing only, what would that be?
2. If I could add a second thing, what would that be?
3. A third?
4. A fourth?
5. A fifth?

If the questions are answered thoughtfully and honestly, the result will be a list of your top five priorities. The key is not just knowing your priorities, but dedicating your full attention to just one priority at a time.[2]

BALANCING LIFE AND WORK

Balancing the many demands of work, family, friends, and personal interests can be a challenge. However, achieving balance is important as it provides peace of mind and energy for each aspect of your life. Spending too many hours on the job without counterbalancing your work with some personal time may cause you to experience burnout and decrease your job satisfaction.

"You must master your time rather than becoming a slave to the constant flow of events and demands on your time."

Determine what really matters to you. Laura Berman Fortgang, an author in the field of personal or life coaching, says, ". . . getting your priorities clear is the first and most essential step toward achieving a well-balanced life. The important point here is to figure out what you want your priorities to be, not what you think they should be."[2] Your goal is to maintain balance in your life so that you are thinking about work when you are at work and about your racquetball strategy when you are on the court. Take time now to complete the Apply It! exercise in this section to determine what matters most to you.

Eliminate unnecessary activities. Once you establish your priorities, eliminate those that didn't make your list as a top concern. Unnecessary activities keep you away from things that matter most to you.

One of Hector's top priorities was to spend time with his son. He enjoyed playing catch with Jake on Saturdays and taking him for ice cream afterward. When his buddies called to ask him to play golf on Saturday, Hector had his priorities straight. He thanked them for the invitation but declined.

Let others help. Others can help you balance your life. Tag team with coworkers—"I'll work this weekend if you will work for me next weekend."

Ask friends and family members to help free up time to take care of your top priorities.

Plan time for you. Build time for yourself into your schedule. These are stress-free periods when you can relax and restore the balance of a busy lifestyle. If you believe that a relaxing activity is important in life, make the time for it and let go of any guilt you have about taking time for yourself.

STRESS MANAGEMENT

How do you feel when your car won't start? When you are at the airport and your coat is on the back seat of the friend's car that brought you there? Chances are you feel stressed. Stress is a simple word with many definitions. A practical way of defining **stress** is the feeling you get from prolonged, unexpressed emotions. Positive emotions do not cause stress because you can express them openly. Negative emotions, however, are often hidden and internalized, thereby causing you to suffer quietly and experience stress.

Prolonged stress can affect your productivity on the job and devastate your health. Stress raises the level of the hormone adrenaline, which can increase your heart rate, respiration, and blood pressure. The more you try to hold your emotions inside, the more the pressure builds up. It is almost impossible to insulate your personal life from work stress. If you are under stress at work, it is difficult to maintain positive and upbeat feelings with your family and friends. Similarly, stress in your personal life is bound to have a negative impact at work.

Photodisc/Getty Images

Keep stress under control by redirecting your thoughts to something more pleasant and relaxing.

Common Causes of Stress

There are many causes of stress. Some *stressors* (factors that create the stress in life) can be eliminated and others must be dealt with as a part of life. With practice, you can learn to survive the emotional down times without allowing stress to overwhelm you. You can also eliminate or reduce controllable stress factors such as running late, procrastinating, or not getting enough sleep.

"Stress is like an iceberg. We can see only an eighth of it above, but what about what's below?"

Everyday events. A few frustrating experiences throughout the day can build up and cause stress. At home, the air conditioning quits or the dog chews your favorite slippers. Common workplace stressors include tight deadlines, conflicting priorities, changing job responsibilities, and conflict with coworkers. In contrast, sometimes not having enough work can create stress. No matter where you work, you will experience some stress.

Life's transitions. Even positive experiences such as an upcoming marriage, a promotion, or moving to a new home can be stressful, especially when you must cope with too many changes at once.

Dwayne is pleased that he is being considered for a promotion to branch manager, but his mother is ill, and he feels responsible for her care. The promotion, if he gets it, will require that he relocate to a branch 65 miles from home. The possible promotion, his mother's illness, and a possible move cause him excessive stress.

Personal finances. Managing your finances can be troublesome regardless of your income level, but it is especially difficult if you must support others. Unpaid bills, misuse of credit, and budget limitations can make life difficult.

Serious situations. Serious circumstances cause stress. Examples are separation from loved ones, job loss, personal illness, or the illness or death of someone close to you. The list goes on.

Understanding the cause of your stress and accepting the fact that you are under stress is important. This may sound obvious, but it requires a deliberate, conscious effort to pause and ponder your situation. Recognize the warning signs of stress and vow to deal with them. Several warning signs are given in the Stress Signals feature box.

"The greatest weapon against stress is our ability to choose one thought over another."

Techniques for Dealing with Stress

With practice, you can build relaxation and stress management into your lifestyle to counterbalance the routine unpleasantness and dangers of stress that you cannot avoid. Several suggestions follow.

Get regular exercise. A healthy body is an excellent weapon to combat stress. A full-blown exercise program can "burn up" the tension that builds in your body during a long period of stress. Activities such as walking, playing tennis, running, and yoga can help you offset the effects of too much stress before it harms you. Many companies offer health and wellness programs designed to maintain and improve employee health. Others support employee wellness by providing an on-site gym or paying a portion of the fee to join a fitness center.

Be easy on yourself. Learn to accept what you cannot change and change those things that are under your control. Do not expect perfection in yourself or in others. Strive to improve yourself, of course, but ask yourself if you are aiming at the reasonable or the impossible.

Stress has a way of creeping into your life and before you know it, you are "stressed out." Here are some common stress signals to watch for as you work to balance life and work.

- Impulsive, irrational behavior
- Frequent headaches
- Insomnia, fitful sleeping
- Anxiety
- Tension in shoulders, neck, and back
- Persistent low energy
- Irregular pulse rate (racing pulse)
- Mood swings
- Inability to concentrate
- Frequent flu or colds
- Increased absenteeism
- Reduced human interaction

STRESS SIGNALS

Take a break. If you have been working too hard for too long, you may find it helpful to "get away from it all." Unfortunately, most of us cannot afford an exotic two-week vacation in the Bahamas, but you can redirect your thoughts to something pleasant and relaxing to "recharge your batteries."

Use stress reducers. Some easy ways to relieve stress are shown in Figure 10-2. Try them to see how well they work for you.

EASY STRESS REDUCERS

1. Sit up straight. Slouching restricts breathing and blood flow and can increase feelings of helplessness. Sitting up straight improves your breathing and gets more oxygen to your brain.
2. Try some simple neck rotating exercises. First rotate to the left and then to the right. Drop your chin. Try this with your eyes closed.
3. Get up periodically and stretch if your job requires you to sit for long periods of time.
4. Drink more water. Because you perspire more when you are stressed, you are left feeling dehydrated. A couple of eight-ounce glasses of water will help.
5. Talk it out. Discussing problems with a trusted friend or counselor can help clear your mind of confusion so you can concentrate on problem solving.
6. Use your lunch break to get away from your work area in body *and* mind.

FIGURE 10-2 Use these techniques to reduce stress.

ANGER MANAGEMENT

Anger is a normal human emotion. But when it gets out of control and turns destructive, it can lead to problems at work, in your personal relationships, and in your life in general. External and internal events can evoke anger. Your anger may be directed at a person (coworker, friend, or supervisor) or an event (traffic jam, delayed flight, or a computer problem).

There are two kinds of anger—passive anger and aggressive anger. **Passive anger** is anger that "slowly burns in your heart." This type of anger usually evolves into pure vindictiveness and often is expressed in secretive or obsessive behavior, manipulation, or self-blame. **Aggressive anger** is anger that explodes quickly on the spot and often is displayed as a threatening outburst.

Anger management refers to the ability of a person to control his/her temperament, particularly in stressful situations. To manage anger, you first must recognize the anger within you, acknowledge how it harms both you and others, and appreciate the benefits of being patient in the face of difficulties. Then apply practical methods to control your reactions, reduce anger, and ultimately to prevent anger.

Reactions to Anger

Three ways in which people react to anger are expressing, suppressing, and calming.

Expressing. People naturally become angry and act aggressively to defend themselves in situations that threaten their survival. But you cannot express anger toward every person or event that annoys you. Yelling, throwing things, and slamming doors are not acceptable reactions to such situations—and they are *never* acceptable in the workplace.

Suppressing. When you suppress anger, you hold it in, stop thinking about it, or try to focus on something else. Over time, anger that is bottled up can lead to physical symptoms such as headaches or hypertension or cause you to get back at others indirectly.

Calming. Tell yourself to calm down. When you make an effort to be calm, you control your outward behavior (aggressive actions or words) and your internal responses, thereby lowering your heart rate, calming down, and letting the negative feelings go away.

Techniques for Dealing with Anger

There are techniques you can use to reduce anger and help you deal with the unsettling situations that are a normal part of life. With practice, you can control your actions, reduce feelings of anger, and channel the emotions into positive behavior. Many emotional reactions result from failure to accept things (and people) as they are. Figure 10-3 shows calming techniques recommended by the Mayo Clinic. Try them to see how well they work for you.

Do you show symptoms of anger management problems? Dr. David Burns, author of *The Feeling Good Handbook*, identifies the following symptoms of anger.[3]

- Explosive outbursts leading to physical attack or destruction of property.
- Exaggerated hostility to unimportant irritants.
- Rapid and harsh judgment statements made to or about others.
- Use of body language such as tense muscles, clenched fist or jaw, glaring looks, or refusal to make eye contact.
- Social withdrawal due to anger.
- Refusing to complete assignments on timely basis.
- Refusing to follow instructions or rules.
- Complaining about authority figures behind their back.
- Refusing to participate in activities when this behavior is expected.
- Authority is challenged or disrespected.
- Verbal abusive language is utilized.

ANGER MANAGEMENT TECHNIQUES[4]

- Take a "time out." Counting to 10 before reacting, or leaving the situation altogether, can defuse your temper.
- Do something physically exerting. Physical activity can provide an outlet for your emotions, especially if you're about to erupt.
- Practice deep-breathing exercises, visualize a relaxing scene, or repeat a calming word or phrase to yourself, such as "take it easy."
- Don't hold a grudge. Forgive the other person. It's unrealistic to expect everyone to behave exactly as you want.
- Practice relaxation skills. Learning skills to relax and de-stress can also help control your temper when it may flare up.
- Use assertive communication rather than aggressive behavior.

FIGURE 10-3 Techniques for managing anger.

checkpoint

1. Identify five techniques for managing time.

_____

_____

_____

_____

_____

_____

2. Explain why it is important to plan and prioritize your day.

_____

_____

_____

_____

_____

3. Why is it important to balance life and work?

_____

_____

_____

_____

_____

_____

4. List four techniques for reducing stress.

_____

_____

_____

_____

_____

_____

5. List five techniques for dealing with anger.

_____

_____

_____

_____

_____

_____

applications

1. Identify key time wasters at home, at school, and at work and explain how you could deal with each one.

_____

_____

_____

_____

_____

2. Create a To Do list of eight things you want to accomplish this week that are related to school, work, and/or your personal life. Use a rating system like the one in Figure 10-1 on page 226.

_____

_____

_____

_____

_____

3. Describe situations in your personal or work life in which you multi-task. Are your multitasking efforts successful? Why or why not?

_____

_____

_____

_____

4. Describe two recent situations that caused you to feel stressed. What physical symptoms did you experience? How did you manage the stress?

_____

_____

_____

_____

5. Describe a recent situation that made you angry. How did you react? Were you able to control your emotions? If so, what technique did you use? If not, what might you do differently the next time you face a similar situation?

_____

_____

_____

_____

Efficient Work Habits

As a family member or an employee, you are expected to "carry your own weight" or, in other words, to do your fair share of the work. Your supervisor and coworkers count on you to assist in daily tasks, decision making, and problem solving. Further, you will be expected to think creatively and use technology efficiently and safely. Remember, you want to work smarter, not harder.

This section will help you understand the decision-making process and present techniques to help you make wise decisions. You will also learn how to think more creatively and use technology responsibly.

MAKING DECISIONS AND SOLVING PROBLEMS

Decision making and problem solving are interrelated. Effective decisions must be made if problems are to be solved satisfactorily. The decisions you make will vary in importance. Some decisions are easy—"What should I wear to class today?" Other decisions take more thought—"Who should I hire for the open position?"

Decision making is the part of the problem-solving process that involves selecting one course of action from several possible alternatives. For example, you decide what to wear to class by considering the alternatives—"I could wear my jeans with the red shirt, the blue pullover, or the striped shirt." You also eliminate other alternatives—the black shirt needs laundering and the tan shirt isn't ironed, etc. Your decision about what to wear to class is based on a study of the available alternatives. Even if you decide to do nothing, you are making a decision. A decision left unmade will result in a "decision by default" or a decision being made for you.

"No trumpets sound when the important decisions of life are made. Destiny is made known silently."

> *Carla's cell phone contract is up, and she is entitled to a new phone if she signs a new two-year contract. At the store, she is amazed at how many models there are. Does she want a cell phone with a digital camera? A speakerphone? Should it be Bluetooth® enabled? What about removable memory? All the choices are too confusing so she decides to do nothing. "No problem," says the sales agent. We'll put you on a monthly contract. That will give you time to make up your mind."*

Uncertainty and Risk

Decision making involves reducing uncertainty and doubt about alternatives. Note that uncertainty is only reduced, not eliminated. Very few decisions can be made with absolute certainty because complete knowledge about all alternatives is seldom possible. Every decision involves some element of uncertainty and risk.

The ideal moment to make a decision is when all accurate information and all possible alternatives are known, and you have unlimited time to make a decision. However, the likelihood of having all the information and time you need is slim. For example, you want to fill your gas tank at the lowest possible price. There are 35 gas stations in your area. Are you going to spend time and your remaining gas checking out all of the alternatives? No, you would likely check out a few stations and fill up at the one offering the best price at the time.

Do you gain anything by delaying a decision? Maybe, or maybe not. Delaying a decision may be a good idea for several reasons: (1) more information may become available, (2) a new alternative may present itself, or (3) your preferences might change. But delaying is not always beneficial. Think about the example of the gas stations. You could run out of gas checking all the alternatives!

Information for Decision Making

You need adequate information to make an informed decision. However, you can become overloaded with information and problems can result. Perhaps you shopped for a digital camera only to find that there were so many alternatives that you couldn't make a choice—and you left the store with nothing. Accumulating too much information can actually diminish the chances for a quality decision.

Your goal should be to consciously select and utilize the information you gather. Make sure you have the necessary, accurate information to make a decision, but eliminate unneeded information. Don't overanalyze the information. Consider each workable alternative and then move on.

"Stay committed to your decisions but stay flexible in your approach."

Briggs is a chain of department stores located throughout the Midwest. Marco is the buyer for the menswear department and goes to the buyers' market each year. He views the selection of winter coats and chooses several styles that he believes will appeal to his customers. As winter temperatures are typically very cold in the cities where the stores are located, he selects coats for warmth as well as style. He reviews last year's sales and finds that very few coats remained for the sales at the end of the season. In fact, several stores tried to order more coats late in the season. Marco decides to increase the total coat order by 10 percent. Winter begins—and coat sales are very slow because the weather is unseasonably mild. The heavy coats remain on the racks and then go on sale for huge discounts at the end of the season. Marco made a decision based on his knowledge, experience, and facts, but the outcome wasn't what he expected.

What do you think about Marco's decision? Would you have made the same decision? Why or why not?

Consequences of Decisions

You gather information, examine alternatives, and make a choice without thinking about previous decisions made by others that created the current situation. But all decisions have far reaching consequences. The decisions made by others often influence the decisions you can make in a situation. Your decisions will affect decisions that others will make.

Frieda goes into her favorite electronics store to buy a digital video recorder. She can buy one of the five models stocked by the store. There may be 40 models of DVRs available, but her alternatives have already been limited by the store's decision to carry five models.

Methods of Decision Making

Some techniques for making decisions are relatively simple, while others are more methodical. An easy way to make a decision is to list the advantages and disadvantages of each alternative. You need to buy a new bicycle so you list the pros and cons of buying each model (bicycle A or bicycle B). After reviewing your list, you decide to buy bicycle B because it has the most advantages. Although this method will work effectively in some cases, in other situations it may be helpful to carry the process a step further and weight the advantages and disadvantages, because some may be more important than others.

Gabriel must decide which laptop to buy (laptop A or laptop B). He writes "Laptop A" at the top left side of a sheet of paper and "Laptop B" at the top right. Down the left side he lists the factors to be rated (memory, size of hard drive, color choice, weight, cost, etc.). He decides on a 5-point scale, with a 5 being the highest rating. Laptop A has 4 GB of memory, which, to Gabriel, is worth 5 points. Laptop B has only 2 GB of memory so he rates it a 3. Laptop A has a 500 GB hard drive, which he rates a 5. Laptop B has a 320 GB hard drive, which he rates a 4. He continues in this manner until he has rated all the factors. Based on the ratings, he decides to buy Laptop A.

A more structured approach to decision making is shown in Figure 10-4. You may find the sequential steps of this method helpful. Note that these steps are similar to the problem-solving steps described in Section 8-2.

Step 1. Identify the goal together with the decision to be made. For example, your goal is to have a relaxing vacation away from work. You need to decide where to go.

Step 2. Get the facts. How much money can you spend on a vacation? How many vacation

EIGHT-STEP DECISION-MAKING PROCESS

1. Identify the goal and the decision to be made.
2. Get the facts.
3. Identify the alternatives.
4. Rate each alternative.
5. Rate the risk of each alternative.
6. Make your decision based on the goal, facts, alternatives, and risks involved.
7. Implement the decision.
8. Evaluate the outcome of your decision.

FIGURE 10-4 Steps in the problem-solving and decision-making process.

days do you have? Are you going to drive or fly? Where would you like to go? Will you spend your entire vacation in one place?

Step 3. Identify the alternatives. Write down possible choices. Gather information on each vacation spot that you want to consider. For example, you might list Fort Lauderdale, Hawaii, and other spots where you feel you could go for a relaxing vacation.

Step 4. Rate each alternative. Consider the good and bad points of each alternative. You might consider cost, time available for travel, method of travel, availability and cost of lodging, vacation packages available, and so on.

Step 5. Rate the risk of each alternative. Every alternative has risks. For example, if you take a vacation during hurricane season, there is a risk of bad weather in Fort Lauderdale. If the trip to Hawaii is costly, future vacations may be at risk.

Step 6. Make your decision based on the goal, facts, alternatives, and risks involved. You may choose Fort Lauderdale because it is the least expensive option offering all the amenities desired. Or, you may decide that you like none of the alternatives. Instead, you might decide to spend the time at home and delay taking a vacation until next year.

Step 7. Implement the decision. If you decided on Fort Lauderdale, you begin by making your lodging and travel arrangements and listing what you need to do before you leave—stop the mail, ask the neighbor to feed the cat, etc. But don't hesitate to "rethink" your decision if a choice isn't working out as planned. For example, you intended to use frequent flyer miles for your airline ticket to Fort Lauderdale. But when you go online to finalize the tickets, you find that you can't get a confirmed flight on the first day of your vacation—you would have to wait until the next day. In which case, you might opt to change your plans.

Step 8. Evaluate the outcome of your decision. Evaluate the outcome of your decision. Ideally, the outcome will prove to be what you expected. You had a relaxing vacation in Fort Lauderdale and all went according to plan. However, outcomes do not always match expectations. The week of your vacation coincided with spring break for hundreds of high-spirited students. Each night was "party time" in the room next door, and the pool was filled with fun-loving young people. You make a mental note to go to the mountains if you ever take another vacation during spring break.

DEVELOPING CREATIVITY

Creativity and imagination are helpful when trying to make decisions, solve problems, or deal with the challenges of everyday life. **Creativity** is the tendency to generate or recognize ideas, alternatives, or possibilities that may be useful in solving problems, communicating with others, and entertaining ourselves.[5] Creative people are problem solvers. Creativity is especially

According to an article that appeared in *Personality Today*, creative individuals have identifiable characteristics.[6]

Creative people:

- Are curious and enjoy a challenge.
- Have a great deal of physical energy, but they are also often quiet and at rest.
- Tend to be optimistic and smart.
- Display a combination of playfulness and discipline, of responsibility and irresponsibility.
- Are comfortable with imagination yet maintain a sense of reality.
- Don't give up easily; they persevere and work hard.
- Are willing to take risks.
- Are very passionate about their work yet can be extremely objective about it as well.

helpful in the workplace, where workers face problems and must make decisions on a daily basis.

What separates the creative person from someone who is not creative? Study the Characteristics of a Creative Personality feature in this section. As you review the characteristics, you will likely conclude that everyone has the capacity to be creative. But it may take time and effort to develop your creativity. Allow yourself to be creative and think beyond the traditional ways of seeing a situation.

Look for Alternatives

When faced with a problem, many people immediately look for a quick solution. Creative people know better. They avoid "vertical thinking," the tendency to look toward one single best answer. The vertical thinker might say, "I need more space—I need to buy a bigger house." The creative thinker, on the other hand, is always looking for alternatives. The creative thinker asks, "How can I get more space in this house? I could have a garage sale to get rid of "stuff" I no longer need. I could convert part of the garage into a storage area. I could finish the basement or add on a room."

Creative thinkers begin by viewing a problem as a creative challenge. If you can turn problems into thought-provoking challenges, your creativity will lead you to solutions. The invention of Post-it® notes is an excellent example of creative thinking.

"A hunch is creativity trying to tell you something."

"In the early 1970s, Art Fry was in search of a bookmark for his church hymnal that would neither fall out nor damage the hymnal. Fry noticed that a colleague at 3M, Dr. Spencer Silver, had developed an adhesive that was strong enough to stick to surfaces, but left no residue after removal and could be repositioned. Fry took some of Dr. Silver's adhesive and applied it along the edge of a piece of paper. His church hymnal problem was solved! Fry soon realized that his "bookmark" had other potential functions when he used it to leave a note on a work file, and coworkers kept dropping by, seeking "bookmarks" for their offices. This "bookmark" was a new way to communicate and to organize. 3M Corporation crafted the name Post-it note for Fry's bookmarks and began production in the late 70s for commercial use."[7]

How Can I Be More Creative?

You want to bring new ideas and be a problem solver, but perhaps you think, "I'm not creative. My ideas are so traditional." The first thing to do is change your thinking. Everyone has the potential to be creative, but some people develop that trait sooner than others. As a child, you likely entertained yourself by being creative. You may have created a "drum" by banging with a spoon on a pan or used blocks of wood to build a "house." Now as an adult, you want to nurture that childhood creativity. With practice, you will find yourself becoming more and more creative. Some suggestions are given here.

Be problem-friendly. Think of a problem as a challenge—not an obstacle. Each problem gives you an opportunity to discover something new or a new way of doing something.

Be optimistic. Trust that there is a solution and do not give up easily. Believe that you can find that solution.

Be curious. Let your mind wander. Ask questions that begin with what, when, why, where, and how. Don't be afraid to question traditional ways of doing things. Look at a procedure and ask, "Is there a better way of doing this?"

Brainstorm by yourself. You learned in Section 8-2 how brainstorming is used in a group setting to generate ideas. The term **brainwriting** is applied to someone who brainstorms alone. Your objective is to identify as many alternatives as you can. Make note of every idea no matter how "far out" it might be. The "out of the box" ideas are sometimes the most creative. Set goals for yourself—"I am going to brainwrite for five minutes and in those five minutes, I am going to list ten ideas." Once the ideas are collected, carefully evaluate the alternatives.

Force yourself to think creatively. Put your mind in training. Make up a problem and write down possible solutions.

Make notes. Always carry a small notebook and a pen or pencil (or use your smartphone). When you get an idea, quickly make note of it.

USING TECHNOLOGY EFFECTIVELY

Technology, used wisely, can help you to work more efficiently. You understand the need to use proper etiquette when using e-mail, voicemail, and texting, and in Chapter 9 you learned how technology can be used to connect people in distant locations for meetings. This section focuses on using technology effectively to manage information and files. Safety and security issues are also discussed.

Information Management

Microsoft Outlook® is an example of an information manager program that can help with everyday tasks such as maintaining an address book (list of contacts), keeping track of appointments, listing tasks (To Do list), and setting reminders.

Maintaining Contact Lists. The contact feature allows you to store contact information (names, addresses, phone numbers, e-mail addresses, fax numbers, pager numbers, etc.) for clients, suppliers, family members, and friends in an address book for easy reference. From your address book, you can create distribution lists or groups of contacts as an easy way to send a single e-mail message to several people at the same time. For example, you might group your family into a distribution list named "Family" and your best friends in a group named "BFFs." Then you could create a single e-mail message to send to all members of a group using the group name rather than key each person's e-mail address separately.

Astrid's responsibilities include sending a monthly e-mail message to members of the marketing team. She creates a distribution list named "Marketing Team" that contains the e-mail addresses of everyone on that team. She enters the group name on the "To" line. When she clicks "Send," her message is sent to every person on the Marketing Team distribution list.

Contact lists require maintenance. Review your contacts regularly. Do not let your list of contacts become unmanageable. Update contact information and delete contacts you no longer need.

Calendaring. Keeping an electronic calendar offers many timesaving options. For example, you can schedule activities in your calendar as appointments, meetings, events, or tasks. You can mark scheduled time as busy, free, or tentative. And if you choose, when it's time to go to a meeting, Outlook will remind you. You can also set your calendar alarms or alerts to remind you of special events such as birthdays and anniversaries. You can synchronize (or link) your work computer, home computer, or other devices (cell phones, iPods, smartphones, PDAs). When you set or delete an appointment, the change is made on *all* of the linked devices. You can also check your calendar through these devices when you're away from the workplace. You can view your calendar a day at a time, a week at a time, or a month at a time.

Inez is driving across Wisconsin to a meeting in Milwaukee. Colin, her administrative assistant, has added an appointment to Inez's Milwaukee schedule. Rather than call Inez on her cell phone while she is driving, Colin enters the appointment in his shared electronic calendar, and Inez's smartphone automatically receives notification of the added meeting as it syncs with Inez's desktop in the home office. Colin enters the information Inez will need for the new appointment in Milwaukee—address, time, contact, and notes so that Inez will be prepared for the meeting.

Some programs offer group calendaring, which facilitates the scheduling of meetings. If coworkers keep their calendars up to date, you can check their availability when you schedule a meeting. You can e-mail coworkers an invitation to the meeting. If they accept your invitation, the date of the meeting is automatically entered on their calendars.

Task Lists. Maintaining an electronic list of tasks is an excellent time-management device. A task can be a one-time only action (responding to a letter) or it can be a recurring item (submitting an article every two months for a newsletter). You can divide a large project into individual parts and track the progress of each task until the project is complete. You can display all tasks, tasks yet to be completed (your To Do list), or completed tasks. You can assign a priority to each task and set an alert to remind you of a deadline. Your To Do list can be integrated with your digital calendar so that the tasks appear on the calendar and can be crossed off as they are completed.

File Management

As with paper files, it is important to establish a logical and easy-to-use file management system to organize your electronic files and enable you to find files quickly. Good file organization begins with giving your folders and file names that are logical and easy to understand. Resist the temptation to use "Miscellaneous" as a filename. All too often these become "junk drawers" where files ultimately are lost. Delete unwanted files and folders from your hard drive monthly to increase hard drive performance. Archive the files you are no longer working on but should retain for historical purposes.

Yuri_Arcurs/iStockphoto.com

Technology used wisely can help you work more efficiently.

Archiving refers to moving data to a secondary storage medium that can be easily accessed, if required. Although archived data may remain on the same computer, archived files are typically stored in a secondary location for backup and historical purposes. You can archive to data disks, a flash drive, an external hard drive, or to a service that provides online data storage service.

Julio has been working on a client's project. After the project is complete, he makes sure the project records (text, audio, and video files) are archived in a secure fashion so they can be accessed easily in the future. As these kinds of files take a good deal of storage space, Julio decides to remove them from his hard drive and archive them on a flash drive.

Safety and Security

Exercise caution in your daily use of the computer. As far as possible, you want to protect your computer against common threats such as viruses and phishing.

Viruses. A **virus** is a software program designed to interfere with the operation of your computer. Computer viruses range from simply irritating to completely devastating. They can display messages, turn documents into templates, or cripple your computer. Viruses are products of malice. The people who create them and the people who knowingly pass them on to others are the same as thieves, stealing time and data from victims and disrupting normal work. Viruses are spread by opening infected documents, using an infected disk, running an infected application, or visiting a website that has a virus built into its code.

You must take precautions to avoid "catching" computer "diseases." While there is no guarantee you won't get a virus, you can reduce your risk by keeping your software up to date. Your computer should never be without up-to-date anti-virus software. As the name implies, anti-virus software continually scans your computer for viruses. Most anti-virus programs automatically download and install updates on a regular basis. New viruses are continually being programmed and released so it is important to keep your virus checker up to date and back up your data on a regular basis.

Backing up data is the only way to completely protect against loss of data due to viruses, improper shutdowns, or equipment crashes. **Backup** refers to making copies of data so that these additional copies may be used to restore the original files after a data loss. These additional copies are typically called *backups*. Backups have two purposes. The first is to restore data following a disaster such as the crash of a computer's hard drive or a fire. The second is to restore a small numbers of files after they have been accidentally deleted or corrupted.

APPLY IT!

Protect your computer against viruses by taking these simple steps:

- Check for periodic updates of your software or take advantage of the many programs that will automatically download and install updates at regular intervals.

- Scan your disks for viruses regularly, especially if you use the Internet frequently.

- Do not open e-mail from any source you do not recognize. E-mail is a frequent carrier of viruses. Some viruses piggyback on spam, luring unsuspecting users into infecting their computers.

- Use a firewall. A **firewall** is an integrated collection of security measures designed to prevent unauthorized electronic access to a networked computer system by limiting "back-door" access to your computer by other computers on the network. Some operating systems come equipped with firewall protection, and some software companies include firewall protection with their anti-virus products.

- Change your password at least every six months. Passwords can help to protect your computer from unauthorized use and protect your various accounts from unauthorized access, which in turn help protect your confidential documents and information.

- Perform routine backups of data from your hard drive to an external hard drive, flash drive, or CD.

Phishing. The act of sending an e-mail that falsely claims to be an established entity (a bank or credit card company, for example) is called **phishing.** It is an attempt to lure people into providing confidential personal and financial information such as credit card numbers, social security numbers, and bank account numbers. This information can be used to empty accounts and steal a person's identity. Be alert and realize that such scams exist. Credit card companies and banks don't ask for this type of information online.

Responsible Use

Always act responsibly when using a computer. Your work may allow you to obtain confidential information (telephone numbers, social security numbers, credit card information, medical records, etc.) that should be used only when you are authorized to do so by your employer or the person to whom it relates. Such information in the hands of an unethical person could do much harm.

Copying material to claim it as your original work is called **plagiarism**. Plagiarism in term papers, reports, or business presentations is a serious offense. Copyright laws protect information, software, and media such as graphics and video. Copyright laws protect individuals or companies from the theft or misuse of their creative, artistic, or literary work. It is illegal to make copies of software programs or copy, share, or download media without permission of the copyright holder. Information on the Web is usually copyrighted and protected by the creators of the website. When using information from the Internet, cite your sources. If you quote material, credit the writer. Cite the website, author, and original source where applicable. Violators of any kind of copyright infringement are subject to prosecution.

checkpoint

1. Explain why decisions are not made in isolation.

   _____

   _____

   _____

2. List the steps in the decision-making process.

   _____

   _____

   _____

3. List five characteristics of a creative person.

   _____

   _____

   _____

4. List three techniques you can use to develop your creativity.

_____

_____

_____

5. Why is it important to back up data regularly?

_____

_____

_____

_____

applications

1. Identify two decisions you have made recently. What alternatives did you consider? What was your final decision? Did the decision meet your expectations?

_____

_____

_____

2. Do you consider yourself creative? Do you tend to "think outside the box" when faced with a problem? If so, which characteristics of a creative person do you posses? If not, how might you develop your creativity?

_____

_____

_____

_____

3. Has your computer (or a friend's computer) been infected with a virus? If so, what was the result? What safety and security measures do you use to protect your home computer?

_____

_____

_____

4. Does your school have an Internet Acceptable Use Policy (AUP) that sets guidelines that govern the access to and transmission of data and information? Do you have a copy of that policy? If not, where is it available?

_____

_____

_____

Public Speaking

You will likely have opportunities to do some form of public speaking in either your personal or work life. For example, you may participate in a panel, give an update of an ongoing project, teach a software application to a group of coworkers, or give a formal speech at a meeting or conference.

Many people have a great deal of anxiety about speaking before others. This anxiety will lessen if you are truly prepared for the speaking experience. Your preparation (whether you will speak to two coworkers or before a large group) includes identifying the interests and needs of the audience, considering what you know about the topic, planning what you will say, and identifying any handouts or equipment needed.

on the job

Tamara is one of several administrative assistants in a large travel agency. She likes her job and has a reputation for being able to work under pressure and meet deadlines. Her time management skills are excellent. Her To Do list is always visible, and she handles large projects by breaking them down into smaller, more manageable tasks. The travel agents she supports are pleased with Tamara's work and have praised her to the agency manager, Robin Marree. Robin is on the board of a local organization that trains women to re-enter the workforce. She asks Tamara to speak to the women and share the time management tips she uses so effectively at work. At first, Tamara is reluctant to agree. "I'm not a public speaker," she thinks to herself. But she eventually agrees to speak. Robin reminded her that she would be sharing information that is meaningful to her, that the group would include only ten women, and that Tamara could determine the presentation length. Tamara prepared for the presentation. First, she asked Robin to identify the specific interests and needs of the women. Next, she decided on five time management tips to share. Then she planned and developed her information points and the slides she would use. Finally, she determined what handouts to provide and arranged to have a media cart available for her laptop. She practiced her presentation until she "had it down cold." On the day of the presentation, she walked confidently into the room, smiled at the audience, and delivered an informative presentation. After the program, she received many compliments on her delivery and content.

What points did Robin make that convinced Tamara to agree to make the presentation? What steps did Tamara take to prepare for the presentation? Do you think Tamara will agree to speak in public again, and if so why?

This section focuses on giving a formal speech. However, many of the principles discussed apply to less formal situations as well. The most important thing to remember is "preparation is the key to effective public speaking." The better prepared you are, the more confident you will be. The more confident you are, the better you will be able to communicate your message.

PLANNING YOUR SPEECH

A **speech** is a formal presentation of information to an audience. Speeches are typically given to inform, persuade, entertain, or inspire. Rarely does a speech serve only one purpose. Most speeches invite the audience to react in one of three ways: feeling, thinking, or acting. For example, a manager speaks to the staff to create enthusiasm for a new project, an instructor gives a presentation to stimulate thinking about a topic, or a coworker from human resources demonstrates how to complete new health insurance forms.

Whether you speak before two people or two hundred people, allow ample time to prepare and conduct research. Developing a good speech takes thought and attention to detail. Real speech preparation means digging something from within you. To deliver a convincing presentation, you must believe in what you say. You want to capture the attention of your audience, convey ideas in a logical manner, and use reliable evidence to support your points.

There are four basic issues you should consider as you think about any speech—the interests and needs of your audience, your knowledge of the subject, how you will organize the speech, and where and how you will present the speech.

The Interests and Needs of Your Audience

Find out as much as possible about your audience so that you can include information that connects to their interests, concerns, expectations, and level of knowledge. This is vital. If you can identify ways to engage your listeners, your speech will be interesting and useful. A speech should make each listener feel that you are talking directly to him or her. Ask yourself these questions about your audience:

- What do they have in common? Age? Interests? Gender? Ethnicity?
- Do they know something about the topic or will the information be new?
- Why will these people be listening to me? Will they be there by choice?
- What level of detail will be effective for them?

Your Knowledge of the Subject

Are you knowledgeable about this topic or do you need to conduct research? Jot down what you know about the subject. You can decide later which information you will actually share with your audience. Your immediate goal is to determine your preparedness level to address the topic. Allow time to research and verify your information or seek new information.

How You Will Organize the Speech

Your audience will have only one chance to grasp the information as you deliver it, so your speech must be well organized and easily understood. In addition, the content of the speech and your delivery must fit the audience. Make sure the topic is appropriate. Topics such as "e-commerce" or "ergonomics" are too broad. Break the topic into manageable points that can be covered and understood by your audience in the time allowed for your presentation.

You will likely have opportunities to do some form of public speaking in either your personal or work life.

Jesse has 45 minutes to present the topic of workplace ergonomics to an audience of insurance agents. He decides to cover two areas of interest to his audience—workstation ergonomics and laptop/PC ergonomics.

Use an outline to organize your speech. Don't make the mistake of thinking you can just "stand up and speak" without first organizing your thoughts. Many people outline their speech on a computer. This is especially useful if you will use slides in your presentation. The slides guide your presentation, and you can use the slides as the starting point for handout materials. Others prefer to write their outline on index cards. The cards are easy to hold and refer to, and you can reorganize your talking points "on the fly" by re-sorting the cards.

There will be times when you must then decide if you will accept the invitation to speak on a specific topic. Ask these questions to help you make your decision.

1. Do I have adequate knowledge of the subject?
2. If I am not familiar with the subject, will I be able to provide my audience with good information? Is there enough time for me to research the topic?
3. Is the subject appropriate for the situation in which I will present?
4. Does the subject have "audience appeal"?
5. Can I make the subject understandable to everyone in the audience?
6. Is the subject of sufficient interest to me that I will be motivated to present it effectively?

Each speech should have three basic parts—an introduction, body, and conclusion.

Design the **introduction** to get the attention of the listener. You might begin with a story, make a startling statement, use an example, ask a question, or share interesting facts. Then give a brief overview of what your speech will cover. Your introduction lets your audience know what to expect and prepares them to be receptive to your message.

The **body** is the "nuts and bolts" of what you want the audience to know. Organize your information into logical, easy-to-understand points. These questions may help as you develop your main points: Will the listeners gain from hearing this? Is this point too brief or too detailed for this circumstance? Will including this point take away from my purpose? Am I including this information for me or for the listeners? Include a good balance of facts, examples, and (if appropriate) anecdotes or stories to keep the attention of your audience. Use transitions to link your main points so that the presentation has an "even flow" from one point to the next.

The **conclusion** provides a brief summary of what you have said. The conclusion is the last chance to get across your message to the audience. What do you want your listeners to remember? Restate your main points so that the listeners will know that they have heard a complete and well-planned presentation. You might use a personal example or a story to reinforce your message.

Plan to cover the topic in the time allotted. No one likes to hear a speaker ramble on and on. Remember, "The mind can absorb only what the seat can endure."

Where and How You Will Present the Speech

"Best way to conquer stage fright is to know what you're talking about."

Sometimes you may stand before a small group in a conference room. At other times, you may stand behind a lectern in a large room. The size of the room, the number of people in your audience, and the subject of your speech will determine what media and equipment are needed. If you are speaking for only a few minutes, you may decide that no equipment is needed—that a short handout will be enough. For a longer speech, you may choose to use slides or other visuals and provide an extensive handout.

Walk-Through of the Planning Phase

You have read about the basics of preparing and presenting a speech. Now let's do a "walk-through" of the process again using an actual situation. Assume that you are the company nurse for Belamy Mining and Extraction. You have been asked to speak at a local business about adopting the community hospital's health and wellness program. You begin by asking yourself questions in the initial planning phase. The answers to these questions will guide you the next step—organizing the presentation.

1. What is the purpose of my speech? The answer to this question should be written in one concise sentence. Is my goal to inform, persuade, entertain, or inspire?

   The purpose of my speech is to persuade the audience that their company should adopt the community hospital's health and wellness program.

2. Who is my audience? What is their main interest in this topic?

   The audience includes managers and representatives from each department. Their main interest is in reducing absenteeism and improving employee well-being, self-image, and self-esteem.

3. What do I know and believe about this topic, and can I relate it to this audience?

   I know the facts about the health and wellness program I am presenting. Qualified physicians and mental health experts developed the program, and it has been successful at Belamy and other area companies. This program has reduced absenteeism rates and improved the well-being and self-esteem of employees. My information relates to the needs of this company.

4. What additional research is needed?

   I need to find information about other local companies that have instituted this program. What percentage of the employees participated in the program? Did the employees need incentives to participate? What was the actual percentage of reduced absenteeism? Have there been any follow-up studies on employee well-being and self-esteem?

5. What are the main points of this presentation?

   - The company should consider adopting a health and wellness program.
   - Experts in the health field designed the program.
   - The program will require very few facility changes.
   - The activities involved in the program include exercise classes, a weight-control program, yoga classes, a strength-training program, and periodic cholesterol and blood pressure screenings.
   - The company can control the cost of the program by the components it selects.

6. What information and examples can I use to support my main points?

   - Health and wellness programs have boosted employee morale in many companies.
   - The outstanding expertise of the people who have developed the program. Mention their education and experience.
   - Testimonial comments from other companies who have adopted the program.

7. Do I have an effective introduction?

Yes. I will begin with statistics that will get the attention of my audience. I will talk about my experience at Belamy, which instituted a health and wellness program and reduced the absenteeism rate by 40 percent in the first year of the program. I will include comments from the human resources director about the improved employee morale and well-being.

8. Do I have an effective conclusion?

Yes. In my summary, I will answer the question, "What's in it for me?" I will restate my main points. I will talk about the reduced absenteeism rates and overall health improvement of participants. I will tell the story of the woman at Belamy who, during a cholesterol screening, discovered that her cholesterol level was dangerously high. Her doctor believes the program may have saved her life.

9. Have I polished and prepared the language and words I will use?

Yes. I have reviewed the speech and decided what words to use that will be most appealing to my audience.

10. What visual aids, if any, do I need?

I will prepare a multimedia presentation that will include the main points, photos of health and wellness programs in operation at various facilities, and a video clip of an employee talking about his experience in the program.

11. What handouts, if any, do I need?

I will print handouts of the slides I use in the presentation.

PRACTICING YOUR SPEECH

"The human brain starts working the moment you are born and never stops until you stand up to speak in public."

You are now ready to practice your speech aloud several times. Practice in front of a mirror or with a friend so that you can work on your gestures, movements, and facial expressions. Make sure your voice is loud enough to be heard, clear and expressive, and that you don't speak too fast. Time your presentation. If it is too short, add some supporting material under your main points. If it is too long, consider deleting one or more sub-points. Practice your opening and closing enough times so that you can keep your eyes on the audience, not your notes.

If you use presentation software to display slides, put your main points on the slides. Practice what you will say when you transition from one slide to the next. Do not try to dazzle your audience with excessive use of animation, sound clips, or gaudy colors. The font size must be large enough to be read at the back of the room. Do not torment your audience by putting a long document in small print on the screen and reading it to them.

If you use index cards for your outline, practice using the cards before you give the speech. Figure 10-5 on page 256 shows a sample outline that might appear on your cards. Do not be concerned about the audience being aware of your cards; the cards signal to them that you are prepared.

Write out and memorize your opening remarks, but do not try to memorize the rest of your speech. Think about what you want to say, but choose the wording as you move from one point to another. That way you will not need to keep your eyes glued to your slides or notes, and your audience will feel like you are talking to them. Slides or index cards are simply devices to help you organize your comments, statistics, and main points.

DELIVERING YOUR SPEECH

Before the day of your speech, take time to go over every part of the experience in your mind. Imagine what the audience will look like, how you will present your talk, what the questions will be and how you will answer them, and so on. Visualize the experience the way you want it to be. You may find that when the time comes to make the actual presentation, it will be "old hat" and much of your anxiety will be gone.

With a "can do" attitude, careful study, and preparation, you can deliver a speech that will communicate your intended message and give you a well-deserved feeling of accomplishment. If you are prepared, your anxiety level will be just enough to support you in giving an animated presentation.

Techniques You Can Use

If you have prepared and practiced ahead of time, there is no reason to be anxious about the delivery. Follow these techniques to put yourself at ease and give an effective speech:

- If possible, make small talk with your audience before your presentation. That way you will recognize some familiar faces when you give your speech.
- Drink a small glass of warm water to open your throat before speaking. (Cold water can cause your throat muscles to constrict.)
- Learn to relax your throat. Yawn. Notice how your throat feels. When you yawn your throat is open. Try to keep this feeling when you are speaking.
- When it is your turn to speak, walk quickly and confidently to the front of the room and wait for everyone's attention before you begin. Look at the audience, smile, take a deep breath, and share your thoughts and ideas.

Connecting with your audience is the key to a making a successful presentation. Follow these tips to communicate your message to your audience.

1. Keep your audience in mind.
2. Speak with conviction.
3. Maintain eye contact with your audience and do not read from your notes.
4. Look for feedback from your audience. Respond to their reactions, adjust, and adapt.
5. Pause periodically. Allow yourself and your audience a little time to reflect and think.
6. Don't let your body language interfere with your message. Avoid extremes: don't be as "stiff as a board," and don't use excessive gestures that can distract attention from what you are saying.
7. Allow time for questions. Before answering, repeat each question for the benefit of anyone who may not have heard the question.
8. Have handouts ready and give them out at the appropriate time. Tell the audience ahead of time that you are handing out an outline of the key points. Listeners who want to note details can write them on the outline.

I. Introduction

Belamy Mining and Extraction instituted a health and wellness program and reduced absenteeism by 40 percent in the first year of the program. A similar health and wellness program could benefit your company.

II. Body

A. Why consider a health and wellness program?
B. Where have health and wellness programs been successful?
C. Who designed and prepared the recommended program?
D. What activities and services are included in the program?
E. What changes to your facility are needed?
F. What does the program cost?

III. Conclusion

Your company can join the ranks of other companies that have reduced absenteeism and improved morale by instituting a health and wellness program. Review key points. Give example of the Belamy employee who discovered a dangerous cholesterol level during a routine screening in the program. Her doctor has said that the program may have saved her life.

FIGURE 10-5 Sample of a speech outline.

- Pick out four or five people in different parts of the room and speak to them, shifting your eyes from one to another.
- Speak to the back of the room so everyone will hear your voice. You will lose your audience in a hurry if they cannot hear you.
- If you are stuck for a word or thought, glance down at your notes or at the slides, think about what you just said, and wait for the word or thought to come. Do not fill in the time with "oh, uh . . ." Don't apologize if you get stuck. Take a deep breath and go on with the speech.
- Use your hands naturally to show conviction or honest enthusiasm. Avoid nervous habits such as fiddling with clothing or jewelry. Do not lean against the podium. Stand on both feet and do not rock from one foot to another.
- Ask your audience to hold questions until the end. Then repeat each question before you answer it. This ensures that everyone has heard the question and gives you some time to organize your thoughts. If appropriate, ask the audience if they have information to add to the response.

checkpoint

1. What are the four basic purposes of a speech?

_____

_____

2. What four things should you consider as you think about a speech?

_____

_____

3. Why is it important to know your subject?

_____

_____

4. What are the three basic parts of a speech?

_____

_____

5. Describe four techniques for putting yourself at ease before a presentation.

_____

_____

applications

1. Describe a situation in which you spoke before a group, even if for only a few minutes. What steps did you take to prepare? How long did you speak? How was your message received? What did you learn from the experience?

_____

_____

2. Prior to speaking before a group, why is it important to find out as much as possible about your audience? Describe a situation in which your needs as a member of the audience were not met. How did you feel at the end of the presentation?

_____

_____

3. Write an opening paragraph for a presentation to persuade your class to raise money for a local animal shelter. Use one or more of the techniques presented in the chapter: begin with a story, make a startling statement, use an example, ask a question, or share interesting facts.

_____

_____

4. Write the closing paragraph for the presentation described in Application 3.

_____

_____

5. What information would you provide about the local animal shelter in Application 3? Where would you find additional information? List some key points based on your research or personal experience.

_____

_____

10 *points to* remember

Review the following points to determine what you remember from the chapter.

✦ Self-management skills enable you to complete tasks independently and take an active role in monitoring and controlling your behavior.

✦ Time-management skills are critical to job success. Start each day with a realistic schedule and remain flexible enough to adjust the schedule when things don't go as planned.

✦ The ability to balance life and work provides peace of mind and energy for each aspect of your life.

✦ Prolonged stress can be devastating to your health and productivity. Practice effective techniques for dealing with stress.

✦ Anger that is out of control can turn destructive and lead to problems. You can learn to control your reactions, reduce anger, and finally to prevent it.

✦ Decision making and problem solving are interrelated skills. Effective decisions must be made to solve problems satisfactorily.

✦ Develop your creativity by thinking beyond your traditional way of looking at things.

✦ Use technology wisely to handle information efficiently and make everyday tasks easier. Protect your stored information from viruses and practice ethical use of information found on the Internet.

✦ View an opportunity to give a speech or presentation as a chance to share your knowledge.

How did you do? Did you remember the main points you studied in the chapter?

KEY *terms*

time management

scheduling

procrastinating

multitasking

stress

passive anger

aggressive anger

anger management

decision making

creativity

brainwriting

archiving

virus

backup

firewall

phishing

plagiarism

speech

introduction

body

conclusion

Want more activities? Go to **www.cengage. com/careerreadiness/masters** to get started.

CHAPTER activities

1. Create a To Do list of things you need to accomplish in the next five days. The tasks may be from your personal, school, or work life. Prioritize your list using the A, B, C system described in Section 10-1. Estimate how much time it will take to complete each task.

_____

_____

_____

_____

_____

_____

2. Describe four stressful situations you have experienced. Opposite each situation, identify a technique you used to manage the stress.

Situation	Stress Management Technique
_____	_____
_____	_____
_____	_____
_____	_____
_____	_____

3. Review the anger management techniques in Figure 10-3 on page 235. List the three techniques that work best for you and explain why.

_____

_____

_____

_____

_____

_____

4. Assume you want to buy a new car. Identify five factors that will influence your final decision (price, fuel efficiency, features, etc.). Research cars you like and narrow your list to two cars. Make your decision based on the goal, facts, alternatives, and risks involved. Which car did you chose? Why?

_____

_____

_____

_____

_____

_____

_____

5. Develop an outline for a 30-minute speech on a topic of your choice. Be sure that you have an interesting introduction, good material in the body of the speech, and a conclusion that summarizes what you said.

Topic: _____

_____

_____

_____

Key points: _____

_____

_____

Conclusion: _____

_____

_____

_____

CRITICAL *thinking*

CASE 10-1 Miguel Triumphs!

Miguel was a member of his Neighborhood Watch program. He had worked on several committees, attended safety conferences, and had helped other neighborhoods form watch groups. The local police chief asked Miguel to speak at a community service organization meeting next month about the benefits of a Neighborhood Watch program and encourage members to form watch groups.

Miguel was terrified. He would have to stand up and speak to 65 strangers. He couldn't tell the chief "no"—he had done so much for the community. He thought of ways to get out of speaking, but he knew this speech was important to the community and worth doing. He read about other Neighborhood Watch groups on the Internet and found statistics showing the value of watch programs and stories of successful programs. He talked to the president of his organization and gathered information about the members. He organized what he wanted to say and outlined the speech on index cards. He practiced his speech in front of a mirror several times and presented it to his parents, who gave him some useful tips.

Miguel's anxiety decreased as his preparation increased. On the day of the presentation, he walked confidently to the podium, smiled at the audience, and gave an informative talk. He received many compliments following the program on his delivery and content. A line formed at the back of the room and the local police chief happily took the names and addresses of those interested in joining Miguel's group or starting a Neighborhood Watch program in their neighborhood.

1. How might Miguel have responded to the six questions in the Apply It activity on page 251?

   1._____

   2._____

   3._____

   4._____

   5._____

   6._____

2. What steps did Miguel take that helped to decrease his anxiety and deliver an effective presentation?

   _____

3. What conclusions do you think Miguel came to as he reflected on his public speaking experience?

   _____

CASE 10-2 Why Did Dora Lose It?

Dora, an assembly plant line supervisor, is ordinarily an easygoing employee who enjoys her work. But this morning she arrived late at work because her son missed the school bus, and she had to drive him to school. Dora was gridlocked in unusually heavy traffic, spilled coffee on her lap, and someone else had parked in her assigned space at work. When she finally got to the line, she found her coworkers idle because the materials they needed hadn't been delivered. At this point, Dora lost her temper and yelled at her assistant Tyron for not taking charge of the problem.

After the situation was under control and everyone was back on the job, Dora went to see the division manager and her longtime friend, Luis. She said, "I blew up at Tyron this morning before I had all the facts. When I got to the line, my workers were doing nothing, and I 'lost my cool' in front of them. The lack of materials was caused by an error in the supply area and totally out of Tyron's control." Luis replied, "Dora, that's not like you. What's going on?" Dora answered, "My husband and I were up most of last night because the baby was sick again, and my son missed the school bus this morning. It was one thing after another on the way to work and I'm exhausted."

Luis said, "You've had some unexpected challenges in your personal life, but you need to remain calm when talking with your coworkers. First, you need to apologize to Tyron. Then take a long lunch and get yourself together. You may find it helpful to talk to one of the counselors in the Employee Assistance Program. A counselor may be able to suggest some ways to avoid and relieve stress."

1. At what point could Dora have paused and gained control of her emotions?

   _____

   _____

2. Luis tells Dora to apologize to Tyron. What would you say to Tyron if you were in Dora's place?

   _____

   _____

3. Using the suggestions in this chapter, write a list of tips for Dora.

   _____

   _____

4. Describe a situation where you faced an accumulation of small incidents that caused you to react in a manner you later regretted. What did you do to correct the situation? How can you react differently when you face a similar situation?

   _____

   _____

Developing Customer Focus

Think About It: Logan works in an exclusive shoe store. He works on commission and prides himself on being the top sales associate each month. A frequent customer comes in and buys several pair of expensive summer shoes. She continues to look around and spots a pair of jogging shoes for her husband. She asks for a size 11. Logan doesn't have that size and tells the customer that he can call the distributor and have the shoes shipped in three to five days. The customer agrees to have the shoes shipped. After the customer leaves, Logan calls the distributor and learns that there are only a few sizes left in that style because it is late in the season. Size 11 is no longer available; however, they have the shoe in size 10½. Logan says, "That's okay, send them to the customer. She'll never notice the size difference." The distributor tells Logan that the customer should receive the shoes in seven to ten days.

Is Logan showing respect and honesty to the customer? What risk is Logan taking by selling his customer this pair of shoes?

Digital Vision/Getty Images

objectives

After completing this chapter, you should be able to:

1. Explain why customers are vital to the success of every organization.
2. Identify what customers expect.
3. Demonstrate how to meet customer expectations.
4. Explain how to maintain good customer relations.
5. Explain why maintaining customer loyalty is important.
6. Deal with difficult customers.
7. Demonstrate proper telephone techniques.

Customer Expectations

All businesses serve someone. Depending on the type of business, the people served may be called customers, clients, buyers, purchasers, guests, patrons, or patients. Regardless of how you refer to them, they expect to be respected, listened to, cared for, and treated fairly. In simple words, customers want to believe that the company values them as individuals and wants their business.

To the customer, you *are* the company. Customers expect you to make the organization work for them. They expect you to answer their questions, solve their problems, share product use ideas, and refer them to the right people. Moreover, they expect you to do all of this in a timely fashion.

WHY CARE ABOUT CUSTOMERS?

Customers are vital to the success of any organization, regardless of its purpose. Without customers, there is no income, no business, and no livelihood. Customers determine the lifespan and success of any business, whether the organization sells cars or provides telephone service. Imagine yourself in a huge discount store with no customers or in a hotel with no guests. Get the picture? No customers means no business.

Customers are important, but *repeat* customers are crucial. The word "custom" is derived from a form of the word "habit." Businesses want customers to make a habit of buying from them. Every organization has a somewhat limited customer base. For example, the local supermarket relies on the continued business of people who live in the area. A steady customer base is the key to a successful business. On average, successful businesses typically get 80 percent of their business from 20 percent of their customers. Repeat business is the backbone of any organization because it provides a steady revenue stream.[1] Therefore, each business must work to meet customer expectations and maintain customer loyalty.

"It is not the employer who pays the wages. Employers only handle the money. It is the customer who pays the wages."

WHAT DO CUSTOMERS EXPECT?

By knowing what customers expect and meeting those expectations, you play an important role in helping your employer keep repeat customers. Any interaction between you and a customer has lasting effects. If you are able to satisfy the customer—to meet customer expectations—you have done your part to encourage the customer to return. In fact, a positive experience with you could erase from the customer's mind all memory of a previous bad experience. Customers may not know your area of responsibility, your job description, or what you can and cannot do for them, but their focus is clear: "Help me with this purchase" or "Solve my problem." Your goals are (1) to treat each customer as you would like to be treated, (2) to make every effort to satisfy customer needs and expectations, and (3) to do your best to make each customer feel valued.

1. To be taken seriously
2. Competent, efficient service
3. Anticipation of my needs
4. Explanations in my terms
5. Basic courtesies
6. To be informed of the options
7. Not to be passed around
8. To be listened to
9. Dedicated attention
10. Knowledgeable help
11. Friendliness
12. To be kept informed
13. Follow-through
14. Honesty
15. Feedback
16. Professional service
17. Empathy
18. Respect

What do customers expect? Naomi Karten, a speaker, consultant, and author, conducts seminars about customer satisfaction. She asks seminar participants to identify factors that matter to them when they're the customer. Some of their responses are shown in the "When I'm a Customer, I Want . . ." feature in this section.[2] Notice that most of the responses are related to the human element.

Quality

All customers expect products and services that are of high quality, fairly priced, clean, and safe. If customers do not receive high-quality products and services, they won't be customers for very long. No business of any size will stay in business if its products or services do not meet consumer expectations.

Some businesses sell products, or tangible items. **Tangible items** can be seen, touched, and usually kept in your possession; for example, a pair of jeans or an HDTV. Customers want a product to be of top quality and, depending on the item, be functional for many years. Other businesses deal in intangible items. **Intangible items** cannot be seen, touched, or possessed. Businesses such as insurance agencies, legal firms, and exterminators sell intangible services. Businesses that sell intangibles must offer the same level of service as those selling merchandise. For example, the customer who hires a plumber to repair a leaky faucet expects the leak to be fixed in a timely fashion with high quality, long-lasting materials.

Reliability

A company that plans to stay in business must be reliable. **Reliability** refers to the ability to supply what was promised in a dependable, efficient, and timely manner. For most consumers, reliability ranks almost as high as price as a top "buy indicator." Customers expect the cars they buy to run efficiently, the jacket they buy online to be the correct size, and the hotel room they reserve to be clean and available for occupancy.

To the customer, the reliability commitment is threefold—the business commitment, the common (or assumed) commitment, and the personal

Your goal should be to treat every customer as you would like to be treated.

Stockbyte/Getty Images

promise. First, there is the business's commitment, which includes promises made in advertising, marketing materials, and published service guarantees. Second, customers make assumptions about what the business can and cannot do for them—this is the assumed commitment or expectation. If a customer has a dentist appointment at 9 a.m., the customer expects to be seated in the dentist's chair at the scheduled time or shortly thereafter. The fact that the dentist is "running late" doesn't change the customer's expectation that the dentist will adhere to the schedule. Failing to meet a customer's expectation (whether or not you were aware of the expectation) has the same impact as breaking a promise.

Finally, there is the personal promise—the promise that comes from you, the company representative. When you tell the customer, "I'll call you back within an hour," the customer expects you to do so. When you say, "You can download that software without any problem," the customer expects the software to download easily. Customers will hold whomever they talk with responsible for all reliability promises made. Provide reasons, not excuses. Customers respond well when they understand the reason you cannot make good on a promise or fulfill a request. Never make an idle promise just to make a sale. A promise not kept could cost you a customer.

> *Adolfo told a customer, "This entertainment center is solid oak. Its construction includes no veneer or pressed wood. It will be delivered tomorrow afternoon." As Adolfo watches the entertainment center being loaded on the delivery truck, he notices that its doors are made of pressed wood. He must call the customer and explain why his promise is not reliable. For example, he might say, "This is Adolfo from Merchandise Bonanza. I sold you an entertainment center yesterday. As it was being loaded for delivery, I realized that it has pressed wood doors and not solid oak as I had stated. This was my error. I apologize for the misinformation, and I regret any inconvenience my error has caused. Do you still want us to deliver the center to you?"*

Adolfo's reliability and honesty will be remembered the next time this customer is in the market for products sold at Merchandise Bonanza.

Timeliness

Customers expect responsive action in a timely fashion. Think of the many businesses that have built their reputations on fast service—McDonald's, FedEx, and LensCrafters, for example. You may use a dry cleaner that promises one-hour service or eat lunch in a restaurant that promises to serve your meal within ten minutes. If you cannot serve customers in a timely fashion, a competitor will be more than happy to do so.

Uncertainty is an aspect of timeliness that causes customer dissatisfaction. Customers who must wait want to know how long the wait will be.

Have you taken your car in for service in the morning, expecting to pick it up after school or work? When you haven't heard from the repair shop all day, you finally call them, only to discover that your car won't be ready until tomorrow. You are upset and disappointed. Now you must get a ride home and figure out a way to get to school or work tomorrow. Some up-front information from the repair shop (or a call during the day with an update) would have saved you a lot of trouble.

What customers consider an acceptable wait varies. Customers ordering fast food expect it within five minutes. Customers in fashionable restaurants see no problem with waiting 20 minutes for a nice meal. Be realistic about wait times and keep customers updated if the time changes. Customers are more tolerant when kept informed about what's happening. Think about waiting for a delayed flight. If you are updated frequently and assured that progress is being made, you will be patient. Statements like "The incoming aircraft will be on the ground in 30 minutes" or "We will begin boarding as soon as we're finished refueling" help customers remain patient.

on the job

Lance works for a private delivery service in a large city. He has a 10 a.m. pickup at a business that stores medical records. The medical records clerk, Saul, tells Lance that the records must be delivered to Dr. Brandt at St. John's Medical Center by 3 p.m. Dr. Brandt must review a patient's records before a surgery scheduled for tomorrow morning. Lance takes his job seriously and double-checks with Saul to make sure he has the correct hospital and doctor's name. He assures Saul that the records will be in Dr. Brandt's hands by 3 p.m. The delivery service that Lance works for has a stellar reputation built on years of reliable service. Lance arrives at the records office at St. John's at 2:30 p.m. The clerk on duty says, "Just set the records here—I'll get to them later." Lance says, "Dr. Brandt is waiting for these records. Can you assure me that they will be delivered to her by 3 p.m.? The clerk replies, "No, I can't. We're very busy today, and we'll get them to her when we have time to deliver them." Lance asks, "Is there any hospital policy that prevents me from delivering the records?" When the clerk says no, Lance picks up the records, checks the hospital directory, and locates Dr. Brandt's office. At 2:45, a nurse in Dr. Brandt's office signs for the records. He thanks Lance profusely, saying that the doctor is eager to review them. Lance calls Saul and tells him that the package has been delivered. Making the phone call wasn't required, but Lance knows that Saul was concerned.

What customer expectations did Lance meet today? Why do you think the medical records storage office will use Lance's company again? How would you describe Lance's service?

Each customer has unique needs and expectations. Customers expect you to understand their situation and respond accordingly. Consider the different needs and expectations of Troy and Alia. Troy wants to buy his wife a sweater. He is nervous about being in the women's department and did not expect so many choices. He is looking to you, the sales assistant, for guidance. Help Troy by asking questions such as, "What color do you have in mind?" "Does your wife like bright or pastel colors?" "Do you know your wife's size?" "Are you looking for a sweater for work or casual wear?" You could then show several sweaters to Troy from which he could make his selection.

Alia is shopping for a sweater for herself. She is comfortable in the women's department, knows what she is looking for, and doesn't need help deciding which sweaters to try on. You offer to answer any questions and then step back and remain available to respond to her questions or requests. In Chapter 7 you read about *empathy*: the ability to look at situations through the eyes of others and understand another person's emotions and feelings. You must be empathetic to the feelings of your customers based on their wants and needs.

Customers expect personal attention from thoughtful, knowledgeable professionals who listen to their concerns and take responsibility for serving them. To a customer, the company begins and ends with you. Using *I* shows that you understand and accept this responsibility. Saying "Company policy is . . ." or "*They* won't allow . . ." tells the customer that you consider yourself "just an employee" and not someone who could be a part of the solution. These feelings won't help the customer, and the customer may view you as part of the problem.

When you are faced with a customer who has a problem, ask questions to be sure you understand the situation. Then take appropriate action. When things go wrong with a product or service, customers often expect an adjustment.

> *Dick works in a large appliance center. A customer storms in and says, "What's wrong with this store? In the past, I could depend on your appliances to be top-quality—but not anymore. I bought this iron from you last week. Its temperature gauge is defective. I burned a hole in a very expensive blouse." Dick replies, "I can understand that you're upset about the blouse and the iron. Let's get this situation corrected to your satisfaction. We'll replace the iron, of course, and check the replacement to be sure it works properly. We'll also reimburse you for the damage to your blouse."*

"Consumers are statistics. Customers are people."

Of course, there are times when your authority is limited and you really can't do anything. But even if all you can say is "Let me talk to my manager and see what we can do," your comment tells the customer that you want to be helpful.

The following statements may be appropriate or inappropriate to say to customers. Place a check before each appropriate statement. Restate each inappropriate statement so it is more empathetic and helpful.

_____ 1. Oh my, that hairstyle isn't at all flattering. Let's try a new style.
_____ 2. I don't work in this department. You'll have to find someone else to help you.
_____ 3. Mora, I'm so glad you came in today. I thought of you when this lovely dress arrived.
_____ 4. Do you have another car you can use in the meantime?
_____ 5. This house needs work. It does not have good marketability.
_____ 6. Mr. Fedele, I'm sorry to hear that you're not happy with the camera you bought yesterday. I'm sure we can find one that better meets your needs.

Recognition

Customers expect to be noticed, and nothing makes someone feel more important than when you recall his or her name. Remembering a customer's name requires work on your part. Begin by making a conscious effort to remember names. If you are introduced to a customer, listen carefully and repeat the name within the first 60 seconds of the introduction. "I understand what you're looking for, Ms. Dembo. This DVD player is very highly rated." If you are not introduced, you can pick up clues from a customer's credit card or office nameplate.

Another technique is to associate the name with an object or another person. For example, you might associate the name "Greenberg" with a mental image of a lush, green lawn. Or ask yourself questions such as, "Is there something unique about this person?" "Does he or she look like anyone I know?" "Do I know someone else with the same name?"

Do not risk offending a customer by being overly informal in any area of the transaction, including using the customer's first name. The safest advice is that, unless you and the customer already know each other, address the person as Mr. or Ms.

Repeat customers often appreciate it when you remember something personal about them—something they bought or returned, a mutual friend, a hobby or something about a family member. For example, you might say "Hi, Ahmed. Are you enjoying your new computer?" or "Hello, Mrs. Sanders, how is your new grandson?"

checkpoint

1. Explain why customers are important to the success of any business.

   _____

   _____

   _____

   _____

   _____

2. List five expectations customers have.

   _____

   _____

   _____

   _____

   _____

3. What are the three types of reliability customers require?

   _____

   _____

   _____

   _____

   _____

   _____

4. Why is it important to respond to customers in a timely fashion?

   _____

   _____

   _____

   _____

   _____

   _____

5. How can you exhibit empathy for a customer?

   _____

   _____

   _____

   _____

   _____

   _____

applications

1. Assume that you want to buy a new laptop. What do you expect of the salesperson? What do you expect of the laptop?

   _____

   _____

   _____

   _____

2. Think of two businesses that you return to frequently. Do your return visits have anything to do with the customer service you receive? Explain.

   _____

   _____

   _____

   _____

3. List five common excuses you may hear from customer service representatives for offering indifferent or poor customer service.

   _____

   _____

   _____

   _____

4. Do you expect the same level of customer service from an online company as you do from a physical store? Explain.

   _____

   _____

   _____

   _____

   _____

5. You are responsible for evaluating the travel specialists who work in the office of Excursions International. These workers are expected to interact effectively with customers and understand their travel needs. What would you expect to observe in order to give an employee a high rating in each of the following areas?

   Attitude: _____

   Knowledge: _____

   Meeting customer expectations: _____

   Dealing with difficult customers: _____

Good Customer Relations

It cannot be overemphasized that customers are vital to the success of any organization. Successful businesses are committed to bringing customers back for more, which is why building good customer relations is so important. Maintaining good customer relations can mean the difference between keeping customers or losing them to the competition. It can mean the difference between the success or failure of a business.

How employees treat customers is a critical factor in sustaining return business. Employees, by their attitudes and customer focus, make a major contribution to building lasting relationships with customers. Building good customer relations is challenging at times, but it does not need to be difficult. Treating each customer as you would like to be treated, identifying his or her needs, and making the person feel valued are important steps toward building good customer relations.

MEETING CUSTOMER EXPECTATIONS

Surveys indicate that customers stop buying from companies where they are treated indifferently. Moreover, unhappy customers usually tell other people why they stopped buying from a particular company. Surveys also show that many dissatisfied customers don't say anything, they just don't come back. Whether you communicate with customers in person or over the telephone, be sure that the message you send is focused on meeting customer expectations. The customer is the reason you have a job. Always remember that you are in the customer service business. Stay tuned to your customers!

You know from your own experiences that customers do not like to be told "That's not my department" or "I don't know." It is unlikely that you would ever verbalize the phrase "I can't be bothered," but your body language can certainly send that message. If you don't know the answer to a question, the correct response is "I don't know, but let me find out for you." Meeting customer expectations by being attentive, knowledgeable, helpful, respectful, and honest fosters good relationships with customers and helps keep you and your company on the track to success.

Be Attentive

Have you walked into a business and been ignored by employees? They might be on the phone, talking to each other, or engaged in an activity that you don't view as important. You may have even walked out wondering how a company can stay in business when its employees don't acknowledge customers.

Jill walked into a gift shop during her lunch hour. She knew what she wanted and was in a hurry. She picked out a stuffed bear and a greeting card and went to the cashier's station, but there was no one there to help her. She looked around and saw an employee restocking

- Stop whatever you are doing when a customer enters. If you can't leave a phone call or what you are doing, immediately say to the customer, "I'll be with you in a moment."
- Greet the customer and give your name (when appropriate).
- Look at the customer and smile.
- Ask how you can be of help.
- Give the customer your total attention.
- Focus more on listening than talking.
- Show or demonstrate products to the customer rather than pointing them out or talking about them.
- Never accept personal telephone calls or carry on a personal conversation in front of customers.
- Treat all customers equally and provide them the same excellent service.

shelves. She called to the employee and said, "I'm ready to check out." The employee took several moments to finish stocking the shelf before going to the cashier's station. He didn't apologize for the delay; he simply rang up the sale and handed the bag to Jill. She was livid. She vowed she would not shop there again, and she shared the negative experience with coworkers, friends, and family.

Being attentive and being a good listener go hand in hand when serving a customer. Focus your full attention on the customer and listen carefully to what he or she says. It is important to ask a customer, "Can I help you?"—but it is even more important to listen to the customer's response.

Be Knowledgeable

Customers today are well informed and demanding. They have more options and know more because of the huge amount of product information available through mass media and the Internet. Customers expect you to know the features, advantages, and benefits of your company's products or services. Product knowledge helps you meet customers' needs and find solutions to customer problems.

Learn all that you can about your company's products or services, as well as those of its competitors. Read material provided by manufacturers and talk with experienced employees about the products or services. In the words of Renee Everson, "Being fully trained about products, services, and company policies will enable you to find the best solution for each customer."[3] Also, be alert to customer comments about products or services so that you can pass them on to other customers. These efforts will prepare you to answer customer questions accurately.

Mr. Valdez, a frequent customer in the hardware store where Rosalie works, asks if the store carries a cleanser he saw advertised on television. Rosalie responds, "Yes, we do. Let me show you where it is located. May I ask how you plan to use this cleanser?" Mr. Valdez tells Rosalie that he needs to clean a heavily stained porcelain sink. Based on her product knowledge, Rosalie replies, "We don't recommend this cleanser for use on porcelain. It's too grainy and rough and could scratch the finish of your sink. Instead, I recommend this one (picks up another product), which is made especially for porcelain. I think you will be happy with it. It is less expensive and smells fresh." Mr. Valdez says, "Thanks for your help. I'll take your advice and give this a try."

Rosalie's product knowledge prevented Mr. Valdez from making a purchase he would regret. Equally important, her actions contributed to maintaining the goodwill of a customer.

Be Helpful

Being helpful to a customer is closely aligned with being knowledgeable. A helpful employee has a firm understanding of the products or services offered and the company's procedures and policies. Whenever a customer comes to you for help, provide assistance by being sensitive to his or her needs. Never humiliate a confused customer in any way because of "misinformation" they share with you. Recognize that the customer is misinformed and provide accurate information without talking down to or obviously correcting the customer. In the following scenario, Isaiah was able to correct the customer without being obvious.

Linda went into the pro shop to buy a putter. She had recently taken up golf and heard it was important to have the right club. When Isaiah, the salesperson, approached her, she said, "I want a female putter." Isaiah smiled, stifled a laugh (he had never heard the phrase "female putter"), and said to the customer, "We have a wide variety of putters for women that I'd be happy to show you. Come right this way."

Figure 11-1 gives examples of acceptable phrases to use when dealing with customers.

USE ACCEPTABLE PHRASES
The left column shows phrases that are unacceptable when serving customers. The column on the right provides acceptable, respectful alternatives.

UNACCEPTABLE	ACCEPTABLE
"I don't know."	"I'll be happy to check and find out."
"This isn't my department."	"I don't work in this department, but let me call someone who can help."
"It's over there (you point)."	"Let me show you where it is."
"That's not my problem."	"I understand that you are upset. Let's find a satisfactory solution to the problem."
"Are you sure you understand?"	"Do you have any other questions about the product?"
"That item is out of stock."	"I'm sorry. That item is currently out of stock, but I'll be happy to check to see how soon we can have one here for you."

FIGURE 11-1 Choose your words carefully when you talk with customers.

Be Respectful

Hold each customer in high regard, and be polite, patient, and positive to everyone. Would you serve a teenager wearing shorts and a faded T-shirt the same way you would serve a person in business attire? You should! Every customer is important and deserves your full attention. Don't make the mistake of judging customers on their appearance. Put aside any biases you may have about certain customers because of the way they dress or because of their age or their race. Your employer hired you to serve and meet the expectations of *all* customers.

> *Toby, dressed in sweats from her workout at the gym, went into the showroom of a dealership that sold expensive sports cars. Cory, the salesperson, sized up Toby and decided (1) she couldn't afford a sports car, and (2) she would request a test drive, but what she really wanted was to buzz around the block a few times in a fancy model. Cory decides to let Toby alone. Toby looked at several models, picked up some brochures, sat in a couple of the showroom models, and finally left. The next day, Cory was driving to work when he noticed in the lane next to him one of the competitor's sport cars, bearing temporary owner tags. Cory looked at the driver. You guessed it; it was Toby. Toby had bought a car from the competition. The competition was happy to acknowledge Toby's presence, answer her questions, and give her the respect all customers deserve.*

Be Honest

If you are to build good customer relations, you must be truthful and sincere when dealing with customers. The phrase "honesty is the best policy" means that you should tell the truth, even when it seems like it would be useful to tell a lie. Lying or misleading a customer invariably leads to far worse problems than telling the truth. The customer may buy the cell phone charger because you told him it would work with any cell phone, but that same customer will return the charger when it does not work with the cell phone he or she has at home. When customers find you to be dishonest, you will have lost their business, respect, and trust.

Peter owns a dry cleaning business. An unhappy customer comes in, throws a suit on the counter, and says, "I specifically pointed out the grease spots on this suit when I brought it in for cleaning, but when I got it home, the spots were still there. Don't you know how to remove grease spots?" Peter was annoyed with the customer's attitude. He replied huffily, "If you had pointed out the spots, the clerk would have noted them on the ticket and the spots would have been removed. It is not a problem to remove grease spots on this type of fabric." The customer replied, "But I *did* point them out!" She pulls out the claim check and shows Peter where the clerk had noted the grease spots visible on the suit. The customer then picked up the suit and said, "I'll take my suit and my dry cleaning elsewhere. I don't appreciate being called a liar. I want the money I paid to have the suit cleaned returned." Peter says nothing; he goes to the cash register and returns the money to the customer.

Why did Peter lose this customer's business? How could he have handled the situation to the satisfaction of the customer?

Customers expect honesty, even when the message they receive isn't the one they want to hear. It is not a pleasant experience to tell a customer that you cannot deliver a product on the desired date. However, misleading the customer into thinking that the product will be available "any day now" (when you know it will be a matter of weeks rather than days) will only annoy the customer. Honesty is the *right* policy.

Make it your policy to be truthful about your products and services. There is no reason to make misleading claims. Along with honesty, be accountable for your actions as you serve customers. If you make a mistake, be up front and admit the error. When you take responsibility for your actions, you will gain the respect of others.

MAINTAINING CUSTOMER LOYALTY

The popular phrase "the customer is always right" is tossed around a lot. Customers may not always be right—but they are always customers and deserve to be treated as special. If the customer is not right, your job is to manage the experience so that the customer remains your customer. Do not let the customer feel that he or she was wrong in deciding to do business with your company.

Just because what the customer says sounds wrong to you, don't assume that it is. Maybe they didn't express themselves very well or the instructions they should have received were vague or missing. Look for opportunities to be helpful. What information could your customer have used before the misunderstanding occurred? Make sure they "get it" now.

Russ (customer): I bought this leaf blower/vacuum from you last week and it doesn't work. It is defective. I thought I could trust your products.

Vicki (clerk): We stand behind all our products. Let's take a look. What seems to be the trouble?

Russ: It won't blow leaves. I want my money back.

Vicki: Assembling these blowers can sometimes be tricky. (Vicki looks at the blower/vacuum and notices that it was put together incorrectly. She disassembles and reassembles it correctly.)

Russ: Mine looked just like that, but it didn't work.

Vicki: Let's see if it will work now. (She sprinkles some packing peanuts on the floor, plugs in the machine, turns it on, and vacuums up the packing peanuts.) There we go. It's working now. Let's try the blower. (She moves the blower pieces into place, drops some more packing peanuts on the floor and they blow everywhere.)

Russ: Well, let me see what you did again.

Vicki (demonstrates): Do you have any questions?

Russ: No, I think I can accept the thing now. Thanks for your help.

Vicki: I'm sorry you had to take the time to bring this back to the store. The directions for assembly could be improved.

Russ: Yes, they certainly could. Thanks again.

In this case, the customer's statement was incorrect. The product was not defective; the real problem was the customer's inability to assemble the product correctly. Note that Vicki handled the situation without telling Russ he was wrong. Vicki listened to his concerns and let him know that she wanted to help. She sent Russ on his way with a working blower/vacuum and a good feeling about her and the company she represents.

DEALING WITH DIFFICULT CUSTOMERS

There are days when not all customers want to be friendly or pleasant. In fact, some can be difficult. You may wonder why they are so difficult. There are hundreds of reasons—a bad day, an unpleasant experience on the way to your business, feeling ill, and so on. Customers are human, and human beings can be annoying, rude, and even abusive. When you deal with difficult customers, do not take it personally. They are not angry with you specifically. Rather, they are upset at a situation. Your job is to build good customers relations with *all* customers—not just those who are pleasant and agreeable.

Complaining customers. What steps can you take when faced with a difficult, complaining customer? First, make every effort to remain calm. By being calm, you will be in a better position to think constructively and find a solution that will satisfy your customer. Begin by asking yourself, "What is the cause of this problem?" This may take a few moments. You have to let the customer "vent" in order to get to the real problem. After listening carefully, restate the problem to make sure that you understand it correctly. Once you and the customer agree on the problem, some additional research on your part may be necessary to resolve the situation.

Rate your ability to meet customer expectations on a scale of 1–4. (If you are not in a position to serve customers, rate how you think you would react if you were.) Give yourself a 1 if you *never* use the skill; a 2 if you *rarely* use the skill; a 3 if you *sometimes* use the skill; or a 4 if you *often* use the skill.

_____ I know my products or services.
_____ I work to meet customer expectations.
_____ I listen when my customers complain or have questions.
_____ I use positive body language when communicating with customers.
_____ I demonstrate empathy toward my customers.
_____ I acknowledge my customers immediately.
_____ I am respectful of *all* my customers.
_____ TOTAL

If your total score is 25 or more, you are doing a good job in meeting customer expectations. If your score is 20 or more, you are doing a fair job. If your score is 18 or below, you need to work harder to meet customer expectations.

Apologize to the customer for any inconvenience the problem has caused. Display empathy—put yourself in the customer's place. Ask the customer for the opportunity to improve the situation. It will be difficult for the customer to continue to be angry when you express a willingness to help.

Now ask yourself, "What can I say to make things right with this customer? What is the best solution I can offer?" Explain that you are going to work to correct the situation. Tell the customer what you *can* do rather than what you cannot do. Don't blame another person or the situation. Ask the customer what he or she would consider to be a satisfactory solution. If that solution is reasonable, do it. (Of course, check with your supervisor for approval if that is what is expected of you.)

Don't take the remarks of an angry customer personally.

Review the situation afterwards and determine what you might do to keep this from happening again. Analyze what went wrong. If appropriate, call the customer in a few days to apologize again and make sure the solution is still satisfactory.

Verbally abusive customers. Unfortunately, you may encounter a verbally abusive customer who may threaten, accuse, or criticize you and your company. If this happens, understand that the customer is upset about something related to the organization (not with you personally), even though some remarks may be directed at you. Focus on determining and satisfying the customer's needs. You (or your supervisor) will need to make some type of adjustment to satisfy the customer and resolve the situation.

Your most unhappy customers are your greatest source of learning.

Never argue with a customer. This will only make the problem worse. Don't try to defend yourself with comments such as, "It's not my fault," "We didn't manufacture the product," or "I wasn't your salesperson." Such remarks will only anger the customer more. Allow the customer to voice his or her frustrations rather than trying to silence the customer with an argumentative statement. Stay calm and professional and try saying, when appropriate, "I understand your anger. Let's find a solution to the problem."

USING THE TELEPHONE EFFECTIVELY

Building good customer relations on the telephone can be more difficult than when serving a customer in person. You cannot use gestures and other nonverbal cues to convey your message, and you cannot see the facial expressions and gestures of the caller. Your voice, speech patterns, vocabulary, and attitude affect a caller's impression of you and your company.

To create a positive impression and build good customer relations, always use the proper telephone techniques shown in Figure 11-2. Practice the techniques and use them when you answer your phone at work. You have only one opportunity to make a good first impression.

TELEPHONE TIPS AND TECHNIQUES

1. Answer promptly and identify yourself.
2. Do not eat, drink, or chew gum when speaking on the phone.
3. Speak clearly and use a pleasant, friendly tone of voice.
4. Listen attentively to the caller's questions and comments.
5. Be patient and helpful.
6. Do not interrupt the caller.
7. Do not give the impression that you are rushed. It is better to return the call when you can give the caller your total attention.
8. Before placing a caller on hold, ask permission first and thank them.
9. It is better to return a call than to keep someone on hold too long.
10. Don't set the receiver down while you search for information; the caller will hear everything being discussed around you. Instead, put the caller on hold.
11. Return all calls as promised and in a timely fashion.
12. Never argue with a caller.
13. Ask for the best phone number and the best time to return a call, especially if someone else will return the call.
14. Generally, the person who places the call should hang up first. Always hang up the phone gently.

FIGURE 11-2 Proper telephone techniques.

"If e-mail had been around before the telephone was invented, people would have said, 'Hey, forget e-mail—with this new telephone invention I can actually talk to people.'"

Answer the call by the third ring. Do you know that your personality comes across in your telephone voice, and that the person you are talking with can "hear" your smile? Take a deep breath; smile before you speak; and control the speed, tone, and volume of your voice. Focus your total attention on the caller. Turn away from your computer, and never eat or drink during a phone conversation.

Project a tone that conveys enthusiasm, confidence, friendliness, and attentiveness. Speak clearly and watch your language. The unacceptable phrases in Figure 11-1 also apply to telephone conversations. Identify yourself by name and include the department and a greeting, if appropriate. For example, "Good morning. Ruben Russell. Graphics Department."

Be prepared to take notes. Write down the caller's name. If the caller doesn't identify him or herself, ask for a name. For example, "Could I have your name please?" or "With whom am I speaking?" Use the caller's name as you continue the conversation.

Ask permission before placing a caller on hold. Always ask callers if they can or want to be on hold. Once you have placed a caller on hold, check back every 30–45 seconds to update them. Thank them for holding and be as accurate as possible about how long they will need to hold. If you don't have an answer in a short period of time, let the caller know you are working on their problem. Allow the caller to decide whether to continue holding, leave a message, or have their call returned later.

Kayla was on the phone with Ken Stewart, a new customer who called to check on his order. Kayla needed to check the company database so she asked Mr. Stewart if she could put him on hold for three minutes while she accessed that information. He agreed. Kayla discovered that the new sofa was somewhere in transit between Atlanta and Cleveland. Before she spent more time researching the problem, she returned to the phone and said, "Thank you for holding, Mr. Stewart. Your sofa is en route, but it may take a few minutes until I can give you a firm delivery date. Would you like to remain on hold or do you want me to call you back once I have the information?" Mr. Stewart asked Kayla to call him back.

Transfer a call. When you need to transfer a call, be polite and ask if the caller would like to be transferred. Always explain why the transfer is necessary. Give the caller the name of the person (if unknown to them) and number in case the call does not go through. Be sure to get the caller's number in case you lose the call during the transfer. Whenever possible, stay on the line until the transfer is complete.

Unfortunately, you may answer the phone to encounter a frustrated customer who has been transferred several times before you get the call. Take ownership of the situation. Apologize for the inconvenience before trying to deal with the caller's concerns. If you don't know how to fix the situation, take the caller's name and number, find the appropriate person, and have that person return the call. Check back with the caller to be sure the situation has been resolved.

checkpoint

1. List five tips for building good customer relations.

   _____

   _____

   _____

   _____

   _____

2. Is the customer always right? Why or why not?

   _____

   _____

   _____

   _____

3. List five "unacceptable phrases" you will not use when talking to a customer.

_____

_____

_____

_____

_____

_____

_____

4. What is the first question you should ask yourself when dealing with a complaining customer?

_____

_____

_____

_____

_____

_____

_____

_____

5. List six telephone tips and techniques.

_____

_____

_____

_____

_____

_____

_____

_____

_____

applications

1. Explain what is meant by the saying, "Each customer is like a tree that branches out everywhere—you never lose just one customer."

_____

_____

_____

_____

_____

_____

2. Identify two companies (physical entities or online companies) that you feel do an excellent job of building good customer relations. Give specific examples of what they do that makes them superior to their competitors.

_____

_____

_____

_____

_____

3. Rewrite the following statements to be more empathetic and helpful.

"Those jeans don't come in your size."

_____

_____

_____

"Your room has been canceled. You should have called ahead and requested a late check-in."

_____

_____

_____

"We discontinued that model of MP3 player."

_____

_____

_____

"We don't make home deliveries of purchases less than $100."

_____

_____

_____

4. Describe a situation where you as a customer had a negative experience while trying to resolve an issue on the telephone. How could the customer service person have handled the situation differently? How was the situation resolved?

_____

_____

_____

_____

_____

_____

11 *points to* remember

Review the following points to determine what you remember from the chapter.

- Customers are important to the success of any business—and *repeat* customers are crucial. Successful businesses work hard to meet customer expectations and maintain customer loyalty.

- Know what customers expect and meet those expectations. Customer expectations include high-quality products and services, reliability, timeliness, empathy, and recognition.

- Meet customer expectations by being attentive, knowledgeable about your company's products or services, respectful, and honest.

- Customers may not always be right, but it is your responsibility to manage the experience so that the customer is satisfied and remains your customer.

- Customers are sometimes difficult, unhappy, and complaining. Take their concerns seriously, but not personally. Identify the concern or problem and offer the best solution possible.

- Providing good service and being courteous with telephone customers is just as important, and sometimes more difficult, than talking face-to-face. Answer the phone by the third ring, be pleasant as you answer, use your best voice, and ignore distractions. When you speak to a customer on the phone, that customer is your number one priority.

How did you do? Did you remember the main points you studied in the chapter?

KEY *terms*

tangible items

intangible items

reliability

Want more activities? Go to **www.cengage.com/careerreadiness/masters** to get started.

CHAPTER *activities*

1. Recall a time when you as a customer were improperly treated in an office or retail business. Describe the situation and explain why you think your expectations were not met.

   _____

   _____

   _____

   _____

   _____

   _____

2. Many businesses provide phone numbers where customers can reach automated voice systems that provide answers to frequently asked questions. Movie theaters and financial institutions are two examples. Describe a situation where your experience with an automated system was positive. Describe a situation where your experience was negative. What do you think are the main drawback of these systems?

   _____

   _____

   _____

   _____

   _____

   _____

   _____

3. Divide into teams of four students. Write a script for the following situation and be prepared to role play your script. Be creative. Let the father be a particularly discourteous customer. Allow Antonio and Theresa to be tactful in resolving the situation to the customers' satisfaction.

   The situation: Antonio and Theresa own a catering business. The day after a wedding reception for 200 people, Mr. and Mrs. Lehto (the father and mother of the bride) storm into the catering office and criticize the food, the presentation, and the serving staff. The true problem, however, is twofold: the parents think the cost of the reception is excessive for what they received, and Mr. Lehto doesn't like tea sandwiches (one of the sandwich choices made by Mrs. Lehto). Laura pulls out the contract Mrs. Lehto signed before the wedding.

   _____

   _____

   _____

   _____

   _____

   _____

4. Call a friend and say that you are conducting an experiment. Ask the friend to focus attention on your voice as you speak. Speak several sentences with a frown on your face. Then smile as you speak the next few sentences. Did your friend notice any difference in your voice?

   _____

   _____

   _____

   _____

   _____

   _____

CRITICAL thinking

Theo works in a small engine shop that specializes in the sale and repair of lawn mowers. Theo sold Roger Klein, a demanding customer, a self-propelled lawn mower. Roger returns to the shop a few days later with the mower in the back of his truck. He storms into the salesroom and states in a loud voice, "You sold me a worthless piece of junk. This is a poor excuse for a lawn mower. It keeps stalling out."

Theo lets Roger "sound off" and waits until he quiets down. Theo then examines the mower and spots the problem, which would be easy to fix. Theo says, "Mr. Klein, I'm sorry you are dissatisfied with this mower. How can I make you a happy customer?" Roger replies, "I want a new mower—in fact, I want a different model." Theo walks to the mower display and says, "This one will serve you well. It is also self-propelled." Roger says, "All right—but this one had better give me better service than the clunker I'm returning." Theo loads the new mower into Roger's truck, and Roger drives away.

Theo, chuckling to himself says, "You dummy! The mower you drove off with isn't as good as the one you returned! It has less power than the original one. I'll clean up the mower you returned and resell it."

1. Did Theo live up to the expectations of his customer? Why or why not?

_____

_____

_____

_____

2. What do you think about Theo's sales tactics?

_____

_____

_____

_____

3. How might Theo's dishonesty and lack of empathy toward his customer catch up with him in the future?

_____

_____

_____

_____

CASE 11.2 Is the Customer Always Right?

Brianna sells an intangible product—homeowners' insurance. She works hard and tries to meet the expectations of her customers. Eva and Murray Shaddock have had an insurance policy for three years. Mr. Shaddock calls Brianna and reports that their roof was damaged during last night's storm. Brianna tells him that she and an adjuster will be out to assess the damage. Brianna and the adjuster go to the Shaddock's home and find that several shingles are missing on the north side of the house.

On examination, the damage to the shingles seems unusual. Normally, Brianna would expect to find a few partial shingles still in place. In this case, it was obvious that eight whole shingles were missing. With Mr. Shaddock's permission, Brianna and the adjuster talk with the neighbors and finds that they have no damage. Further, they find eight shingles partially concealed in the trash. They examine the roof damage again and, based on what they see, suspect that the shingles were pulled out of place. Brianna and the insurance adjuster agree that the damage was not caused by the wind.

1. Should Brianna tell the Shaddocks that she and the adjuster concluded that the shingles were pulled off the roof and not removed by wind? If so, what should she say?

   _____

   _____

   _____

2. To keep the Shaddocks as customers, should Brianna file a report that says the roof damage was caused by the wind and should be covered by the insurance policy? What might be the result of this filing?

   _____

   _____

   _____

3. What consequences might the Shaddocks suffer for falsely claiming damage to their roof?

   _____

   _____

   _____

4. Is "honesty the best policy" in this case?

   _____

   _____

   _____

   _____

Valuing Diversity   **12** chapter

Think About It: Kirsten grew up in Montana big sky country. Her grandparents were immigrants from Norway, and she remembers some good-natured teasing about her blond hair. She also remembers hearing ethnic stories. Norwegian farmers were stereotyped as stubborn and not particularly intellectual. But underneath it all was pride and appreciation of Scandinavian culture. After completing a two-year degree in accounting, Kirsten went to work in a local bank where she eventually moved into a management position. Yesterday she was told that management was offering her an exciting challenge if she wanted it. They were sending her to El Paso, Texas, to set up the accounting system in a new branch bank where she would train personnel from Hispanic backgrounds. While she was well qualified for the assignment, she was nervous about accepting it. In discussing it with George, a trusted friend and coworker, she said, "I have never worked in a place where the culture is so different from mine. What do I know about the people and their customs in El Paso? Will I be at a disadvantage because I'm not fluent in Spanish, as my coworkers and many of the bank's customers will be?"

Are Kirsten's concerns about accepting this opportunity justified? What can Kirsten do to adjust to a culture so different from her own?

© Golden Pixels LLC, 2009/Used under license from Shutterstock.com

12.1 Our Diverse Society

12.2 Understanding Other Cultures

12.3 Fairness in the Workplace

objectives

After completing this chapter, you should be able to:

1. Describe the changing American workforce.
2. Explain how employers manage diversity and how workers can adapt to diversity in the workplace.
3. Describe how discrimination, prejudice, and stereotyping can cause cultural conflict.
4. Explain why it is important to understand other cultures.
5. Explain how employers are required to recognize and avoid unfair or illegal discrimination and prejudice in the workplace.
6. Explain what sexual harassment is and how to deal with it.

Our Diverse Society

What if everyone around you were just like you? What if they were all your age, your race, and your size with your background, abilities, and beliefs? You may think that interpersonal relations would be easier because there would be so much common ground. Of course, not everyone is like you. **Diversity** refers to differences among individuals based on gender, race, age, religion, culture, and other characteristics. There is increasing diversity in American society. People come in all shapes and sizes, and all ages, races, religions, and ethnic backgrounds.

Building common ground with people who are not like you is one of the most important skills you can develop in today's multicultural world. As you work on developing this skill, you will find that understanding people who are different from you can enrich your life as well as theirs. If you have the attitude that you can learn something from everyone you meet, you will expand your horizons much more than if you close your mind to these opportunities.

"Diversity is the one true thing we all have in common. Celebrate it every day."

LEARNING FROM DIVERSITY

If you approach your personal and professional relationships with an open mind, you may find that some of the lessons learned about diversity appear to be negatives ones. For example: how *not* to judge people you consider to be "foreigners"; how *not* to be biased against a particular ethnic group; how *not* to assume that the man who works at the bank is the manager and the woman in the next cubicle is his assistant. But most of the lessons will bring positive results. You will increase your understanding, gain the ability to look at problems from different viewpoints, and find new ways of developing solutions in cooperation with people from different backgrounds. Cultural diversity may make our lives more complicated, but it also makes our lives more fulfilling and more productive.

> *When Chris's good friend Patrick transferred to another office, management hired a man who had moved to the United States from Vietnam as a young child. Chien Nguyen kept to himself. He brought his lunch to work and left for home immediately after work. He spoke English without an accent—when he spoke to Chris at all. Chris missed working with his buddy Patrick. One day his mother gave him an article from a magazine about the local Vietnamese community. Chris showed the article to Chien, who knew some of the people written about. A few weeks later, Chien invited Chris and his mother to his home for dinner with his family. Chris's mother and Chien's aunt were nurses in the same health care group and had met a week earlier at a training session about the upcoming flu season. What a small world!*

How diverse is your world? Give yourself 1 point for each *yes* answer.

1. I have a passport.
2. I have visited another country.
3. My parents or grandparents were born in another country.
4. I speak more than one language.
5. I socialize with people from other cultures.
6. I work with people from other cultures.
7. I have taken a class with or worked with a person with disabilities.
8. I have watched a foreign-made movie with subtitles.
9. I enjoy listening to music from other cultures.
10. I follow the news every day.
11. I am familiar with the customs and history of my own ethnic background(s).
12. I have asked someone from another culture to explain something about his or her culture.
13. I have asked someone from another culture for his or her observations about my culture.
14. When I meet a person with disabilities, I focus on what that person *can* do.

Did you score more than 12 points? Felicitaciones! (That's "congratulations" in Spanish.) No matter what you scored, think of other creative ways you can become more aware of the diversity in your community.

BIAS AND STEREOTYPES

During your childhood and teenage years, you develop your attitudes and values from people around you: your family, friends, classmates, teachers, and neighbors. It is easy to absorb attitudes and values from others without thinking much about them. Or you may have a bad experience with a member of another race or ethnic group and then generalize a negative attitude toward everyone from that group. When you are intolerant of people unlike you, it is often because of biases based on unfair assumptions you make about a group they belong to or a particular background they have.

A **bias** is a way of thinking that prevents you from being impartial about a situation, issue, or person. If your friend raved about her accounting instructor and you are about to take accounting with the same person, you probably have a positive bias toward the class and the instructor. If your sister is serving in the military and is stationed overseas, you may be biased against anti-war demonstrators who are picketing at the Veterans' Day parade.

A stereotype is the belief that certain groups of people all have certain qualities or characteristics. **Stereotyping** occurs whenever you assume that all members of a group have the same characteristics instead of viewing the members of the group as individuals. When you stereotype someone, you assign to that person characteristics that may be unfair and undeserved.

For the sake of illustration, suppose that you were raised to believe these fictitious stereotypes:

- Thin people are stingy.
- People who have blue eyes can't be trusted.
- People who have small feet are terrible cooks.

Of course, all three of these made-up stereotypes are ridiculous. If you examine your own stereotypes and the ones you hear others express, you will find that they are equally irrational. No doubt there are some thin people who are stingy, but you would never assume that they all are. It would be absurd to assume that you can't trust anyone with blue eyes or that people with small feet are bad cooks. Stop and think about real stereotypes you may have heard. If you analyze them carefully, do they make any more sense than the three absurd examples above?

The trouble with generalities is that they are rarely true. Even if you assume that certain groups have positive qualities, the reality is that some in the group probably do and some probably do not. Some far-fetched examples may help you to understand this. Suppose you assume that:

- People who use wheelchairs are brilliant mathematicians.
- Left-handed people have great singing voices.
- People who wear glasses are generous.

You can see that generalities still don't hold water, even if they are based on positive qualities. When you find yourself making assumptions about someone because of race, nationality, gender, or appearance, think again. Judge people based on their own conduct and qualities, not on generalizations you assume apply to their group.

Discrimination and Prejudice

Discrimination is behavior based on an unfair attitude. If you believe a particular race of people tends to be lazy, you display a discriminatory attitude. If you were an employer and refused to hire people of that race, you would be guilty of discrimination.

Prejudice is a term that is often used in connection with discrimination. It means to prejudge or form an opinion without taking the time and effort to judge fairly. If you have decided that people belonging to a particular group are inferior, you will likely prejudge all people you meet belonging to that group. When you prejudge a person based solely on being a member of some group, rather than on what he or she is like as an individual, you are showing prejudice.

Reaching out to neighbors and coworkers from backgrounds unlike yours can expand your horizons.

Photodisc/Getty Images

Subtle Discrimination

Subtle discrimination is discrimination that is not obvious and is seldom brought out in the open. It is based on appearance, values, or some other personal characteristic. Examples are discrimination against short people, tall people, single people, or divorced people, to name a few. You may be a victim of this type of discrimination, or you may be guilty of subtle discrimination against others. Although this subtle discrimination may not be illegal, it is unfair and counterproductive in the workplace.

Drew couldn't understand why Mr. Cunningham hadn't hired any Mexican-American workers. The insurance office served a multicultural mix of people, but lately many Mexican Americans had moved into the neighborhood. Adding a Mexican American to the staff would better reflect the changing community. When Drew asked Mr. Cunningham, he said, "I don't know. I guess I haven't found anyone who I thought would be a good fit for this office."

Keep in mind that the effects of prejudice and discrimination are destructive. Make every effort to eliminate prejudice by developing acceptance and tolerance of people who are unlike you.

TREAT OTHERS FAIRLY

Are you aware of your own biases?

- Examine your own attitudes. Are you prejudging others? Do you need to unlearn some prejudices?
- Ban from your vocabulary all negative terms for ethnic and other groups.
- Learn and use the preferred terms for identifying group members. For example, refer to "people with disabilities," not "crippled people." The United States Department of Labor website has a helpful guide to preferred terms.
- Avoid using a person's minority group label to identify the person. For example, say "Deliver the package to the receptionist" instead of "Deliver the package to the Latina woman at the front desk."
- Resist and expose prejudice when you encounter it. Find a tactful way to bring intolerance out in the open.
- Bring up the subject of discrimination. You may influence others to be more aware of and sensitive to these problems.

FIGURE 12-1 Become aware of your own biases.

Overcoming Unfair Judgments

Discrimination, prejudice, and stereotyping can become so much a part of your life that you hardly notice them. These unfair judgments often feel right simply because they are a habit. If you make an effort to rethink your preconceived ideas about a particular group, you can overcome your tendency to stereotype and prejudge people. It's not just a question of being politically correct. It's a question of being fair.

As you become aware of and sensitive to discrimination (including your own), you will find opportunities to resist unfairness at work and in society. Figure 12-1 has several suggestions.

CULTURAL PRIDE AND TOLERANCE

It is natural to take pride in your own cultural heritage and to feel most comfortable with it. You can celebrate your own heritage as well as that of other groups. The key is not to assume that yours is superior or inferior to theirs. Your heritage is not necessarily better or worse—it's just different. This tendency to believe in the superiority of one's own culture is called **ethnocentrism**.

Naturally, you view the world from your own perspective, which is based on your background and experience. Take care that this natural tendency does not turn into seeing and appreciating only your own individual point of view, which can give you a narrow and distorted image of reality.

Balancing Viewpoints

Ethnic food is one of the most pleasant ways to experience other cultures. You may think that your Puerto Rican grandmother's spice cake is the best in the world. It probably is—in your family—but it is not necessarily better than a spice cake made by someone else's Italian grandmother or another person's Scottish grandmother. It's just different. The same is true of attitudes, behaviors, and customs. You can love your own cultural heritage without mocking others. You can learn to make use of the attitudes and behaviors you find good in other cultures and tolerate the ones you find less valuable.

When Jen returned from being an exchange student in Sweden, she began taking off her shoes when she entered the house. Jen explained that Swedes never wear their "outside" shoes inside their homes. Many families keep a pair of wooden shoes beside the door for each family member. Jen asked her family to try taking off their shoes at the front door for one week. A month later, Jen's father and sister were still following this custom. They keep flip-flops in the hall closet to wear inside, and Jen's father is thinking about making a "shoe tray" for the front hallway.

Remind yourself to treat everyone else's culture and world view with respect and consideration, expecting the same in return. If you think someone is treating you with disrespect *because* you are a woman, or *because* you are overweight, or *because* you are of Middle Eastern descent, calmly challenge his or her stereotyping. Find a quiet, private moment to have this conversation. You can be assertive in discussing a perceived problem without being angry or confrontational. Sometimes just talking about a perceived bias can ease everyone's discomfort. The person you are challenging may not even have been aware of treating you differently, or seeming to.

The more you learn about different groups and cultures, the more you will come to appreciate them. Here are some suggestions:

- Attend cultural events, festivals, parades, and other activities sponsored by ethnic groups in your area.
- Explore an ethnic grocery store or go to an ethnic restaurant and sample a new cuisine.
- Take the initiative in getting to know people from different ethnic groups.
- Participate in diversity workshops or other training activities sponsored by your employer or your school.
- Volunteer to help with fundraising events for people with disabilities.
- Read or listen to authors and politicians speaking about issues affected by ethnic diversity.

EXPAND YOUR MULTICULTURAL HORIZONS

Arlene is a senior designer for a clothing manufacturer. Her record as an employee is excellent, but she has a tendency to worry about her job. During dinner with her friend Marilyn, Arlene said, "I think I'm in for real trouble." "What's the problem?" Marilyn asked. Arlene replied, "They've added another designer in my division—a young Korean woman. The boss probably wanted someone who will work twenty-four hours a day and all weekend. You know how 'foreigners' are. She will probably work for next to nothing." Her friend responded, "I don't know why you're so concerned. You're very talented and everyone compliments your work." Arlene continued, "She has a strong accent. In the two minutes we talked, I could hardly understand a word. I don't know why they couldn't hire one of the hundreds of local designers who are dying to get into the business." Marilyn responded, "You need to slow down and stop jumping to conclusions. You talked to this woman for two minutes. Put yourself in her shoes: she knows she has an accent, and she had all of two minutes to meet the senior designer. I'm sure she was very nervous. The best thing you can do, for both of you, is keep an open mind. She will probably be grateful to learn from you." Arlene smiled and replied, "Fourteen years ago when I moved here from Atlanta, I was practically in the same situation. Mr. Olson used to laugh at my Southern accent, but he was a wonderful mentor to me."

Is Arlene's attitude toward her new coworker reasonable? Why can Marilyn see the situation more clearly than Arlene can?

TODAY'S CULTURALLY DIVERSE SOCIETY

You have no doubt heard the United States described as a "melting pot" of different cultures. Earlier in American history, the term "melting pot" described the blending of immigrants from other cultures into the dominant American culture sometimes described as the WASP (White Anglo-Saxon Protestant) majority. It was expected that immigrants would try to look, sound, and think like this majority.

Today this multicultural concept has evolved into the widely accepted value of *inclusion*—including people who may have been excluded at one time. In the past, women, people with disabilities, African Americans, Hispanics, and Native Americans were often excluded from jobs and educational opportunities.

Even today, when age discrimination is illegal, older and younger workers often must overcome negative assumptions in the job market and workplace. If you find yourself assuming that the oldest person in your workplace lacks computer skills or that the youngest person lacks good judgment, ask yourself if you may be biased because of the person's age. Make an effort to judge people as individuals, not stereotypes.

Today's value of inclusion embraces the harmonious mixing of cultures rather than the impossible goal of trying to make us all alike. Figure 12-2 shows how the population of the United States is expected to change by mid-century.[1]

Diversity in our society will only increase. Your individual success in both your personal and professional life will depend, in part, on how well you adapt to these changes.

The country's population is expected to increase to 419.9 million people in 2050, from 305.5 million in 2009. White Americans have dominated American society and the American workforce for generations, but government projections show them declining in coming years to less than half of the population. The major ethnic groups are growing at different rates.

- Today, white non-Hispanics make up about 65 percent of the American population. That percentage will decline steadily until it is below 50 percent by 2045. Government projections show whites composing 46.3 percent of the population in 2050.
- Hispanics make up 16 percent of the population. That will increase to about 30 percent in 2050.
- Asians are 5.3 percent of the population today and will increase to about 9 percent in 2050.
- The African-American population, now at 13.6 percent, will rise to 15 percent by 2050.

FIGURE 12-2 Projected changes in American population by 2050.

checkpoint

1. What is diversity and how does it affect your personal and work life?

_____

_____

_____

2. Explain why each of the following statements is *wrong*.

a. Diversity is the same as inclusion.

_____

_____

_____

b. Ethnocentrism is an appropriate reaction to changes in society.

_____

_____

_____

c. Whites have always been and will probably always be the majority in the American workforce.

_____

_____

_____

_____

3. What is the difference between a bias and a stereotype?

_____

_____

_____

_____

4. What is subtle discrimination? Give two examples.

_____

_____

_____

_____

5. What does it mean to describe the United States as a "melting pot" of different cultures?

_____

_____

_____

_____

applications

1. Think about people you know who come from other cultures. List three of them by their first names and describe differences you have noticed between the way you view things and the way they do.

_____

_____

_____

_____

2. Do you think men and women hold different stereotypes? Why or why not?

_____

_____

_____

_____

3. Talk to older adults about diversity. Do they view diversity differently from the way you view it? Explain your answer.

_____

_____

_____

_____

4. Think about your sensitivity to the values, dress, and customs that may reflect other people's cultures. For example:

a. You're in a grocery store when you hear people speaking a language you do not understand. How do you react?

_____

_____

_____

_____

_____

_____

b. You're attending a diversity-training workshop. Your partner for an activity introduces himself as Ito Ichiro and asks you to call him Ito-san. He doesn't make eye contact and has a nervous smile on his face the entire time. How do you react?

_____

_____

_____

_____

_____

_____

c. You're in the doctor's waiting room when a woman who covers her head with a hajib (a traditional Muslim head scarf) sits down beside you. How do you react?

_____

_____

_____

_____

_____

_____

d. The couple sitting across from you in the food court are speaking French and eating their sandwiches with knives and forks. How do you react?

_____

_____

_____

_____

_____

_____

Understanding Other Cultures

Cultural diversity enriches our lives in many ways, but it can also lead to misunderstandings. Problems that arise among people from different racial and ethnic backgrounds are called **cultural conflicts**. **Culture** refers to a learned and shared system of knowledge, beliefs, values, and attitudes. Ethnocentrism (the tendency to see and appreciate only our own individual point of view) is behind many of these difficulties. Nevertheless, cultural conflict can usually be avoided if you are aware, open-minded, and respectful to cultural values, attitudes, and beliefs different from your own.

on the job

Peter and Misuki are coworkers at a lumber company that has been acquired by a Japanese company. They are on a break from a training session where they were learning how to interact with Japanese customers. Peter's assignment during the session had been to meet with two Japanese men who were playing the role of purchasing agents negotiating to buy a large quantity of lumber. Misuki (who had moved from Japan when she was a teenager) was assigned to observe the interaction. Peter was told to give his usual sales pitch and then evaluate the meeting with Misuki at break time. Peter thought he had done his homework. He had samples of the wood that would work best for interior door and window frames. He had calculated a discounted price and shipping costs to the Tokyo harbor. He was sure the bid was a great deal. Still, he felt discouraged. He told Misuki, "I couldn't figure out how to relate to those guys. I was uncomfortable and I know they were, too. I just couldn't connect with them." Misuki replied, "I think you tried to relate to these Japanese customers just as you would to Americans. Let me explain what I observed."

What additional homework could Peter have done to prepare for these negotiations? Why was it a good idea to have Misuki react to what she observed?

If you have not already done so, read the On the Job scenario. Here is how Misuki, who is from Japan, coached Peter on his negotiations with the Japanese buyers. She told Peter he had underestimated the influence cultural differences would have on the negotiations, and she explained how Japanese attitudes and behaviors differ from those in American culture.

"When Mr. Suko handed you his business card," Misuki said, "You tucked it into your planner without really looking at it. In Japanese culture, it is more polite to take a few moments to read the card respectfully. The Japanese also like to spend more time on polite social conversation before approaching the business of the meeting. Americans think a much shorter time is enough. To the Japanese buyers, you jumped too quickly into your sales proposal.

You need to be patient until the Japanese client introduces the subject. Don't misinterpret this as not being serious about the business at hand."

Misuki continued, "Eye contact can be another communication conflict. I was watching you. You would try to make eye contact, and they would try to avoid it. They would lower their eyes, and you would look right at them. When you looked down at your notes, they would look up."

"You probably felt uncomfortable because they were often silent during the negotiations. You may have thought this meant they were uninterested or dissatisfied. Among the Japanese, respectful silence is a way of being polite. Facial expressions also enter into it. If things are not going well, Americans expect to see frowns. A respectful, tolerant smile is a courtesy in Japan, but Americans may misread this smile as approval or agreement."

"There's also a cultural difference in the way they view their relationship to their company. I think the word that got you into the most trouble was *you*. It's better to ask a Japanese representative, 'What does your company think?' rather than 'What do you think?' "

Peter was fascinated by Misuki's explanations. "I'm glad this was a training session!" he said, "This was a hard way to learn, but I know the lesson will stick. I never want to experience that again!"

RESPECTING DIFFERENCES

Many cultural conflicts occur because people simply do not know what matters in another culture. In dealing with people from other backgrounds, try not to assume that they will share your attitudes, behaviors, and customs. Here is an example of a cultural conflict and how it might have been eased.

Svetlana grew up in Moscow and had recently moved to the United States. After several weeks of working with Svetlana, her new friend Andy invited her to dinner at his house. Andy was very specific in his invitation. He and his wife Ellen planned to serve appetizers at 5:30 p.m. and dinner at 6 p.m. When Svetlana arrived at 6:30, she cheerfully greeted Andy with a hug, and when introductions were made, she put her arm around Ellen and greeted her warmly. Ellen wriggled away from what she felt was inappropriate touching. She kept backing away from Svetlana, who stood very close to her when they spoke.

Your own background will influence how you react to people's behaviors and attitudes in this story. In traditional Russian culture, being punctual is not important. Svetlana did not mean to insult Ellen by arriving late. Svetlana was accustomed to a different sense of both time and personal space than Andy and Ellen were used to. According to former foreign service officer Yale Richmond, author of the book *From Nyet to Da: Understanding the New Russia*, "Russians stand very close when conversing, often less than 12 inches apart, which is closer than many Westerners will find comfortable. They gesture more and do not hesitate to make physical contact and invade the other person's space."[2]

One of Svetlana's greatest challenges in adjusting to life in the United States will be to learn to respect the American sense of time and personal space. If Andy and Ellen had understood that these behaviors are culturally determined, everyone would have been more comfortable.

DEALING WITH LANGUAGE BARRIERS

Language is probably the most obvious source of cultural barriers. You may have experienced this firsthand as a tourist trying to find your way in a foreign country. Or perhaps a foreign tourist visiting the United States stopped you and asked directions. What can you do when you find yourself unable to understand or make yourself understood? First, and most important, you can avoid making unfair assumptions.

Assuming that a person is poor or illiterate because he or she speaks broken English is unfair and unrealistic. In fact, that person's limited English probably exceeds your ability to speak their language. Would you want to have someone judge your intelligence by your ability to speak a foreign language? You can generally assume, however, that they would like to speak English better. You can help them by speaking clearly and by using standard English and not slang, which may be harder to understand. You can take the time to explain words that are unfamiliar to them. It is also helpful to avoid using culturally based metaphors, as in the following example.

Jane and Tim were complimenting Anjali on a presentation she gave for Stanley, who was ill. Anjali was headquartered in Mumbai, and she was on a three-month assignment in the United States. "You really hit that one out of the park," Tim said. "You can pinch hit for me any time you want!"

Jane added, "I was nervous for you when I heard that Stanley had to take a rain check. Even though your projections are just ballpark figures, they are exactly what we needed. Today is the first day I don't feel like we have two strikes against us. Maybe we can finally get off first base. Please touch base with us when you have the final figures."

Did you notice all the baseball metaphors in the scenario? Anjali is from the land of soccer and cricket, and she had a hard time following Jane and Tim. The conversation is exaggerated to make an important point. Use standard English when you talk with someone who learned English as a second language, and watch the person's body language for signs that you have not been understood.

Digital Vision/Getty Images

Learn to look beyond appearances to understand people from other cultural backgrounds.

In today's global society, it is wise to make an effort to learn other languages. Although you cannot master every language you will encounter in the workplace, you can learn to become conversational in at least one. If you have frequent contact with speakers of a particular foreign language, start by learning how to express common terms such as "please," "thank you," "hello," and "goodbye."

Jordan's new classmate Frieda was originally from Germany. She speaks excellent English, but with a slight accent. They have become good friends and often arrive at class together. Jordan decided to learn a few phrases in German. The next day, he said, "Guten Morgen. Wie geht es dir?" Freida smiled broadly. "Jordan, I'm impressed! You just wished me a good morning and asked how I am!"

ADJUSTING TO A MULTICULTURAL SOCIETY

As part of your effort to adapt and feel comfortable in a society where there is so much diversity, you should take advantage of opportunities to make cultural adjustments. Figure 12-3 lists some ways to do this.

Reaching out to neighbors and coworkers from backgrounds unlike yours can expand your horizons. Explore what you can learn from others who may feel isolated or subject to discrimination—young entry-level workers, men or women who may be a minority in your workplace, people with disabilities, older workers, and those whose educational and social backgrounds are different from yours.

The Internet is a tremendous resource for finding information about other cultures, countries, and traditions. Conduct a search on a particular area of interest, or simply search "cultural diversity" for links to interesting websites, research, and articles. You can find a lot of information on the U.S. State Department's website as well as foreign government websites and online newspapers, television, and radio stations.

1. **Study at least one foreign language.** You can take courses through adult and community education programs. Bookstores and libraries have books and CDs.

2. **Listen to online radio stations** that broadcast in the language you are learning. This is a good way to hear the language spoken clearly at a conversational speed.

3. **Sharpen your skills by speaking** the language instead of English with friends or coworkers who are fluent in the language. Ask them to correct your mistakes and coach you in pronouncing and speaking correctly.

4. **Ask someone who knows the** language to translate the words and also help you to interpret silences, gestures, and facial expressions from an unfamiliar cultural context.

5. **Go to the Meetup website and** search for groups in your area that meet to practice speaking the language.

LEARN ABOUT OTHER CULTURES

Learn about the cultures of your neighbors and coworkers:

- Study other cultures. Books, magazines, newspaper articles, television programs, and movies can all be good resources.
- Study the problems and issues that create misunderstanding and cause division.
- Make friends with people from different cultural backgrounds. Ask them to explain some of their customs, beliefs, and practices.
- Offer guidance if you see people having a difficult time adjusting, but do so with sensitivity and respect. Explain aspects of local culture that they may not understand. Help them to feel welcome, to understand, and to fit in.
- Explain your own culture to those from other cultural backgrounds. Compare cultures by finding similarities as well as differences.
- Observe people from other cultures in their interactions with one another. Notice gestures, facial expressions, and posture while they are talking.
- Take a stand on issues that promote respect for and appreciation of diversity.

FIGURE 12-3 Make the effort to learn about other cultures.

Interview someone from a culture or minority group that interests you. Then answer these questions:

1. What are some interesting and unusual (to you) customs and behaviors in that culture?

_____

_____

2. How does the person explain the importance of the customs and behaviors?

_____

_____

3. Which of your customs and behaviors does this person find strange? Why?

_____

_____

4. How do you explain these customs and behaviors to this person?

_____

_____

checkpoint

1. List two things you can do to avoid conflict due to cultural differences.

_____

_____

_____

_____

2. What is the most noticeable source of cultural barriers?

_____

_____

_____

_____

3. List four ways you can help those from other countries make cultural adjustments in the workplace or at school.

_____

_____

_____

_____

4. Why is it important to use standard English when speaking with people whose first language is not English?

_____

_____

_____

_____

5. List four ways you can learn about other cultures.

_____

_____

_____

_____

applications

1. Do you agree with these statements? Explain your answer.

   a. People from other countries who come to the United States to live should be required to learn English well before they come.

   _____

   _____

   _____

   _____

   b. Americans don't need to know any language other than English.

   _____

   _____

   _____

   _____

   c. Arriving on time is valued in every culture.

   _____

   _____

   _____

   _____

   d. People who gesture a lot with their hands are nervous and high strung.

   _____

   _____

   _____

   _____

e. It is impolite to wear a hat indoors.

_____

_____

_____

_____

f. A man should always shake a woman's hand when they are introduced.

_____

_____

_____

_____

2. Make a list of things people say that reflect cultural stereotypes. Two examples are listed to get you started: The French are romantic. Germans drive fast.

_____

_____

_____

_____

3. Where have you traveled outside the United States? What were your reactions to the culture? What did you learn about yourself?

_____

_____

_____

_____

4. If you speak or understand another language, how has this helped you adjust to multicultural situations?

_____

_____

_____

_____

5. As a result of reading this section, what steps do you intend to take to improve your relationships with people from other cultures?

_____

_____

_____

_____

Fairness in the Workplace

Everyone has an inner sense of fairness, and when it is violated, it is natural to feel uncomfortable, hurt, and sometimes angry. Nothing is more important than fairness for bringing harmony to the workplace. If you treat others unfairly, you cause resentment, grudges, and ill will. Fairness comes down to treating others as you would like to be treated. It means behaving toward others with kindness and honesty and without bias. A fair person does not take advantage of others. A fair person carries his or her share of the workload, without expecting others to do it for them. A fair person may get an idea from someone else, but does not claim it as his or her own; the person who had the idea is given full credit for it.

Fairness also means treating people equally, without discriminating based on prejudices and stereotypes. The word discrimination originally meant recognizing differences. Over time, however, it has developed a negative meaning: unfair treatment of a particular person or group based on race, gender, religion, or physical disability. Such treatment is unfair because it is based on stereotypes rather than on objective observations and judgments.

"Diversity may be the hardest thing for a society to live with, and perhaps the most dangerous thing for a society to be without."

on the job

Rahina's interview for a position as the receptionist at a health clinic was conducted by two men, the clinic administrator and a doctor. She was young and wearing a wedding band, so the interviewers assumed she was married. They seemed to be very concerned about how long she would stay in the position. They asked a lot of questions about her long-term plans, and the manager said, "What about your family?" Rahina sensed that he was trying to find out if she had children or planned to have them. She knew that would be an illegal question to ask, so she simply said, "My family would be delighted if I came to work here."

Are the interviewers entitled to know about Rahina's family? Did Rahina handle the question well?

DIVERSITY AND AFFIRMATIVE ACTION

Diversity—the demographic, cultural, and personal differences among individuals—is sometimes confused with affirmative action. **Affirmative action** is a legal concept that requires employers to take positive steps to create employment opportunities for minorities and women.

Affirmative action began with the 1964 Civil Rights Act, which prohibited discrimination in voting, public places, government programs, and employment. It was designed to create equal opportunities for all regardless of race, color, religion, sex, or national origin. In spite of its attempt to right past wrongs, affirmative action has been controversial and has been challenged in the courts by some who argue that it has made white males the objects of unfair discrimination. Nevertheless, women and minorities have made great gains in the workplace since 1964. Businesses have embraced diversity and inclusion as being good for business and as a means of creating new ideas, new markets, and new opportunities for expansion.

Angela had been a stay-at-home mom for 10 years. Now that her children were grown, she wanted to reenter the job market. Her neighbor, Henry, suggested that she apply for an opening at the Highway Department where he had worked for 20 years. He knew Angela liked being outdoors, and the state job had good benefits. "But wouldn't I be the only woman working there?" Angela asked. "As a matter of fact, you would. But when I started, I was the only African American working there, which probably seems impossible to you." Henry answered. "It's about time they hired a woman, and you would be really good at the job."

Reverse Discrimination

As employers changed their policies for recruiting, selecting, and hiring, the problem of reverse discrimination emerged. **Reverse discrimination** is discrimination against members of a social or racial group that is considered to be dominant in a society. In the United States, whites, especially white men, have been affected by reverse discrimination. The objective of affirmative action was to create a workforce with fair representation of women and minorities. Giving preference to women and minorities, however, left many white men complaining of unfair discrimination. While affirmative action may seem to be a reasonable effort to resolve imbalances in the workplace, it left some white men thinking they were not hired or promoted *because of* their gender and race.

Kevin had interviewed for six jobs as an administrative assistant, but every job had gone to someone else. "I feel like white males are a persecuted minority," he complained to his wife. "If I were a woman or a minority, I know someone would have hired me by now." "You really should have the same opportunities no matter what your sex or race," his wife replied. "Maybe we should rehearse your interview answers some more. I know someone is going to offer you a job. Maybe there's more we can do to market you."

EQUAL EMPLOYMENT OPPORTUNITIES

The U.S. Equal Employment Opportunity Commission (EEOC) receives complaints of unfair discrimination and evaluates them and then either tries to work out the problem or refers the complaint to the courts. It develops guidelines to help organizations create and put fair hiring programs into practice. This agency is supported by state and local government agencies such as community action boards, human relations commissions, human rights offices, and citizens' review boards concerned with discrimination by employers and government agencies.

It is important to know your legal rights in the workplace. You do not need a law degree to understand workers' basic rights. For example:

- Employers are not allowed to discriminate in any area of employment based on race, color, religion, sex, national origin, disability or family status.
- It is illegal for employers to discriminate in recruiting, hiring, promoting, discharging, classifying, or training employees.
- It is illegal to treat women and minorities differently from the way white males are treated in the payment of wages or benefits, working conditions, and work responsibilities.

Some state and local laws also protect groups based on other characteristics, such as sexual orientation. Figure 12-3 shows the U.S. laws that protect workers' rights.[3]

Knowing your rights to fair treatment in the workplace is the first step in ensuring fairness. Every worker should be aware of these basic rights, which have evolved over many years. Understanding them will not only ensure that you are treated fairly but it will also remind you to treat others fairly.

LAWS PROTECTING WORKERS

The Federal laws prohibiting job discrimination are

- **Title VII of the Civil Rights Act of 1964**, which prohibits employment discrimination based on race, color, religion, sex, national origin, disability, or family status.
- **The Equal Pay Act of 1963**, which protects men and women who perform substantially equal work in the same establishment from sex-based wage discrimination.
- **The Age Discrimination in Employment Act of 1967**, which protects individuals who are 40 years of age or older.
- **Title I and Title V of the Americans with Disabilities Act of 1990**, which prohibit employment discrimination against qualified individuals with disabilities in the private sector and in state and local governments.
- **Sections 501 and 505 of the Rehabilitation Act of 1973**, which prohibit discrimination against qualified individuals with disabilities who work in the federal government.
- **The Civil Rights Act of 1991**, which, among other things, provides monetary damages in cases of intentional employment discrimination. It prohibits discrimination for or against employees or job applicants on the basis of race, color, national origin, religion, sex, age, or disability. The act is also interpreted to prohibit discrimination based on sexual orientation.

FIGURE 12-3 U.S. laws against employment discrimination.

PROHIBITED JOB INTERVIEW QUESTIONS

U.S. Department of Labor regulations make it illegal for job interviewers to ask certain questions. An interviewer or application form may ask whether the applicant is a citizen of the United States. Questions about an individual's ability to speak or read a foreign language are also permitted. However, questions about ancestry or native language are not allowed. For example, asking "What language do you speak at home?" is illegal. But "What languages do you speak?" is a legal question.

Government regulations also guard against discrimination based on religion. As a job applicant, you should be advised concerning normal hours or days of work required by the employer. An employer may ask if you are willing to work the required schedule. An employer may not, however, question you about your religious denomination, practices, affiliations, or holidays.

Sex discrimination. Discrimination based on sex is a complicated issue. As traditional roles for women changed, particularly after World War II, more women entered the workforce. Today, women make up more than half of the workforce. Many men have been rethinking the roles they play at home in search of the right balance between work and family. These redefined roles have caused some concern on the part of employers. Employers may be concerned about how family obligations might interfere with work, but it is unfair to assume that women are more likely to miss work than men for family reasons.

Marital status. A potential employer may not ask about your marital or family status. You do not need to provide information about whether you are single, engaged, married, divorced, or separated. Employers may not ask questions about a spouse's income, the number and ages of your children, or plans for pregnancy. As an applicant, you may be asked if it will be possible for you to meet specific work schedules or if there are any activities, commitments, or responsibilities that may hinder you from doing your job.

Other questions that may allow the employer to learn about your family status (without asking directly) can relate to your expected duration on the job or anticipated absences. These questions may only be asked if they are asked of all applicants and weighed equally in evaluations for both sexes.

Age discrimination. Discrimination against workers over the age of 40 is also illegal. Discrimination because of a person's age is referred to as **ageism**. Employers cannot legally prefer younger workers because they think they will be less expensive, more flexible, and willing to learn. Some employers may view older workers as good hires because of their experience, knowledge, and maturity. Others may discriminate against them in the belief that they are less likely to adapt to new methods and technologies.

Younger workers can also be discriminated against. The national unemployment rate for workers aged 16–24 is always higher than for older workers. In a recession, young workers are more likely to be laid off than older workers, and they may experience subtle discrimination when they compete against older, more experienced, workers for jobs. Young workers are more likely to be hired as temporary workers: more than 50 percent of all temporary workers are under the age of 35. To avoid violating child labor laws, an employer may require a work permit issued by school authorities to prove the applicant is old enough to work. However, the employer may not require a birth certificate as proof of age.

Criminal background. Traditionally there has been discrimination and prejudice in the workplace against those whose character does not meet with the general standards of society. Convicted criminals, members of subversive organizations, people with poor credit ratings, and others considered to be "undesirable" may have difficulty finding jobs even when they have the skills and abilities to perform the job.

U. S. law prohibits discrimination against people who may have been arrested for, but not convicted of, a crime. It bars the potential employer from asking whether a job applicant has ever been arrested. Questions about an applicant's conviction (and if so, when, where, and the disposition of the case) are allowed.

Pregnancy. The law also prohibits an employer from refusing to hire a woman because of a pregnancy as long as she can perform the major functions of her job. Women affected by pregnancy or any related condition must be treated the same as other applicants or employees with similar abilities.

Physical and psychological disabilities. The 1990 Americans with Disabilities Act (ADA) protects the rights of people with disabilities. Interviewers may ask the applicant whether he or she can perform the essential tasks and functions of the job, which is a fair question for any applicant. The employer is not required to hire a person who is not able to do the job, but a candidate with physical limitations cannot be subjected to a physical exam as a condition of employment unless every candidate is required to have one.

pryzmat/iStockphoto.com

Employers are required to make reasonable workplace accommodations for individuals with disabilities.

ACCOMMODATING PEOPLE WITH DISABILITIES

You will find people with disabilities working in virtually every sector of the economy. After a worker with a disability is hired, the employer must make reasonable accommodations so that the employee will be able to stay on the job and perform effectively. Some examples are discussed here.

Work assignments may be adjusted to accommodate the worker with disabilities. An employee who is being treated for stress and depression might have trouble concentrating and meeting deadlines. The employer might relieve the person of particularly stressful tasks, such as greeting clients, and move the employee to a quiet workspace. An employer might accommodate an employee who is being treated for cancer by granting unpaid leave on days when chemotherapy is scheduled.

For each area, write a legal and an illegal question that might be asked during a job interview.

Sex discrimination

Legal: _____

Illegal: _____

Marital status

Legal: _____

Illegal: _____

Age discrimination

Legal: _____

Illegal: _____

Criminal background

Legal: _____

Illegal: _____

Physical or psychological disabilities

Legal: _____

Illegal: _____

"Things which matter most must never be at the mercy of things which matter least."

The workplace and its facilities must be accessible. For example, if the door to the lunchroom is too narrow to accommodate a wheelchair, it may have to be widened. An employee may need to bring a service animal to work. Because many people with multiple sclerosis cannot tolerate heat, an employee with multiple sclerosis may need a parking space closer to the building in the summer to minimize the time spent outside.

Special equipment may be needed, or existing equipment or devices may need to be modified, to accommodate the worker with a disability. For example, an employee who returns to work after a stroke may need speech recognition software for dictating e-mail. An employee with one hand may need a smaller keyboard for efficient one-hand typing.

An employer can avoid making accommodations if it can show that being expected to make them is unreasonable. The employer must show that the accommodations would entail "undue hardship, difficulty, or expense."

PROTECTION FROM SEXUAL HARASSMENT

You have a legal right to be free from sexual harassment in the workplace. **Sexual harassment** is coerced, unethical, and unwanted intimacy. It is not only an issue of sex; it is also an issue of power. Sexual harassment can occur at any level of an organization. Men can harass women and vice versa. Subordinates can harass supervisors and vice versa.

Sexual harassment is illegal under Title VII of the Civil Rights Act of 1964. The Supreme Court has ruled that remarks, gestures, and even graffiti can be considered forms of sexual harassment. Rude sounds, suggestive whistling, jokes about sex, derogatory rumors, notes or signs posted in a person's work space, brushing up against bodies, and unwelcome touching are forms of sexual harassment.

Sometimes the perpetrator is not aware that his or her behavior is considered harassment. What may be intended as friendly teasing can come across as bullying. Flirting may come across as sexual harassment. The difference depends upon how the person targeted feels about it. Most acts of sexual harassment are power plays that are degrading in nature.

Remedies for Sexual Harassment

If you are being sexually harassed in the workplace, you should speak up. Ignoring or tolerating the situation can lead to a cycle of ongoing harassment and victimization. You need to be assertive and establish strong personal boundaries. If the problem persists, you can take your complaint to the human resources department of your company or to your union. You may also file complaints on a federal level with the EEOC and on a local level with human rights agencies. See the Dealing with Sexual Harassment feature in this section.

OVERCOMING DISCRIMINATION

You may be able to overcome discrimination with positive resistance over time, and with patience. If you work for employers who think everyone of your race is lazy, prove them wrong. If your bosses think women cannot handle complex technology, prove them wrong. Your quiet, positive resistance and determination may change a person's mind.

Many organizations offer some form of diversity training to prevent or reduce problems. **Diversity training** programs aim to teach employees how to get along in a diverse workplace and how to work harmoniously with people from different backgrounds. Employees learn how companies benefit from the mix of different skills and perspectives. Diversity training workshops often use videos, scenarios, and team assignments.

If you feel that you are the victim of sexual harassment, there are several steps you can take:

- **Confront the person who is harassing you.** Tell the person how you feel about what is happening and make it very clear that you want the unwanted behavior to stop.

- **Write down exactly what happened and what you both said.** Note who witnessed the incident, if anyone. Keep copies of all communications about the incident.

- **Talk to your coworkers about the incident.** Sexual harassers are often "repeat offenders," and an employer may be more likely to respond to complaints from more than one person.

- **Tell some friends and family members.** If needed, they can testify to your reactions at the time of the incident.

- **If the harassment continues,** explain the situation to your supervisor. If the perpetrator is your supervisor, go to his or her supervisor, to the human resources department, your union, or government agencies in charge of protecting your rights.

Employers may not retaliate against employees who report sexual harassment. Simply turning and walking away may seem like the least painful option, but it leaves you with little satisfaction and the harassment may continue. If you leave your job to avoid harassment, the individual who violated your rights may harass others in that workplace.

Be aware that if you have a legal case against your employer for discrimination, you must be prepared to face a not-always-sympathetic public that may include your coworkers. If you decide to proceed with court remedies, do not make the mistake of thinking it will be easy.

Moving Forward

Employers and employees today are more accepting of diversity than in the past. But diversity in the workplace sets the stage for problems, such as prejudice, stereotyping, sexual harassment, and subtle discrimination. To help avoid and overcome these problems, many employers are voluntarily using affirmative action programs. They are working to accommodate workers with disabilities, and they are working to avoid and eliminate sexual harassment. They are making changes that will help workers who are somehow different to fit in, get along, and feel accepted and appreciated.

checkpoint

1. What form of discrimination can apply to older or younger workers?

_____

_____

_____

2. What actions may sexual harassment include?

_____

_____

_____

3. List four questions that are NOT legal in employment interviews and on applications.

_____

_____

_____

4. List reasonable accommodations that an employer might make to enable a person with disabilities to stay on the job and perform effectively.

_____

_____

_____

5. Why is failing to report sexual harassment not the best choice?

_____

_____

_____

applications

1. Do you think reverse discrimination is a problem in today's workplace? Why or why not?

_____

_____

_____

_____

2. What is different about the terms "deaf man" and "man with a hearing impairment"? Why is the second term more respectful?

_____

_____

_____

_____

3. Discuss in a small group how you might respond to an interviewer who asks questions during an employment interview that you know are illegal. Role play an interview. Remember that some interviewers may be inexperienced and may not know that a question is illegal, so practice answering in a way that takes this into account.

_____

_____

_____

_____

4. Describe a situation where you or someone you know was treated unfairly in the workplace. What was the cause? How was the situation resolved?

_____

_____

_____

_____

5. Identify accommodations that you have observed at school and in various workplaces that make life easier for people with disabilities.

_____

_____

_____

_____

12 points to remember

Review the following points to determine what you remember from the chapter.

- Today's workforce is diverse. There are more women, more ethnic minorities and immigrants, and more people with disabilities.

- While diversity in the workplace is increasingly viewed as a positive force, it can create problems, which must be faced and solved.

- Working and interacting with people who are unlike you can enrich your understanding of the world and your effectiveness on the job.

- Discrimination is unfair treatment based on a person's race, gender, religion, nationality, or other characteristic. Subtle discrimination may be based on physical characteristics or private conduct.

- Prejudice, stereotyping, and ethnocentrism are underlying causes of discrimination in the workplace.

- Affirmative action plans were designed to correct the effects of past discrimination by encouraging employers to hire and promote more women and minority workers.

- American law prohibits most discrimination in the workplace. Some unlawful practices include asking questions or using selection criteria that would permit the employer to give preference to or reject job applicants because of race, color, national origin, religious affiliations or practices, gender, family status, age, and disabilities.

- The Americans with Disabilities Act (ADA) protects workers with disabilities. Other laws protect workers from sexual harassment and age discrimination in the workplace.

How did you do? Did you remember the main points in the chapter?

KEY terms

diversity

bias

stereotyping

discrimination

prejudice

subtle discrimination

ethnocentrism

cultural conflicts

culture

affirmative action

reverse discrimination

ageism

sexual harassment

diversity training

Want more activities? Go to **www.cengage.com/careerreadiness/masters** to get started.

CHAPTER *activities*

1. Finish the following sentences with your first thoughts. As you review your answers, examine them for prejudicial content.

   a. People my parents' age _____

   b. Teenagers today _____

   c. Bosses _____

   d. Alcoholics _____

   e. Foreigners _____

   f. People who are physically challenged _____

   g. People who have been laid off _____

2. Do you have prejudices? What are they?

   _____

   _____

   _____

   _____

   Do members of your family or close friends have prejudices? What are they?

   _____

   _____

   _____

   _____

3. Describe a time when you met someone from another culture. What did you do to demonstrate respect for that person's culture?

   _____

   _____

   _____

   _____

4. Describe an experience of subtle discrimination against you or someone close to you.

   a. What was the discriminatory action or behavior?

   _____

   _____

   _____

   _____

   b. What do you think was the reason or underlying motive for the discrimination?

   _____

   _____

   _____

   _____

   _____

   c. How did the victim of the subtle discrimination (you or someone close to you) react or respond?

   _____

   _____

   _____

   _____

   d. What was done, or what might have been done, to prevent future occurrences of this kind?

   _____

   _____

   _____

   _____

5. Emma is a copyeditor for a mail order publisher. Most of her coworkers are male. Consider each of the following situations and decide whether it is a case of sexual harassment. Explain why or why not. Discuss with your classmates how Emma should react and what she might do to prevent further problems.

   a. A coworker puts up a calendar with scantily-clad women in the employee break room.

   _____

   _____

   _____

   _____

   b. Her supervisor asks her for a date.

   _____

   _____

   _____

   _____

   c. She wears a low-cut blouse to work and gets catcalls from her coworkers.

   _____

   _____

   _____

   _____

   d. The office manager calls her "honey" and "dear" and puts his arm around her.

   _____

   _____

   _____

   _____

   e. A coworker invades her personal space when he talks with her, and his eyes seem to examine her from head to toe.

   _____

   _____

   _____

   _____

CRITICAL *thinking*

Greg, an assistant manager in an auto parts store, has been transferred from his job in Cincinnati to a position in the predominantly Arab-American neighborhood of Dearborn near Detroit. The transition has been difficult for Greg, partly because he finds himself in an unfamiliar environment. Everybody around him seems so different from the people knows. They even have a different religion. The customers all seem to feel more comfortable with the rest of the staff, who are all Arab-American.

Greg feels uncomfortable when coworkers speak Arabic to one another. He does not understand Arabic, and he feels as though they are talking about him or just wasting time. He finds himself getting irritable with them when really all they have done is to speak their language. He feels like an outsider and doesn't know how to connect with his coworkers. Lately, he is starting to think he was wrong to accept the transfer.

1. What can Greg do to adjust to living and working in an environment where he feels like an outsider?

   _____

   _____

   _____

2. How can Greg start learning some Arabic so that he can at least join in small talk with his coworkers?

   _____

   _____

   _____

3. Should the store manager just tell the other workers to speak only English in the shop? Why or why not?

   _____

   _____

   _____

4. Where can Greg learn more about his coworkers' cultural heritage?

   _____

   _____

   _____

CASE 12.2 The Customer Knows Best

After Selena lost her job as a clerk in a small gift shop, she started working in a store near her home that specialized in cosmetics, hair products, wigs, and hair pieces for women of color. The shop imported beauty and hair supplies from all around the world that matched many different skin tones and hair textures as well as hard-to-find accessories that appealed to minority groups such as Asian and African immigrants as well as American minorities. Before she started working there, Selena, who was Hispanic, had loved shopping there because the store carried cosmetics that perfectly suited her complexion and hair accessories she could not find anywhere else.

The owners worked hard at supplying a wide variety of unusual products from all over the world, such as Indian sandalwood soaps and exotic brightly colored hair nets from Kenya. As a clerk, she needed to be able to answer customers' questions about hair products, wigs and other hair pieces, and accessories for African and Asian hair.

One day a group of African-American teenagers came into the shop and began talking about their hair. Selena listened to their concerns about how fragile their hair was, how straightening could damage it, and how hard it was to find a style that was easy to maintain. She decided to start reading beauty magazines aimed at black women so that she would be more aware of their needs.

1. If you were Selena, would you have joined the conversation with the teenaged customers and asked questions about their concerns? Why or why not?

_____

_____

_____

_____

2. What can the shop owners do to help train Selena?

_____

_____

_____

_____

3. What can Selena do to let customers know that she is genuinely interested in helping to solve their grooming challenges?

_____

_____

_____

_____

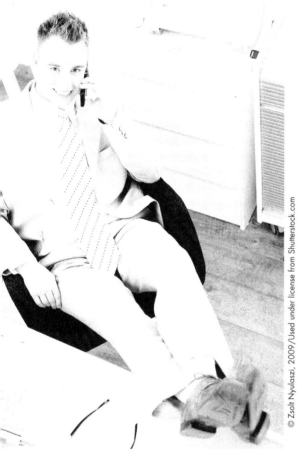

© Zsolt Nyulaszi, 2009/Used under license from Shutterstock.com

objectives

After completing this chapter, you should be able to:

1. Explain the meaning of integrity and ethics.
2. Describe situational ethics.
3. Understand what it means to act with integrity and have a personal code of ethics.
4. Describe ethical standards that employees expect from employers.
5. Describe ethical standards that employers expect from employees.
6. Discuss unethical business practices.

Think About It: Sarah and Miguel, supervisors in a mail order distribution center, were sharing a table in the lunchroom. "I haven't seen Yvonne this week," Sarah remarked. "Does she still work here?" "Well," Miguel replied, "I wonder if she ever did really *work* here. It seemed like every time I walked past her desk, she was doing her accounting homework. Anyway," he added, "She was let go. The manager told me it was because Yvonne was working for Yvonne." "I think I know what you mean," Sarah said. "I could never find her when I wanted to ask a question. It seemed as though she was always taking a break. I heard her manager was furious when Yvonne gave a copy of our mailing list to a friend who works for another company. That could really make our customers angry if they start receiving junk mail. I wondered what her manager was going to do about her." "One weekend," said Miguel, "I came in to catch up on paperwork. I found her using the office manager's computer, and there were copies of a yard sale flyer in the printer. I wouldn't trust Yvonne to work for me."

If you were an employer, would you trust Yvonne to work for you? What did Miguel mean when he said that Yvonne was working for Yvonne? What did Yvonne do that demonstrated unethical behavior and a lack of integrity?

Leading an Ethical Life

Ethics refers to accepted standards of right and wrong. Every day you have to make decisions: at home, at school, at work, while shopping, even while commuting. As you make these decisions, you consult your *moral compass* that tells you what is right. In some cases, the right choice may be clear. In other cases, you have to weigh the good against the bad and find the solution that does the most good or the least harm. Right and wrong are often not as clear as distinguishing black from white. In many choices you make, there are many shades of gray between them. The term **situational ethics** describes the gray areas where the "right" thing may depend on the circumstances.

ETHICS AND SELF-RIGHTEOUSNESS

Some people think there are universal truths that apply to all times, all cultures, and all situations. When this attitude is carried to extremes, it causes self-righteousness. **Self-righteousness** is self-satisfaction based on the belief that one's own morals are superior to the morals of others. Self-righteous people are inflexible because they believe they are better people than those around them. They are blind to those gray areas between right and wrong, and they judge others harshly. Self-righteousness is sometimes associated with hypocrisy. **Hypocrisy** is a kind of insincerity in which someone publicly pretends to follow superior moral standards, while privately acting against those principles.

Self-righteousness is something to think about when judging other people's choices. You may think you would have made a better choice in the same situation, but nobody has faultless judgment. That's why forgiveness is often the right choice when someone else has wronged you or others. If you have ever carried a grudge over something that happened to you, you know that dwelling on the misdeeds of others can take over your thoughts and do you more harm than the original misdeed.

MORALS AND ETHICS

The words *ethics* and *morals* are closely related and often used interchangeably. The word *ethics* came into English from classical Greek, and the word *morals* from Latin. Morals are personal beliefs about what's right and what's wrong. Your "moral compass" guides your behavior and is the basis for your personal character. Ethics refers to the standards or codes of behavior expected by a group to which an individual belongs. Countries, organizations, and social groups have ethics, and individuals in the group are expected to act ethically.[1]

Kara made a big mistake when she clicked Send. She was writing an e-mail to her supervisor Adam to complain about the way the receptionist Susan handled phone calls. Kara had never liked Susan because she was hired to replace Kara's friend Alice. Kara was so angry that she used the e-mail to complain about every single thing she thought Susan had ever done wrong. If Kara had reread the e-mail before she clicked Send, maybe she would have noticed that she was sending it to everyone in the company. Kara had never mentioned any problems with Susan to

Adam, so Adam was shocked. Susan feels humiliated, and Kara knows that everyone is laughing at her behind her back.

It may be hard to let go of anger and resentment, but when you do, it will free you from the burden of holding a grudge or trying to punish people, including yourself.

on the job

Gavin, a new server in a popular seafood restaurant, noticed that some of the wait staff consistently received larger tips than he received. He was puzzled because this seemed to happen on every shift. He had been a server in another restaurant and knew that he provided good service to his customers. After several weeks, he discovered the reason. Amelia, the person assigned to train Gavin, explained it this way: "What it amounts to is giving free refills and desserts," she said. "They give customers items they didn't order and tell them they're on the house. And when the restaurant is especially busy, they frequently 'forget' to add a side order charge to the check. Customers include in the tip some of the money they 'saved' on the meal. Money that should have gone to the restaurant for food or beverages goes to the server."

What should Gavin do if he is to maintain his own personal integrity and ethics? How would you feel if you were Gavin's employer?

RIGHT AND WRONG IN THE REAL WORLD

There are generally accepted notions of right and wrong in private life and at work, but to say something is *always* right or *always* wrong raises problems. This is where situational ethics may apply. You may say, "It is always wrong to steal from others." Consider the case, however, of Jean Valjean, a character in Victor Hugo's novel *Les Miserables*, who is sent to prison for stealing food to feed his starving family. Was he wrong to steal food?

You may say, "It is always wrong to take a life." However, most people condone killing in war, and many Americans are in favor of the death penalty. You may say, "It is always wrong to lie." What about the people in Amsterdam who hid Anne Frank and her family from the Nazis during World War II? Were they wrong to lie about where the family was? This is a case where lies prolonged lives and served the greater good.

Ethical decisions come down to how you treat other people, how you treat other people's belongings and resources, and how you treat public property and the environment. As you read this

© iofoto, 2009/Used under license from Shutterstock.com

The right thing to do is not always crystal clear. Actions have consequences, both good and bad.

chapter, you will become more aware of the attitudes and standards to follow to be a good employee and a good member of your community. You will have opportunities to think about situations where it may not be a simple question of right or wrong.

STRIVING FOR INTEGRITY

Integrity refers to consistency in adhering to moral principles. When you act with integrity, you do what you have determined is right, even if the choices you make may cause complications for you or for others. When choices are difficult, the outcomes need to be carefully considered. You have to consider what harm your choice may do as well as what good it may do.

When an employee fails to act with integrity, everyone in the workplace, including the employer, may be affected. When a business fails to act with integrity, the consequences may affect many people: customers, investors, employees, business leaders, even the general public. Consider the frustration that resulted from the lack of integrity on the part of Dynamic Designs.

> *Evan is confident that his team picked the best company to develop its new website. Dynamic Designs' proposal listed everyone who would work on the project and described their relevant experience. Four weeks later, the project hasn't gotten off the ground. The project manager hasn't returned Evan's calls, and the sales rep's phone goes directly to voicemail. Evan calls Jorge Marco, the webmaster listed in the proposal, and is surprised when a person named Simon Ashwell answers. Simon explains that Jorge has been reassigned to a job that's having a major deadline crisis and that he, Simon, is completely "up to speed" on Evan's project. Simon then asks Evan some questions that indicate he hasn't looked at the sample websites or the project schedule.*

Sometimes people behave ethically not because it is the right thing to do, but because they are afraid of negative consequences. Even if nobody ever finds out what you did wrong, it may continue to bother you simply because you betrayed your own values. When personal integrity drives your decisions, you do what is right simply *because* it is right, and not because you may be punished if you do the wrong thing.

> *It is Jenna's first day back at work after a week's vacation. At her afternoon break, Jenna goes down to the lobby for a pick-me-up smoothie. Maryann, the barista, surprises Jenna by handing her her umbrella, which Jenna didn't even know she had lost. Maryann said, "I observe my customers closely. You were in a hurry when you stopped in before your vacation, and you left your umbrella here. I kept it behind the counter for you."*

The reverse is also true. When you do something that does not feel right, you violate your own values and damage your self-image.

Ethical Business Conduct

Many companies and professions have an official **code of ethics**, which provides written guidelines for workers to follow based on specific ethical standards and values. The official code of ethical business conduct is often available on a company's website and may be mailed to customers and shareholders as a normal practice. A portion of The Hershey Company's Code of Ethical Business Conduct is shown in Figure 13-1.[2]

The Hershey Company's entire code of conduct is 44 pages in English. It is available in the languages of the other countries where the company does business. Everyone connected with Hershey is expected to follow the code: "All employees, officers, and directors must act according to the principles set forth in our Code. We expect everyone working on our Company's behalf, including consultants, agents, suppliers, and business partners, to adhere to our ethical standards. We may never ask a third party to engage in any activity that violates these standards."[3]

CODE OF ETHICAL BUSINESS CONDUCT

At its website, The Hershey Company posts its Code of Conduct in the language of every country where they do business. Here is the high-level overview:

- OUR COMMITMENT TO FELLOW EMPLOYEES. We treat one another fairly and with respect, valuing the talents, experiences and strengths of our diverse workforce.
- OUR COMMITMENT TO CONSUMERS. We maintain the trust consumers place in our brands, providing the best products on the market and adhering to honest marketing practices.
- OUR COMMITMENT TO THE MARKETPLACE. We deal fairly with our business partners, competitors and suppliers, acting ethically and upholding the law in everything we do.
- OUR COMMITMENT TO STOCKHOLDERS. We act honestly and transparently at all times, maintaining the trust our stockholders have placed in us.
- OUR COMMITMENT TO THE GLOBAL COMMUNITY. We comply with all global trade laws, protecting our natural resources and supporting the communities where we live, work and do business.

FIGURE 13-1 The Hershey Company's Code of Conduct (overview).

Most companies and organizations take ethics very seriously. Some require all employees to re-sign the code of ethics every year. In some companies, employees who violate company code are suspended with or without pay while the matter is reviewed, and, if confirmed, the ethical violation may lead to their dismissal.

In addition to wanting to do the right thing, companies want to avoid liability for the wrongful acts of its employees. Organizations can incur legal penalties and government fines for such violations even in cases where its officers were unaware of the misdeeds. The company is also at risk for private lawsuits from people harmed by the employee's actions.

Personal Code of Ethics

Perhaps without realizing it, you have been developing your own code of ethics since you were a young child. This code affects your behavior in the workplace and at home. You can learn a lot about the ethics you apply in your daily life by putting your values into words. A sample personal code of ethics offered by the Life Lesson Network is shown in Figure 13-2.[4] The Life Lesson Network website is a nonsectarian resource for parents and other adults who teach children about ethical problems and solutions. Consider it a starting point, not an end product.

Assume that you want to give advice to a niece or nephew who is going off to college. This person means a great deal to you, and you want to share your personal code of ethics with her or him. List five topics you would cover and the advice you would give.

1. _____

2. _____

3. _____

4. _____

5. _____

MY PERSONAL CODE OF ETHICS

- **Integrity:** I will be honest in everything I do—always forthright—always sincere—always reliable—always dependable.
- **Caring:** I will care about others—always considerate—always fair—always willing to help those in need—never ridicule or intentionally hurt others.
- **Excellence:** I will do the best at everything I do—always strive for excellence—never accept mediocrity—never procrastinate.
- **Attitude:** I will maintain a positive attitude—always respectful—always loyal—always humble—never arrogant.
- **Courage:** I will stand up for what is right—never give in to negative peer pressure—never allow fear of failure to prevent trying.

FIGURE 13-2 Have you given thought to your personal code of ethics?

Let your personal code of ethics be your guide every time you have to make a decision that could possibly do harm to others, to your company, or to the environment.

checkpoint

1. What is situational ethics? Give an example.

_____

_____

_____

_____

2. Who may be affected when a company does not act ethically?

_____

_____

_____

_____

3. Who may be affected when an employee does not act ethically?

_____

_____

_____

_____

4. Why would an organization have an official code of ethics?

_____

_____

_____

_____

5. Do you think most people have a personal code of ethics? Why or why not?

_____

_____

_____

_____

applications

1. What ethical behaviors that you learned at home are likely to carry over to the workplace?

_____

_____

_____

_____

2. Describe someone you have read about or have seen on television or on YouTube who has demonstrated hypocrisy. Why do you think the person acted that way? What do you think you would you have done in the same situation?

_____

_____

_____

_____

3. The Hershey Company's code of ethical conduct includes this statement: "We expect everyone working on our Company's behalf, including consultants, agents, suppliers, and business partners, to adhere to our ethical standards." Why does the Hershey Company expect other people

and organizations to follow Hershey's code of ethics? Do you think others will comply? Why or why not?

_____

_____

_____

_____

_____

4. Assume your friend is a clerk in a discount store that sells items for $1 or less. Your friend thinks it is okay for him to take a candy bar now and again. How would you respond if your friend said:

a. "It's just a 50-cent candy bar. What's the big deal?"

_____

_____

_____

_____

_____

b. "I need an energy pick-me-up when there are lots of customers in the store."

_____

_____

_____

_____

5. Why do you think people are self-righteous? What issues are you self-righteous about?

_____

_____

_____

_____

6. You promise to keep a secret, but to keep the secret you will have to lie to someone. Would you keep this promise? Explain your answer.

_____

_____

_____

_____

_____

Right and Wrong in the Workplace

Even though ethical choices may not always be easy, employers expect people to bring their consciences to work with them. In return, employees expect the organizations they work for to be honest and responsible. Each expects the other to show integrity in the workplace and in the business world.

Given the choices faced every day at work and in private life, a person with integrity will do the right thing—to the best of his or her judgment. He or she will follow that interior moral compass to tell right from wrong, fair from unfair, honest from dishonest. A person with integrity makes choices based on moral values and principles knowing that in the real world, mistakes will be made. When that happens, learning from your mistakes can help you to grow your integrity. Self-forgiveness can help you get to the point where you can learn from your mistakes.

THE INTEGRITY OF THE EMPLOYER

You read in Chapter 7 that it is acceptable to have expectations of your employer. When you are hired to do a job, there is an understanding that both the employer and employee will act with integrity. The employer agrees to pay you a fair wage for your work, and many employers provide benefits such as health insurance, paid vacation, and sick leave. You also have a right to expect honesty and fairness from your employer. Here are some examples of what is expected from the employer:

- To provide a safe, healthful, reasonably comfortable workplace.
- To provide the tools, equipment, and supplies employees need to do their jobs properly and safely.
- To treat employees equally, without regard for their sex, age, ethnicity, race, religion, or disability.
- To base raises, bonuses, and promotions on merit and productivity, not on personal relationships.
- To conduct an honest, responsible business. If the company produces products, they should be safe and effective, and the advertisements for them should be honest. If the business provides a service, the best interests of customers and clients should be the driving force behind the way business is done.
- To keep accurate and honest records and accounts.
- To respect the environment.
- To follow local, state, and federal laws.

Codes of Ethical Conduct

Many professions, such as medicine and journalism, have written codes of ethics that apply to the work they do. These documents address specific issues that come up in the course of working in that profession. Individual organizations in these

Jefferson-Madison Regional Library in Charlottesville, Virginia, encourages employees to strive for the highest level of ethical conduct, and to that end employees will:

1. Provide the highest level of service through appropriate and usefully organized collections, fair and equitable circulation and service policies, and skillful, accurate, unbiased, and courteous responses to all requests for assistance.
2. Resist all efforts by groups or individuals to censor library materials.
3. Protect each patron's right to privacy with respect to information sought or received, and materials consulted, borrowed, or acquired.
4. Make a good faith effort to recognize and respect intellectual property rights.
5. Adhere to the principles of due process and equality of opportunity in peer relationships and personnel actions, treating coworkers and other colleagues with respect and fairness, and fostering workplace conditions that safeguard the rights and welfare of all employees.
6. Distinguish clearly in their actions and statements between their personal philosophies and attitudes and those of an institution or professional body.
7. Avoid situations in which personal interests might be served or financial benefits gained at the expense of the library patrons, colleagues, or Jefferson-Madison Regional Library.

FIGURE 13-3 Library employees' code of ethics.

professions may have additional guidelines or word them slightly differently. Figure 13-3 shows the Code of Ethics for library workers at Jefferson-Madison Regional Library in Charlottesville, Virginia.[5] Notice that resisting censorship, respecting intellectual property, and respecting their patrons' privacy are important values.

Unethical Behavior by Organizations

There are many ways in which an organization may engage in unethical behavior, including bribery and kickbacks. In recent years, the news has been full of reports of corporate ethics violations. Companies and their leaders have been prosecuted for cheating investors, some of whom lost their entire life savings. Not only did these individuals and groups defraud investors and the public, they put a great deal of energy into covering up their crimes in order to continue to misuse other people's assets.

APPLY IT!

An employee who discovers that the employer is not following ethical standards is in an awkward position. Assume that you are the employee faced with the following five situations. Think about each situation and decide what you should do. Consider who you might talk to if you decide that speaking up is the right thing to do.

1. You believe there is a substantial risk of injury because your employer is not supplying the required safety equipment to workers. Should you bring the problem to the employer's attention? Why or why not?
2. You know that your company is producing a faulty product. Should you report it? Why or why not?
3. You know that your company is dumping toxic waste into a stream. Should you try to stop it? Why or why not?
4. You know that your company is falsifying records. Should you speak up? Why or why not?
5. You know that your company is advertising falsely in the local newspaper. Should you bring it up? Why or why not?

Many employees who had their retirement funds invested with these companies lost not only their jobs but also the value of their retirement accounts. Even though the executives responsible for the misconduct may be prosecuted and punished, the damage they have done still hurts thousands of people.

PERSONAL INTEGRITY

An employer who hires, trains, and pays a worker expects the worker to share the values and pursue the goals of the organization. The employer should be able to rely on you. The values behind your conduct on the job should be driven by your own moral standards as well as by those of your employer and society in general. Your employer has a right to expect that you are acting throughout the day with goodwill and a positive attitude to serve the needs and interests of the organization. Loyalty is highly valued by employers.

Ethics and Productivity

As an employee, you are expected to come to work every day on time and to focus on your work throughout the day to support your employer's purposes and goals. When you waste time on the job, you are wasting the employer's time and money. When you are unproductive, you are short-changing your organization. When you waste the employer's resources, you are adding to the costs of doing business. Make sure you always have your employer's best interests in mind.

Ibrahim takes the 6:30 a.m. train to work, walks three blocks to the office, and enters the lobby at 7:45 on the dot. He takes the elevator to his floor and immediately starts his computer and checks his electronic calendar. He's settled in and ready to work at 7:55, five minutes before the office officially opens. Ralph, who lives in the same suburb, takes the 7:00 express train, buys a pastry in the lobby, and is usually at his desk just before 8:15. Ralph can't understand why Ibrahim leaves home for work 30 minutes earlier than necessary. Do you know why?

Some people may think that the little ways in which they abuse their position don't amount to much. Consider this: if all the employees are looking out for themselves and not for the organization, the business will eventually fail and its employees will find themselves out of a job. The success of the organization depends on the goodwill and conscientious effort of its workers as well as its leaders.

Respect for the Employer's Property and Resources

You should take care to use your employer's equipment, supplies, and facilities wisely. Paper is a good example. When you waste it, you may be contributing to deforestation as well as to the costs your employer incurs to replace it. Avoid printing or photocopying more pages than needed. Print on both sides of the page when possible. Reuse scrap paper for projects that are less important, and recycle paper whenever possible.

Treat the employer's equipment with respect. Avoid using equipment such as a computer or printer for personal projects, unless your employer gives you permission to do so on your own time. Avoid using the employer's copier for personal documents. It is easy to find copy shops where you can quickly and inexpensively make personal copies.

Some people see no problem installing software from work on their home computer. This is not only wrong but also illegal. Unless you or your employer has paid the proper licensing fees to the software manufacturer, this amounts to stealing software applications. The same is true of lending the installation disks to friends or relatives. The fact that you have access to the disks does not give you the right to install the software on any computer other than those included in the license agreement.

on the job

Valerie is the receptionist in the office of a popular radio station. All employees are required to sign in and out of the office indicating where they are going, for what purpose, and when they will return. The station's general manager, Phil, has hired his son Ira to work as a technician at the station for the summer. Valerie cannot help noticing that Ira comes in late to work every day and gets four or five personal calls a day. He changes the conversation or wanders off when one of the more experienced technicians tries to show him a new procedure, and he rarely follows through on his repair assignments. Some technicians have had to stay late fixing things he was supposed to take care of. Ira signs out to visit the station's "transmission tower" to do "maintenance" almost every day, which no other technician at the station considers a daily chore. He stays at "the tower" for three to four hours at a time and sometimes comes back just as the office is closing. Everyone is fed up with Ira and irritated with Phil for not noticing, or maybe ignoring, the issues.

Should Valerie say anything to Phil about his son's behavior? Would Phil and Ira consider this any of her business?

Following Rules

You are expected to follow the organization's rules and guidelines, which may be spelled out in an employee handbook. Your employer expects you to take breaks as allowed, such as a ten-minute break in the morning or an hour for lunch. Taking more time than allowed is a form of stealing because it deprives your employer of the work you are paid to do during that time. If you occasionally need to take a longer lunch break to run an errand, ask your supervisor for permission and make up the lost time.

One rule common to many organizations is that employees are prohibited from romantic relationships with their coworkers—not only in the workplace but privately as well. Aside from the concern that someone might be exploited by a person in power, there is also the concern that romantic relationships among employees may interfere with the effective operation of the organization. It is better to maintain a professional relationship with everyone at work, without the complications that romantic relationships may bring to the workplace.

Fairness to Others

An ethical worker is kind and fair to others, treating coworkers, customers, and the public with respect and consideration, no matter what their race, religion, ethnic background, gender, or age. There may be times when a customer tries your patience and you have to control yourself so you do not react. There may be days when personal concerns put you under stress that sours your relations with coworkers. If you find yourself snapping at others or being impatient, apologize sincerely and try to control your ill temper. Everybody has "off" days, but keep in mind that your personal problems and concerns belong at home.

Roxanne tries to see the silver lining in tough situations, but today is a particularly challenging day that is testing her resolve to be positive. The latest crisis is a last-minute push to mail five copies of a proposal to an important client by the end of the day. When Michael stops by to see if the mailing is ready, she glares at him without speaking. But she realizes that his concern is genuine and that she gains nothing by being unpleasant. She tells him they finished printing the proposal and are putting the copies into binders. "Thanks for the update," he replied. "Let me know if I can help!"

Digital Vision/Getty Images

Treat coworkers as individuals, without making assumptions based on age, religion, or race.

If you have a coworker who is slow to learn the ropes, or who has qualities or habits that annoy you, do not assume that these traits are because of the person's age, religion, or race. Treat your coworkers as individuals, without making assumptions based on the group they belong to. Look at the situation from the other person's point of view and find a way to help.

Petty Theft

Some workers take small things from their employer without giving it much thought. It may be small tools, postage stamps, or reams of paper for their personal use. When inexpensive items like these are taken, it is called petty theft.

According to University of the Pacific business professor Chuck Williams, studies show that one-third to three-fourths of workers admit that they have:

- Stolen from their employer.
- Committed computer fraud.
- Embezzled funds.
- Vandalized company property.
- Sabotaged company projects.
- Faked injuries to receive workers' compensation benefits or insurance.
- Taken "sick" time off when they were not really sick.

These problems cost companies as much as $66 billion a year, or about 6% of their income.[6]

Petty theft is the illegal taking of another person's property without that person's freely given consent. These items may not be worth a lot of money, but they belong to your employer; you do the employer wrong if you thoughtlessly walk off with them. Even if you think "everyone does it," it is clearly unethical.

Make it your goal never to take anything belonging to your employer or your coworkers. You may think nobody would ever take another person's lunch, drink, or snack from the break room refrigerator, but this is a common complaint in the workplace.

You may think that most employees don't cheat their employers. However, those who do cost businesses some $66 billion dollars a year, as you can see in the feature Who Cheats at Work? If a coworker takes building supplies from the construction site and sells them online, would that make you think of doing the same? Hold yourself to a higher standard when you witness this kind of behavior, which can be contagious. Challenge your coworker about what he or she is doing. The person may not look at it as stealing, but it clearly is. Even if you do not report the theft, the unethical coworker may be caught and punished—by being fired, by facing criminal charges, or both.

Alcohol and Drug Abuse

You may think that an employee's conduct outside the workplace is private and should not enter into the employer–employee relationship. However, when it comes to drug and alcohol use, there is room for debate. It is obvious that you should not come to work under the influence of alcohol or drugs, which may impair your ability to do your work and may make you more likely to be injured or injure others. Still, what if you use drugs on the weekend when you are not working? Does the employer have a right to dismiss you for what you do in your private time?

An increasing number of employers are insisting on "zero-tolerance" policies in the workplace. These employers may require that employees undergo periodic medical tests to ensure that they are not using illegal substances. Since evidence of drug use may remain in your system for many weeks, even if you stop using the substance the week before you start a new job, tests may detect it. A positive test may make the employer withdraw the offer of employment.

"If you don't want anyone to know it, don't do it."

FRAUD IN THE WORKPLACE

Fraud is defined as intentional deception made for personal gain or to damage another individual. There are many types of workplace fraud. Four of the most common types are discussed here.

Conflicts of Interest

Many offices and professions have policies on conflicts of interest. A **conflict of interest** means that you take unfair advantage of your situation to benefit yourself or others instead of putting the employer's interests first. You have probably heard the term applied mainly to lawyers and politicians. For example:

- Judges should remove themselves from presiding over cases that involve members of their family because the judge could not be impartial.
- Members of Congress should not propose or promote laws that benefit a business or industry that has contributed heavily to their campaigns for the same reasons.
- The purchasing agent for the city should not award a big construction job to his or her brother-in-law, unless the brother-in-law offered the lowest and best bid.

One way to avoid this kind of conflict of interest is to let someone else—someone who can be impartial—make the decision. Government institutions have guidelines to help members avoid conflicts of interest. Figure 13-4 shows the guidelines followed in the U.S. House of Representatives.[7] As you read the guidelines, think of recent examples in the news of these codes being followed—or not.

You may think that these issues only apply to people in positions of power. However, people at all levels should think about possible conflicts of interest. If you are a cashier in a supermarket and your best friend gets in your line, you should not "forget" to ring up a few items to save your friend money. If you do this kind of thing, you are misusing your power, however slight it may be. Both you and your friend are stealing from your employer.

CODE OF ETHICS FOR GOVERNMENT SERVICE

Any person in Government service should:

1. Put loyalty to the highest moral principles and to country above loyalty to Government persons, party, or department.
2. Uphold the Constitution, laws, and legal regulations of the United States and of all governments therein and never be a party to their evasion.
3. Give a full day's labor for a full day's pay; giving to the performance of his duties his earnest effort and best thought.
4. Seek to find and employ more efficient and economical ways of getting tasks accomplished.
5. Never discriminate unfairly by the dispensing of special favors or privileges to anyone, whether for remuneration or not; and never accept for himself or his family, favors or benefits under circumstances which might be construed by reasonable persons as influencing the performance of his governmental duties.
6. Make no private promises of any kind binding upon the duties of office, since a Government employee has no private word which can be binding on public duty.
7. Engage in no business with the Government, either directly or indirectly, which is inconsistent with the conscientious performance of his governmental duties.
8. Never use any information coming to him confidentially in the performance of governmental duties as a means for making private profit.
9. Expose corruption wherever discovered.
10. Uphold these principles, ever conscious that public office is a public trust.

FIGURE 13-4 Code of ethics for government service.

Audrey works in an office where she is responsible for stocking supplies such as copier paper and printer cartridges. It's almost quitting time, and her friend Otto arrives a few minutes early to take her to dinner. "Are those new flash drives?" Otto asks, pointing to several USB drives on her desk. "Yes," Audrey replies. "As soon as I put these in the supply room, I'll be ready to go." "My flash drive has only 2 GB of memory, and these have 8 GB," Otto replies. "Could you give me one? You have several there so I doubt anyone will miss one." Audrey was stunned by Otto's request. "No, I most certainly cannot give you one," she replied. "The flash drives aren't mine to give—they belong to the company. And I would appreciate it if you wouldn't put me in this position again."

Abuse of Fringe Benefits and Other Privileges

Many employers provide paid sick leave, personal leave, and vacation time. Unfortunately, people often abuse their fringe benefits and other privileges. Paid sick leave is one example. Employees may be tempted to "call in sick" when they are quite well. Sometimes this is a gray area of abuse. For example, if the employer allows paid time off when you are sick but not to care for your sick child, you may be tempted to tell the employer that you are sick so you can stay home and care for your child.

Sherry is the business manager for a small nonprofit organization that provides free tutoring to inner-city children who may be struggling in school. Recently Sherry has needed more time off to cope with some personal problems, so she "forgets" to record two of the personal days she has already taken.

In situations like this, it is better to level with your supervisor. You could ask for a day or two off without pay, for example, until your child is well enough to return to school. Most employers understand that personal problems like this happen. If you are a valued employee, your employer may bend the rules a little for you. When a family member is ill for an extended period, there is also the Family and Medical Leave Act (FMLA) of 1993, which allows most workers to take time off to care for a family member. Unfortunately, personal leave is sometimes abused.

© iofoto, 2009/Used under license from Shutterstock.com

An ethical employee tries to keep costs down on expense accounts.

Injury and Disability Fraud

In some cases, workers go beyond abusing sick time. Some go so far as to fake accidents and injuries at work to collect workers' compensation payments or social security disability payments. Workers' compensation (also called *workers' comp*) is a type of insurance managed by the state in which you work. It is designed to pay medical and other costs for people who are hurt on the job. These payments may be extended if you are temporarily disabled. If you are permanently disabled, you can apply for social security disability payments from the federal government. Unfortunately, some people fake or exaggerate injuries and disabilities to collect these payments when they are actually able-bodied. They may claim payments even if the injury was due to their own carelessness. The website for Online Lawyer Source estimates that "as many as 25% of all filed claims involve some form of workers' compensation fraud."[8]

This kind of fraud is so common that it has become a subspecialty for lawyers who defend employers against false claims and lawyers who support workers who file claims. Any claim, true or false, can cause an employer's insurance premiums to rise dramatically, so employers want to make sure payments go only to those who really need them. Figure 13-5 is from a poster published by the Alabama Attorney General's Office and the Alabama Department of Industrial Relations that lists the kinds of fraud that take place.[9]

WORKERS' COMPENSATION FRAUD CAN BE:

- Reporting an off-the-job accident as an on-the-job accident.
- Reporting an accident that never happened.
- Complaints of accident injury symptoms that are exaggerated or nonexistent.
- Malingering to avoid work when injury is healed.
- Not reporting outside income from other work-related activities while drawing workers' compensation benefits from another employer.
- Making false or fraudulent statements for the purpose of obtaining workers' compensation benefits.

FIGURE 13-5 Examples of workers' compensation fraud.

Expense Account Abuse

Some employees, especially sales representatives and executives at all levels, have expense accounts for things such as airfare, meals, hotels, and mileage driven in their own cars. Other workers, such as those who fix problems in other offices or in the field, may also have travel expenses that the employer pays. Other employees travel for business less frequently, perhaps attending conferences and annual professional meetings away from their home office.

Some companies have liberal expense accounting policies. They trust employees to keep personal records and report what they spent. Other companies have strict rules and regulations and require receipts. These detailed rules and recordkeeping procedures are designed to protect the employer from employees who might misuse the expense accounting system to get money to which they are not entitled.

> *The accounting department at Fernandez Electronics was auditing the expense accounts of its sales force because of a steep rise in expenses reported. They discovered that Jose was reporting much lower expenses than any of the other sales staff. Wondering how Jose kept his expenses so low, they called him in to review his expense accounts. It turned out that Jose had traveled at inconvenient times to get lower airfares. He took buses or walked instead of taking taxis. Where he did not skimp was on entertaining clients. In those cases, he took the clients to nice restaurants and reported exactly as much as the meals cost.*

What can the rest of the sales force learn from Jose's thrifty habits?

checkpoint

1. Why do many professions and businesses have specific codes of ethics that apply to the work they do?

_____

_____

_____

_____

_____

2. What is conflict of interest? Give several examples.

_____

_____

_____

_____

_____

3. Explain what workers' compensation fraud is.

_____

_____

_____

_____

_____

4. What expenses do employers typically cover?

_____

_____

_____

_____

_____

5. What should an employee tell the employer if he or she needs to stay home with a sick child?

_____

_____

_____

_____

_____

applications

1. Why do you think petty theft is common in some workplaces? List businesses that might be most susceptible to petty theft.

_____

_____

_____

2. Explain why respect for the environment is an ethical issue.

_____

_____

_____

3. Is an employee's use of drugs or alcohol on the weekends any of the employer's business? Why or why not?

_____

_____

_____

_____

4. Re-read issue #2 of the code of ethics for library workers at Jefferson-Madison Regional Library on page 326. Give examples of groups or individuals who may try to censor library materials.

_____

_____

_____

_____

5. Identify someone whose ethics you admire. Write a paragraph explaining why you consider this person a role model.

_____

_____

_____

_____

6. Why do professional codes of conduct such as those for doctors and paralegals not always prevent unethical behavior on the part of members?

_____

_____

_____

_____

13 points to remember

Review the following points to determine what you remember from the chapter.

- Ethics refers to accepted standards of right and wrong that you apply to choices in your personal life and at work.
- Many ethical choices are not as clear as black and white, but are more like shades of gray in which you must balance possible good effects against the possible harm of a decision.
- Integrity refers to consistency in adhering to moral principles. Employers and employees expect one another to show integrity in the workplace.
- Among other things, employees expect employers to provide the equipment and supplies to do the job properly and safely; to conduct business honestly; to follow local, state, and federal laws; to treat employees equally; and to base raises, bonuses, and promotions on merit and productivity.
- Employers expect employees to be loyal, dependable, and honest, to make ethical decisions in the workplace, and to treat the employer's time, facilities, equipment, and supplies with respect.
- Employers expect workers to treat one another with respect and consideration.
- Common types of workplace fraud include petty theft, abuse of fringe benefits, and abuse of expense accounts.

How did you do? Did you remember the main points you studied in this chapter?

KEY terms

ethics

situational ethics

self-righteousness

hypocrisy

integrity

code of ethics

petty theft

fraud

conflict of interest

Want more activities? Go to **www.cengage.com/careerreadiness/masters** to get started.

CHAPTER *activities*

1. Your objective is to develop a code of ethics for your class. First, divide into small groups of four to six students. Each group writes its interpretation of a code of ethics. Then as a class, discuss and compare the various codes, pulling the best elements from the different lists in order to develop a single code of ethics for the class.

   _____

   _____

   _____

   _____

   _____

2. How can your class monitor compliance with the ethical code written in Application 1? What actions should be taken against people who break the code?

   _____

   _____

   _____

   _____

   _____

3. Is it honest and ethical to take home things that the employer has no use for and/or wants to dispose of, such as used packing boxes, surplus or waste building materials, scrap paper, and free samples of merchandise? Explain your answer.

   _____

   _____

   _____

   _____

   _____

4. You work in a clinic where one of the surgeons is being sued for malpractice. You are in a position to see some of the correspondence between the surgeon and the lawyers who are working on the case. A friend of yours is a patient of the surgeon. Should you share information about the malpractice suit with your friend?

   _____

   _____

   _____

   _____

   _____

5. List several things office workers can do to put respect for the environment into action.

   _____

   _____

   _____

   _____

   _____

6. A friend wants to look at your homework. She did not have time to finish hers because of a family emergency. Would you show it to her? Why or why not?

   _____

   _____

   _____

   _____

   _____

CRITICAL *thinking*

Maria is a safety coordinator in the human resources office of a tanning factory that prepares animal hides for the leather industry. She is also responsible for keeping track of occupational health and safety records for the factory, including safety precautions employees should take with the chemicals used in tanning.

The factory employs many Hispanic workers who speak limited English. Part of Maria's job is to explain policies and procedures to them in Spanish, as needed. Maria has tried to keep the workers advised of how toxic these chemicals can be and what precautions should be taken. Unfortunately, the factory manager has refused to pay for new safety gloves, masks, and other protective items that obviously need to be replaced. She is most concerned about the protective gloves because she worries about the chemicals getting on workers' hands. Maria has also seen workers dump chemicals into the stream behind the plant. She is pretty sure, but not positive, that the chemicals are toxic.

Today a safety inspector from the Occupational Safety and Health Administration (OSHA) came in for a spot check of safety procedures. Maria is not sure whether she should tell the inspector everything she knows. She wants to be loyal to her employer, and she really needs to keep her job.

1. What are Maria's ethical obligations in this situation?

   _____

   _____

   _____

2. Do you think Maria would be disloyal to disclose what she knows about possible safety violations? Why or why not?

   _____

   _____

   _____

3. Does Maria owe her allegiance to the factory owners or to the workers?

   _____

   _____

   _____

4. If you were in Maria's place, what would you do? Why?

   _____

   _____

CASE 13.2 Follow Local Customs?

Dmitri works as a sales representative for East-West International Partners, a company that sells raw materials to companies and governments abroad. Dmitri, who was born in Moscow and came to the United States when he was 12 years old, was hired specifically to sell to customers in the former Soviet Union. Dmitri speaks English and Russian fluently and has an excellent sales background. He is also familiar with Russian customs and culture, which is one of the reasons he was hired. The company is sure his understanding of the area will help him serve existing customers and generate new business there.

The company has a strict code of ethics that forbids employees to offer or accept bribes and kickbacks. Dmitri knows that among some of his customers, bribes and kickbacks are considered a part of doing business. It is simply expected that you "line some palms" along the way to get the deal through. He also knows that he has to account for all his expenses for each customer. Dmitri and his American-born boss are traveling in Russia and are meeting with a client tomorrow, and Dmitri is pretty sure the client will want a kickback.

1. How should Dmitri approach this dilemma? If you think he should discuss the problem with his boss, what should he say?

_____

_____

_____

_____

_____

2. If you were Dmitri, would you operate on American values, local values, or some balance among them? Explain your answer.

_____

_____

_____

_____

_____

3. Do you think that Dmitri's boss and the other managers are completely unaware of the issue? Why or why not?

_____

_____

_____

_____

_____

4. If your answer to question 3 is *no*, what suggestions do you have for Dmitri?

_____

_____

_____

_____

_____

_____

5. What suggestions do you have for Dmitri's boss and the other members of management:

a. If your answer to question 3 is *no*:

_____

_____

_____

_____

_____

_____

b. If your answer to question 3 is *yes*:

_____

_____

_____

_____

_____

_____

Part 4

It's all about

Workplace Success

kstock/Getty Images

Workplace Focus

Bob Stecher is a self-employed realtor working for Coldwell Banker Residential Brokerage in Atlanta, Georgia.

Before changing careers to real estate just four years ago, Bob worked in several other industries. He knows firsthand how change in the workplace—whether it's your task list or your entire profession—is a certainty. "I believe no matter what the change is, your positive attitude can be the biggest resource you have," says Bob. "Even if you had no control over what caused the changes that have taken place, address them promptly and logically, and do your best to make the outcome an asset for you professionally and personally."

Implementing or adapting to change requires superior leadership skills. "I define leadership as the ability to guide a group of people toward a goal by helping them believe in a common vision and gain consensus. In other words, a leader helps his or her team perceive that the steps they take toward that goal are theirs as a group, not just the leader's. You need to be open to understanding how people think, communicate, and learn from mistakes to produce results."

For Bob, networking is the skill at the heart of leadership, managing change in the workplace, and job searching. "Networking can help you gain support from others, share information, and brainstorm ways to improve in the position you are in or find the position you want most. If you consistently make an effort to connect with other professionals in your field and beyond, doors will open that you never knew existed."

© Bob Stecher

Developing Leadership Skills and Managing Change

Think About It: When Will was in high school, he started working at Ruiz Insurance Company as a clerk. He filed documents, made copies, and entered data in the company's customer database. After he had been there about a year, Mrs. Ruiz started to assign him more responsibility. He learned enough about homeowners' and auto insurance to answer routine phone calls from customers.

Are Will's concerns reasonable? What can he do to help his coworkers adjust to his new position?

He wrote routine letters for Mrs. Ruiz to review. He assembled packets of information with cover letters to be mailed to prospects. He created and updated spreadsheets detailing each salesperson's prospects, proposals, and results. Will attended a local community college after he graduated from high school and went on to complete an associate's degree in business. He was thinking of transferring to a university to complete a B.S. in accounting, perhaps going on for an M.B.A degree. However, Mrs. Ruiz thought he would make an excellent insurance salesperson and offered him a job just after he completed the associate's degree. Will was flattered that Mrs. Ruiz thought he was ready for such a responsible position. After talking it over, they decided that Will could work during the day and take classes at night. Will was thrilled with this opportunity, but wondered how the secretary and receptionist he had trained under might feel about his promotion over them.

Stockbyte/Jupiter Images

objectives

After completing this chapter, you should be able to:

1. Describe the qualities and skills common to most leaders.
2. Compare various leadership styles.
3. Explain the importance of empowering others.
4. Explain how leaders can influence others.
5. Describe how leaders bring about change and innovation.

14.1 What Makes a Leader?

14.2 Empowering and Influencing Others

14.3 Leading Change and Innovation

What Makes a Leader?

You may think you are a born leader. You may think you have no leadership skills at all. Either way, you are probably wrong. The notion that "leaders are born, not made" has been largely dismissed by scholars who study leadership. Although business leaders have many attitudes and attributes in common, these are not necessarily qualities they were born with. Becoming a leader takes hard work and commitment to developing leadership skills. But if you are motivated to lead, you can acquire these skills and become an effective leader.

The terms *management* and *leadership* are often used almost interchangeably, but not every manager is a leader, and not every leader is a manager. The authority that a manager has to set goals, develop plans, and assign work makes that person a *boss*, not a leader. Leaders have personal qualities that motivate others to follow their direction and work toward a common goal. The most effective leaders encourage, teach, and guide *followers*—not subordinates.

Warren Bennis, business professor at the University of Southern California, says the primary difference is that leaders are concerned with *doing the right thing*, while managers are concerned with *doing things right*.[1] Another view is that while managers are concerned with control, leaders are more concerned with expanding people's choices.[2]

"Managers solve problems so that others can do their work, while leaders inspire and motivate others to find their own solutions."

QUALITIES OF LEADERS

What separates a leader from a follower? What can you do to develop the attitudes and behaviors you will need in order to lead? You can build qualities and skills that make others want to follow you. Some of these attitudes, behaviors, and skills have been covered in other chapters, but they also apply to learning leadership. Some of the attributes commonly accepted as essential to leaders are listed in Figure 14-1.

Ambition means wanting to get things done. Ambitious people are self-motivated to accomplish as much as they can. Usually, ambition is a positive force that drives people to pursue a task, a goal, an idea, or an ideal. Ambitious people focus their energy on initiating projects and getting them done. At its best, ambition is not a selfish quest for power. However, when an ambitious person pursues a goal that is corrupt, misguided, or just plain wrong, ambition can lead to colossal business failures, such as the Wall Street "meltdown" that began in September 2008.

Many people have a natural internal drive to better themselves and the world. If you find yourself having trouble getting motivated, review Chapter 2, especially the sections "Set Goals" and "Develop Action Plans."

ESSENTIAL LEADERSHIP QUALITIES

Ambition	Persistence
Integrity	Persuasiveness
High energy	Assertiveness
Intelligence	Decisiveness
Self-confidence	Sensitivity to the feelings and needs of others
Creativity	

FIGURE 14-1 Leadership qualities.

When you find yourself having trouble with a decision:

- Make sure you have all the facts.
- Write down the pros and cons of each alternative.
- Weigh the potential benefits you have written down against the potential risks.
- Think of the best outcome each alternative could bring.
- Think of the worst outcome each alternative could bring.
- Ask yourself whether the worst outcome is catastrophic or manageable. If you believe you can handle the worst outcome, it may be worth the risk.
- Make your decision and evaluate the outcome.

Put your goals in writing and describe the steps to reach them. You also need to prepare to deal with setbacks. Write down the obstacles to success and the strategies you plan to use to overcome them. Pursue your goals one step at a time, and be sure to appreciate each accomplishment along the way.

Integrity means being honest and trustworthy. Leaders with integrity do not lie or mislead others. You can believe what they say and trust their motives. People with integrity take pride in doing the right thing. They have the greater good in mind and strive to do what is best for everyone involved.

Energy is the effort you apply to getting things done. Energy means the intensity you bring to an effort, which can energize those around you. It means approaching tasks with enthusiasm and determination. It begins with initiative in starting tasks and projects and continues with the determination and diligence to see them through.

Intelligence is the ability to think, solve problems, and learn. Intelligence means more than just wisdom, and it is a very individual trait. You may be great at math but not at writing, or the reverse. You have your own "brand" of intelligence that you can focus on the task at hand, and you know when to call on the intelligence and skills of your coworkers to supplement your knowledge and skills.

Self-confidence is belief in yourself and your abilities. Self-confidence comes with time as you learn to understand yourself, motivate yourself, discipline yourself, and give yourself credit for your accomplishments and abilities. In Chapter 1, you learned some techniques for building self-confidence. Here is a brief review:

- Give yourself recognition, praise, and positive self-talk each day.
- Know your strengths and weaknesses, and set goals to overcome your weaknesses.
- Talk with others about your good qualities.
- Focus on your achievements, regardless of how large or small.

Creativity means having original ideas, or thinking about old things in new ways. Creative people generate ideas and look at problems from fresh perspectives. Creative people are curious and willing to take risks. They are enthusiastic about exploring new approaches to problems. They have the ability to focus their energy, and they face tasks with passion and imagination. You may think that you are not very creative, but creativity is something you can develop.

Persistence is sticking to a task until it is done well. It can be tempting to give up when you see obstacles in the way or face serious setbacks. In Chapter 2, you learned how to develop an action plan as a strategy for reaching your goals. Review this chapter for ways to develop persistence, such as charting a route, defining the steps it will take to reach your goal, and staying on track. Do not be afraid to modify steps and strategies when needed. Keep your eye on the goal—and be flexible about how you get there. Self-discipline is another important leadership quality. Before you can discipline anyone else, you must be able to discipline yourself.

Persuasiveness is the ability to influence and motivate others. Most persuasion takes place through words. For example, a person who makes a case for a point of view and influences others to accept those ideas is being persuasive. When trying to influence others, it is important to think through the supporting points and present them in the most positive light to get others to see things as you do. Explain the benefits of the outcome you want. Then explain how you have thought through the steps needed to get there, so that your followers will understand *how* the results can be reached.

Assertiveness is the ability to put forth your own ideas with confidence. In Chapter 6, you learned that assertiveness is the ability to express your thoughts and feelings and to assert your rights while respecting the feelings and rights of others. You learned how to make your own thoughts clear in an open, direct, and honest way while acknowledging other points of view.

Decisiveness is the ability to reach decisions and carry them out. It is important to take action without too much hesitation. In Chapter 10, you learned techniques for solving problems and making decisions, including gathering all the facts and considering alternatives before deciding. Your chances at success are usually higher if you explore the possibilities with others. You will make some mistakes. Everyone does. Still, it is obvious that acting too late is likely to make problems harder to solve.

Sensitivity means that you care about the people around you and their success. In Chapter 7, you learned about being sensitive to the feelings of others and trying to make them feel at ease. You learned about empathy, the art of recognizing the feelings of others and responding to those feelings with a "you" orientation. In Chapter 5 and in Chapter 7, you learned how becoming a better listener can improve your ability to influence, persuade, and negotiate. These qualities are essential to leadership.

> "Leadership should be born out of the understanding of the needs of those who would be affected by it."

STYLES OF LEADERSHIP

Your leadership style is how you behave when you are trying to influence the performance of others. It is the way you supervise or work with others. An Internet search will show you that there are hundreds of books, theories, and models of leadership in various settings. There may be something to be learned from all of these interpretations, and you can incorporate useful ideas from them into your unique style. You learned about the three basic leadership styles in Chapter 7: laissez-faire, democratic, and autocratic.

- A *laissez-faire leader* gives responsibility to followers to carry out their duties without a great deal of direction or close supervision. This kind of leader sets goals and provides information and guidance when asked, but allows employees to determine how to reach the goals.
- A *democratic leader* encourages followers to participate in solving problems and making decisions and practices moderate control over the followers. This kind of leader welcomes suggestions from followers but still makes the final decisions and accepts responsibility for outcomes.
- An *autocratic leader* makes plans and decisions alone, telling followers what to do and when and how to do things. This kind of leader expects followers to do as they are told and does not seek opinions and ideas from the group.

People who study leadership describe other styles of leading, including *charismatic leadership, transformational leadership*, and *servant leadership*, which overlap the styles described above.

The Charismatic Leader

The word *charisma* comes from an ancient Greek word meaning "divine gift." A **charismatic leader** has extraordinary magnetism that inspires others to follow him or her with devotion. Charismatic leaders may have a positive or negative impact. Examples include religious leaders and political leaders such as the Rev. Dr. Martin Luther King and President John F. Kennedy. These leaders inspire people to follow their lead with extraordinary devotion and loyalty.

The Transformational Leader

Transformational leadership is similar to charismatic leadership. It describes leadership based on the personal vision and passion a leader may have that inspires and transforms others. A **transformational leader** inspires followers to act in the interests of the group, helping and supporting each other and working in harmony toward a common goal. Mahatma Gandhi, who lead the nonviolent civil disobedience that ended British rule in India, and Nelson Mandela, who lead the anti-apartheid movement in South Africa, are two examples of transformational leaders. Transformational leaders often have an enormous, life-changing impact on their followers and their times.

"I skate where the puck is going to be, not where it has been."

The Situational Leader

The style a leader uses may also depend upon the situation, the qualities and abilities of the followers, and the task in question. This is called *situational leadership*. A **situational leader** might tell the custodian, "Make this office look, smell, and be really clean," describing the intended results but not the steps to get there. This approach assumes that followers will come up with their own ways of getting things done.

There are other situations, however, when a leader has to determine the exact steps to be taken to reach the results. For example, a manager of a medical clinic might tell the staff, "Wash your hands with soap and hot water and use the antibacterial lotion every time you use the restroom and every time you enter an examination room." In many situations, letting the follower determine how to get the intended results is the most effective approach because the follower is using his or her own problem-solving skills and "buying into the task." In others situations, a leader may need to describe the each step needed to reach the goal.

The way a person leads can depend on the situation and the people involved.

Effective leadership requires flexibility and adaptability. What works in one situation may not work in another. What works with one follower may be ineffective with another, depending on the person's personality, maturity, skill level, and other qualities. If the situation is urgent, even a democratic leader may implement a quick solution with the idea of refining it later, after listening to other ideas.

OPPORTUNITIES TO LEAD

As you progress through your career, look for opportunities to lead and seek feedback. Ask what you did well and what you could have done better. Then use this information to help you in your next leadership role.

Asking for honest feedback takes some courage. At the end of a difficult undertaking, nobody feels eager to think about what he or she did wrong. Still, there is always something you could have done better. The point is to know what mistakes you made, which may not be obvious to you. When you know how others viewed your performance, you can acknowledge your mistakes, learn from them, and think of ways to avoid repeating them. If possible failure were a reason not to lead, there would be few leaders. Everyone has ideas and visions to offer others. Even if your vision is not fulfilled exactly as you had hoped, you will learn from the experience.

When Vanetta's company decided to switch to a new integrated software package, she told her supervisor that she had learned to use the new software in a night school class she took last semester. She offered to coach the other administrative assistants at a brown bag lunch meeting, where she tried to show them what she had learned. When she asked the group if the meeting had been helpful, several of her coworkers said there was too much to take in all at once and asked her to e-mail screen shots and instructions. Vanetta developed a set of "one-point lessons" and put them on the share drive.

LEADERSHIP SKILLS

Successful leaders know how to motivate others to get the results the leader envisions. Interpersonal skills are essential to this process, including reading how others are reacting to you, your ideas, and your suggestions.

Emotional Intelligence

Emotional intelligence is the ability to recognize your own and others' emotions and react appropriately. People with emotional intelligence use their self-awareness and self-control to manage group relationships in a positive way. They can perceive the changing feelings and moods of others and adjust their words and behavior accordingly. It may be as simple as delaying a difficult conversation until the other person is in a more receptive mood.

Harold had been with the company as head of the sales department for five months when all the departments were told to develop a plan to reduce spending by 20 percent. At the biweekly sales meeting, Harold announced this newest "challenge" and talked about the "exciting opportunities" the department would have to try some new ideas. He asked his coworkers to divide into three groups and spend the next eight minutes brainstorming ways to cut costs. He set a kitchen timer and sat down with Frank and Betty as part of their group. The three of them came up with 18 ideas. When the timer rang, Harold asked Julia and Ari to lead the next part of the meeting—collecting each team's ideas, combining similar ideas, striking out duplicates, and writing the ideas on the whiteboard. When Julia and Ari stood up, Harold told the group he had to run an errand and would be back in 720 seconds. Harold returned in 12 minutes—with the company's first aid kit—just in case, he said, anyone was worried that the person sitting to their left might pass out from the stress and anxiety. After that, Harold was all seriousness as they talked about the ideas on the whiteboard. When they took a break 45 minutes later, the group had several valuable ideas to consider.

What were Harold's goals for the meeting? What are some of his leadership skills? What is his leadership style?

Scholars who study emotional intelligence emphasize that these abilities, like the other leadership traits, can be *learned*. Social relationships are complicated because people are complicated. Their moods and feelings—and your own—change for reasons that will not be apparent unless you pay close attention. A book or course can tell you what to pay attention to and provide helpful advice and activities to practice what you are learning, but you will not become a leader by *studying* emotional intelligence or any of the leadership traits. Developing these traits takes place in the real world through observation, introspection, practice, patience, and hard work.

Diplomacy and Tact

The best leaders have mastered the arts of diplomacy and tact, which are among the communication skills you have been learning throughout this book. A diplomatic person is skilled at considering how words, gestures, and actions may be interpreted from different points of view, in order to avoid offending others. A tactful person has the ability to say or do the right thing without hurting another person's feelings. Diplomacy and tact require sensitivity to what is appropriate in dealing with others, including speaking and acting without causing them pain, embarrassment, or discomfort. Tactful people treat others with great respect and consideration.

> Ashley was a paralegal assistant in a legal firm where the paralegals all worked in adjoining cubicles without much privacy. For months, she had been seething when her supervisor Lila pointed out errors she had made. Lila had a right to point them out, but she always seemed to do it in front of Ashley's coworkers, which embarrassed her. One afternoon as Lila was pointing out an error Ashley had made, Lila thought she noticed tears in Ashley's eyes. She took her aside later and asked if everything was all right. It had never occurred to Lila that she was the cause of Ashley's distress. When Ashley told Lila what was making her so miserable, Lila apologized and thanked her for pointing this out. "I must have embarrassed others in the same way. You have taught me an important lesson."

Effective Communication

The ability to communicate effectively—to listen carefully to others and to get your message across—is an essential leadership skill. Writer Stephen Covey put it well when he advised, "Seek first to understand, then to be understood."[3]

Leaders are excellent listeners. When you are focused entirely on getting your own point of view across, you lose the advantage of hearing different ideas and frustrate the people around you by ignoring their suggestions. Listening to others helps you look at problems from different viewpoints, which opens the door to new solutions. It enhances your ability to learn, influence, persuade, and negotiate. It shows others that you care about and respect their views.

Leaders are effective speakers. If you think about leaders you have known, you will find that they express themselves clearly and forcefully. People listen attentively when they speak. Some leaders have a natural talent for speaking, but these skills can also be learned. There is a difference, of course, between speaking casually to a small group and giving a formal speech to a large group. Leaders are generally good at both.

Matt is a drafter at an architectural firm. One of the architects has told Matt that he considers him the most skilled drafter they have. Grant wants Matt to arrange and lead some workshops to teach the others how he gets the results he achieves. Matt is confident that he knows some helpful techniques and tips, but he's not sure how to lead a workshop. He thinks back to his best teacher, who met with students one-on-one to look at their drawings. Matt knows there isn't time for this approach at work, but he asks the group to send him anonymous examples of their work three weeks before the workshop. He posts the drawings on the intranet with some questions about each drawing to think about before the workshop.

Whether the group is large or small, formal or informal, eye contact is important to getting your message across. You may have noticed how highly effective speakers like President Barack Obama make eye contact with individuals, whether speaking in front of a crowd or in a small group.

You learned previously how the rate at which you speak, your tone, pitch, volume, inflection, enunciation, pronunciation, and vocabulary affect your image. You also learned the importance of speaking clearly and effectively. These skills are essential for leaders who want to persuade others to adopt their point of view.

checkpoint

1. What is the difference between management and leadership?

_____

_____

_____

_____

2. Describe transformational leadership.

_____

_____

_____

_____

3. What is situational leadership?

_____

_____

_____

_____

4. Why is it important to be aware of leadership opportunities?

_____

_____

_____

_____

5. Why is emotional intelligence an important leadership quality?

_____

_____

_____

_____

applications

1. Identify a leader you have known (a parent, teacher, or business person, for example). Describe the leadership style this person used and give examples of that style.

_____

_____

_____

_____

2. Of the leadership styles described in this chapter, which do you prefer when you are a follower? Why?

_____

_____

_____

_____

3. Describe a situation when you had to use diplomacy or tact. Who was involved? How did you feel after the situation was resolved?

_____

_____

_____

_____

4. Do you think emotional intelligence can be learned? Why or why not?

_____

_____

_____

_____

5. Identify the qualities these people have that make them effective leaders. How are they alike? How are they different?

a. The Rev. Dr. Martin Luther King, Jr.

_____

_____

_____

_____

b. Warren Buffett

_____

_____

_____

_____

c. President Barack Obama

_____

_____

_____

_____

d. Secretary of State Hillary Clinton

_____

_____

_____

_____

e. Donald Trump

_____

_____

_____

_____

Empowering and Influencing Others

As a leader, you will need to understand the importance of empowering others. Obviously, a leader cannot do everything alone. Leaders need empowered followers. To **empower** others means to give others the authority and responsibility to carry out tasks or solve problems that the leader has defined. Sometimes the task will be assigned to one person, other times to a team. This is not to say that teams always come up with better solutions than individuals do. Sometimes creating a team to solve a problem may actually slow down the process. As you gain experience, you will learn when a team is the better option.

Leaders understand how to divide work among individuals and teams so that efforts are coordinated and people use their time efficiently. Empowering others shows that you respect their abilities. Be supportive as your coworkers take on new tasks you have given them.

©iofoto, 2009/Used under license from Shutterstock.com

An effective leader needs empowered followers.

DELEGATING TO OTHERS

A leader *delegates,* or turns over, the planning and/or execution of a task to others. Assigning specific tasks to individuals or teams is an art as well as a science. You will want to take advantage of each individual's strengths while developing and enhancing their skills and encouraging them to learn and grow. You will find that when you empower others, they come up with ideas and solutions that would not have occurred to you. You must expect that they may make some mistakes. As their leader, you can help them become aware of mistakes and learn from correcting them. Your group can help you analyze what went wrong and determine how to do it better next time.

Many theorists believe that it is best to describe the results you want and let the employee or team figure out how to get those results. For example, giving instructions to the grounds crew of a park, a manager might say, "I want this park to look clean, green, and the way nature intended." The staff would know that this means they should pick up litter without the manager dictating that detail. However, on a cleanliness issue that is more specific, the manager might simply give instructions: "Every employee must use a hand sanitizer after handling money."

Imagine that you are the office manager of a busy doctor's office. The doctor in charge has asked you to lead an ad hoc committee to research medical software packages for putting the office's records online. She wants the committee to meet with sales reps for the different vendors and narrow the list to two programs to consider. She thinks the committee will need two months to accomplish its goal.

1. Who will you ask to be on the committee?
2. What will you discuss at the first meeting? Develop an agenda for this meeting. (Look back at Chapter 9 if necessary.)
3. After talking with some friends in other medical offices and doing some preliminary research, you think that the work will take longer than two months. Outline an e-mail message to the doctor explaining your reasons and asking for more time. (Add details to make the scenario realistic.)

"Never tell people how to do things. Tell them what to do and they will surprise you with their ingenuity."

When you empower someone in your group, you give that person the authority to make certain decisions and carry them out without close supervision. You make the person responsible for the results, letting him or her decide how to reach those results. For example, a manager might give the cashier at a bookstore the authority to decide how best to speed up lines at the cash register. She may decide that a second cash register or faster barcode scanners should be added. Most people perform better when they are allowed to participate in choosing plans, solutions, and procedures. They "own" the problem when they are thinking about and taking responsibility for the outcome.

When you delegate to others, you give the people in that responsibility for the results. Several minds are often better than one at solving problems. A group has the advantage of looking at problems from many viewpoints and drawing on the experiences of many people instead of only one person.

MENTORING OTHERS

Mentoring means taking someone under your wing, guiding and teaching that person so that he or she benefits from your experience and skills. Such nurturing relationships have always existed, as between parent and child or between teacher and student. In the workplace, mentoring is an excellent way to develop individual potential. A more experienced and knowledgeable person is matched with someone who can benefit from learning what the mentor has to teach. The person being mentored is called the *mentee, protégé,* or *apprentice.*

Today, many companies have established formal mentoring programs that match mentors with mentees. Some business leaders see formal mentoring as an essential employee development tool. In those cases, the mentor and mentee may be assigned to work together, and the mentor may be held accountable for the mentee's progress. In other workplaces, informal relationships develop on their own between interested individuals. In either case, these relationships can be very valuable to a person learning a new field or expanding knowledge in a familiar field.

> *Omar could see that Andrea, the new mailroom clerk, was feeling lost. Omar had started in the mailroom five years ago, and he remembered how confusing it could be to sort and deliver dozens of letters, documents, and packages throughout the building. As he passed the mailroom he stopped and said, "Hi, Andrea. How's it going?" She looked very unhappy. "I don't know, Omar. I thought being the mail clerk would be easier. I keep delivering things to the wrong person or the wrong department. Then people have to call me to pick things up and redeliver them to the right place." "Did you know that I started out here in this job?" Omar asked. He continued, "Would you like to meet at break to go over some of the problems you're having? I think I may be able to help. And feel free to call my extension anytime something confusing comes up."*

Mentoring is not always a case of an older person guiding a younger person. In a process called "reverse mentoring," a younger person, perhaps someone skilled at newer technology such as smartphones, guides someone from the previous generation in learning new skills. The older person may in turn offer insights into something else that the younger person wants to learn. The terminology may be modern, but the process is not. Coworkers learn from each other and always have.

Erin is a sales agent at a busy real estate agency. Regina, the office manager, has asked Erin if her teenaged daughter Meghan can shadow her for two days for a school assignment. Erin is glad to help and encourages Meghan to use her laptop to view some of the houses and condominiums listed for sale. Erin is pleased when she comes back from lunch and finds Meghan busily reviewing layouts and home prices. Erin can see that Meghan is genuinely interested in learning about the business. The next day, Erin has prepared some assignments for Meghan. She invites Meghan to go with her on a sales call and briefs her about the property on the drive over. She gives Meghan her laptop and suggests that she ask the clients if they would like to see the neighborhood's website and blog. On the trip back to the office, Erin asks Meghan to summarize the sales call in an e-mail message to her and Regina.

Meghan is lucky that Erin has emotional intelligence and likes the role of mentor. How could the sales call have gone wrong if Erin did not have have emotional intelligence? How would the agency have been affected?

Throughout your career, it is likely that you will have more than one mentor and that you will mentor more than one other person. You may find someone you admire and ask him or her to be your mentor. Most people enjoy the process. Then, when you are more experienced, you may find someone who needs your guidance and offer to mentor him or her. Acting as a mentor to someone new to your field helps you as well as the mentee, because you must focus your attention to describe processes and procedures. You will find both experiences very rewarding.

SETTING AN EXAMPLE

Self-management and self-discipline build self-confidence, a key quality for leadership. Before you can motivate or discipline anyone else, you have to motivate and discipline yourself. If you are confident that the path you are taking will get the job done, you will be motivated. Some leaders simply decide what to do and inform their followers of how and when to carry out their plans. This is the autocratic leadership style, which most theorists consider to be the least effective method of leading others.

You will probably find it easier to motivate those around you if you involve them in solving problems with you, deciding together on a course of action. If they have not participated in the plan, they are less likely to be enthusiastic about it. There may be some who resent having the solution imposed upon them without discussion and who will find subtle ways to thwart it. You need their good will. Showing respect for them and their ideas is the best way to build goodwill.

George is in charge of buying new desk chairs for the office staff. He had a budget and had looked at a lot of options. Then he decided to ask several coworkers which type of chair they wanted—and got a different answer from everyone. Scott wanted a "balance ball chair" from a yoga store, Angie wanted a special chair that supported her back, and Zach wanted a chair with a mesh seat and back. George decided that, as long as the group stayed within the budget, everyone could choose the chair they wanted. His coworkers were pleased to be allowed to choose the chair that suited them.

As a leader, you are a role model for your coworkers. You need to behave as you want them to behave. You influence their behavior through your own behavior. This includes basics such as arriving on time, staying

To show your supervisor and coworkers that you are a capable leader, practice the following techniques.[4]

- **Complete tasks.** Show your supervisor that you can complete tasks without constant supervision.

- **Don't stop working when there's a foul-up.** Don't let glitches stop you in your tracks. Look for solutions, and avoid displaying frustration or helplessness.

- **Pick up the slack.** Doing what needs to be done, even if it is not part of your job description, is a good way to make yourself needed and appreciated.

- **Learn to translate "boss speak."** When bosses don't want to sound bossy, they say things like, "We're running out of paper." What they mean is, "Go get some more."

- **Deal with small problems yourself.** Don't complain about small things.

- **Choose the right moment to make a suggestion or a complaint**—not when the group is rushing to meet a deadline or leave for a conference.

- **Tell the truth.** Being honest about problems and mistakes will boost your credibility.

- **Let others win.** Be open-minded and supportive of others; no one wants to work with a know-it-all.

- **Know the organizational culture.** Be aware of the role your job plays in the big picture. Pay attention to what's going on around you.

on task, managing your time well, meeting deadlines, and treating everyone around you with respect and consideration. It includes planning, prioritizing, and setting reachable goals, skills which you have studied in other chapters of this book. It will involve decision making and problem solving.

Your own attitudes and behaviors can be as persuasive as your words—perhaps even more persuasive. Still, strong communications skills can contribute greatly to your effort. Find the clearest, simplest, and most compelling way to make your case. Choose a time when the people you want to persuade can really listen and think about what you say. Give examples of similar approaches to problems that have worked in comparable situations. Even if your plan sounds risky, followers will go along with it if they trust you.

Trust is something you build over time. Be frank about the risks, if any, of the path you advocate. Make it clear that you will take responsibility if the plan does not succeed. Then ask for their help. Invite them to voice their reservations, and ask them to help you modify the plan to prevent whatever problems they anticipate.

RESPONSIBILITIES OF LEADERSHIP

Leading others gives you authority and power over your followers. There is an ancient saying that tells us that "power corrupts." Perhaps there is a tendency, or at least a temptation, for people to take advantage of or even misuse power when they get it. Keep this in mind as you find yourself in a position to influence or even control others. Leaders who take advantage of power simply to impose their will on others are not going to be as effective as leaders who use more democratic styles.

Remind yourself to use your authority wisely and responsibly for the greater good as well as for your own peace of mind. Your personal integrity is essential to your long-term success and will serve you well the next time you have an opportunity to lead.

checkpoint

1. What does it mean to empower others?

_____

_____

_____

_____

2. Give an example of mentoring.

_____

_____

_____

_____

3. Why is it important for a leader to set an example?

_____

_____

_____

_____

_____

_____

4. Explain why a group might make a better decision than a person acting alone.

_____

_____

_____

_____

_____

_____

5. Explain why a leader's actions are as important as his or her words.

_____

_____

_____

_____

_____

_____

applications

1. Describe a situation when a leader might persuade others without using words.

_____

_____

_____

_____

2. Think of a time in history when power corrupted a leader. Who was the leader? What were the circumstances? What was the result?

_____

_____

_____

_____

3. What skills and knowledge do you possess that you could pass on to another person? Describe a situation in which you could serve as a mentor to a family member, a friend, a classmate, or a coworker.

_____

_____

_____

_____

4. Why is it important for leaders to have personal integrity?

_____

_____

_____

_____

5. Use a two-column table to contrast the qualities of an effective and ineffective leader.

   a. Think of someone who you feel is an extremely effective leader. The person could be any person in a leadership position. In the left column, list the positive leadership traits of this person.

   _____

   _____

   _____

   _____

   b. Now think of someone who you feel is an extremely ineffective leader. In the right column, list the negative leadership traits of this person.

   _____

   _____

   _____

   _____

   _____

   c. Select one of the qualities listed in the left column. Write a paragraph about why that quality is so important in today's workplace.

   _____

   _____

   _____

   _____

   _____

Leading Change and Innovation

Organizations and people change for many reasons. It may be that they decide to change in order to improve what they do or how they do it. They may be forced to change in order to stay competitive in changing economic times. For example, people sometimes find themselves out of a job in mid-life. If there are no jobs in their current field, they may have to start all over learning a new trade or career. This is never easy, and it probably becomes more difficult as you grow older. They may have invested many years in the field where they had been working. Starting over can seem overwhelming. The alternative, however, is continued unemployment. Once someone begins this process, it can become less frightening and actually turn out to be energizing and fulfilling.

The same is often true of organizational change. At first employees think, "Why do they have to change this? I don't see anything wrong with the current procedure, but now they are going to change it." If you make up your mind to cooperate and face the new challenge, you will probably find out that the change really is for the better. When personal computers were first introduced, many workers wanted to stick to their typewriters. Today, who would choose a typewriter over a computer? Who today would argue that personal computers have not increased individual productivity and created new job opportunities?

Change usually comes from the top of an organization. However, increasingly, managers are listening to ideas for innovation from people throughout their organization. After all, the people who actually do a particular task have a clearer idea of how to do it better. Improvements may occur to them that the manager never considered because he or she does not have the same day-to-day hands-on experience. Although the goal is always to improve productivity, performance, efficiency, or competitiveness, even positive change can be disruptive. That is why leaders must plan for change, communicate with followers about it in a timely and clear fashion, and then monitor and measure progress.

It has been six months since Marivel expanded her eight-year-old bakery by renting the space next door and opening a breakfast and lunch spot, which has turned out to be quite successful. Unexpectedly,

©AVAVA, 2009/Used under license from Shutterstock.com

An effective leader communicates why changes are being made.

a business acquaintance approaches Marivel about renting space in her kitchen to open a catering business called Dinner Divas. That same week, a friend asks her if she is interested in taking him on as a partner to turn the daytime coffee <u>shop</u> into an evening coffee <u>house</u>, with easy chairs and an espresso machine. Marivel did not expect either of these offers and does not know if they would be good or bad for her business. Still, she is smart enough to know that she should thoughtfully consider each one.

CHANGE IS INEVITABLE

The world around us is always changing, so you would think that we would accept change as inevitable. Instead, we often resist it consciously or unconsciously. This is true partly because it takes work to change. It usually seems easier in the short run to do what you have been doing. In the long run, however, people who do not change are left behind as everything around them changes. When a leader comes along who wants to change goals, procedures or routines, many of us balk, drag our feet, or complain. Yet no enterprise or person can prosper over the long term without healthy change.

Murray, the longtime lab director in the R&D (research and development) department, has announced his retirement. Marianne, the head of R&D for three years, has received great advice from Murray on every topic she has asked him about. Murray is a modest man, but she suspects that he knows more about their department than the rest of the group put together. They meet in his office to talk about ways Murray can document his knowledge so that it doesn't "walk out the door" with him when he retires. Murray shows Marianne dozens of binders and several file cabinets filled with one-of-a-kind documents that predate the use of personal computers and electronic files. He suggests that he spend the rest of his time labeling everything and putting together a list of what he has. Marianne has a different idea. She appreciates Murray's interest in preserving the past, but she believes it is essential to capture his perspective on the new technologies, new products, and new processes that have been implemented over the years. She wants to put together an ad hoc committee to work with Murray. She asks him to meet with her in two days to talk about the committee and what can be accomplished before Murray retires.

Why does Marianne want to preserve Murray's perspective on the changes he has been part of? How can Murray and the committee accomplish Marianne's goals?

Any business, organization, or person who wants to grow must not only accept change, but also anticipate it and seek it. It is not a question of change for the sake of change. It is a question of making progress. Failing to change is the same as standing still. It means staying in the same rut without learning, growing, and making progress.

HOW LEADERS BRING ABOUT CHANGE

A leader must start with a vision of what he or she wants to accomplish. In order to make this vision reality, the leader is often asking others to change what they do or how they do things. Sometimes the leader is changing who does what, which can make people feel insecure in their jobs. One of the leader's most important priorities should be to make followers feel comfortable with proposed changes. Sometimes the changes a leader proposes will mean the elimination of positions or significant changes in what individuals do. It is not always easy for followers to accept these possibilities and adapt to them.

The first step in bringing about change is clear communication. A good leader explains how and why changes are needed. The leader will be patient in answering followers' questions about how the changes will affect them individually and as a group. Inviting followers to participate in how changes take place is more likely to get them to "buy into" your plan than is simply imposing it on them. Inviting them to voice their apprehensions and explaining how you plan to avoid what they fear will help ease their discomfort.

THE RATE OF CHANGE

Gradual, controlled, and well-thought-out change is usually easier to manage than sudden and drastic change. An effective leader is looking ahead enough to start changes before the situation becomes a crisis. Incremental and gradual changes are usually easier to put in place and easier for followers to accept.

Incremental change is change that occurs in a series of small, planned steps. If you set up a plan to measure progress in stages, your followers will better understand how the other steps will be manageable. When problems arise or followers fall behind schedule, address the problems as soon as you are aware of them. Incremental change allows followers to appreciate the progress they are making toward larger goals. It also gives both leaders and followers a chance to fine-tune subsequent steps based on what they have learned from completed steps.

TIPS FOR MANAGING CHANGE

- **Look at the change as a new opportunity.** One of the very best ways to predict the future is to create new possibilities for yourself.

- **Believe in yourself.** Focus on your past successful experiences and sources of personal strength that may help you realize what strategies to use to face current challenges.

- **Stay positive.** Don't allow yourself to stay stuck in negative feelings, self-pity, worry, anger, or bitterness. That will only make you feel worse. Focus on the future, and think of the change as a challenge that you will conquer.

- **Spend energy on things you can change.** Keep in mind when one door closes, invariably other doors of opportunity can open up. When you take positive steps on your own behalf, things can start to change for you.[5]

TAKING RISKS

Whenever you make a change, there is a chance that something will go wrong. This should not keep you from taking risks. Think ahead and ask yourself, "What could go wrong if I do this?" Careful planning will help you anticipate the risks and develop a plan for addressing problems that may arise. If you understand and accept the possible negative consequences, you can weigh the benefits against the risks of a change and make wiser decisions. It is a matter of managing risk, not avoiding it altogether. Rarely do important changes go smoothly without any rough spots.

> *Florence and Larry Mueller own Mueller and Associates, a small accounting firm. Tax season is as busy as ever, but business the rest of the year is down and they need to cut costs. This summer, two visits from a computer technician (at $75 an hour) cost $450. Florence heard about a new community-focused program at the community college. She met with the director of the computer department there and arranged to pay a monthly retainer fee to have students maintain the company's computers. She was nervous about letting the lab install a program to monitor their computers remotely, but the student who made the first service call was so knowledgeable and helpful that she and Larry decided to go ahead with the remote system. The new process is saving money, and it's reassuring to know that Mueller and Associates' files are being routinely backed up.*

INNOVATION AND CONTINUOUS IMPROVEMENT

Change and innovation are not identical concepts. When you **innovate**, you create something significantly new or a new way of doing something. Innovation is the successful application of a new idea. Most scholars who study innovation in business agree that a change must result in a considerable difference in order to be innovative. Innovations make a product or service more valuable to customers, or they substantially improve a procedure or process for greater efficiency or creativity. Economists cite innovation as a major force in growing the economy.

Apple is one of the most innovative of the Fortune 100 companies (the largest 100 companies in the United States). Apple was the first company to find a way to make money selling digital media on the Internet through its immensely popular iTunes Store, where users buy and download music, videos, audio books, applications, television shows, and movies. Another Apple innovation, the iPod portable media player, is so popular that the term *podcast* was coined for it, although it is not necessary to have an iPod to receive and play podcasts.

The concept of continuous improvement is related to innovation. **Continuous improvement** is a management process that constantly monitors what the enterprise is doing and how people are doing it. This enables leaders to identify and address problems and foster growth through ongoing improvement of products, services, procedures, and processes. This is not a bad principle to apply to your own self-improvement. True leaders—the people whom others instinctively look to for direction—are lifelong learners and observers who are constantly looking for ways to do things better.

Flexibility and Adaptability

Continuous improvement requires both leaders and followers who are flexible and adaptable to changing technologies, procedures, and strategies. Something as simple as upgrading to a new version of a word processing program can throw people off. Are you on "auto pilot" when you key a document or enter data into a spreadsheet? Like everyone, you are used to doing things a certain way. It takes time and effort to learn and adapt to a newer version of the software. Although the change may slow you down in the short run, it will probably make your job easier in the long run. It is likely that you will find yourself learning entirely new kinds of software without formal training in how to use it. In cases like this, you need to take a deep breath and face the challenge with determination. You will learn the new software as you are using it—and it may even be fun, as challenges often are.

APPLY IT!

Read each situation and determine if it describes a change (C) or an innovation (I).

_____ Anderson Auto Parts is putting a new number-coding system on its parts to make them match manufacturers' number codes.

_____ Tellers at First National Bank have been told to start wearing business casual clothes to work instead of the suits and jacketed dressses they have worn for years.

_____ The owner of Randy's Riding Stable has decided to require all trainers to be certified, even if they have done their jobs well without certification.

Fatima's Fabric Store is considering making several changes. They are thinking about:

_____ Stocking an environmentally certified line of "green" fabrics.

_____ Stocking scrapbooking and wall stenciling supplies.

_____ Teaching upholstery classes.

_____ Offering in-home decorating assessments and services.

_____ Selling reupholstered chairs and sofas on consignment.

_____ Renting the back room to a jewelry maker who sells jewelry supplies and teaches daytime and evening jewelry-making classes.

If a leader is to be effective, the changes he or she brings about should make followers more efficient, more effective, and more creative. In order to achieve these outcomes, a strong leader will maintain a creative work environment where followers are encouraged to suggest innovations. This does not mean that every idea they have will be implemented. It does mean that they will be encouraged to think about better ways of doing things and that their ideas will be treated with respect. It is through constant striving to improve that situations and outcomes change.

Whether you are leading or following, it helps to understand and embrace the process of change. Leader or follower, you will undergo many changes in your work life. This is how people and enterprises grow.

checkpoint

1. Name a major obstacle to implementing change.

_____

_____

_____

_____

2. Give an example of incremental change.

_____

_____

_____

_____

3. What is continuous improvement?

_____

_____

_____

_____

4. Explain the difference between change and innovation.

_____

_____

_____

5. Why must leaders take risks?

_____

_____

_____

applications

1. Why do you think some people fear change? Recall a time when you resisted change and explain why you resisted.

_____

_____

_____

_____

2. Describe a time when you played a leadership role. What type of leadership style did you use? Were you able to accomplish your objective? Why or why not?

_____

_____

_____

_____

3. Describe a creative environment that you have experienced (for example, in a job, at school, or in a club or organization). What did you learn from the experience?

_____

_____

_____

_____

_____

4. Explain how continuous improvement works.

_____

_____

_____

_____

_____

5. List some major changes that are taking place in your community. How will existing businesses be affected? What new business opportunities are being created? What old businesses are being replaced?

_____

_____

_____

_____

_____

14 points to remember

Review the following points to determine what you remember from the chapter.

- Leaders have qualities that include ambition, energy, intelligence, self-confidence, creativity, persistence, persuasiveness, assertiveness, decisiveness, and sensitivity.
- The main leadership styles are laissez-faire, democratic, and autocratic. Other styles include charismatic, transformational, and situation leadership.
- Leaders are skilled at diplomacy and tact, listening well, speaking well, treating others with respect, taking risks, and accepting responsibility.
- Leaders empower others through delegation and mentoring.
- Leaders must set an example for followers, who will model the leader's behavior and attitudes.
- Leaders speak and listen well to persuade others and collaborate with them on solving problems.
- The world around us is always changing. We must adapt by accepting and embracing change.
- Failing to change can mean being left behind.
- Innovation and continuous improvement drive progress.

How did you do? Did you remember the main points you studied in the chapter?

KEY terms

charismatic leader

transformational leader

situational leader

emotional intelligence

empower

mentoring

incremental change

innovate

continuous improvement

Want more activities? Go to **www.cengage.com/careerreadiness/masters** to get started.

CHAPTER *activities*

1. Which qualities common to leaders do you think you already have? Which qualities do you think you need to develop?

   _____

   _____

   _____

2. Set SMART goals for developing each leadership quality you listed in Activity 1 as one you need to develop. (If necessary, refer to Figure 2-3 on page 24 for a review of SMART goals.)

   _____

   _____

   _____

3. Describe a time when someone helped you accept an unwelcome or unexpected change, or when you helped someone else. What did you learn from the experience?

   _____

   _____

   _____

   _____

4. For two of the leadership styles described in this chapter, write a short "best case" scenario depicting that style of leader interacting with his or her followers. Include enough details to make the scenarios interesting and useful examples.

   _____

   _____

   _____

   _____

5. Explain how a leader can help others to accept change.

   _____

   _____

   _____

   _____

   _____

6. Ping is a groundskeeper in a city park. He loves working outdoors and wants to do his work well. However, his supervisor, Jake, wants to control what Ping does and exactly how he does it right down to each step. Ping comes from China, where respect for elders is highly valued. He would like to suggest easier ways of doing a few things, but is hesitant to approach Jake about them.

   a. What advice would you give Ping about this dilemma?

      _____

      _____

      _____

      _____

      _____

   b. What could Jake do to become a more effective leader?

      _____

      _____

      _____

      _____

CRITICAL *thinking*

CASE 14.1 Kamilah's Story

Kamilah is one of eight administrative assistants in the human resources department of a large insurance office. Kamilah's manager has asked her to select and lead a team of assistants in drafting a revision of the employee handbook. Kamilah is the youngest administrative assistant at the company, and she has been there only two years. She knows that some of her coworkers are envious of the authority her supervisor gives her. Some of them have even seemed hostile. Kamilah knows that the manager wants her to handle this situation without much further supervision.

The existing handbook that they need to revise is unclear in places and it leaves out important issues such as a dress code, equal opportunity employment, grievance procedure, disability policy, and leave-of-absence policies. After the team completes a draft of the handbook, it will be distributed to company officials for their review, so it needs to be well done. Kamilah feels unsure of her leadership skills. She feels uncomfortable even approaching the others about the assignment.

1. What should Kamilah's first steps be? Should she include all seven of her fellow assistants in the handbook revision group, or should she limit it to a few people?

   _____

   _____

2. What can Kamilah do to get the others to accept her as their leader? What does she need to communicate to the others at the outset?

   _____

   _____

3. Write the e-mail that Kamilah will send to the assistants asking them to join the team and explaining the project. Prepare an agenda for the first meeting of the handbook revision team.

   _____

   _____

4. Assume that Kamilah and her team have completed the draft of the employee handbook. Create a brief questionnaire that Kamilah might use to ask the team members to evaluate her performance.

   _____

   _____

CASE 14.2 Planning the Holiday Party

Brandon worked as a paralegal assistant in a law firm specializing in immigration. He volunteered to lead the team planning the firm's holiday party to be held Friday, December 13. The holiday party was an annual tradition, and the law partners considered it an important event.

Brandon asked his two best friends at work to help with the planning. They met at a local restaurant after work and decided how to divide up the work. Brandon would choose the location and work with the staff on the menu and other details. Annette would take care of entertainment. Vijay would e-mail the invitation. Time was limited so they did not talk much about details. They agreed to meet again on Friday, November 30 to make sure everything was in order. Friday morning, Brandon and Vijay had a voice-mail message from Annette, who explained that she was taking a personal day. Brandon postponed the meeting until Monday.

On Monday, Brandon announced that he had booked Beal's Steakhouse, a popular restaurant near the law firm, for 8 o'clock to midnight Friday evening. Annette pointed out that she and four coworkers she knew personally were vegetarians—and there were probably more on the staff. Vijay told Brandon and Annette that he and the two Hindu lawyers did not eat beef. Annette had hired a friend who was a hip-hop DJ to provide the entertainment, which Brandon thought some of the older partners were unlikely to enjoy. Vijay was concerned that the party started so late; what were people supposed to do between the end of the workday and 8 p.m.? With only eight days left to make arrangements, the group was scrambling—and Vijay had not sent out the final announcement yet.

1. What could Brandon have done to prevent the last-minute scramble?

   _____

   _____

2. Was Brandon right to put his friends on the team? Why or why not?

   _____

   _____

3. With eight days left to finalize plans for the party, what should Brandon do next to fix the problems?

   _____

   _____

4. What do you think Brandon and Annette and Vijay have learned from this experience?

   _____

   _____

chapter 15

Getting the Job

Blend Images/Jupiter Images

objectives

After completing this chapter, you should be able to:

1. Analyze your personal values, traits, interests, aptitudes, and skills.
2. Prepare a worksheet showing your experiences and qualifications.
3. Investigate possible resources and plan a successful job campaign.
4. Prepare a resume, job application form, and cover letter.
5. Present yourself as a strong candidate during a job interview.
6. Prepare a thank-you note or letter as a follow-up to a job interview.

Think About It: Dan Hensen is enrolled at the local community college. However, his current financial situation permits him to take only night school classes and makes it necessary for him to look for daytime work. His interview for a job at a customer center for a wireless provider went well. Dan was impressed by the newly remodeled workplace. He liked the people he would work with, and the training would take place on the job. He was offered the position and started work enthusiastically. Within a few weeks, Dan realized that this was not the job for him. He had trouble learning the features of the various phones and remembering the fine print on all the different contracts, and he became anxious when customers asked questions he could not answer. He was not an outgoing person, and he was uncomfortable serving a steady stream of customers. He began to realize that he needed to think about his future and get a job where the work suited his personality, interests, skills, and aptitudes.

What questions should Dan have asked during the interview? What is your advice for Dan as he prepares to think about other positions?

Analyze Your Interests and Qualifications

You now have one of your greatest challenges ahead of you: finding the right job. Although you may not find a perfect fit right away, it is important to aim for a job that matches your interests, needs, skills, training, and your likes and dislikes.

Finding a job is hard work, and it is very likely that you will be launching a job search several times throughout your working life. The U.S. Bureau of Labor Statistics reports that American workers, on average, change jobs every five years.[1] The National Longitudinal Survey of Youth (1979) estimated that the average worker would have about ten different jobs between the ages of 18 and 38.[2] Now, more than thirty years later, the turnover is very likely higher than that.

Consider each job search and each interview a learning experience, even if you are not hired. Review your strategies, your answers to interview questions, and other details so that you learn from your mistakes.

YOUR SELF-ASSESSMENT

Whether you are starting out or starting over, finding a job requires preparation and planning. The first step is a thorough, honest self-assessment. What do you value in life? What are your personal traits? What do you enjoy doing? What are your aptitudes and skills? What are your career goals? You will want to keep these interests and characteristics in mind as you explore job possibilities and market your strengths to prospective employers.

Self-assessment is an ongoing process that changes with your growth and experiences. If you are to take charge of yourself and become successful in your life and work, you must have a clear, realistic image of where you are now and where you want to be in the future.

Muriel has been working as a medical secretary for the past year. In general, she enjoys her work. But lately, she finds herself wishing she had a greater opportunity to use her creativity. The medical terminology and coding system make her work very exacting—something that is becoming frustrating. She makes a list of her transferable qualifications and decides to look for an administrative assistant position in an advertising agency.

Identify Your Personal Traits

Like everyone, you have a variety of personal traits that will affect what type of work you will most enjoy. For example, how well you do under pressure? Are you resourceful? How sociable are you? How easily do you adapt to new situations? You will be happiest at a job that complements your personal traits. Look at the list of traits in Figure 15-1. Which traits would you use to describe yourself?

Use this checklist adapted from *Getting a Job Process Kit* by Robert Zedlitz to evaluate your interest in these things.[4]

I would like a job where I:

(0) No interest   (1) Some interest   (2) Strong interest

a. _____ Work outdoors

b. _____ Fix things

c. _____ Work with my hands

d. _____ Work alone

e. _____ Solve problems

f. _____ Explore situations

g. _____ Work with new ideas

h. _____ Work with other people

i. _____ Help people

j. _____ Manage people

k. _____ Sell

l. _____ Travel

m._____ Work with numbers

n. _____ Key reports and other documents

o. _____ Write documents

p. _____ Work in an office

q. _____ Work with computers

r. _____ Work in a structured setting

s. _____ Work in an informal setting

Review your rankings; what five things would you like in your ideal job?

Define Your Interests

Your interests are the things that you enjoy doing. Think of several things that you find satisfaction in and do well. What do they have in common? For example, you may find that the activities you enjoy most are those that involve working with a variety of people. Or, conversely, you may find you are happiest when working alone. If you find a career that involves

SAMPLE PERSONAL TRAITS[a]

adaptable	determined	generous	persuasive
assertive	direct	idealistic	positive
caring	disciplined	independent	reflective
cautious	efficient	loyal	resourceful
consistent	energetic	objective	self-confident
creative	enthusiastic	open-minded	sociable
dependable	fair	organized	steady
detail-oriented	flexible	patient	tactful

FIGURE 15-1 Sample personal traits.

doing what you are interested in and enjoy, you are more likely to enjoy your job and advance in it.

When Steve and his friends talked about their first jobs, Steve usually skipped over his three summers as a counselor-in-training at the community center's day camp. After all, everyone knew that the counselors-in-training spent a lot of time "babysitting" the younger campers. When Steve admitted to himself how much he liked that job and working with young people, he researched Teach for America and applied for a position as an elementary teacher.

Consider all of your interests when thinking about your job choices.

Identify Your Aptitudes and Skills

An **aptitude** is a natural talent, ability, or capacity to learn. Having an aptitude for something makes learning things related to that aptitude much easier. For example, if you have an aptitude for math, working with figures comes more easily for you than for someone who doesn't have an aptitude for math. A **skill** is an aptitude that you have put into practice and improved. Employers are interested in both transferable skills and technical skills. **Transferable skills** can be used in many different work settings. Keyboarding, for example, is a skill that can easily be used in a variety of workplaces. **Technical skills** are specialized skills needed for specific jobs. For example, the ability to read blueprints is a technical skill required of an architect or engineer. Figure 15-2 lists transferable and technical skills. Review the skills in each category as you think about your own skills.

SAMPLE SKILLS[5]

Transferable Skills		Technical Skills	
creating	organizing	baking	home decorating
doing math	persuading	childcare	photography
fixing	planning	cooking	plastering
inspecting	public speaking	driving a truck	playing an instrument
interpreting	researching	environmental tests	reading blueprints
keyboarding	selling	exterior painting	roofing
leading	sorting	farming	sewing
marketing	teaching	fitting eyeglasses	taking blood pressure
mediating	writing	helping patients	welding

FIGURE 15-2 Sample transferable and technical skills.

Corry applied for a position as a ticket agent for a major airline. He found the ad online and thought the job sounded like something he would enjoy. He submitted his application and was called to take a screening telephone interview. (The company had already determined that people who did well on the phone interview would be interviewed in person.) Corry was asked, "Do you meet the qualifications for this position?" He answered, "Yes, I guess so." He was asked if he was interested in the airline industry, to which he replied, "I certainly like to fly whenever I have the chance." Next question: "Tell me about your experience with computers." Corry: "My previous jobs have been in sales. Other than sales data entry, I haven't worked with computers much." Last question: "Can you lift 70 pounds?" Corry: "No, I hurt my leg playing rugby." The interviewer cut the conversation short at this point and said, "I don't think you have the qualifications we are seeking."

Was Corry prepared for this interview? Had he thought about his personal traits, interests, and skills?

INVENTORY YOUR EXPERIENCE AND QUALIFICATIONS

As you evaluate what you have to offer an employer, you may find it helpful to create a personal inventory worksheet detailing your experience, training, skills, interests, and personal traits and aptitudes that would make you a valuable employee. Create a table like the one shown in Figure 15-3 and write down your qualifications in these areas:

- Education and training (schools attended; dates; certificates, degrees, and honors)
- Work experience (full time and part time)
- Skills
- Interests
- Personal Traits

EXPERIENCE AND QUALIFICATIONS WORKSHEET

Education and Training	Work Experience	Skills	Interests	Personal Traits

FIGURE 15-3 Personal inventory worksheet.

Keep your personal inventory worksheet in a prominent place for easy reference. Having your experience and qualifications in worksheet form will be helpful as you complete job search documents such as a resume, cover letter, and an employment application form.

checkpoint

1. Why is a self-assessment a necessary part of finding a job?

_____

_____

_____

_____

_____

2. Why are you more likely to advance in a job that involves doing things in which you are interested?

_____

_____

_____

_____

_____

3. What is the difference between an aptitude and a skill? Give two related examples of each; for example, being "musical" and playing the saxophone.

_____

_____

_____

_____

_____

4. What are transferable skills? Why are employers interested in transferable skills?

_____

_____

_____

_____

5. What are technical skills? Why are employers interested in specific technical skills?

_____

_____

_____

_____

applications

1. Look at the personal traits listed in Figure 15-1 on page 373. Select the five traits that best describe you and that you think will help you achieve your goal of finding meaningful employment. Describe a situation in which you demonstrated each trait.

_____

_____

_____

_____

_____

_____

2. Your family and friends may know more about you than you think. Ask someone from each group what type of job or career they can picture you being happy in and to explain why. Did any of their responses surprise you?

_____

_____

_____

_____

_____

_____

3. Having assessed your interests and abilities, identify two jobs in which you would be most interested. What about these jobs would you find most enjoyable?

_____

_____

_____

_____

_____

4. It is easy to see why a person would enjoy doing things he or she has an aptitude for. Can you also understand why someone might not enjoy doing something he or she does well? Explain.

_____

_____

_____

_____

_____

Networking and Other Sources of Job Leads

The more resources you use for your job search, the more choices you will have and the more likely you are to find a suitable job. How can you learn about job openings? The Internet, your college career counseling center, and local newspapers are places to start. This section will discuss these, along with other options such as networking, employment agencies, career fairs, and volunteering. Determining where the jobs are takes imagination and initiative because many jobs are never advertised.

Jolene is very interested in getting a job in one of the hospitals or medical facilities in her community. She has the credentials and experience to work in respiratory therapy. She sees an ad on a local website describing positions at Bayside Hospital. The ad does not specifically mention openings for respiratory therapists, but Jolene calls the contact person listed in the ad and talks with him about her qualifications. Jolene explains that she is new in the community and that she has credentials and experience in respiratory therapy. She realizes that the web's ad does not mention openings for respiratory therapists and asks the contact if he anticipates any expansions or openings in this area. He tells her that Bayside is well staffed and suggests that she call the St. Thomas Medical Center, where he has heard from a friend that they are looking for respiratory therapists.

What job resources did Jolene use? What did she do well? Will you consider her technicque when you look for a job?

NETWORKING

About 65 percent of job-seekers report finding their jobs through networking. **Networking** is defined as developing contacts or exchanging information with others in an informal network to further one's career. It involves developing relationships with people who can assist with your job search and find job leads. It involves telling people you know that you are looking for a job and asking them to contact you if they hear of any openings.

Talk to your family, friends, former employers and coworkers, teachers, neighbors, members of professional organizations, and everyone else you can think of and tell them that you are looking for a job. The more people you talk to about your job search, the more leads and information you will discover. Encourage others to tell you about their job search experiences so you can learn from each other.

Susan got the bad news in February: the dentist she works for as a dental hygienist is retiring in April and moving to Arizona. She tells everyone she knows that she is looking for a new position, but it's a small community without many job openings. At Dr. Marple's retirement party, her friend and fellow hygienist Jean surprises everyone with the news that she and her husband have joined the Peace Corps. Jean introduces Susan to her employer, Dr. Beam, who invites Susan to stop by his office next week to talk about his unexpected opening for a dental hygienist.

Move out from your base of family and acquaintances by looking for ways to expand your networking opportunities. Check your library and local newspaper and websites for groups of job seekers to meet with to share ideas and leads. Do not be too proud to ask for help in getting a job. The old saying that "It's not what you know, but who you know," holds some truth. There is nothing wrong with having a friend or family member help in your search to get a job for which you are qualified. Since networking is the most productive source of job leads, focus your efforts on this approach.

During your job search, learn about career fields, specific employers, and specific jobs. This information can turn up job leads and help you stand out during interviews.

- **Career fields.** Follow industry trends. Learn about educational requirements, job descriptions, growth outlook, and salary ranges.
- **Specific employers.** Learn as much as possible about the companies where you hope to work: their products and services, markets and customers, divisions and locations, number of employees, predicted job openings, salary ranges, and benefit plans.
- **Specific jobs.** Get job descriptions, identify the required education and experience, and learn about working conditions, career paths, salary ranges, and benefit plans.

SOURCES OF JOB LEADS

Networking is powerful, but smart job seekers know they need to use as many ways as possible to locate job openings. This section covers other important sources of leads: local advertisements, college career centers, career websites, career fairs, state and private employment agencies, small businesses, and unpaid positions in organizations in your career field (through volunteer work, internships, and cooperative education).

"There is no such thing as a self-made man. You will reach your goals only with the help of others."

Local Advertisements

Advertisements in local newspapers, business journals, and websites are not only a source of job openings, but also show trends of the types of jobs openings that are most common in your area. The websites mentioned later in "Online Career Sites" also have information about jobs in different parts of the country. Follow the local business news carefully while you are searching for a job.

College Career Centers

Your school's career center is an excellent source of information and resources. You can learn about industries, companies, jobs, and local employers. At most centers, you can participate in mock job interviews with the staff and sign up for real interviews with companies that are recruiting for new employees.

Rita's first job on campus was at the career placement center. She could have worked at the bookstore, but she heard the center might be able to help her find an internship in accounting, her planned major. After observing how committed the center's staff was and seeing how many ways they helped students, Rita began to think that she wanted to spend her own career helping people whose lives are in transition. She used the center's resources to explore her new interest and changed her major to human resources.

Career Websites

"A job search that doesn't have a definite plan is likely to become a search with no job."

The number and variety of employment websites is immense, but there are three general categories: government-sponsored websites, for-profit websites, and career sites of professional organizations and industry trade groups.

Government-sponsored websites. Two examples are CareerOneStop and Career Voyages. CareerOneStop is maintained by the U.S. Department of Labor. It has career resources and tools for exploring careers and conducting job searches. The Resume Advice section, for example, has guidelines and tools for creating and improving resumes, plus samples and templates. The America's Service Locator section of CareerOneStop has state and federal information, such as information about federally funded training programs for laid-off workers, veterans, and older workers. Career Voyages, a collaboration between the U.S. Department of Labor and U.S. Department of Education, "is designed to provide information on in-demand occupations along with the skills and education needed to attain those jobs."[7]

The U.S. Bureau of Labor Statistics has excellent resources for job-seekers, including the *Occupational Outlook Handbook*, with detailed information about hundreds of jobs: "training and education needed, earnings, expected job prospects, what workers do on the job, [and] working conditions."[8] Many states also have websites with information useful to every job seeker, such as California's JobStar site.

For-profit websites. Two examples are QuintCareers.com (Quintessential Careers) and CareerBuilder.com. These comprehensive sites have lists of job openings and information about every topic imaginable related to careers and job searches. CollegeGrad.com is an excellent site for students and recent graduates. All of these sites are free to job-seekers, but free registration is required to use some of the resources and tools. Compare the services at several sites before you join one.

Career websites maintained by professional organizations and industry trade groups. For example, the American Art Therapy Association's website has an extensive career section. The Association for Information Technology Professionals (AITP) website provides an events calendar and chapter locations. It also provides AITP members with educational opportunities, forums, and resources for networking with experienced IT professionals and those new to the field.

It is easy to become overwhelmed by all the online job-search websites. Job-Hunt.org is a good site to visit early in your search. It offers job search advice and tips as well as an Online Job Search Guide.

Career Fairs

Career fairs (also called *job fairs* or *career expos*) are an efficient way to learn about many potential employers at the same time. You can gather company literature, talk to recruiters, check out companies in the same field, and network with other job seekers. Dress professionally and come prepared with business cards and copies of your resume. Read about the fair online before you attend so you can make the best use of your time.

Many educational institutions sponsor multiple job fairs throughout the year, with each geared to a specific discipline. The campus-sponsored job fair is ideal for most college students since it is convenient, and the employers have established a recruiting relationship with the school.

©Bob Daemmrich/Photo Edit

Career fairs are a way to investigate many potential employers and to network with other job seekers.

State Employment Agencies

Every state has a job service agency that helps people find employment. Your state agency will have many job listings in a wide variety of occupations, and the staff in these agencies know about the business, industry, and government jobs available in the state. You can visit the local branch of the agency or check it out online. In many states, you can submit your resume out online for private companies to review.

Employment services at state agencies include career counseling, career and personal assessments, help with resumes and interviewing skills, and job search workshops. Most sites have computers for job-seekers to use, and they may have access to online databases that are not available to the general public. State agencies do not charge for their services. The goal of these agencies is to make as many placements as possible to keep unemployment low and keep the state economy healthy. Use the free, and valuable, services in your state.

Private Employment Agencies

Private employment agencies can also be useful. If you contact a private agency, remember that the agency is in business to make a profit. When you complete their application form, you will be asked to sign a contract. *Read the contract before you sign it.* Ask what services the agency offers and what period of time the contract covers.

Many private agencies charge fees to employers to find competent, qualified workers, but some charge the applicant for this service. The fee may be an up-front dollar amount or a percentage of the wages you will earn in the job placement. Most private employment agencies will help prepare resumes and letters and give aptitude tests. These services and others may be included in the fee or may cost extra.

If you decide to use a private agency, make sure you understand who will pay the fee for a match between you and the employer. Verify what the procedure is if the job does not work out and you are dismissed for any reason during the first year of employment. Will the agency find you another position? Will there be an additional fee? Before you sign up with any private agency, check it out thoroughly. Call the Better Business Bureau and ask people who have used the agency if they were satisfied with the service provided.

Small Businesses

Small businesses employ more than 50 percent of the private workforce. Learn about them through the chamber of commerce, your college career center, and through newspapers and business journals (and their websites). The websites of trade associations are good places to learn about individual businesses in specific fields, such as solar energy companies or companies in the homeland security industry. Job-Hunt.com has an extensive list of these types of websites.

Volunteer Work, Internships, and Cooperative Education

Volunteer work is a great way to learn about a field of interest. Most opportunities are at nonprofit organizations that need help filling their goals and meeting deadlines. As a student, you may also qualify for supervised internships in workplaces. Some educational institutions have cooperative education programs, which place students in paying jobs in their fields while they are in school.

checkpoint

1. What percentage of jobs is found through networking?

_____

_____

_____

2. Identify and describe two government-sponsored websites for job seekers.

_____

_____

_____

_____

_____

_____

3. Why do states have agencies to help their citizens find jobs?

_____

_____

_____

_____

_____

_____

4. How do private employment agencies make money?

_____

_____

_____

_____

_____

_____

5. What are the advantages of researching your occupational field?

_____

_____

_____

_____

_____

applications

1. Are you currently working? If so, what sources did you use to get that job?

_____

_____

_____

_____

_____

2. Why do you think most people find jobs through networking?

_____

_____

_____

_____

_____

3. Describe a situation where you networked. What were the circumstances? What results did your networking bring?

_____

_____

_____

_____

_____

4. List 10 people you would feel comfortable talking with about your job search and qualifications. Explain how each person might be able to help your job search.

_____

_____

_____

_____

_____

5. Research upcoming career fairs in your area. Who runs these fairs? Which employers will attend? In what ways are the fairs different from each other?

_____

_____

_____

_____

_____

6. Visit your college career center. Look at the books, journals, and online resources at the center's library. List five resources that look helpful and describe how they may be useful in your job search.

_____

_____

_____

_____

_____

Job Search Documents

How does a prospective employer judge whether or not you possess the qualifications needed for a job? Since the employer probably does not know you personally, he or she can make an evaluation based on how well you sell yourself—how effectively you market your strengths. You can highlight your strengths by using a resume, cover letter or letter of application, and an employment application.

An important part of your job campaign is your resume. A **resume** is a concise, well-organized summary of your education, work experience, and other qualifications. You will also need to write a cover letter, or letter of application, to send with your resume. A **cover letter** is used to introduce you to a prospective employer and request an interview. Many companies request that you also complete an employment application. These documents are your first introduction to most prospective employers, and you will want to make a good first impression through attractive, readable documents that highlight your skills and experience. Your goal is to present yourself as the best person for the job and gain a job interview.

Maya and Serena are sorting through 55 cover letters and resumes. Who knew so many people wanted to be a store manager? "Here's another one with a photo enclosed," Maya says. "Do they really think good looks are a prerequisite for the job? And what about these one-size-fits-all cover letters? I think some of these people didn't even read the job description." "I can't get over the number of typos I've seen," Serena said. "Don't these people proofread their work? Take this cover letter, for example. It has a typo in the very first sentence! Or this resume where the word *experience* is misspelled. When I see errors like these, I immediately reject the application. If an applicant doesn't take care when preparing these documents, then he or she likely won't give attention to detail when on the job." In the end, Maya and Serena identified the six most qualified applicants that they wanted to call in for an interview.

Do you think it's likely that only six of the 55 applicants had the skills and qualification to do the job? What criticisms did Maya and Serena have about the resumes and cover letters?[9]

RESUME

Think of a resume as an advertisement for yourself. Its purpose is to "sell" you and your skills and gain an interview. It should be written to effectively set you apart from other applicants by focusing on your achievements.

You can leave your resume with prospective employers, attach it to an application, send it with a cover letter, and share it with people in your network. It is a wise practice to share your resume with everyone who is interested in helping you find a job. Also, expect to update your resume as you advance in your career. Your work experience, skills, and abilities change over time so you will want to keep your resume current.

There are many acceptable formats for resumes. Websites, libraries, bookstores, and textbooks have numerous resources that discuss the merits of various formats for different purposes in various stages of your career. The resume must always be keyed with care. Errors on a resume are totally unacceptable. Your resume should be well organized and without any marks or smudges. It should be a factual presentation of your education, experience, skills, and accomplishments. Because the first "reader" may be a scanning device or a software program, avoid fancy typefaces, italics, or underlining. Use space, boldface type, capitalization, or type size to separate or highlight information. The resume should be a brief, one-page document produced on high-quality paper.

A prospective employer may require you to submit an **electronic resume**. An electronic resume, also called a *scannable resume*, is a plain text (ASCII) or HTML document often submitted online with an employment application. If so, information about the requirements for submitting your resume online can usually be found on the employer's website.

A common approach to organizing a resume is to use headings to separate the text into important sections that are easy to scan. Your resume should include sections that are most appropriate for your experience and be in the order that best highlights your qualifications. The following sections are typically included in a resume.

Contact Information

At the top of the resume, list your name, mailing address, telephone number(s), e-mail address, and website address (if appropriate). Omit the title *Resume* and the words *Contact Information*. Use a professional-sounding e-mail address that includes your name, such as Miriam.Frankel@email.com. Some employers are turned off by an applicant who uses an unprofessional e-mail address.

Objective

The next section of a resume is usually a concise job objective. Briefly state your employment goal or the type of position you are applying for. The employer will use this section to match your interests with the company's needs. Your objective may be general or specific. For example, a general objective might state: "Full-time position as an executive assistant." A more specific objective might say: "Full-time position as a legal secretary in a multinational law firm."

The objective is optional. Omit it if you are unsure what the employer is seeking or if you want to use the same resume for several positions. However, using the same resume for several positions may be a disadvantage. It is better to customize your resume to fit each job opening to give yourself the best chance for an interview.

Qualifications

This optional section is a bulleted list of your key strengths that show an employer that you can do the job. Figure 15-4 shows a resume for a person applying for the position of office manager in a travel agency. Kimberly has not worked in a travel agency, but she lists her qualifications in a section called "Skills and Capabilities" immediately below the Objective. She hopes that after skimming this section, the reader will be receptive to her work experience even though it is not in the travel field.

Education

An employer will look for schooling or training that is essential for doing a job. List the highest level of education you have successfully completed. List the school, the address, the dates you attended, and your area(s) of study. If you graduated and earned a diploma or certificate, include these accomplishments. If you excelled academically, list any scholarships, awards, and honors (or put these in a separate section if they are especially strong).

Any special courses, on-the-job training, or military service should be listed in this section. (You can also describe your military service in a separate section.)

As you begin your career, your education is probably your strongest asset, and that is why it appears below the objective. As you progress in your career, your work experience will become more important and relevant, and the Education section will follow the Experience section. The general exception would be if you were changing careers and have taken special courses related to your new objectives. The key is to put the qualifications most likely to "sell" you closest to the top of the resume.

Work Experience

Prospective employers want to see your work experience. List your previous jobs in reverse chronological order; that is, list your current or most recent job first, then the next most recent, and so on. Include the name of your employer, location, employment dates, job title, duties, and accomplishments or specific skills used. Be truthful about all aspects of your work experience. And yes, you should list jobs from which you have been fired. There is no need to indicate you were dismissed, but be prepared to explain the circumstances in the interview. It is not uncommon to have a less-than-perfect work history.

Kimberly Corcoran

828 Edgewood Drive ● Flint, MI 46507 ● 810-555-8515 ● kimcork@provider.net

OBJECTIVE	Office manager for a travel agency
SKILLS AND CAPABILITIES	**Management and Supervisory** • Manage the Rental Property Group. Supervise two clerical staff. • Oversee and coordinate advertising, insurance, leases, contracts, estimates, and maintenance. • Maintain financial records of rental transactions and operating expenses. • Extensive contact with public, vendors, and real estate agents. **Computers and Training** • Virtual Travel Master: Deliver Travel Services on the Internet, distance learning, Certificate of Achievement. • Evaluated rental property software management system; selected and implemented Quicken Rental Property Manager 2009. • Trained agents and office staff on GoldMine Mobile Edition; developed customized PowerPoint presentation. • Microsoft Office 2007 and Adobe Acrobat.
EXPERIENCE	**Office Manager; September 2009–Present** Everest Real Estate Services; Flint, MI. Maintain agency website. Prepare online sales and rental listings. Maintain sales and commissions log. Maintain and balance bank accounts for sales transactions and operating expenses. Compile prospect lists. **Administrative Assistant; July 2007–August 2009** Everest Real Estate Services, Flint, MI. Part-time during college (20 hours a week). First person to hold this position. Expanded and maintained agency website. Trained agents and office staff on GoldMine Mobile Edition. **Sales Associate; May 2005–August 2007** The Office Factory; Flint, MI. Part-time in school year; full-time summers. Sold office furniture and accessories. Duties included sales, recordkeeping, stocking, and inventory.
EDUCATION	**Associate Degree in Applied Business Technology, August 2009** Linden Valley Community College, Springdale, MI. GPA in major: 3.8. **Virtual Travel Master Certificate of Achievement, December 2008.** All Aboard Travel Agency Training, Inc. *Deliver Travel Services on the Internet*, distance-learning course, 12 modules.
ACTIVITIES AND ACHIEVEMENTS	Completed 5 marathons on 3 continents; on track to complete marathons on all 7 continents by 2014. Founded the Girls Can Run club at Elms Montessori.

FIGURE 15-4 Sample resume.

Use precise action verbs to describe your skills and achievements. For example, *collaborated* is a good word to use to emphasize your skills as a team player. Other descriptive verbs are:

- administered
- acquired
- approved
- assisted
- conducted
- designed
- developed
- evaluated
- forecasted
- illustrated
- installed
- introduced
- led
- maintained
- monitored
- negotiated
- organized
- planned
- prepared
- recorded
- scheduled

Certifications or Special Licenses

In this section, list any special certifications or licenses you have obtained that are relevant to the position for which you are applying. For example, a person applying to work in a daycare center would list the date he or she received his or her First Aid and CPR Certification.

Related Experience

Use this section to demonstrate how well-rounded you are. Be sure to highlight other experiences related to your job objective, such as school, social, and service organizations. Use a heading that is the most appropriate for your achievements and experiences, such as Awards and Honors, Volunteer Work, Community Service, or Activities and Achievements.

Organizing Your Resume

Refer again to Figure 15-4, which shows Kimberly Corcoran's resume to apply for the position of office manager. Because Kimberly has an impressive work history for a recent college graduate, she places her work experience before her education. She also includes the "Skills and Capabilities" section immediately under her job objective. Note that Kimberly lists her online training in the use of the Internet to deliver travel services in two sections of her resume—Skills and Capabilities, where she simply lists it, and Education, where she gives more information about the course. If she uses the same resume with a different career objective, she would remove the online course from the Skills and Capabilities list. There is no one-size-fits-all resume formula. You should tailor your resumes to specific job titles, job advertisements, and employers by using terminology that addresses their employment needs.

There are three main organizational patterns for resumes. Kimberley's resume is organized chronologically. The **chronological resume** lists employment and education information by date, starting with the most recent (reverse chronological order). Kimberly uses the chronological pattern to emphasize her steady work experience that is related to the position she is applying for. This structure is also well-suited to students and entry-level workers who do not have highly specialized skills.

The **functional resume** focuses on personal characteristics, skills and abilities, and work experiences. The functional format is useful for applicants who lack work experience directly related to the position, who have changed jobs frequently, or who have gaps in employment. It is also recommended for job seekers who are changing careers or returning to work after a long absence.[10] These patterns can be combined, as Kimberly does when she includes the "Skills and Capabilities" section in what is otherwise a chronological resume. This combined pattern is called a **combination resume**.

Your goal is to craft the best resume that you can. It will take more than one try to get the resume that works best for you. The companion website for this textbook has sample resumes. Also, look at the samples and templates on the many online career sites.

References

References are those people who know your academic ability and/or work habits and are willing to recommend you to a prospective employer. List your references on a separate page, not on the resume. Include the name and title, address, phone number, and e-mail address of three or four people who can attest to your skills and personal qualities. Your references might include an employer or coworker, an instructor, or possibly a career counselor. Do not use relatives or personal friends as references.

You must get permission from your references before you use their names. Figure 15-5 shows references for the resume in Figure 15-4. While employers expect applicants to have references, they differ in their preferences about when and how they want to see a list of references. Take the list with you to the interview and be ready to provide it if asked.

tacojim/iStockphoto.com

Check your resume very carefully to be sure it is error free.

REFERENCES FOR KIMBERLY L. CORCORAN

Oliver Upton (Accounting Instructor)
Linden Valley Community College Springdale,
MI 49771
231-555-8970
upton.oliver@lvcc.org

Rinji Mori (Vice President)
Everest Real Estate Services
Flint, MI 48519
810-555-6060
rmori@everestrealestateservices.com

Martha Overton (Real Estate Agent)
Everest Real Estate Services
Flint, MI 48519
810-555-6060
moverton@everestrealestateservices.com

FIGURE 15-5 Sample list of references.

COVER LETTER

A cover letter is a letter of inquiry or application that you submit with an application and/or resume. Its primary purpose is to present a target message that will help you get an interview. It should be assumed that there will be many applicants for a position and that few will be interviewed.

If you really want the position, invest the time to create a brief, but strong, message. The letter must be keyed and formatted so that it is easy to read. It must be organized logically, be clean and neat, and be concise. If you are mailing your resume and cover letter, the cover letter and resume should be on good quality, matching paper. Some experts recommend sending your resume and cover letter in a large envelope so that they will lie flat on the reader's desk.

Keep your cover letter short (typically one page). If the letter is longer than one page, you may be trying to include too much information. Do not repeat everything that is in the resume. Employers are busy, and they are looking for a brief introduction to each job applicant. Figure 15-6 describes the seven parts of a successful cover letter. Figure 15-7 shows a sample cover letter.

Errors of any kind in the cover letter are totally unacceptable. Proofread your letter several times, and ask someone else to look over it too. Notice as you proofread and edit your letter how many sentences begin with "I." Rewrite most of them to make the activities the subject of the sentence. Use action words such as *administer, supervise, develop, coordinate,* and *train.*

As the human resources manager, Amy gets hundreds of job applications a month. She has to read through them quickly. Sometimes she finds a resume and cover letter that are impressive and well done but not right for the current position. She keeps them on file for future reference. Applications that are messy, unclear, poorly written, or that have typographical errors go right into the shredder.

ELEMENTS OF A GOOD COVER LETTER

Include these seven elements in your cover letter:

1. **Your address.** Include your street address, city, state, and ZIP code.
2. **Date.** The month, day, and year of the letter.
3. **Letter address and salutation.** Key where the letter is going to and to whom. A greeting to the person receiving the letter is called the salutation. If you know the person's name, use it. If you do not know who will receive the letter, use a general salutation such as *Dear Human Resources Manager.*
4. **First paragraph of the letter.** Explain why you are writing the letter. Keep your statement simple. You are writing a letter to apply for a job. Tell the reader where you learned about the job opening.
5. **Second paragraph of the letter.** This important paragraph explains why you are the ideal candidate for the position. Write two to three good sentences that focus on what you think will be important to the employer. The job listing should give you a good idea of what information to include and which skills or aptitudes to highlight. Refer the reader to your enclosed resume.
6. **Final paragraph of the letter.** Ask for an interview. Tell the reader where, when, and how to reach you. Invite the reader to contact you. It is also acceptable to say, "I'll contact you in a few days [or by the end of the week]." If you say you are going to contact the person, be sure to do so.
7. **Closing.** Use a business closing to the letter. A good closing is "Sincerely." Sign the letter. Key the word "Enclosure" below your keyed name to call attention to your enclosed resume.

FIGURE 15-6 The elements of a good cover letter.

Kimberly Corcoran

828 Edgewood Drive ● Flint, MI 46507 ● 810-555-8515 ● kimcorc@provider.net

September 21, 20--

Ms. Marilyn Mendelssohn, Owner
Near 'N Far Travel
2277 Colorado Blvd.
Denver, CO 80123

Dear Ms. Mendelssohn

This letter is in response to your advertisement for an office manager at Near 'N Far Travel. My family and I are in the process of moving to Denver, and I am very much interested in the travel business. I recently completed the Virtual Travel Master online training course. My instructor, Maria Sanchez, of All Aboard Travel Agency Training, Inc., suggested I contact you because of your desire to expand your agency's Internet profile and online services.

In my current job as manager of a real estate agency, I have a good deal of experience interacting with the public and handling unique situations that can change quickly. My associate's degree in Applied Business Technology has given me a strong foundation in customer service, marketing, and office technology. I hope you agree that my enclosed resume shows that my work experience and travel interest would make me an asset to your agency.

I will be in Denver October 5-8 to run in the Denver Marathon. I will call you next week to determine your interest in meeting with me at that time.

Thank you for your consideration.

Sincerely

Kimberly Corcoran

Enclosure

FIGURE 15-7 **Sample cover letter.**

EMPLOYMENT APPLICATIONS

Most employers will require you to complete an **employment application** or *job application*. A completed application form provides information that the company needs in a format that is easy for them to process. The form is used by employers to gather basic information from everyone who applies for positions. In today's job environment, you might find yourself filling in a printed form, completing an application on the employer's website, or filling in an application at a kiosk in a mall or store.

Printed Applications

When you decide to apply for a position or visit the employment office of the business, go to the human resources office. Go alone. Do not take a friend or relative. The employer is interested only in you. Have your social security number, a black pen and pencil, your resume, and information you have put together about former jobs, your education, your references, and your military service (if any).

A sample printed application form can be found on the companion website for this textbook. You may want to print this form and complete it at home for practice and take it with you as a guide in completing the employer's application form. However, each company has its own application form, and each form is a little different. Follow the instructions on the application form you are given.

Take the completion of the form seriously. The form shows the potential employer basic information about you, including how well you follow directions and how neat you are. If you did not understand a question on the form, ask the person who gave you the form for assistance. See the feature "Tips for Completing a Job Application."

Figure 12-3 in Chapter 12 describes the U.S. laws against employment discrimination. A job application form can only ask job-related questions. The employer cannot legally ask if you are married, divorced, or single, because marital status does not affect your ability to do a job. The only question that may be asked legally about your age is whether you are 18 or older.

If the application asks for a desired salary and you have little or no experience, write *starting wage*. If you are experienced and have extensive education, write *negotiable* to indicate that you want to discuss the salary. Carefully read the questions and your responses one last time before signing your name.

APPLYING ONLINE

If you find a job opening on a website, you will probably apply online. To be allowed to apply, you will need to register at the site by supplying your e-mail address and selecting a user name and password. Choose a professional-sounding e-mail address.

At some sites, you will need to complete an online application form. Online application forms are typically a mix of blank fields (in which you will enter text) and pull-down menus (from which you will select a response). Be sure to follow all instructions carefully. The form may have fields for entering contact

IMPORTANT: Read through the entire application before you start writing anything!

- **Follow the directions.** Read each question carefully and enter only the information that is requested. If the form says please print, then print. If the form says to circle your answer, circle it.

- **Be specific.** If the form has a space to write the position you desire, enter the position(s) you are interested in. Never write *anything* or *anything available*. Be as specific as you can about the job you want to apply for.

- **Be neat.** Print or write clearly so that your answers can be read easily. Use a black pen unless instructed otherwise. (Black ink photocopies best.) Avoid crossing out answers, writing too large or too small, or making smudges on the paper.

- **Plan ahead.** Skim through the application to see if the answers are written above or below the questions. Think about each answer and gauge the space for it before you start writing.

- **Give honest answers.** Your signature on the form means that you answered every question truthfully and to the best of your ability. A signed application is a legal document, and being untruthful is considered grounds for refusing employment. If you are hired, you can be dismissed for having been untruthful on the application.

- **Fill in the application completely.** Write NA (not applicable) if a question does not apply to you. If you leave the space blank, the employer may think you skipped the question accidentally.

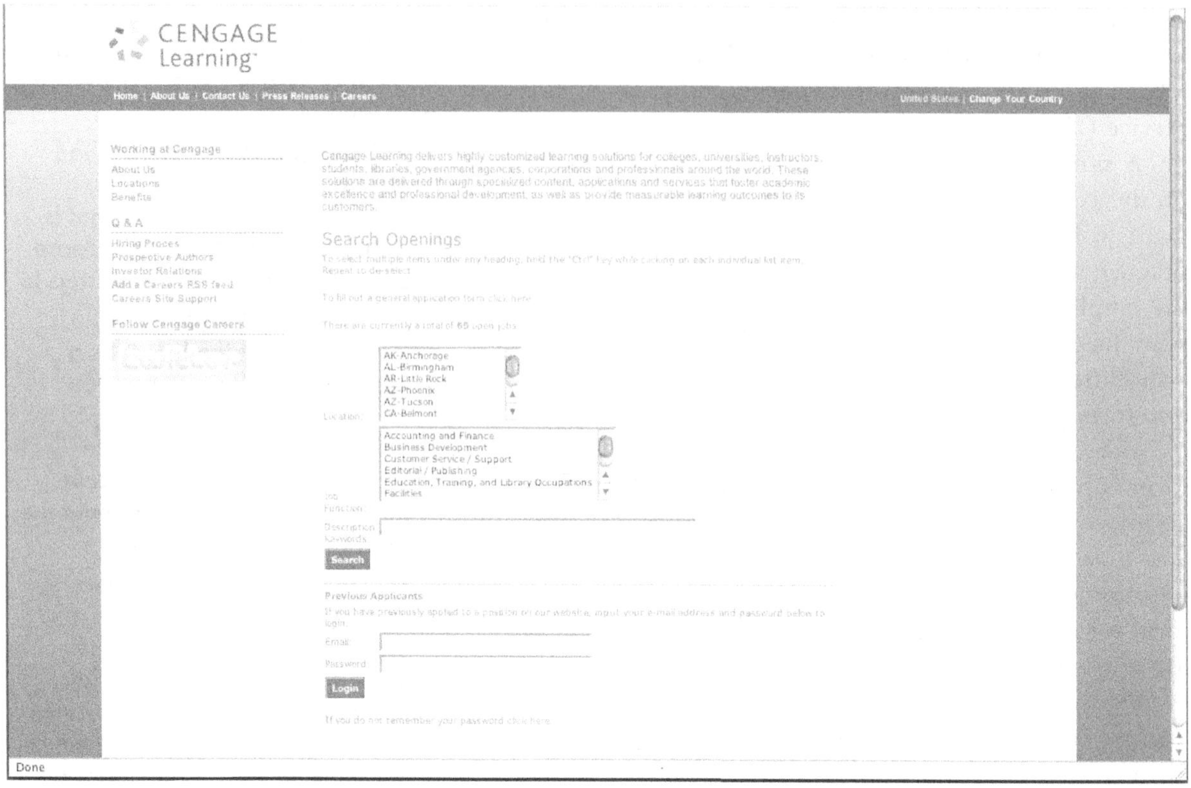

FIGURE 15-8 Partial online employment application.

information, degrees earned, training certifications, and job history. At some sites, you will enter your contact information and then be able to attach your resume and/or cover letter. Other sites may have a field for pasting portions of your cover letter into fields in the application. Figure 15-8 shows a portion of an online application form.

Keep in mind that online applications are scanned by computer programs that search for certain minimal qualifications. The computer may weed you out if you do not have those terms in your application or resume. The job description is a good place to find these key terms. Try to "echo" the terms used there—provided, of course, that they match your background and experience.

checkpoint

1. When would you omit the Objective section of a resume?

_____

_____

_____

_____

2. Why is it important that your resume and cover letter be free of errors of any kind?

_____

_____

_____

_____

3. When would you list your work experience before your education in your resume?

_____

_____

_____

_____

_____

4. Why should you write a short cover letter?

_____

_____

_____

_____

5. Which resume format is recommended for job-seekers who do not have highly specialized skills?

_____

_____

_____

_____

applications

1. Action verbs are power words that stand out in a resume. Write an "action statement" that describes an accomplishment of yours. For example, "Selected and organized files to be scanned and archived." Use the words below or substitute other action verbs.

a. Developed _____

_____

b. Maintained _____

_____

c. Coordinated _____

_____

d. Supervised _____

_____

e. Tested _____

_____

f. Analyzed _____

_____

g. Operated _____

_____

h. Installed _____

_____

i. Communicated _____

_____

2. Write a job objective for a resume to be submitted for each of job opening:

a. Imported car dealer. Sales representatives needed. Will train.

_____

_____

b. Seattle Airlines has full-time position available for a customer service agent. Good communications skills required.

_____

_____

3. List five people who can act as references for you. List how you know each person.

a. _____

b. _____

c. _____

d. _____

e. _____

4. Write a script that you can use to ask people be a reference for you.

_____

_____

5. Why would you want to customize your resume for different job openings? What things might you change in different versions?

_____

_____

The Job Interview

This is your big chance. You have filled out the job application and submitted your resume along with a cover letter. Being granted an interview tells you that the person doing the hiring considers you among the strongest applicants. You are being seriously considered for the job! Although you may feel some anxiety about the interview process, be proud that you were among the few who were chosen for an interview. Most of your competitors did not make it this far. Most employers have time to interview only four to six applicants, even though hundreds may have applied.

It is natural to feel pressure as your interview date approaches. However, you should adopt the attitude that whether you are hired or not, you will learn something from the interview process. As you become more experienced at being interviewed, you will become more relaxed, confident, and effective.

This section has advice about preparing for interviews, making the best case for yourself during an interview, and following up after an interview.

PREPARING FOR THE INTERVIEW

A successful interview starts long before the actual meeting. You need to learn as much as you can about the organization, organize the material you are taking with you, and give attention to your personal appearance.

Do Your Homework

The more you know about the company or organization, the better. You should be aware of whether the company is privately or publicly owned, for profit or not-for-profit. Search for recent articles about the organization. Read the version of the company's mission statement posted online so that you understand what matters to its leaders. Learn the names of the CEO and other top management. If the company makes products, be sure to know what they are and, if possible, what competing products are on the market. If the company provides a service, make sure you understand the service and its role in the community and/or the economy. If it is a charitable or arts organization, learn how it serves the community and what its challenges are.

Search the name of your interviewer to learn about him or her. If you are being interviewed by more than one person, such as a search committee, ask ahead of time for the names and titles of the people you will be meeting. Think about topics for discussion, such as a company product you have used, an advertisement you have seen, or an issue related to the company's industry.

Get Organized

The night before the interview, go through the documents you will be taking along to make sure you have everything in order. These may include a copy of your social security card, copies of your resume and reference list, copies of awards and certifications, and, possibly, samples of your work. For some positions, such as a draftsperson, photographer, or computer designer, it is easy to think of samples that you would want to show. For other positions, or if you do not have experience in the position you are interviewing for, consider bringing samples of your school work, such as a spreadsheet or newsletter article. If you have a busines card, bring several to hand out. Put the papers in a portfolio or file folder to keep them neat.

A day or two before the interview, go to the location so that you will know exactly where it is and be aware of any challenges, such as distant parking, which might add to the time it takes to get to the office. Make sure that you consider rush-hour traffic and possible traffic jams, leaving plenty of room for unexpected delays. Allow time to arrive at least a few minutes before the scheduled interview but not so early that you might inconvenience the interviewer, who no doubt has others things to attend to. Be sure to take some black pens and pencils along so that you do not have to borrow something with which to write. Taking along a notebook is fine, but ask permission to take notes before you begin writing.

Make a Good First Impression

Pay careful attention to your appearance for the interview. The clothes you choose should be determined by the kind of job for which you are applying. If you are applying for an office or sales job, wear business attire. Usually a dress shirt, tie, and slacks are appropriate for men, and in some workplaces, a suit or jacket with slacks is the norm. Women should wear a business-like dress, suit, pantsuit, or skirt and blouse. Dress codes in many offices have relaxed in recent decades, making "business casual" the norm. If you are applying for a construction or factory job, you may want to wear neat and clean work clothes.

If you are in doubt about how employees are expected to dress, go to the company ahead of time and observe what employees are wearing as they enter or leave the workplace. This will give you an idea of the company's dress code. It is a good idea to dress a little better than the typical employee if attire is casual. It is not necessary to buy new clothes for the interview, but what you wear should be immaculate and in perfect repair. You want the interviewer to remember you, not your clothes, so stay away from bright, flashy, or unusual outfits. Make sure you and your clothes look neat and clean—well-groomed hair, shined shoes, pressed clothes. You want to make a good first impression.

Keep jewelry and other accessories such as scarves to a minimum. Too many accessories can make you look cluttered. If you have tattoos or facial jewelry, cover them or take them out for the interview. Your hands should be clean and neatly manicured. Avoid overly ornate manicures which could give the impression that your nails will get in the way of keyboarding or other work activities. If you wear makeup, don't overdo it, and check just before the interview to be sure it is not smeared or smudged.

"Never wear a backward baseball cap to an interview unless applying for the job of umpire."

Of course, good personal hygiene is essential. Shower or bathe, brush your teeth, and be sure to use deodorant. Avoid strong perfumes, colognes, and aftershave scents. You may love the fragrance, but it is best not to assume that your interviewer will agree. In any case, you want the interviewer to remember you, your qualifications, and your answers to questions—not your scent.

on the job

Christina applied for a position as a print services coordinator in an advertising firm. She read their ad in a local jobs website and was confident that she met the qualifications. She applied and was invited to come in for an interview. She arrived wearing a tailored pantsuit and carrying an attractive leather portfolio. She was a few minutes early and spent the time quietly looking through the material in her portfolio. When Mr. Henderson arrived to interview her, she gave a firm handshake and repeated his name as she greeted him. Inside his office, she set her portfolio on her lap and asked permission to take notes during the meeting. When Mr. Henderson agreed, she took out a notepad opened to a page with some questions she wanted to ask. She smiled at Mr. Henderson and waited for his first question.

What steps did Christina take to create a good first impression? What are some of the questions that might have been written on Christina's notepad?

INTERVIEW QUESTIONS

You want to be as prepared as possible for questions the interviewer may ask. Rehearsing typical questions and your responses with a friend or family member can help you prepare simple, clear, and effective replies. Your school may provide an opportunity for you to be videotaped before you take a job interview. Think about how your education and experience will help you in this job, and be prepared to give specific examples when they will reinforce your point. For some questions, there is no "right" answer. Be honest, sincere, positive, and upbeat. You can find many resources on the Internet to help you rehearse. You will find some common questions in Figure 15-9.

STANDARD INTERVIEW QUESTIONS

Tell me about yourself.
Tell me what you know about this company.
Why do you want to work for this company?
Why does this job opening interest you?
How did you become interested in this company?
What jobs have you held?
Why did you leave those jobs?
Do you prefer working alone or with others?
What are your strengths? What are your weaknesses?
How well do you work under pressure?
What do you want to be doing in five years?
What do you like to do in your spare time?
What makes you think you can do this job?
Why should I hire you?

FIGURE 15-9 Sample interview questions.

Be prepared for open-ended questions, and make sure you provide real information that will help the interviewer evaluate you. For example, if you are asked to describe a time when you had to handle an unreasonable customer, choose an example with a positive outcome that reflects your interpersonal skills.

Make sure you have prepared a clear, concise summary in answer to the common question, "Tell me about yourself." You should carefully prepare a short statement that summarizes your education, experience, and skills that apply to this position. When you are thinking about and refining this summary of your qualifications, it may help you to write it out, or to make a bulleted list of points you want to make. However, do not read it to the interviewer. Your statement should not sound like a memorized recital. It should sound like a simple story you are telling to describe how your background fits the job.

If the interviewer's questions fail to uncover everything you'd like the interviewer to know about you, volunteer the information. Look for opportunities to make job-benefit statements. A **job-benefit statement** is a brief explanation of how an individual's skills can benefit the company.

Lauren was interviewing for the newly created position of marketing coordinator at a small electronics firm. She explained briefly how she would apply her skill with various software packages to support marketing initiatives.

Often, an interviewer gives you this opportunity toward the end of the session, but be prepared to take the initiative.

THE INTERVIEW PROCESS

Arrive for your interview a little early. You are neatly dressed and well-groomed. A calm, composed job applicant will make a better impression than a rushed, frantic one. If someone gives you a ride, ask the driver to wait nearby until your interview is over. Have your documents, pens and pencils easily accessible. You do not want to fumble for things when you need them. Before the interview starts, turn off your cell phone. You do not want a ringing phone to interrupt the interview and annoy the interviewer.

Introducing Yourself

Introduce yourself to the person at the reception desk. Give your name and the name of the person you are scheduled to meet, making certain to pronounce the interviewer's name and title

Make sure the interviewer's first impression of you is a good one.

©iofoto, 2009/Used under license from Shutterstock.com

correctly. It is important to greet this person with a friendly smile and a confident voice. Be courteous and professional to everyone you meet. Remembering and using the names of people you meet can help them to remember you. If the person at the desk is not too busy, it is alright to engage in some small talk about the weather, or how long the person has worked for the company. You will no doubt be asked to take a seat and wait until the interviewer is ready for you.

Body Language and First Impressions

Your **body language** is the nonverbal signals you send, including your posture, bearing, stride, handshake, eye contact, gestures, and facial expressions. Whether you introduce yourself to the interviewer or the receptionist introduces you, smile, make eye contact, and shake the person's hand firmly if a hand is offered. You do not want your handshake to be limp, nor do you want it to be crushing. Use the interviewer's name, making sure you have the pronunciation right. For example, you might say, "Good morning Ms. Schmidt. I'm Peter Wayne. Thank you for taking the time to meet with me this morning."

As you enter the interview room or office, remain standing until you are invited to sit down. Your sitting posture should be straight but not rigid. Focus on looking relaxed and confident. Do not slouch or fidget. Do not put your bag, briefcase, or papers on the interviewer's desk. Place them in your lap, at your side, or on the floor until you need them. Figure 15-10 has some tips about effective body language.

Responding to Questions

As the interviewer begins asking questions, answer each question honestly and specifically. It is likely that you will be asked open-ended questions that will give you an opportunity to describe your skills and accomplishments.

When you prepared for the interview, you wrote a clear, concise summary in answer to the common question, "Tell me about yourself." When you answer this question, look the other person in the eye and *tell* about your-

WHAT IS SAID WITHOUT WORDS

- An upright, confident posture reflects your sense of self-worth.
- Eye contact shows you are listening and are interested in what the interviewer has to say.
- A smile shows that are you relaxed and confident. Keep your facial expressions friendly, calm, relaxed, and positive.
- A firm handshake conveys that you are professional and enthusiastic. Avoid a weak or overly aggressive handshake.
- Leaning slightly forward toward the interviewer conveys that you are interested. Leaning back can give the opposite impression.
- Be aware of the interviewer's body language to help you sense when you are losing the person's attention or when you are going into too much detail.

FIGURE 15-10 Body language in an interview.

self in a smooth and conversational tone. Your statement should not sound like a memorized recital. It should sound like a simple story you are telling to describe how your background fits the job.

Another common question may be, "Tell me what you know about our company." This is where your homework will pay off. Show that you are familiar with the overall structure of the company, its products or services, and its leaders. If the company has been in the news lately in a positive context, you should mention that you read about it. If there has been a recent development or trend in the field, or a new product introduced, you can show that you are well informed about the matter.

> *The interview was almost over when the interviewer leaned forward and smiled sweetly and asked Jenny the question everyone told her to expect: "What is your greatest weakness?" Jenny had prepared an answer that presented one of her strengths as a weakness. She replied, "It's important to me to do what I say. I can get impatient when something isn't completed on time."*

Listening

Because the interview is a two-way communication process, listening is an essential skill in a job interview. Before answering any question, be sure that you have really listened and understood it. If you are not quite clear about what the interviewer is asking, restate the question in your own words

APPLY IT!

Are you ready for the job search? Use this checklist to prepare. Place a check beside each item as you complete it.

I have:

1. _____ Determined my qualifications and interests.
2. _____ Discussed my aptitudes with others.
3. _____ Networked with friends and people who may be able to help me find a job.
4. _____ Checked other sources of job leads.
5. _____ Prepared my resume.
6. _____ Practiced interviewing.
7. _____ Prepared my list of references.
8. _____ Prepared a job application letter.
9. _____ Proofread my application documents.
10. _____ Reviewed the job application and filled it in carefully.
11. _____ Planned what to wear and what to take to the interview.
12. _____ Studied the prospective employer (products and/or services, etc.).
13. _____ Prepared questions to ask the interviewer.
14. _____ Sent a thank-you follow-up note or letter.

and ask, "Did I understand that correctly?" Many interviewers like to ask questions such as "Tell me about a time when you had to complete a task or project that you disliked, and how you managed to complete it," or "Tell me about a time when you had to resolve a conflict between your personal life and your job." It is alright to pause for a moment to think about your answers, saying, "Let me give that some thought."

Do not interrupt the interviewer by jumping in too quickly with your answer. Pause to make sure the interviewer has finished asking the question before you start to reply. You want to answer the interviewer's questions thoughtfully and thoroughly without burying the points you want to make under too much detail. If you see the interviewer's eyes and attention drifting, wrap up your answer so that you don't lose your audience.

If you do not know the answer to a question, tell the interviewer honestly that you do not know. You can easily get yourself in difficulty if you try to fake knowledge or skills that you really have not mastered. You might add, however, that you are a quick learner and are confident that you could get quickly up to speed in this area of the job. You might want to mention something similar that you have recently mastered on your own to show that you have the ambition and aptitude to learn. Eagerness to learn and grow is a quality highly valued in the job market.

> *Dubois Publishing, the company where Samantha wanted to work, used Microsoft Access software for its database. Samantha had never used the program, although she was very familiar with other Office products. In the interview she was asked about her experience with Access. "I have worked with three other database software packages, but I haven't used Access yet," Samantha told the interviewer. "However, I'm confident that I can learn it quickly. It's installed on my computer, and I started taking the online tutorial a couple of days ago. I see lots of similarities with the database programs I've used. I also bookmarked several free tutorials for learning Access."*

Asking Questions

At some point in the interview, usually near the end, the interviewer will likely ask you if you have any questions about the job or the company. The interviewer may already have told you about what the job pays and what the benefits the company provides. But if not, now is *not* a good time to ask how much the job pays, what the fringe benefits are, and how much vacation time you will get. Questions regarding these matters may lead the interviewer to conclude that you are interested only in what the company can do for you rather than what you can do for the company. Save those questions to ask when and if you are offered the job.

Your impression will be more positive if you ask questions that show you are really thinking about how you will fit into the company and where this job might lead. You could ask what qualities and skills the interviewer thinks most important to success in the position, and then take the opportunity to

How would you describe the responsibilities of the position?
How would you describe a typical week/day in this position?
Is this a new position? If not, what did the previous employee go on to do?
Whom does this position report to? If I am offered the position, can I meet him/her?
How many people work in this office/department?
What is the typical work week? Is overtime expected?
What are the prospects for growth and advancement?
Would you like a list of references?
If I am extended a job offer, how soon would you like me to start?

FIGURE 15-11 Sample interview questions to ask.

point out examples in your background of those qualities and skills. Or you might ask about the working relationships within the department in which you will work.

Before the interview, prepare a list of questions you might ask. Place the list in a folder where you can easily refer to it. Figure 15-11 lists some questions to ask if the interviewer does not provide the information.

Do not ask questions that make you look uninformed (What does the company do?) or interested in the wrong things about the position (How long is the lunch break? How long would I have to work until I'm eligible for a raise?).

Closing the Interview

The interviewer will decide when to end the meeting. He or she will signal to you that it is time to go by thanking you for your time, standing up, and perhaps escorting you to the door. Thank the interviewer for giving you this opportunity to interview. Express your enthusiasm for the job, and briefly summarize how well your background fits the company's needs. Do not expect a job offer during the interview.

This is a good time to ask the interviewer when a hiring decision is expected, and whether it would be appropriate for you to check with the office in a few days or a week to find out if the job has been filled. If the interviewer tells you to wait until the company contacts you, be sure to wait. You want to appear eager, but you do not want to pester them before they have completed all the interviews and made a decision.

While the interview is fresh in your mind, jot down notes to help with future interviews. Reflect on the interview and what you learned from it. What better answers could you have given? When similar questions come up in another interview, you want your responses to be more polished. Think about points you made that seemed effective and points that would have been better left out. Discuss the interview with a friend or relative. Ask their opinion of how you could have responded better to difficult questions.

Immediately after the interview, send the interviewer a thank-you note or letter. Thank her or him for the time spent interviewing you and telling you about the position. Make it clear where you can be reached when a decision is made. This is an opportunity to mention any brief point that you may not have covered in the interview. It would also be alright to enclose a sample of a particular kind of work discussed in the interview, such as a sample spreadsheet you have created. Mail the thank-you note or letter right away so that it arrives promptly. There is no harm in also thanking the interviewer via e-mail. Figure 15-12 is a sample thank-you note. Sample thank-you letters are available on the website for this textbook.

"If opportunity doesn't knock—build a door."

Dear Mr. Hamish

Thank you for meeting with me this morning to discuss the opening you have for a records processor. I enjoyed meeting you and learning more about Hamish Enterprises and hope you agree that my qualifications and your needs are a good match.

If there is any further information you need to help you make your decision, please call me at 513-555-4449 or email me at beverly.smith@gnet.com. I look forward to hearing from you soon.

Sincerely

Beverly Smith

FIGURE 15-12 Sample thank-you note.

If the interviewer has encouraged you to check back with the company, make sure you do so within the requested timeframe. Ask to speak directly with the interviewer, if available. If not, leave a simple message that you are checking in with the company about the opening and express your continued interest in the position. Leave your name and phone number for a return call.

AFTER LEARNING THE EMPLOYER'S DECISION

If you are offered the job and have accepted it, your career is on its path. If you interviewed with other companies, inform them that you have accepted another position. If you did not get the job, be gracious and grateful when you are informed that someone else has been chosen. Make it clear to the company that if any other positions open, you would like to be considered for them. You may go through several interviews before you find the right job. Make each interview a learning experience.

checkpoint

1. List three common questions asked in job interviews.

   _____

   _____

   _____

   _____

   _____

2. Explain how body language can affect the outcome of an interview.

   _____

   _____

   _____

   _____

   _____

3. What are some of the things you might want to know about the company before your interview date?

   _____

   _____

   _____

   _____

   _____

4. Why is it important to listen carefully during an interview?

   _____

   _____

   _____

   _____

   _____

5. Why is it important to follow up after the interview?

   _____

   _____

   _____

   _____

   _____

applications

1. Identify a job in which you would be interested. Write a short statement that summarizes your education, experience, and skills that apply to that position.

_____

_____

_____

_____

2. If you are currently working, how did you dress when you interviewed for the job you now hold?

_____

_____

_____

_____

3. Explain how you can prepare for the question, "Tell me about yourself."

_____

_____

_____

_____

4. Why should you prepare some questions to ask during the interview?

_____

_____

_____

_____

5. How can being aware of the interviewer's body language be helpful during an interview?

_____

_____

_____

_____

6. You have read about how your personal appearance affects the people you meet at the interview. Describe how your personal appearance also affects *you* during the interview process.

_____

_____

_____

15 points to remember

Review the following points to determine what you remember from the chapter.

- As you explore career fields and job possibilities, keep your personal traits, aptitudes, and skills in mind.

- Create a personal inventory list of the education, training, experience, skills, interests, and traits that will make you a valuable employee.

- Because most people find their jobs through networking, the ability to network is critical to a successful job search.

- Ensure that your resume is error-free and that it sells your strengths in relation to the job for which you are applying.

- Your cover letter should be neat, brief, and logical—and it should persuade the reader to interview you for the job opening.

- Employment application forms vary, so follow the directions carefully. Fill in the application completely and be sure to sign it.

- Many job openings require an online application.

- Prepare carefully for every interview. Learn as much as you can about the organization, select which documents to take, and make plans to get to the interview on time.

- Look your best. Body language can tell an interviewer as much about you as your words.

- Come to the interview with a prepared summary statement about yourself. Rehearse answers to common interview questions and prepare a list of your own questions. Immediately after the interview, send the interviewer a thank-you note or letter.

How did you do? Did you remember the main points you studied in the chapter?

KEY terms

aptitude

skill

transferable skills

technical skills

networking

resume

cover letter

electronic resume

chronological resume

functional resume

combination resume

employment application

job-benefit statement

body language

Want more activities? Go to **www.cengage.com/careerreadiness/masters** to get started.

CHAPTER *activities*

1. Look at the list of sample transferable skills listed in Figure 15-2.

   a. List 10 transferable skills you have.

   _____

   _____

   _____

   _____

   _____

   b. For each skill, write a statement that describes how you could use this skill in a job.

   _____

   _____

   _____

   _____

2. Look at the list of sample technical skills in Figure 15-2 on page 374.

   a. List 5 technical skills you have.

   _____

   _____

   _____

   _____

   b. For each skill, write a statement that describes how you have you used this skill in school or at work.

   _____

   _____

   _____

   _____

3. Research three career fields you are interested in. For each field, answer these questions.

   a. What education and training are needed?

   _____

   _____

   _____

   b. What do workers do on the job?

   _____

   _____

   _____

   c. What is the expected job growth? Where are most of the jobs?

   _____

   _____

   _____

   _____

   d. What are the earnings?

   _____

   _____

   _____

   e. What are the working conditions?

   _____

   _____

   _____

4. Choose a company where you would like to work. Research the company, its products and/or services, and rehearse answering the question, "What do you know about our company?"

_____

_____

_____

_____

_____

5. Divide into groups of three or four people and practice answering the common interview question, "Tell me about yourself." Give each other ideas for improving your statements.

_____

_____

_____

_____

_____

6. Visit your college career center. List the services they provide in each of these areas and describe how you can use these services in your own job search.

a. Finding job leads

_____

_____

_____

_____

_____

b. Preparing resumes

_____

_____

_____

_____

c. Writing cover letters

_____

_____

_____

_____

_____

_____

_____

_____

_____

_____

d. Mock interviews with staff employees

_____

_____

_____

_____

_____

_____

_____

_____

_____

e. Interviews with company representatives who are recruiting at the college

_____

_____

_____

_____

_____

_____

CRITICAL *thinking*

CASE 15.1 Changing Direction

James spent a year in community college studying criminal justice, but he left school without graduating and worked as a host in a fashionable restaurant. The work was okay, but he knew this wasn't the career for him. One week, two things happened at work to change his career plans. On Tuesday evening, an elderly man collapsed during dinner. The next day, a delivery person slipped in the ice in the parking lot and broke his ankle. In both cases, James could help—but only by calling 911. He was impressed with how efficient, calm, and knowledgeable the emergency responders were and wondered if he could do this work. He visited the local fire station where the emergency medical technicians (EMTs) were based and talked to the two EMTs who were on call at the time. They told him how they had become EMTs and talked about how much they loved their work. When James mentioned that he had attended the local community college, they recommended that he explore the college's EMT program. They also encouraged him to come back to the fire station with a list of questions for their director and gave James the director's hours and contact information.

1. Write three or four questions James should ask the EMT director.

   _____

   _____

   _____

   _____

   _____

2. What resources of the community college should James use in exploring this new direction in his career? Be specific in your answer.

   _____

   _____

   _____

   _____

3. What online resources should James use?

   _____

   _____

   _____

   _____

CASE 15.2   Is This Job for Barry?

Barry had always been a quiet, shy person who was happiest when he was reading something, whether it was in print or online. He learned a great deal about a lot of things over the years, and it seemed like he could find anything on the Internet. He was thrilled when he learned about a job opening as a page in a research library. His job would be to locate books, manuscripts, and records, deliver them to the library desk, and reshelve them when the researcher finished using them. However, the librarian told him that the page position had been filled and the only opening she had was on the reference desk helping students and other researchers find what they needed to do their research. Barry wanted to work in a library, but was nervous about interacting directly with the library's patrons. He wasn't sure that working the reference desk was the best job for him.

1. Should Barry consider a job that doesn't fit his personality and interpersonal skills? Why or why not?

_____

_____

_____

_____

_____

_____

2. Should he tell the librarian he is nervous about interacting with the public?

_____

_____

_____

_____

_____

_____

3. If you were the librarian, what advice would you give Barry?

_____

_____

_____

_____

_____

_____

chapter 16

Taking Charge of Your Career

Stockbyte/Getty Images

objectives

After completing this chapter, you should be able to:

1. Set career goals and establish a career path.
2. Identify the elements essential for keeping a job.
3. Conduct yourself professionally in a performance appraisal.
4. Determine if and when you should change jobs.
5. Explain the importance of networking throughout your career.

Think About It: Cynthia was eager to begin her new job at Riverside Pharmaceuticals. When she arrived on her first day, her supervisor Todd took her to the human resources department, where she spent most of the morning completing forms for new employees. Todd picked Cynthia up at HR and took her to her work area. He introduced her to her coworkers and reviewed various company policies and procedures. Luckily, the person who held the job previously had left several pages of instructions *Do you think Cynthia had a typical first day on the job? Do you agree that she did not do any real work?* and advice, which Cynthia read carefully. Then the information technology person arrived to set up her computer and e-mail account and explain the online tutorial for the department's custom software. Cynthia spent the rest of the day reading the employee handbook, looking at the company's intranet (the internal website for employees), and reviewing the folders and files on her computer that she needed for her job. There was a lot of information to absorb, and she was concerned that she had not done any "real" work by the end of the day. A new coworker Dianne said, "There's a lot to take in at first, but each day will get easier. You'll see." Cynthia smiled and replied, "Thanks for saying that. See you tomorrow!"

Getting Off to a Great Start

When you start a new job, any job, it is natural to feel a little lost at first. Your coworkers will find it much easier to learn your name than you will to learn theirs, because you will have many names and faces to connect. Working in a new setting with an unfamiliar telephone system and unfamiliar computer can be stressful. You are naturally eager to make a good impression, so you may be a little nervous and self-conscious. Often the first week on a job is more about learning the ropes than about getting things done, which can be frustrating for someone who has a strong work ethic and likes to make a real difference in the workplace.

Although it is important to learn the company policies, procedures, and written and unwritten rules, you must realize that it will take time to become acclimated to your workplace and responsibilities. Be patient with yourself and with the process. When you have everything organized, you can dazzle them with your efficiency. For now, you simply need to settle in and learn.

"Regardless of how you feel inside, always try to look like a winner."

TAKING CARE OF PAPERWORK

There is no getting around the paperwork required for starting a new job. Your supervisor or someone from the human resources department will give you the necessary forms and be available to answer your questions. Be sure to fill out all forms completely and honestly. Read each form carefully. If you are unsure about the meaning of an item on a form, ask for clarification.

Employment Forms

One of your first orders of business at a new job will be to complete payroll and benefits forms. You should be prepared to show your driver's license and social security card for identification and payroll purposes. Every month a portion of your paycheck will be put into a federal social security account called *FICA*, an abbreviation for Federal Insurance Contributions Act. Your employer matches that sum by putting an equal amount in your account. You will appreciate the contributions you and your employer have made when you reach retirement age and begin to draw on the benefits.

One of the first forms you will complete is **Form W-4**, the Employee's Withholding Allowance Certificate. The form tells your company's payroll department how much money to withhold from your paycheck each pay period for federal and state income taxes. The amount withheld from your check depends on your income, your marital status, and the number of dependents you claim. Some people like to withhold more money than they think they will owe, so that they get a bigger refund at tax time. Although it can be an easy way to put aside some money you might otherwise be tempted to spend, it is not the best way to save, since this money earns no interest.

Your employer will send your W-4 form to the U.S. Internal Revenue Service (IRS), which monitors federal income tax. At the end of the year, you will receive a **Form W-2**, the Employee's Wage and Tax Statement, which reports to the IRS and to you how much estimated tax was withheld for federal, state, and local income taxes. It will also tell how much you paid for social security taxes, which your employer matches, and for Medicare taxes, as well as information about other health and retirement benefits you may have received.

Federal law also requires that the employee and employer jointly fill out an Employee Eligibility Verification document known as **Form I-9**. This form from the Department of Homeland Security requires both the employer and the employee to attest that the worker is authorized to work in the United States. A completed I-9 form is required not just for immigrants but also for citizens born here. Your employer will again ask to see two forms of identification such as a driver's license, social security card, passport, or voter registration card. The employer is required to keep this completed and signed form on file to ensure that the employer is not hiring illegal aliens who are not authorized to work in the United States.

Employee Handbook

At most companies, you will receive an **employee handbook** that spells out specific policies and rules governing the employer–employee relationship. Read the handbook carefully and note any questions you have. You may be asked to sign a document confirming that you have read the information, understand it, and will follow the policies and procedures detailed in the handbook. Figure 16-1 shows the types of information typically covered in an employee handbook.

Many companies have a program called **orientation**, the purpose of which is to introduce new employees to the company. Such programs may be formal or informal. Formal orientation programs are common in large companies where a number of new employees are beginning their jobs at the same time.

TOPICS IN AN EMPLOYEE HANDBOOK

Work and compensation issues, such as compliance with Equal Employment Opportunity laws for hiring and employment; attendance and reporting to work; work hours and schedules; recording hours worked; pay period; overtime pay; holidays; personnel files; performance evaluations.

Workplace standards and expectations, such as safety; care of equipment and supplies; drug-free workplace; appearance and dress; conflicts of interest; code of ethical conduct; personal calls and visits; business expenses; procedures regarding electronic resources and communications; confidential and proprietary information; disciplinary procedure; responding to customer inquiries and problems.

Benefits, such as paid time off, leaves of absence, health insurance; 401(k) retirement accounts.

FIGURE 16-1 Typical topics covered in an employee handbook.

"There are no menial jobs, only menial attitudes."

A large banking institution planned an orientation program for its 20 new employees. The morning program consisted of introductions of key staff and an explanation of policies and procedures that apply to all employees. At lunch, all new employees and their supervisors were introduced. The afternoon sessions were held in the individual departments where the new hires would be working and were conducted by the supervisors.

Insurance Forms

If your employer provides medical, dental, optical, disability, and life insurance, count yourself lucky. Not all organizations can afford to offer such benefits. You will want to spend some time concentrating on filling out these forms accurately so that you get the benefits to which you are entitled. Do not be afraid to ask questions. If there are options for different medical plans, for example, you may want to take home the written information and review it before you sign. Review all of the material carefully and decide which options are affordable and best meet your needs.

Paul had never had a job with health insurance benefits, so many of the terms and concepts were unfamiliar to him. He took the forms home so his sister-in-law, Rita, who worked in human resources at another company, could give him some advice. He also asked her a couple of questions he had jotted down about things he did not understand in the employee handbook. Rita was happy to help with the insurance forms, but she encouraged Paul to ask his supervisor or someone in HR at his organization his questions about the employee handbook, since procedures, rules, and policies are different in every organization.

Other Benefits

The employee handbook will list the company's policies on vacation, sick days, and personal leave time. Read these carefully. If you do not know whom to contact when you are too ill to work, ask. Also, make sure that you are using the personal leave time as the company intends. Your employer may also offer assistance with parking costs and a pre-tax withholding account for dependent care, such as child daycare.

You may also be asked to fill out forms for a 401(k) or other retirement plan, which you may choose to join (sometimes after a waiting period of up to a year). The employer may match the money you put aside for retirement up to a certain limit. Even if these savings withheld from your paycheck make your budget tight, when retirement age comes, you will be glad you chose to participate.

ADJUSTING TO YOUR NEW JOB

This section describes some of the key issues that you will face as you adjust to a new job, such as meeting your coworkers, learning company policies and procedures, and setting up your work area.

MAKE IT A GOOD FIRST DAY

- Report to work on time.
- Bring two forms of identification with you for the Form I-9 verification.
- Make sure you have information such as birth dates and social security numbers for your dependents. You will need this information to fill out insurance forms.
- Bring contact telephone numbers for family, friends, or neighbors who should be notified in case of an emergency.
- Be sure that your appearance is neat, clean, and professional. People notice everything about you, including your smile.
- Dress appropriately. When in doubt about what to wear, dress conservatively and professionally.
- Be polite, friendly, relaxed, and professional even though you may be feeling nervous.
- Listen carefully to instructions and take notes.
- Exhibit a genuine desire to learn.

Meet Your Coworkers

You will meet some of your coworkers during the first day on the job. Make every effort to be polite and appear competent and professional. Also strive to remember their names. It may help to repeat names as people are introduced. Many of your coworkers will automatically introduce themselves. If you have not been introduced to someone, introduce yourself. Say something like, "Hi, I'm Shelley. I just started working in the accounting department." If you do not hear or understand the full name, ask the person to repeat it. "I'm sorry. I didn't catch your name." Look people in the eye when you are introduced and offer a firm handshake.

It may take you a few weeks to feel totally comfortable around the other workers. But, if you exhibit a genuine desire to learn and improve, you will be accepted into the work environment.

"Watch, listen, and learn. You can't know it all yourself. Anyone who thinks they do is destined for mediocrity."

Understand Your Job Description

You may have received a job description during the job interview process, but it is a good idea to review it when you start the job. A job description is a written explanation of the tasks, duties, and responsibilities of a particular job. Job descriptions are important because they:

- Clarify who is responsible for what within the organization.
- Help to define relationships between individuals and departments.
- Help the employee understand the responsibilities of the position. This enables the employee to assess the importance of everything he or she is accountable for and provides a sense of where the job fits into the company as a whole.
- Assist job applicants, employees, supervisors, and human resources professionals at every stage in the employment relationship. They provide information about the training, knowledge, and skills needed for a job and can prevent misunderstandings by telling employees what they need to know about their jobs.
- Help management analyze and improve the company's organizational structure and reveal whether all responsibilities are adequately covered.
- Provide a basis for job evaluation, wage, and salary adjustments.

Your job description is a very important document. Read it and ask questions about it. After you have been on the job for a while, review it to be sure that it adequately represents what you are doing on the job. If not, talk with your supervisor about amending it. Figure 16-2 is a sample

ADMINISTRATIVE ASSISTANT[1]

- Relieve management of administrative detail.
- Coordinate work flow.
- Compose correspondence and reports.
- Maintain the boss's calendar and arrange travel.
- Train and supervise part-time employees.
- Recommend software upgrades.
- Supervise the work of office staff who report to the administrative assistant.
- Set up and facilitate meetings and conferences.
- Prepare handouts and presentations.
- Greet clients and visitors, as needed.
- Maintain departmental records.
- Conduct online research, as needed.
- Manage website.
- Perform general office duties.

FIGURE 16-2 Sample job description for an administrative assistant.

job description for an administrative assistant from the website of IAAP, the International Association of Administrative Professionals.

Learn the Policies and Procedures

Policies and procedures differ from company to company. As a new employee, you will want to learn these rules and make every effort to comply with them. Ask about anything in the employee handbook that you do not understand. If there is no handbook, this does not mean there are no rules. It simply means that they are unwritten. Make sure you learn how your employer wants you to conduct business. Some of the issues you should be aware of are:

- Expected work hours.
- Meal breaks and other rest periods.
- Security and identification procedures.
- Parking arrangements.
- Use of company equipment and services—e-mail, Internet access, telephone, fax, and copier.
- Vacation, sick, and personal leave policies.
- Whom to call if you are ill or unable to come to work for a good reason.

Some of these basic policies and rules may have been explained at the interview. If not, be sure you ask about the policies before the end of your first work day. You may find it helpful to keep a notebook handy to jot down your questions and the answers you receive.

In many workplaces, there are issues of confidentiality and privacy. Some companies require workers to sign a confidentiality agreement to protect the organization's intellectual property. **Intellectual property** is intangible property that is the result of creativity. Examples are musical, literary, and artistic works; discoveries and inventions; strategies; and ideas, phrases, and designs. If you work in a medical, dental, optical, or pharmaceutical setting, you will need to understand the rights of patients under *HIPAA*, the Health Insurance Portability and Accounting Act, which covers the privacy of medical records, conversations, and other communications.

Learn the Safety Rules

Some companies also have safety rules that are posted for all employees and possibly published as well in a safety manual. These rules ensure that workers have a safe working environment and equipment or procedures to protect them against workplace hazards, including exposure to toxic substances. If you are employed in a manufacturing setting or an area where there is heavy equipment, dangerous conditions, or hazardous materials, make sure you understand the risks and preventive measures you should take to protect yourself. You may be required to wear safety shoes, gloves, glasses or goggles, a mask, or clothing that protects you against hazardous conditions. Your company must enforce these rules to meet government and insurance standards.

Every employee has the right to safe working conditions. If you are unsure about how to operate a piece of equipment, ask for help. Never begin using machinery or equipment until you have been trained to use it safely. Observe all safety rules and report any unsafe conditions immediately to your supervisor.

"You have to learn the rules of the game. And then you have to play it better than anyone else."

Learn the "Understood" Rules and Expectations

Every workplace has some expectations and rules that are simply understood rather than written down. For this reason, they are sometimes called "unwritten" rules. For example, a company may prefer that no one wear T-shirts with lettering to work. This may not be a written policy. It is simply "not done" in the company. You will learn these rules by observing, listening, and questioning. It is wise to learn these unwritten rules quickly—and follow them.

The most important of these unwritten expectations is that you will put in an honest day's work for an honest day's pay. Other expectations you can assume are that you need to come to work on time every day and return from lunch and breaks on time. In any position, it may not be written, but you are expected to be kind, courteous, and respectful to customers and coworkers.

Set Up Your Work Area

A professional appearance is important in any workplace. This includes not only how you look, dress, speak, and write but also how your workspace looks. When it is well-organized and tidy, your work area leaves a professional impression on coworkers as well as outsiders. A family photograph on your desk may be all right, but make sure you do not overdo it. You should not turn your work area into an elaborate interior decorating project. Religious and holiday symbols and decorations should always be minimal. Being orderly and organized also makes your job easier.

Your employer is required to provide a safe place for you to work. If there is a problem with your area, tell your supervisor so the problem can be corrected. If you share your work area with others, you must respect their rights and feelings in order to help maintain a good, safe work environment for everyone.

"The victory of success is half won when one gains the habit of work."

EXHIBITING WINNING WORK ATTITUDES

This section describes key personal characteristics that you will want to exhibit on the job to ensure that you keep your position, such as establishing good work habits, accepting responsibility for your job, and treating everyone with respect.

Establish Good Work Habits

Among the unspoken expectations discussed earlier in this chapter is the understanding that you will focus on your work throughout the day and be as efficient as possible. It goes without saying that you must not abuse or

GOOD WORK HABITS FOR EVERY JOB

• Do not waste supplies.	• Ask questions when you don't understand something.
• Listen carefully and follow directions willingly.	• Be kind and helpful to others.
• Follow the "unwritten" rules.	• Admit your mistakes and learn from them.
• Ask questions—and remember the answers.	• Be objective and fair in your relationships with others.
• Dress appropriately for the type of work you are doing.	• Accept responsibility for your job.
• Be pleasant and friendly.	• Treat everyone with respect.

FIGURE 16-3 Good work habits to develop.

misuse company property, equipment, or supplies. Treating customers, clients, the general public, and coworkers with consideration is basic to any job. Arriving on time each day and sticking to schedules are both important. Develop the habits in Figure 16-3 to get off on the right foot with your employer.

Have a Strong Work Ethic

Employers want workers who take pride in their work and in the company or organization. When you have a strong work ethic, you work as steadily and efficiently as you can, not wasting time or goofing off. Pausing to chat with coworkers is all right, as long as you keep it brief. You want to be on friendly terms with everyone, but you are there to work, not to socialize. If coworkers spend time complaining or gossiping, take care not to join them. Your attitude should be upbeat no matter how negative those around you may be.

"You don't get paid for the hour. You get paid for the value you bring to the hour."

Most employers do not quantify exactly how much you have to accomplish in a day, but if you are not productive, it is unlikely that you will keep your job. Make up your mind to be self-motivated, setting standards and goals for yourself if your supervisor does not set them for you. Always have the employer's best interests in mind. If you have to deal with a difficult customer, remind yourself that you represent your employer, and you need to be a positive representative no matter how difficult the customer may be. Treat the employer's property as you would treat your own, not carelessly or thoughtlessly.

Look for Ways to Improve

Employers value workers who are eager to learn and grow in their jobs. There may be several ways of completing a particular task. Pay attention to useful techniques or ideas of coworkers that might make you more efficient or productive. Ask your supervisor or coworkers about any aspect of your job that you do not understand. If opportunities for training are available, sign up.

The more you learn and do on the job, the more valuable you are to your employer. Use your creativity to generate new solutions to problems in the workplace. If you think of a more efficient way to handle a procedure or task, think it through and then suggest

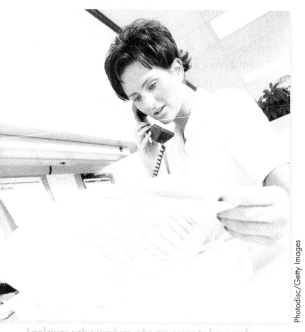

Photodisc/Getty Images

Employers value workers who are eager to learn and grow in their jobs.

it to your supervisor. However, if the supervisor decides against the change you suggest, do it the current way without complaint.

Accept Responsibility for Your Job

Accept responsibility for your assigned job responsibilities and also for any mistakes you may make. And you will make mistakes, because you are human. Do not be afraid to admit your errors, but be sure to learn from them. Taking ownership for your mistakes is a sign of growth and maturity. Whatever you do, do not try to hide your mistakes or blame them on someone else or ignore them. Keep upgrading your work habits and your work skills. The more confidence you have, the fewer mistakes you will make.

Learn all you can about your job, the company, and the work environment. Keep informed about new policies and procedures and put them into practice. Become familiar with the company's new products or services.

Accept Criticism Positively

Treat suggestions from your supervisor or coworkers as opportunities to learn how to improve. Accepting suggestions and criticism helps you grow as a person and as a worker. Sometimes you may be completely unaware of something you are doing wrong, or something you could do better, until someone else brings it to your attention. Even when you do not agree with the criticism, try to adapt as your supervisor wants you to. Do not over-react and think that you have failed. Keep striving to meet your supervisor's expectations.

Use this checklist every week that you are on the job, and see what you can accomplish with a "can-do" attitude. Show your good attitude by:

_____ Giving a day's work for a day's pay.
_____ Striving to meet your employer's expectations.
_____ Showing a desire to please.
_____ Listening to suggestions.
_____ Not making excuses for errors.
_____ Respecting the ideas and opinions of others.
_____ Trying to see things from the point of view of others.
_____ Being open to change.
_____ Being passionate about what you do.
_____ Helping, encouraging, and praising others.
_____ Smiling often.

Keep a Sense of Humor

Laughing and light-heartedness can ease tense situations and make difficult tasks easier to get through. This includes an ability to laugh at yourself. Taking yourself too seriously makes everything seem harder. Lighten up!

Having a sense of humor does not include telling jokes that are crude or in poor taste. You are bound to offend others if you engage in that sort of humor. Also avoid being sarcastic about other people and their work, which can lead to bad interpersonal relations in the workplace.

Keep workplace humor under control and in perspective, taking care not to step over the line into unprofessional behavior. Constantly telling jokes, being the "company clown," and playing practical jokes can backfire on you by undermining your professional image and reputation. You do not want to be seen as someone who is always goofing off and clowning around.

Treat Everyone with Respect

Most people lose their jobs not because they could not do the work, but because they failed to fit in and get along with others. Nobody enjoys working with an irritable or mean-spirited coworker. Don't you prefer to work with people who are positive and pleasant? Don't you prefer to work with people who treat you with kindness and respect? Don't you prefer to work with people who are cooperative and supportive? Make up your mind to be that positive, kind, and cooperative worker if you want your career to stay on track. Interpersonal skills and friendly attitudes can make you a valued employee even if you are still learning to accomplish the work itself.

Just as you want to be treated fairly and as an individual, your coworkers want you to treat them well. This means treating others with consideration and respect no matter what age, race, religion, nationality, or gender. As you learned in Chapter 12, embracing diversity in the workplace is an important way to broaden your horizons and learn from others.

FINDING A MENTOR

As you transition into a new position, you may receive help from a *mentor*, a person assigned to help a new employee with orientation and training. As you learned in Chapter 2, a mentor may offer advice, answer questions, help a new employee understand the culture of the business, share expertise and experiences, and serve as a role model. Your mentor can be a very valuable resource and can help you quickly learn the rules, including the "understood" rules and expectations you read about earlier in this chapter.

If your company does not have a formal mentoring program, find someone you admire and ask him or her to help you learn and grow. When you find that mentor, let the person lead the way, but do not be afraid of asking questions or asking for help. Most people enjoy guiding and teaching

"People often say that motivation doesn't last. Well, neither does bathing—that's why we recommend it daily."

Martin was eager to start his new job as an administrative assistant in the city records department. He spent most of the morning in the human resources department taking care of paperwork. Then he went to his supervisor Latoya's office, where he met Nancy, Latoya's executive assistant and Martin's assigned mentor. The three of them talked about some departmental policies and procedures, and then Nancy and Martin went to a conference room to talk. Nancy gave Martin a copy of a recent proposal passed by the city council to hire an outside vendor to convert paper records being stored off-site into an electronic system and then shred the original paper records. She explained her role and Martin's role in interviewing vendors, selecting a vendor, and overseeing the work. This project would take about 75 percent of Martin's time for at least six months. She gave him an overview of his other projects and ongoing assignments, and they arranged to meet in a week to discuss how things were going. She suggested that they meet for breakfast in the cafeteria once a month during Martin's four-month probationary period. When Martin arrived at work the next day, he had an e-mail from Nancy recapping their mentoring arrangement. Attached to the e-mail was an article about the architectural history of City Hall that she thought he might find interesting.

Is Martin's job off to a good start? Do you think Nancy is a good mentor? Why or why not?

others, and each of you can learn from the other no matter what your skill level. These relationships can also be very important when problems arise in the workplace. Your mentor can help you resolve conflicts and solve problems.

UNDERSTANDING WORKPLACE POLITICS

Politics seem to exist in every workplace. Certain people form alliances, certain others dislike each other or are jealous of others' talents or successes. Some are concerned with protecting their own job security, gaining a promotion, or having more power in the organization. Some are out for their own advancement, not for the good of the company. It is difficult to avoid getting caught up in these political intrigues and struggles. They just seem to be part of human nature.

If the politics in your workplace appear to be unproductive or even destructive, try to hold yourself above them. Do not participate in gossip or any other kind of undermining of coworkers, even if you dislike the coworkers. Just walk away, and vow to treat everyone fairly and honestly—as you want them to treat you.

checkpoint

1. Why is it natural to feel a little lost when starting a new job?

_____

_____

_____

_____

2. Why should you review your job description carefully?

_____

_____

_____

_____

3. What should you do if you make a mistake on the job? What should you *not* do?

_____

_____

_____

_____

4. Why is it important to learn the company's "unwritten" rules and expectations?

_____

_____

_____

_____

5. Why is it unwise to get involved in workplace politics?

_____

_____

_____

_____

applications

1. List four unwritten rules and expectations in your current job. If you are not currently working, use your most recent job.

_____

_____

_____

2. List four unwritten rules and expectations for the executive assistant to the president or dean of a community college. (Feel free to speculate.)

_____

_____

_____

3. Assume you want to find a mentor on your own.

   a. What qualities would you look for in a mentor?

   _____

   _____

   b. How would you approach someone and ask if he or she would be interested in mentoring you?

   _____

   _____

   c. What would you do and say if the person declined your offer because he or she did not have the time to mentor you?

   _____

   _____

4. Think of a situation where a coworker acted "silly" and said or did what he or she thought were humorous antics.

   a. How did your coworkers react?

   _____

   _____

   b. Did the person gain anything by acting this way?

   _____

   _____

   _____

   c. Was he or she considered immature?

   _____

   _____

   _____

5. List five types of intellectual property in the organization where you work. If you are not currently working, use your most recent organization.

   _____

   _____

   _____

Planning Your Career

You are responsible for taking charge of your career.

©Robert Kneschke, 2009/Used under license from Shutterstock.com

A career doesn't just happen. It is your responsibility to take charge of your career and make it happen. An important first step is to create a vision for what you want your career to look like. Your chances of long-term success will be greater if you plan and prepare to be successful in your current position and in the various jobs that will become part of your career path—a plan that you can follow that will lead to a position with more responsibility, satisfaction, and income.

Success in advancing a career consists of discovering your potential and developing it. It includes making the most of what you have to offer the employer, of sharpening your skills, and of keeping up with what is new in your chosen career. Your on-the-job hours should be satisfying—adding to your self-fulfillment and contributing to your professional growth and personal happiness. If you are happy during your hours at work, your overall mental and emotional health will be enriched.

VISUALIZE SUCCESS IN YOUR CAREER

There are no shortcuts to success. There are no substitutes for planning your career if you want to build a satisfying one. Visualize where you want to be in your career in two years, five years, in ten years, or at retirement. One of your life goals should be to move ahead in your career to reach your full potential.

Set Goals and Devise Action Plans

The most common reason people do not reach their potential is because they do not have a career strategy that includes clear and attainable goals and action plans. A **career strategy** is a plan of action to reach your goals. You read in Chapter 2 about setting goals and creating action plans. Set specific, realistic goals for your career. Write down short-term and medium-term goals as stepping stones to meet your long-term goal(s).

June's long-term goal is to be a head pediatric nurse in a large community hospital. Many years ago she set a short-term goal to do volunteer work with sick children in a local hospital. She also set a medium-term goal to find a job paying good wages in the health field to support herself while she took classes in nursing. Volunteering at the Children's Hospital Medical Clinic one Saturday a month for three years during high school—her short-term goal—gave June a great deal of satisfaction and assured her that she had chosen the right career. One of the nurses at the clinic helped June find a job as a part-time administrative assistant in a physical therapy center while she was in college—her medium-term goal.

You may need to change your goals because of life circumstances: health issues, economic conditions, or a family situation, for example. The workplace may also change. Career fields can shift in this rapidly changing technological world. You may move far beyond your expectations and exceed your goal earlier than you planned. If changes occur, you need to be flexible and set a new long-term career goal.

Energize Yourself about Your Goals

Having written goals is a good start, but not an end in itself. As you plan for your future career, never neglect your current job. Your current job is important; you are building your reputation as a worker. You are gaining knowledge and skills, and you are making contacts that will be important as you move toward your goals.

Share your career goals with people who are supportive of you and who will encourage and help you along the way. Sharing your goals with others will also increase your sense of responsibility, and you will have someone to help motivate you and share in your successes. Believe that you can accomplish your goals, and you will have a much greater chance of achieving them. If you set realistic, specific goals, you know that they are achievable.

KNOW THE DIFFERENCE BETWEEN A JOB AND A CAREER

A *job* involves performing a designated set of responsibilities and duties for a specific employer. A *career* encompasses a "family" of jobs. Your career is your life's work. "High school math teacher at Charleston High School" is a job, and "teaching" is a career. Unless you know the difference, for you, between a job and a career, you may spend time and money and energy changing careers when what you need is to change jobs. Or you might change jobs repeatedly and still be dissatisfied because you are in the wrong career. Before you change your job or your career, analyze whether your discontent is with your specific job or your career choice. Do not change your career just because you do not like your supervisor, and do not keep changing jobs when you really are not well suited for your career.[2]

PERFORMANCE APPRAISALS

Companies require competent workers. In many companies, the supervisor for whom the employee works conducts a job performance appraisal at least once a year. A **performance appraisal** is a system of determining how well an individual employee has performed his or her job during a period of time compared to a predetermined set of standards. In many companies, the performance appraisal is considered part of career development. The appraisal will largely determine if you keep your job, receive a promotion, or receive a pay raise. In the case of new employees, the evaluation may come at the end of a trial period or *probationary period*. The so-called trial period may extend over 3, 6, or 12 months. The length of the trial period may be determined by the complexity of the job and the level of skills possessed by the new employee.

The two basic types of performance appraisals are *criteria-based* and *goal-based*. In the more traditional criteria-based appraisal, the employee's work is rated according to standardized company criteria for productivity, quality of work, and so on. Because standardized criteria and ratings may not accurately reflect an employee's assigned tasks, many employers have moved to goal-based appraisals. Together, the employee and supervisor agree on goals for the employee to meet during the evaluation period. At evaluation time, they separately assess how goals have been met, compare their assessments, and make a final report that includes both of their assessments.[3]

Your performance appraisal will include a face-to-face meeting with your supervisor. This meeting gives your supervisor a formal opportunity to talk about your job, its responsibilities, and the potential for growth. Your supervisor can tell you how you fit in the company, if you need extra training, and if you are making the best use of your skills. Discussing your weaknesses is meant to help you become a better worker. It is not meant as a way to pick on you or lower your self-esteem. The evaluation session also gives you a chance to speak openly about problems you see with your job, to ask questions, and to offer your suggestions for the betterment of the company.

When your evaluation session is over, both you and your supervisor will sign the appraisal form. The original copy will become part of your permanent personnel file. You will get a copy for your own records. It is important to make a good impression during the appraisal conference. The conference may determine future promotional opportunities for you. Employees who make an effort to improve their work are often rewarded with raises and promotions.

RAISES AND PROMOTIONS

Your short-term and medium-terms goals will likely include efforts to get raises and promotions. Keep in mind that your ability to do your current job well impacts your ability to get raises and promotions.

Requesting a Raise

In most organizations, your performance appraisal is directly related to any increase in pay you may receive. A good appraisal may result in a pay raise. If your company has no pattern set for wage increases, it may be appropriate for you to request a raise based on a satisfactory performance evaluation.

Before you ask for a raise, think about your accomplishments of the past year. Be prepared to justify why you feel you are worthy of a salary increase. Tell your supervisor:

- What new responsibilities you have taken on in the past year.
- What new skills you have acquired and are using on the job.
- How your strengths have contributed to meeting company goals.

Base your request for a raise in pay on your work and accomplishments. Do not talk about your financial needs or obligations.

Working Toward a Promotion

Part of getting ahead on the job is climbing the career ladder by getting a promotion to a higher level. Promotion opportunities usually come from getting a positive performance evaluation. The positive appraisal says that you have proven your ability to accept more responsibility and do more challenging work.

In addition to getting a good appraisal, be the best at what you do, set and meet goals for yourself, and know the company and the promotion policies. Also, it may be necessary to blow your own horn—but without bragging. Be positive and enthusiastic about your job. When you talk with coworkers or your supervisor, speak with confidence about your experiences and accomplishments, but avoid making too many "I" statements.

Elaine has been an events coordinator at Harmony Gallery for three years. She enjoys the work and her schedule allows her to spend time with her two small children. Elaine is a single parent. She is offered the position of Acquisitions Director of the gallery, with a salary of $850 a week. Her new duties will include supervising four people who are currently her coworkers, handling their performance appraisals, attending board meetings one evening a month, and being responsible for implementing the goals set by the board. Elaine will also be expected to attend regional auctions to search for new works for the gallery. Elaine's current position is hourly. She earns $17 an hour and works 40 hours a week. She gets time and a half for overtime, and in the summer, when the gallery has the most visitors, she sometimes works 44 to 48 hours a week. As a supervisor she will not be eligible for overtime. Elaine carefully weighs the pros and cons of the promotion and thinks about her future and the future of her family.

What is your advice for Elaine? What issues should she consider? Does she need any additional information to make this decision? If yes, what should she ask her employer?

In most organizations a promotion means that you will have more responsibility. Before you accept a promotion, weigh the advantages and possible disadvantages of accepting the promotion. The promotion should be in line with your career goals. If the promotion is not in line with your plan, you will have a decision to make: do you change your goals or turn down the promotion? A higher salary and a new title are not always good reasons to accept a promotion.

UPGRADING YOUR SKILLS

In the changing workplace environment, it is essential to keep up with changes in technology. Your technical skills can become obsolete if you are not careful about maintaining them. For example, you may have become proficient on a certain software package that your employer decides to upgrade or replace. Or you may find that the methods, systems, and routines of a new position are entirely different from those you learned in school or used in another organization. What should you do?

It is important to keep a "learning attitude." Take advantage every day to learn and improve. Pay attention to what's going on around you. Ask questions when faced with a new challenge. Ask for demonstrations of new systems or procedures. Take advantage of training opportunities, such as on-the-job training for employees who need to learn new skills. Welcome the opportunity to learn something new. New information and new skills are guaranteed to improve your effectiveness and security. When you consider job opportunities, select an organization that provides, promotes, and supports ongoing training as part of its policy.

The local community college or university may offer coursework related to your employment. Many community colleges have partnerships with local businesses and industries. These courses provide an outstanding opportunity for the ambitious employee to improve and expand his or her knowledge and potential. You can find dozens of tutorials, many free, online.

Consider taking courses or participating in webinars in human relations, public speaking, and team building. These skills are essential for supervisory roles. Keep a record of the training and courses you take and discuss them at your performance appraisal. It is a good idea to maintain a *career portfolio* in which you keep documents and other items that provide evidence and examples of your work accomplishments, certifications, and training. Also, include letters and other documents of recognition for a job well done.

"Get happiness out of your work or you may never know what happiness is."

CHANGING EMPLOYERS

The time may come when you consider changing employers. This is part of navigating your career path. Changing jobs can be difficult and stressful because of the relationships you have developed and the security you feel within the job. Changing jobs is an important decision and should not be taken lightly. Be sure you change jobs for the right reasons. It is important to do your homework and carefully evaluate any new opportunity.

You may want to consider a job change if:[4]

_____ Your current employer cannot offer any advancement.
_____ Your current job does not further your career goal.
_____ The economy causes layoffs.
_____ Your department or job is eliminated.
_____ You do not agree with the policies and goals of the organization.
_____ You want to move to a new part of the country.
_____ You want a new challenge.
_____ You have a new career goal and your job does not fit into your plan.

Do Your Homework

It is not a good idea to quit your current job until you find a new one, and avoid rushing into a job change without doing some homework and planning. Begin by listing the reasons to either stay in your current position or move on to a new position. Look at all aspects of your current job and any new job you find tempting. Another job or company may look good on the surface, but be careful. If you do not do your research, you could end up working with a difficult supervisor; you could be given a heavy, unpleasant workload; or you could find yourself in a position with no growth potential.

Take the time to examine the activities that you like and dislike, with an emphasis on those you like. Also, don't limit yourself to similar jobs when making a change. Look for jobs that take advantage of both your skills and your interests. But always keep your career goals in mind. If the job change does not fall in line with your career objectives, think again about making the change.

"The best way to appreciate your job is to imagine yourself without one."

Evaluate New Opportunities Carefully

As you seek to build a satisfying career, do not sell yourself short just to obtain immediate employment. Your goal is to market your skills for the best possible measure of job stimulation and challenge, security, appreciation, and other rewards. The most important question to ask yourself before accepting a new job is, "Does this position move me toward reaching my long-term career goals?" Other questions to consider before taking a new job include:

• How stable is the company?
• What is the company's reputation?
• How stable is the position?
• What are the opportunities for advancement?
• What are the organization's promotion policies?

- Will I need more education if I stay with this company?
- What security does the position offer?
- Will the work be interesting and challenging enough?
- Do I have the interests, qualifications, and aptitude for this position?
- Are there any negative issues about the job?

Jobs do not last forever, and it is important to know when and how to leave. The best time to plan for advancement is before you make a job change. One of the considerations to weigh is whether the job offers the possibility of promotion. For example, a well-established firm may offer more security than advancement. A new firm, on the other hand, may provide rapid advancement to those employees who are promotable; yet the position may be less stable than with the established firm. You will need to examine the options. Figure 16-4 lists some of the issues to take into account when you are considering changing employers.

ADVANTAGES OF GOING OR STAYING[5]	
ADVANTAGES OF STAYING WITH YOUR CURRENT EMPLOYER	**ADVANTAGES OF CHANGING EMPLOYERS**
Consider these possible advantages of seeking advancement or growth with your current employer:	While it may be more comfortable to stay where you are, there may also be advantages to making a change:
• You do not need to adjust to new surroundings and new coworkers. • Your reputation for job stability is better if you do not change jobs frequently. • You will not lose accumulated benefits, such as vacation time and the employer's contributions to your retirement account. • If your current job offers health insurance and other benefits, it can be risky to give them up. When you consider a job change, always consider the benefits, not just the compensation.	• You may increase your job interest by becoming involved with a new job challenge. • You may advance more quickly in the new organization than you would by seeking a promotion in your current organization. • You may receive a better salary or benefits package. • You may gain knowledge, broaden your experience, expand your network, and perhaps expand your career growth opportunities.

FIGURE 16-4 Advantages of staying with your current employer or changing employers.

When You Leave a Job

If you decide the best course of action is to leave your current job (or if you are asked to leave), do so professionally and courteously. Throughout your working life, references from past employers will be requested. For this reason, you must leave your job on a pleasant and positive note. Do not leave angry or in a huff, even if you were dissatisfied with the position. You want to maintain a reputation for fairness. Give your employer at least two weeks' notice that you are resigning, and be sure to be "on the job" right up to your last working day. Say goodbye to your coworkers and supervisors. If the job experience has been valuable, tell them so.

Before you walk out the door, you have several things to do that are in your best interest.

1. Check to see if you are entitled to *severance pay*, an allowance usually based on length of employment that is payable to a terminating employee. There is no law requiring severance pay; nevertheless, some employers offer this benefit to employees who are laid off because of downsizing or because the position has been eliminated.

2. Check to see how your final paycheck will be delivered to you and when it will be available.

3. Check to see if you are eligible to receive payment for unused vacation days or sick leave.

4. Check to see what happens to your health insurance benefits. The federal *COBRA* law (the Consolidated Omnibus Budget Reconciliation Act, passed in 1986) and various state laws provide continuation of health benefits for a period of time when an employee quits, is laid off, or is fired for any reason other than misconduct. The human resources department should help you with your insurance benefits paperwork.

5. Check into unemployment insurance in your state's Department of Labor. If you lose your job temporarily or permanently you may be eligible for financial assistance. These benefits vary greatly from state to state.

checkpoint

1. Why is it important to visualize where you want to be in your career?

_____

_____

_____

_____

2. Why should you set short-term and medium-term goals?

_____

_____

_____

_____

3. What should you be prepared to tell your supervisor when you request a raise?

_____

_____

_____

_____

4. How should you decide whether to accept a promotion?

_____

_____

_____

5. What are some of the advantages of staying with your current employer?

_____

_____

_____

6. What are some of the advantages of changing employers?

_____

_____

_____

applications

1. List three career goals that you have considered for yourself. Describe how you might reach these goals.

_____

_____

_____

2. List some events that have changed your career goals.

_____

_____

_____

3. Write a specific, realistic long-term career goal for yourself.

_____

_____

_____

4. Write short-term and medium-term goals for the long-term goal above.

_____

_____

_____

5. Explain how you would prepare yourself to ask for a raise in your current position. If you are not currently working, use your most recent job.

_____

_____

_____

Networking—It Never Stops

No matter how comfortable and content you may be in your job, chances are that things will change. Change is inevitable. It may be an improvement, or it may be a development that will make you want to move on. In an economic downturn, you can find yourself without a job through no fault of your own. Take time periodically to update your resume and stay aware of openings that are available. Even if you are not interested in changing jobs, you may be able to help someone who is looking, and that person may someday help you.

NETWORKING FOR YOUR CAREER

You have learned in previous chapters how important interpersonal relationships are in the workplace. They are also critical in the broader context of your career development. It is usually through some personal contact that people find new jobs. This is why networking is so important. Networking is developing and maintaining personal connections in your field of work, including your personal contacts, friends, neighbors, and family. Even if they are not involved in your professional field, the people you network with may have contacts who may have contacts who may know of an opening somewhere. Envision a web of these interconnections to visualize how far-reaching and useful a network can be.

"Find something that you're really interested in doing in your life. Pursue it, set goals, and commit yourself to excellence."

INTERNAL NETWORKING

Most people think of networking as a practice that occurs outside of one's current workplace. On a professional level, you will want to develop positive relationships both inside and outside your organization. *Internal networking*—developing and maintaining positive relations with people who work within your company—is important to achieving career success.

By being friendly, cooperative, and supportive, you can nurture relationships with people throughout your organization who may be able to help you advance in your career. Helping your supervisor and coworkers meet tight deadlines creates a bond among you, which makes them want to help you as well. Be aware of what is going on in the organization, and make it a point to be friendly with people in other departments even if you do not interact with them routinely.

Comstock Images/Jupiter Images

Maintain an extensive network throughout your career.

Informal Communication Networks

Every organization has informal communication networks that do not follow the established lines of authority. Even if you are not interested in changing jobs, informal networking can help you do your job better. Some examples of these casual interactions are:

- Sharing ideas.
- Giving and receiving tips.
- Discussing common problems and solutions.
- Comparing notes on working conditions and challenges.

Make Yourself Visible

Many companies prefer to promote people who already work in the company instead of hiring an unknown person from outside. Make sure your supervisor and others know that you would like to grow into a job with more responsibility. You can call attention to yourself without seeming too aggressive. Be patient and keep trying. Make an effort to be more visible in the company. For example, you can volunteer to serve on or lead an interdepartment committee assigned to address a company-wide issue. Even volunteering to serve on the holiday party committee can help you to be more visible.

Make an effort to stay "in the loop" with developments in your organization. Take a sincere interest in its challenges and try to be part of the solutions. Understand who the decision-makers are and make an effort to know them. Welcome new employees warmly and help them adapt to the workplace. You never know whether the person you were kind to will start his or her own company and offer you a job there.

> Brian's supervisor Sharon asked him to represent their department on the company-wide committee to study cost-cutting options that could help the company avoid layoffs. Brian was interested in all the ideas he learned about, especially telecommuting. He volunteered to interview employees who were currently telecommuting and report to the committee on their experiences. Reggie, the first person he interviewed, worked in Brian's department. A few days after the interview, Sharon forwarded Brian an e-mail she had received from Reggie, who praised Brian's professionalism and his work on the committee.

Serve Your Internal Customers

"Coming together is a beginning; keeping together is progress; working together is success."

Pay attention to the needs of your internal customers. **Internal customers** are the people in your department or other departments within the company who are served or supported by the work you do. If you work in the marketing department, the sales department is one of your internal customers. The sales department relies on your market research and the data you collect about potential customers. When calling on customers, the sales representatives use the marketing material you create. If you work in human resources, every employee in the company is an internal customer in some way or another, through the organizational "paperwork" that HR handles for employees. Keep your relationships with your internal customers positive. Try to please the people you interact with just as you would an external customer.

Contacts outside your workplace can offer many ways to learn, grow, and find opportunities to advance your career. *External networking* refers to developing and maintaining positive relations with people outside your company. Not all of the suggestions that follow involve "active" networking with individuals. Some of the suggestions will plant seeds that may yield results later in your career.

Keep in touch with the people you meet throughout your education and career. For example, when a coworker or supervisor leaves your company for a new job, make an effort to stay in touch. There may be opportunities for you at the coworker's new employer, or other connections outside your current employer.

It is also a good idea to stay in touch with former classmates, teachers, and academic advisors. Many schools and college post job opportunities for graduates and alumni. These connections can be very important when it comes time to look for a new job or explore other options.

Professional Organizations

A professional organization consists of individuals with similar job positions or interests. For example, the International Association of Administrative Professionals (IAAP) is dedicated to enhancing the success of career-minded administrative professionals by providing growth opportunities through education, community building, and leadership development.[6]

Going to meetings, conferences, and conventions related to your work can help you make new contacts in your chosen field. Professional organizations rely on volunteers and there are many ways to get involved. Taking a leadership role in the local chapter of a professional group will make you visible locally in your industry. Volunteering to edit the local chapter's newsletter would put you in touch with people and developments in the field. Making a presentation at a local meeting or regional or national conference would give you credibility with your peers and enhance your leadership and speaking skills. Serving on or leading a committee on industry issues could make you known throughout the professional organization.

Online Networks

In today's world, it is important to network with people you may never meet in person but who are part of your **online social network**, an online community of people with shared interests who directly or indirectly interact with one another online.

Online communities such as Facebook and LinkedIn are important networking tools. Facebook is primarily a social tool for staying in touch with friends and meeting people who have similar interests, but it can also be used to find and maintain business contacts. LinkedIn is a business-oriented social network that allows registered users to maintain a list of contact details about people they know and trust in business. They can use these *connections* to meet new people, find a job or business opportunity, and help others do the same. Many employers list job openings on LinkedIn and use the site to find potential candidates.

Facebook and LinkedIn are general sites. There are also social networking sites for specific industries, such as the fashion industry and travel industry.

Community Involvement

Every workplace is a community, and you are also a member of a larger community outside work. To achieve balance in your life, get involved in that community. Volunteer to work for a charity or organization that fits your interests. Attend local chamber of commerce meetings or check its online events calendar to find activities of interest. Use these opportunities to learn new skills, sharpen old ones, and expand your network.

Lifelong Learning

Rapidly changing technology has created a fast-changing world. Jobs and careers have changed dramatically in recent years and will continue to change as technological innovations are introduced to the workplace. To have a successful career, you must be a lifelong learner by developing and sustaining the habit of continuing your education, either formally or informally. To have a successful career, you must continually update your skills and add new skills. New skills and additional job responsibilities can always be added to your resume, thus making you more employable.

Making learning a priority includes staying up to date in your field through professional organizations, websites, and industry publications. Take in-person workshops and college courses, and use the resources on the Internet. Take time to review the section "Upgrading Your Skills" on page 430. The basic skills and knowledge you have now provide a firm foundation upon which to build your career. If you recognize the opportunities that change offers and work hard to attain your goals, you should enjoy a rewarding career.

checkpoint

1. Why is it important to continue to network even after you have a job?

_____

_____

_____

_____

_____

2. What is internal networking?

_____

_____

_____

_____

_____

3. What can you learn from informal communication networks in your organization?

_____

_____

_____

_____

_____

4. What is an internal customer?

_____

_____

_____

_____

_____

5. What are the benefits of getting involved in professional organizations in your field?

_____

_____

_____

_____

_____

_____

applications

1. How can you make yourself more visible in your current job? If you are not currently working, use your most recent job.

_____

_____

_____

2. List several things you have learned informally at work or at school that have helped you to improve your own job skills.

_____

_____

_____

3. Think of three of your department's internal customers. Describe how you could improve the services you provide each person or group. If you are not currently working, use your most recent job.

_____

_____

_____

_____

4. Identify a professional organization in your career field.

   a. What is the purpose of the organization?

   _____

   _____

   b. Is there a local chapter? Where (and how often) are meetings held?

   _____

   _____

   c. What professional growth opportunities and services does it offer?

   _____

   _____

5. Identify a person in your class or at work who might be of help to you in furthering your career. Network with that person. Then list what you learned from your networking experience.

   _____

   _____

   _____

   _____

16 *points to* remember

Review the following points to determine what you should remember from the chapter.

- Bring two forms of identification (a social security card and a driver's license, passport, or voter's identification card) with you on the first day of a new job.
- Read the employee handbook, if there is one, carefully and thoroughly. Follow the rules (written and unwritten), policies, and procedures in your organization.
- Know what is expected of you. Understand your job description; review it periodically to ensure that it adequately represents your job assignments. Set up your work area efficiently and keep it neat.
- To keep your job, exhibit good work habits and demonstrate a strong work ethic. Accept responsibility for your job, accept criticism positively, and treat everyone with respect.
- Take full advantage of having a mentor. If you are not assigned a mentor, try to find someone who will serve in this role.
- Do not get involved in destructive workplace politics.
- Keep good records throughout the year for your performance appraisal. Tell your supervisor about your accomplishments and new skills.
- Lifelong learning is the norm. Keep up with changes in your field and develop new skills.
- Consider all the issues carefully before changing employers.
- Network to develop and maintain connections in our field of work, including your personal contacts, friends, neighbors, and family.

How did you do? Did you remember the main points you studied in this chapter?

KEY *terms*

Form W-4

Form W-2

Form I-9

employee handbook

orientation

intellectual property

career strategy

performance appraisal

internal customers

online social network

Want more activities? Go to **www.cengage.com/careerreadiness/masters** to get started.

CHAPTER *activities*

1. Practice "first day of work" introductions with three or four of your classmates.

   a. Introduce yourself to a classmate.

   _____

   _____

   b. Introduce your classmates to each other.

   _____

   _____

2. Explain the purpose of the following forms: Form W-4, Form W-2, and Form I-9.

   _____

   _____

   _____

3. "Understood rules" are evident in both the classroom and the workplace. List several of the most important "understood" rules in the classroom and at a job you currently hold or held previously.

   a. In the classroom:

   _____

   _____

   b. At a current (or previous) job:

   _____

   _____

4. Review the list of good work habits in Figure 16-3. Add four suggestions from your personal experience.

   _____

   _____

   _____

5. You read about the importance of setting a career goal. What is your long-term career goal?

   _____

   _____

   _____

   a. List two or three short-term goals that will help you meet your long-term goal.

   _____

   _____

   b. List two or three medium-term goals that will help you meet your long-term goal.

   _____

   _____

6. You want to continually update your skills and abilities.

   a. List new skills that you have mastered in the last year, along with any workshops or courses you have taken.

   _____

   _____

   b. How will these new skills and knowledge help you to achieve your career goal?

   _____

   _____

   c. Identify two new skills that you would like to acquire in the next year. Why are these skills important to your career goal?

   _____

   _____

CRITICAL *thinking*

CASE 16.1 Is a Promotion in Order?

Lilli has been working at the Computer Superstore retail chain as a salesperson for several years. She knows the products well and has proven herself to be a dependable worker who generates high-volume sales.

The position of buyer becomes available. Lilli wants the position because it involves travel and a pay increase. It also would be a step toward her career goal to be a district manager of a chain of computer stores. The buyer would negotiate with major software and hardware suppliers across the country for the best prices. But Lilli is not a "negotiator," although she makes an extra effort to smile when talking with customers and to listen carefully to determine their needs. Lilli is also opinionated and works harmoniously with only a few of the large sales staff. In a few instances, she's had loud disagreements that were overheard by management. Lilli's performance appraisals have been satisfactory, and she ranks among the top ten in sales volume. However, at each session her supervisor has reminded her that she needs to work on her "people skills" with the internal staff.

1. Will Lilli get the promotion? Why or why not?

_____

_____

_____

_____

_____

2. Would you hire Lilli as a district manager? Why or why not?

_____

_____

_____

_____

3. If you were Lilli's friend, what advice would you give her?

_____

_____

_____

_____

_____

CASE 16.2   Is It Time for a Change?

Noah has worked as a technician in a county government environmental planning office for three years. His appraisal reports have been excellent, and he is well-liked by his coworkers and supervisors. He doesn't get along with one county official, but Noah overlooks this since he does not report to this person.

Noah's experience and training are in environmental planning and he is a true environmentalist. The government paperwork, bureaucracy, outdated codes, rules, and regulations are a constant annoyance to him. His current work is to monitor housing developers to make sure that the "urban sprawl" does not interfere with the natural beauty of surrounding mountains. His toughest task is to keep the developers within the rules and codes established by the elected county officials.

Noah has been offered an environmental planning position in another state where he would be doing similar work for a nongovernmental agency. The new position includes a pay raise of $12,000 per year. His work will be to assist land developers design attractive, environmentally neutral developments.

1. What factors should Noah consider as he explores the offer to change positions?

_____

_____

_____

_____

_____

2. Do you see any drawbacks if Noah decides to remain in his current position?

_____

_____

_____

_____

3. What additional information would you need to help Noah decide whether to take the new position?

_____

_____

_____

_____

Chapter 1

1. Peale, Norman V. *The Power of Positive Thinking.* New York: Simon and Schuster, 2002. Print.

2. Dalton, Marie, Dawn G. Hoyle, and Marie W. Watts. *Human Relations,* 2nd Edition, Thomson Learning. Cincinnati: South-Western Educational Publishing, 2000, p. 35. Print.

Chapter 2

1. Falconer, Eric. *"10 Ways to Instantly Build Self-Confidence."* 25 July, 2007. Web. Accessed 12 May, 2009. http://www.pickthebrain.com/blog/10-ways-to-instantly-build-self-confidence.

2. Covey, Stephen. *Seven Habits of Highly Effective People.* New York: Simon and Schuster, Inc., 1989, p. 71. Print.

3. Nikitina, Arina. "SMART Goal Setting: A Surefire Way to Achieve Your Goals." Goal Setting Guide, GoalSettingGuide.com. Web. Accessed 12 May, 2009. http://www.goal-setting-guide.com/smart-goals.html.

4. Williams, Felicia A. Willings. "Personal Action Plans. A surefire Road to Success." 17 November, 2007. Web. Accessed 22 May, 2009. http://changing-personal-habits.suite101.com/article.cfm/personal_action_plans.

5. Downing, Skip. *On Course: Strategies for Creating Success in College and Life,* 5th Edition. Boston: Houghton Mifflin Company, 2008, p. 71. Print.

Chapter 3

1. Sasson, Remez. "The Power of Positive Attitude." SuccessConsciousness.com—Awakening the wisdom and power within you. Web. Accessed 14 May, 2009. http://www.successconsciousness.com/positive_attitude.htm.

2. Bauer, Chuck. "Top 7 Strategies to Overcome Negative Attitudes in the Workplace." Web. Accessed 14 May, 2009. http://top7business.com/?id=561.

3. Nauert, Rick. "A Negative Attitude is Contagious." PsychCentral—Learn, Share, Grow. Web. Accessed 18 May, 2009. http://psychcentral.com/news/2007/10/05/a-negative-attitude-is-contagious/1374.html.

Chapter 4

1. Ruble, Peter. "Is Perception Reality?" Accessed 18 May, 2009. Web. http://ezinearticles.com/?Is-Perception-Reality?&id=271062.

2. "Posture for a Healthy Back: Sitting, Driving and Sleeping." Cleveland Clinic—Health Information Center. Web. Accessed 21 May, 2009. http://www.spineuniverse.com/displayarticle.php/article2023.html.

3. Post, Peggy. *Excuse Me, But I Was Next. . .* New York: HarperCollins Publishers, 2006, p. 47. Print.

Chapter 5

1. "Communication Skills Start Here—Why You Need to Get Your Message Across." Mind Tools: Essential Skills for an Excellent Career. Web. Accessed 23 May, 2009. http://www.mindtools.com/CommSkll/CommunicationIntro.htm.

2. Axtell, Roger E. *Gestures: The Do's and Taboo's of Body Language Around the World,* Revised and Expanded Edition. New York: John Wiley & Sons, 1997, p. 9. Print.

3. Performance Research Associates. *Delivering Knock-Your-Socks-Off Service,* 4th Edition. New York: American Management Association, 2007, p. 100. Print.

4. "Active Listening: Hear What People are Really Saying." Mind Tools: Essential Skills for an Excellent Career. Web. Accessed 22 May, 2009. http://www.mindtools.com/CommSkll/ActiveListening.htm.

5. Downing, Skip. *On Course: Strategies for Creating Success in College and Life,* 5th Edition. Boston: Houghton Mifflin Company, 2008, p. 132. Print.

Chapter 6

1. Scott, Elizabeth. "Reduce Stress with Increased Assertiveness." Web. Accessed 6 March, 2009. http://stress.about.com/od/relationships/p/profileassertive.html.

2. Fiore, Dr. Tony. "4 Steps to Assertive Communications." Web. Accessed 7 March, 2009. http://www.selfgrowth.com/articles/Fiore4.html.

Chapter 7

1. "19 Ways to Enhance Your Sense of Humor." Stealth Health. Web. Accessed 27 May, 2009. http://www.rd.com/living-healthy/19-ways-to-enhance-your-sense-of-humor/article16125.html.

2. Saulny, Susan. "Students Stand When Called Upon, and When Not." *The New York Times,* 25 February 2009: A1. Print.

3. Fripp, Patricia. "A Team is More Than a Group of People." Web. Accessed 17 June, 2009. http://www.fripp.com/art.team.html.

4. Bixler, Susan and Lisa Scherrer. *5 Steps to Professional Presence.* Avon, Massachusetts: Adams Media Corporation, 2001, pp. 94–95. Print.

5. Choney, Suzanne. "Obama Gets to Keep His Blackberry." MSNBC.com. Web. Accessed 8 June, 2009. http://www.msnbc.msn.com/id/28780205.

Chapter 8

1. "About Conflict." Academic Leadership Support. Web. Accessed 7 June, 2009. http://www.ohrd.wisc.edu/onlinetraining/resolution/aboutwhatisit.htm#conflictisnormal.

2. "Managing Conflict: A Guide for Managing Watershed Partnerships." Know Your Watershed Information Network. Web. Accessed 7 June, 2009. http://www.ctic.purdue.edu/KYW/Brochures/ManageConflict.html.

Chapter 9

1. Everard, Kenneth E. and James L. Burrow. *Business Principles and Management,* 11th Anniversary Edition. Mason, OH: Thomson, South-Western, 2004, pp. 252–253. Print.

2. Knowlton, Nancy and Bob Hagerty. "Do Your Meetings Measure Up to Your CEO's Expectations?" Interview on EffectiveMeetings.com. Web. Accessed 25 March, 2009. http://www.effectivemeetings.com/meetingbasics/ceo_expectations.asp.

3. Yip, Jason. "It's Not Just Standing Up—Patterns of Daily Stand-Up Meetings." MartinFowler.com. Web. Accessed 12 June, 2009. http://martinfowler.com/articles/itsNotJustStandingUp.html.

4. Knowlton, Nancy and Bob Hagerty. "Do Your Meetings Measure Up to Your CEO's Expectations?" Interview on EffectiveMeetings.com. Web. Accessed 25 March, 2009. http://www.effectivemeetings.com/meetingbasics/ceo_expectations.asp.

5. Covey, Stephen R. *The 7 Habits of High Effective People.* New York: Simon & Schuster, 1989, p. 94. Print.

6. Farivar, Cyrus. "How to Run an Effective Meeting." Web. Accessed 12 June, 2009. http://www.bnet.com/2403-13059_23-61211.html.

Chapter 10

1. Wallis, Claudia (quoting Mayer, David). "The Multitasking Generation." *Time,* 26 March 2006. Web. Accessed 11 July, 2009. http://www.time.com/time/magazine/article/0,9171,1174696-6,00.html.

2. Roth, Sherry (quoting Fortgang, Laura Berman). "5 Tips for Better Work-Life Balance." WebMD.com. Web. Accessed 14 April, 2009. http://www.webmd.com/balance/guide/5-strategies-for-life-balance.

3. Axis-One Resource Center. "Symptoms of Anger." Axis-One, Inc. Web. Accessed 15 April, 2009. http://www.axis-one.com/anger/symptoms-of-anger.html.

4. Mayo Clinic Staff. "Anger Management Tips: Tame Your Temper." Web. Accessed 16 April, 2009. http://www.mayoclinic.com/health/anger-management/mh00102.

5. Franken, Robert E. *Human Motivation,* 3rd Edition. Thomson Brooks/Cole, Pacific Grove, CA 1988, p. 396. Print.

6. Czikszentmihalyi, Mihaly. "The Creative Personality." *Psychology Today,* 1 July1996 (updated 14 October, 2008). Web. Accessed 15 April, 2009. http://www.psychologytoday.com/articles/199607/the-creative-personality.

7. Bellis, Mary. "Post-it Note." About.com: Inventors. Web. Accessed 13 April, 2009. http://inventors.about.com/od/pstartinventions/a/post_it_note.htm.

Chapter 11

1. "Ten Tips to Build Customer Loyalty." *All Business.* Web. Accessed 28 June, 2009. http://www.allbusiness.com/sales/customer-service/1961-1.html.

2. Karten, Naomi. "What Do Customers Want Anyway?" Web. Accessed 25 April, 2009. http://www.hotelnewsresource.com/article16368.html.

3. Evenson, Renee. *Award Winning Customer Service: 101 Ways to Guarantee Great Performance.* AMACOM, a division of American Management Association, 2007, p. 13. Print.

Chapter 12

1. "Census Bureau Projects Tripling of Hispanic and Asian Populations in 50 Years; Non-Hispanic Whites May Drop To Half of Total Population." *U.S. Census Bureau News*. Web. Accessed 29 August, 2009. http://www.census.gov/ Press-Release/www/releases/archives/ population/001720.html.

2. Richmond, Yale. *From Nyet to Da: Understanding the New Russia*. Boston: Intercultural Press, Inc., 2008. Print.

3. Federal Equal Employment Opportunity (EEO) Laws. Web. Accessed 29 August, 2009. http://www. eeoc.gov/abouteeo/overview_laws.html.

Chapter 13

1. Adapted from WiseGeek. Web. Accessed 30 August, 2009. http://www.wisegeek.com/ what-is-the-difference-between-ethics-and-morals.htm.

2. The Hershey Company. "Code of Ethical Business Conduct, "p. iii. Web. Accessed 3 September, 2009. http://www.thehersheycompany.com/about/ conduct.asp.

3. The Hershey Company. Code of Ethical Business Conduct, page 1. Web. Accessed 3 September, 2009. http://www.thehersheycompany.com/about/ conduct.asp.

4. The Premier International Foundation. Web. Accessed 30 August, 2009. http://lifelessonnetwork. org/a_personal_code_of_ethics.html.

5. Jefferson-Madison Regional Library in Charlottesville, Virginia. Web. Accessed 24 August, 2009. http://jmrl.org/policy/section2-11.pdf.

6. Williams, Chuck. *MGMT,* 2008 Edition. Mason, OH: Thomson South-Western, 2009. Print.

7. U.S. House of Representatives Ethics Committee. Web. Accessed 24 August, 2009. http://usgovinfo. about.com/blethics.htm.

8. OnlineLawyerSource.com. Web. Accessed 24 August, 2009. http://www.onlinelawyersource. com/workers-compensation/fraud.

9. The Alabama Attorney General's Office and the Alabama Department of Industrial Relations. Web. Accessed 24 August, 2009. http://dir.alabama.gov/ docs/posters/wc_fraudposter.pdf.

Chapter 14

1. Bennis, Warren. "Why Leaders Can't Lead." *Training and Development Journal.* 43, No. 4, 1989. Print.

2. Zaleznik, Abraham. "Managers and Leaders: Are They Different?" *Harvard Business Review* No. 55, 1977: 76–78. Print.

3. Covey, Stephen R. *The 7 Habits of Highly Effective People.* New York: Simon and Schuster, Inc., 1980, p. 235. Print.

4. Adapted from *Interpersonal Communication* by the Agency for Instructional Technology. Mason, OH: South-Western Publishing, 2002, p. 63. Print.

5. State of Michigan Employee Service Program. Web. Accessed 1 August, 2009. http://mich.gov/ documents/corrections/MANAGING_CHANGE_ ARTICLE_224471_7.pdf.

Chapter 15

1. Mullins, John. "Career Planning the Second Time Around." Occupational Outlook Quarterly Online, Summer 2009. Web. Accessed 31 October, 2009. http://www.bls.gov/opub/ooq/2009/summer/ art02.pdf.

2. "Lifetime 'Career' Changes." Grab Bag. Occupational Outlook Quarterly Online, Summer 2006. Web. Accessed 31 October, 2009. http://www.bls.gov/ opub/ooq/2006/summer/grabbag.pdf.

3. Zedlitz, Robert. Adapted from *Getting a Job Process Kit* by Robert Zedlitz. Cincinnati, OH: South-Western Publishing, 1998, p. 2. Print.

4. Ibid, p. 4.

5. Adapted from the Texas Workforce Job Hunter's Guide. Web. Accessed 24 October, 2009. http:// www.twc.state.tx.us/news/tjhg/s1exercise4.html.

6. Levitt, Julie Griffin and Lauri Harwood. Adapted from *Your Career: How to Make It Happen*. Mason, OH: South-Western Cengage Learning, 2010, p. 80. Print.

7. Career Voyages. Web. Accessed 3 November, 2009. http://www.careervoyages.gov/about-main.cfm.

8. Occupational Outlook Handbook (OOH), 2008-09 Edition. Web. Accessed 3 November, 2009. http:// www.bls.gov/oco.

9. Adapted from *Personal Effectiveness* by the Agency for Instructional Technology. Mason, OH: South-Western Publishing, 2002, p. 58. Print.

10. Kushner, John A. and Doris D. Humphrey. Adapted from *How to Find and Apply for a Job*. Cincinnati, OH: South-Western Publishing, 2001, p. 40. Print.

11. Adapted from "Interview Questions and Answers." About.com: Job Searching. Web. Accessed 31 October, 2009. http://jobsearch.about.com/od/interviewquestionsanswers/a/interviewquest2.htm.

Chapter 16

1. Adapted from "Administrative Support Job Descriptions." International Association of Administrative Professionals. Web. Accessed 4 November, 2009. http://www.iaap-hq.org/resources/keytrends/JobDescriptions.html.

2. Levitt, Julie Griffin. Adapted from *Your Career: How to Make It Happen*. Mason, OH: South-Western Cengage Learning, 2006, p. 322. Print.

3. Adapted from *Personal Effectiveness* by the Agency for Instructional Technology. Mason, OH: South-Western Publishing, 2002, p. 26. Print.

4. Levitt, Julie Griffin. Adapted from *Your Career: How to Make It Happen*. Mason, OH: South-Western Cengage Learning, 2006, p. 323. Print.

5. Ibid, p. 324.

6. International Association of Administrative Professionals home page. Web. Accessed 11 November, 2009. http://www.iaap-hq.org.

7. Allen, Scott. "The Importance of Being Memorable." About.com. Web. Accessed 27 November, 2009. http://entrepreneurs.about.com/od/businessnetworking/a/memorable.htm.

glossary

A

Action plan A strategy to achieve a specified goal or outcome.

Ad hoc meeting A meeting called to address a specific issue or situation.

Adjustment The measures that are necessary to put into action the settlement agreed upon by the parties involved in the conflict.

Affirmative action A legal concept that requires employers to take positive steps to create employment opportunities for minorities and women.

Ageism Discrimination because of a person's age.

Agenda A list of topics to be addressed at a meeting.

Aggressive anger Anger that explodes quickly on the spot and often is displayed as a threatening outburst.

Aggressive communication Occurs when someone communicates strong feelings in a vigorous manner without regard to the rights and feelings of others.

Anger management The ability of a person to control his or her temperament, particularly in stressful situations.

Aptitude A natural talent, ability, or capacity to learn.

Archiving Moving data to a secondary storage medium that can be easily accessed when required.

Assertive communication Occurs when someone expresses feelings and asserts his or her own rights while respecting the feelings and rights of others.

Attitude Your outlook on life; how you respond to people and events.

Autocratic leader An "in charge" person who exercises unlimited power or authority.

B

Backup Making copies of data so that these additional copies may be used to restore the original files after a data loss.

Behavior A manner of acting or reacting to a general set of circumstances.

Behavior modification A system of motivation that emphasizes rewarding people for doing the right things and punishing them for doing the wrong things.

Bias A way of thinking that prevents you from being impartial about a situation, issue, or person.

Board meeting A formal meeting held for administrative purposes.

Body The "nuts and bolts" of your speech; what you want the audience to know.

Body language The nonverbal signals you send, including your posture, bearing, stride, handshake, eye contact, gestures, and facial expressions.

Brainstorming Typically, a group technique used to generate a large number of ideas or solutions to a problem.

Brainwriting The process of brainstorming alone.

C

Career strategy A plan of action to reach your career goals.

Character Distinctive personal qualities or traits.

Charismatic leader Someone with extraordinary magnetism that inspires others to follow him or her with devotion.

Chronological resume A resume format that lists employment and education information by date, starting with the most recent (reverse chronological order).

Closed questions Questions that require single-word or very short answers.

Code of ethics Written guidelines for workers to follow based on specific ethical standards and values.

Colloquialism Words or phrases often used in a specific geographical area and more informal settings and most common in conversation.

Combination resume A resume that combines elements of the chronological and functional formats.

Communication The act of transmitting information and meaning from one individual or group to another.

Conclusion A brief summary of what you have said in your speech.

Conflict A difference of opinion caused by opposing attitudes, behaviors, ideas, needs, wants, or goals.

Conflict of interest Taking unfair advantage of a situation to benefit yourself or others

449

instead of putting the employer's interests first.

Conflict resolution Managing conflict by defining and resolving issues between individuals, groups, or organizations.

Continuous improvement A management process that constantly monitors what the enterprise is doing and how people are doing it.

Conversation The two-way spoken exchange of thoughts, opinions, and feelings.

Cover letter A document used to introduce you to a prospective employer and request an interview.

Creativity The tendency to generate or recognize ideas, alternatives, or possibilities that may be useful in solving problems, communicating with others, and entertaining ourselves.

Critical listening Separating facts from the opinions.

Cultural conflicts Problems that arise among people from different racial and ethnic backgrounds.

Culture A learned and shared system of knowledge, beliefs, values, and attitudes.

D

Decision making The part of the problem-solving process that involves selecting one course of action from several possible alternatives.

Democratic leader A person who encourages employees to participate in the management process.

Discrimination Behavior based on a prejudicial or unfair attitude.

Diversity The differences among individuals based on gender, race, age, religion, culture, and other characteristics.

Diversity training A program designed to teach employees how to work harmoniously with people from different backgrounds.

E

Ego Your consciousness of your own identity and self-worth.

Ego conflict A difference of opinion in which the individuals view "winning" or "losing" the conflict as a measure of their expertise and personal worth.

Electronic resume Also called a *scannable* resume, is a plain text (ASCII) or HTML document often submitted with an employment application.

E-mail A system for sending and receiving messages electronically over a computer network.

Emotion A state of feeling or a conscious mental reaction (positive or negative) toward a specific object or event.

Emotional intelligence The ability to recognize your own and others' emotions and react appropriately.

Empathy The ability to look at situations through the eyes of another with a true understanding of what the person is actually feeling.

Employee Assistance Program A program intended to help employees deal with personal problems that might adversely impact their work performance, health, and well-being.

Employee handbook A company manual that spells out specific policies and rules

governing the employer–employee relationship.

Employment application A form used by employers to gather basic information from everyone who applies for positions.

Empower To give others the authority and responsibility to carry out tasks or solve problems that the leader has defined.

Enunciation Pronouncing each part of each word clearly.

Envy Resentful desire of something that someone else has.

Ethics Accepted standards of right and wrong.

Ethnocentrism The tendency to believe in the superiority of one's own culture.

Etiquette The customs or rules of behavior regarded as correct in social and work life.

F

Fact Information that can be proven.

False conflict A perceived difference of opinion that does not really exist.

Feedback Information returned to the sender that indicates whether the message is' understood.

Firewall An integrated collection of security measures designed to prevent unauthorized electronic access to a networked computer system.

Form I-9 This form, Employment Eligibility Verification, requires both the employer and employee (citizen and noncitizen) to attest that the worker is authorized to work in the United States.

Form W-2 This form, the Employee's Wage and Tax Statement, reports to the IRS estimated taxes withheld for federal, state, and local income taxes purposes.

Form W-4 This form, the Employee's Withholding Allowance Certificate, is used to figure the right amount of federal and state income tax to have withheld from an employee's paycheck.

Fraud Intentional deception made for personal gain or to damage another individual.

Functional resume A resume format that focuses on personal characteristics, skills and abilities, and work experiences.

G

Gender-neutral language Language use that aims at minimizing assumptions about gender.

Goals Clearly stated results that you want to achieve within a specified time period.

Goal-setting The overall process for achieving your goals.

H

Hypocrisy A kind of insincerity in which someone publicly pretends to follow superior moral standards, while privately acting against those principles.

I

Icebreakers Topics used to lessen tension or awkwardness at the beginning of a conversation.

Image The set of qualities and characteristics that represent perceptions of you as judged by others.

Imaging A deliberate effort to picture your life as you would like it to be.

Incremental change Change that occurs in a series of small, planned steps.

Inflection The rise and fall of the voice.

Information overload An excessive amount of information being provided, which makes processing and absorbing the information very difficult.

Innovate To create something significantly new or a new way of doing something.

Intangible items Items that cannot be seen, touched, or possessed.

Integrity Consistency in adhering to moral principles.

Intellectual property Intangible property that is the result of creativity (i.e., artistic works, inventions, phrases, and designs).

Internal customers People in your department or other departments within the company who are served or supported by the work you do.

Internship program A coordinated classroom and laboratory training program that includes on-the-job training in the work environment.

Introduction Comments at the beginning of a speech used to get the attention of your audience.

J

Jargon Technical terminology or characteristic words and ideas that belong to a specific type of work or field of knowledge.

Jealousy A feeling of rivalry toward one who you believe has an advantage over you.

Job-benefit statement A brief explanation of how an individual's skills can benefit the company.

Job description A written statement of what a job holder does, how it is done, why it is done, and the skills needed to perform the job.

L

Laissez-faire leader A person who gives responsibility to employees to carry out their duties without a great deal of direction or close supervision.

Leadership style The method a supervisor uses to manage and communicate with people who directly report to him or her.

Listening The process by which we make sense out of what we hear.

M

Management meeting A meeting at which management or administrative staff report on their areas of responsibility and learn about new policies, procedures, and challenges.

Meeting A formal or informal assembly of two or more individuals who come together to discuss one or more topics.

Mentor A trusted counselor or guide.

Mentoring Taking someone under your wing, guiding and teaching that person so that he or she benefits from your experience and skills.

Message The thought, idea, or information transmitted.

Minutes The written record of what took place at a meeting.

Monotone Speech in an unvaried key or pitch.

Morale A sense of common purpose within a group.

Multitasking Attempting to do more than one task at one time.

N

Networking Developing contacts or exchanging information with others in an informal network to further one's career.

Nonverbal communication Wordless messages.

O

Online social network An online community of people with shared interests who directly or indirectly interact with one another online.

One-on-one meeting The most frequent meeting type, either informal or formal, between two people.

Open questions Questions phrased to elicit longer answers and encourage others to participate in the conversation.

Open-minded Having or showing receptiveness to new and different ideas and the opinions of others.

Opinion Information based on personal beliefs or feelings.

Oral communication Spoken messages.

Orientation Formal or informal program used to introduce new employees to the company.

P

Passive anger Anger that "slowly burns in your heart."

Passive communication Occurs when someone allows their rights to be violated because they fail to express honest feelings.

Perception The process of attaining awareness or understanding based on sensory information; an immediate reaction to the senses.

Performance appraisal A system of determining how well an individual employee has performed his or her job during a period of time compared to a predetermined set of standards.

Personal space The space you put between yourself and others in order to feel comfortable.

Petty theft The illegal taking of another person's property without that person's freely-given consent.

Phishing The act of sending an e-mail that falsely claims to be an established entity (a bank or credit card company, for example).

Pitch How high or low the voice sounds.

Plagiarism Copying material to claim it as your original work.

Prejudice To prejudge or form an opinion without taking the time and effort to judge fairly.

Probing questions Questions used in seeking more detail to help clarify or verify what has just been said.

Procrastinating Delaying an action to a later time.

Pronunciation Saying a word correctly.

R

Receiver The individual to whom the thought, idea, or information is transmitted.

Recurring meeting A meeting held periodically.

Reinforcement The reward or benefit used to reinforce positive behavior.

Reliability The ability to supply what was promised in a dependable, efficient, and timely manner.

Resentment A feeling of displeasure, ill will, and deep anger over something you believe (correctly or incorrectly) to be a wrong or an insult to you.

Resolution The phase of conflict in which the main issues are out in the open and the parities can propose solutions and come to a decision that is agreeable to all.

Resume A concise, well-organized summary of your education, work experience, and other qualifications.

Reverse discrimination Discrimination against members of a social or racial group that is considered to be dominant in a society.

Rhetorical questions Questions that are not true questions because they don't require an answer.

S

Scheduling The process by which you plan the use of your time and set deadlines for completing tasks.

Selective listening Hearing only what you want to hear.

Self-actualization The process of growing to reach your greatest potential.

Self-confidence A sense of personal strength and a belief in one's abilities.

Self-esteem Belief in your abilities and your worth or value.

Self-image The mental picture of who you are.

Self-pity Feeling sorry for yourself without looking at the good things in your life.

Self-righteousness Self-satisfaction based on the belief that one's own morals are superior to the morals of others.

Sender The originator of a thought, idea, or piece of information.

Series meeting A meeting held at the same time each month but the topic discussed varies.

Sexual harassment Coerced, unethical, and unwanted intimacy.

Simple conflict A difference of opinion—typically over a fact or a piece of information—that is seldom serious and usually easily resolved.

Situational ethics The gray areas where the "right" thing may depend on the circumstances.

Situational leader A person whose leadership style depends upon the situation, the qualities and abilities of the followers, and the task in question.

Skill An aptitude that you have put into practice and improved.

Small talk Light, informal conversation that has no agenda; a way to acknowledge a person's presence and create a comfortable environment.

SMART goals Goals that are well-focused, specific, measurable, attainable, relevant, and timely.

Speech A formal presentation of information to an audience.

Staff meeting A meeting that is typically called by a team leader or manager for those who report to that manager either directly or indirectly.

Status meeting A meeting that provides current information about something that is ongoing.

Stereotype A generalized perception or first impression based on oversimplified beliefs or opinions about a person, event, group, or object.

Stereotyping Occurs whenever you assume that all members of a group have the same characteristics instead of viewing the members of the group as individuals.

Stress The feeling you get from prolonged, unexpressed emotions.

Subtle discrimination Discrimination that is not obvious and is seldom brought out in the open.

Supervisor An employee whose key responsibility is to ensure that the employees being supervised produce the assigned amount of work on time and within acceptable levels of quality.

Sympathy The ability to identify with the person and feel sorry for another but without having a true understanding of what the person is actually feeling.

T

Tact Sensitivity to what is appropriate in dealing with others, including the ability to speak or act without offending others.

Tactile communication Communication through the sense of touch.

Tangible items Items that can be seen, touched, and usually kept in your possession.

Team An identifiable group of people who are committed to a common purpose for which they hold themselves accountable.

Team player Someone who emphasizes group accomplishments and cooperation rather than individual achievement.

Teamwork People working together cooperatively to accomplish established team goals and objectives.

Technical skills Specialized skill needed for specific jobs.

Teleconferencing Technology that enables two or more people to hold a meeting via a telephone or a network connection.

Text messaging Sending short text messages (160 characters or fewer, including spaces) from a mobile device to a cell phone, PDA, or pager.

Time management The planning and using the hours and minutes of a workday in the most effective and efficient manner possible.

Transferable skills Skills that can be used in many different work settings.

Transformational leader A person who inspires followers to act in the interests of the group, helping and supporting each other and working in harmony toward a common goal.

Try-out experience A program that provides an actual on-the-job opportunity for a limited period of time.

V

Values and beliefs conflict A difference of opinion that occurs when people differ in their feelings about an aspect of life, and those differences are brought into focus on a particular issue.

Videoconferencing Technology that enables people at different sites to come together for an electronic meeting where they can see still or real-time video images of each other.

Virtual team A group of people physically separated by time and/or space and whose members primarily interact electronically in cyberspace.

Virus A malicious software program designed to interfere with the operation of your computer.

Vocabulary The sum of words used by, understood by, or at the command of a particular person or group.

Voice and video chatting Technology that enables people connected electronically to have a conversation with someone or even chat face to face.

Voicemail A centralized electronic system for answering and routing telephone calls.

Volume The loudness or softness of the voice.

W

Web conferencing Technology used to conduct live meetings or presentations over the Internet.

Webinar Short for *web-based seminar*, it is a type of web conference that refers to a lecture, presentation, workshop, or seminar transmitted over the Web.

Work ethic A set of values based on the virtues of hard work, diligence, and caring about your work and your coworkers.

Written communication Information received in writing.